For a Better Life

GENERATIONS

A History of Canada's Peoples

For a Better Life
(Za Bolji Život)

A History of
the Croatians in Canada

Anthony W. Rasporich

Published by McClelland and Stewart Ltd. in association
with the Multiculturalism Directorate,
Department of the Secretary of State
and the Canadian Government Publishing Centre,
Supply and Services Canada.

Catalogue No. Ci44-7-1982E

McClelland and Stewart Limited
The Canadian Publishers
25 Hollinger Road
Toronto, Ontario
M4B 3G2

CANADIAN CATALOGUING IN PUBLICATION DATA
Rasporich, Anthony W., 1940-
For a better life = Za bolji život

(Generations: a history of Canada's peoples)
Bibliography: p.
ISBN 0-7710-7308-9 (pbk.)

1. Croatian Canadians – History.   I. Canada. Multiculturalism Directorate.   II. Title.   III. Title: Za
bolji život.   IV. Series.

FC106.C93R37   971'.00491823   C82-094423-8
F1035.C7R37

Printed and bound in Canada

Contents

Editors' Introduction

Canadians, like many other people, have recently been changing their attitude towards the ethnic dimension in society. Instead of thinking of the many distinctive heritages and identities to be found among them as constituting a problem, though one that time would solve, they have begun to recognize the ethnic diversity of their country as a rich resource. They have begun to take pride in the fact that people have come and are coming here from all parts of the world, bringing with them varied outlooks, knowledge, skills and traditions, to the great benefit of all.

It is for this reason that Book IV of the *Report of the Royal Commission on Bilingualism and Biculturalism* dealt with the cultural contributions of the ethnic groups other than the British, the French and the Native Peoples to Canada, and that the federal government in its response to Book IV announced that the Citizenship Branch of the Department of the Secretary of State would commission "histories specifically directed to the background, contributions and problems of various cultural groups in Canada." This series presents the histories that have resulted from that mandate. Although commissioned by the Government, they are not intended as definitive or official, but rather as the efforts of scholars to bring together much of what is known about the ethnic groups studied, to indicate what remains to be learned, and thus to stimulate further research concerning the ethnic dimension in Canadian society. The histories are to be objective, analytical, and readable, and directed towards the general reading public, as well as students at the senior high school and the college and university levels, and teachers in the elementary schools.

Most Canadians belong to an ethnic group, since to do so is simply to have "a sense of identity rooted in a common origin ... whether this common origin is real or imaginary."[1] The Native Peoples, the British and French (referred to as charter groups because they were the first Europeans to take possession of the land), the groups such as the Germans and Dutch who have been established in Canada for over a hundred years and those who began to arrive only yesterday all have traditions and values that they cherish and that now are part of the cultural riches that Canadians share. The groups vary widely in numbers, geographical location and distribution and degree of social and economic power. The stories of their struggles, failures and triumphs will be told in this series.

As the Royal Commission on Bilingualism and Biculturalism pointed out, this sense of ethnic origin or identity "is much keener in certain individuals than in others."[2] In contemporary Canadian society, with the increasing number of intermarriages across ethnic lines, and hence the growing diversity of peoples ancestors, many are coming to identify themselves as simple Canadian, without reference to their ancestral origins. In focusing on the ethnic dimension of Canadian society, past and present, the series does not assume that everyone should be categorized into one particular group, or that ethnicity is always the most important dimension of people's lives. It is, however, one dimension that needs examination if we are to understand fully the contours and nature of Canadian society and identity.

Professional Canadian historians have in the past emphasized political and economic history, and since the country's economic and political institutions have been controlled largely by people of British and French origin, the role of those of other origins in the development of Canada has been neglected. Also, Canadian historians in the past have been almost exclusively of British and French origin, and have lacked the interest and the linguistic skills necessary to explore the history of other ethnic groups. Indeed, there has rarely ever been an examination of the part played by specifically British – or, better, specifically English, Irish, Scottish and Welsh – traditions and values in Canadian development, because of the lack of recognition of pluralism in the society. The part played by French traditions and values, and particular varieties of French traditions and values, has for a number of reasons been more carefully scrutinized.

This series is an indication of growing interest in Canadian social history, which includes immigration and ethnic history. This may particularly be a reflection of an increasing number of scholars whose origins and ethnic identities are other than British or French. Because such trends are recent, many of the authors of the histories in this series have not had a large body of published writing to work from. It is true that some histories have already been written of particular groups other than the British and French; but these have often been characterized by filio pietism, a narrow perspective and a dearth of scholarly analysis.

Despite the scarcity of secondary sources, the authors have been asked to be as comprehensive as possible, and to give balanced coverage to a number of themes: historical background, settlement patterns, ethnic identity and assimilation, ethnic associations, population trends, religion, values, occupations and social class, the family, the ethnic press, language patterns, political behaviour, education, inter-ethnic relations, the arts and recreation. They have also been asked to give a sense of the way the group differs in various parts of the country. Finally, they have been asked to give, as much as possible, an insider's view of what the immigrant and ethnic experiences were like at different periods of time, but yet at the same time to be as objective as possible, and not simply to present the group as it sees itself, or as it would like to be seen.

The authors have thus been faced with a herculean task. To the extent that they have succeeded, they provide us with new glimpses into many aspects of Canadian society of the past and the present. To the extent that they have fallen short of their goal, they challenge other historians, sociologists and social anthropologists to continue the work begun here.

Jean Burnet
Howard Palmer

[1]   *Report of the Royal Commission on Bilingualism and Biculturalism.*
[2]   Ibid. Paragraph 8.

Author's Preface

Ethnic histories are rarely the product of any one individual's efforts. By their very nature they must represent a collaborative effort, for ethnic groups themselves are a vast network of people, organizations, traditions, and feelings. Some of their memories may remain in letters and albums stored in family attics and basements, and yet others are buried in archives and newspaper morgues, but all are a part of a collective group memory of enormous complexity and diversity. To uncover this network is a difficult task, and no single historian can hope to discover all of the facts or come to know more than a small number of the nearly sixty-five thousand Croatians in Canada and all of their ancestors and descendants. The historian therefore stands on a bridge in time between Croatia and Canada over which a hundred thousand or so migrants have passed back and forth since the turn of the century. Some faces and names are familiar – most are not – but if one carefully observes the manner of the people and listens to their concerns, their hopes and aspirations, one can tell much about them. Moreover, if one listens carefully to reports of what other observers such as newspaper editors, writers, and group spokesmen have said, one can piece together a reasonably accurate account of those who have come and gone over that same bridge.

The reader may well ask, what are the particular lights by which this author sees on the bridge of Croatian-Canadian history? As a Canadian-born son of first- and second-generation immigrants, my own perspective is rich in the folk memory of immigration and assimilation but also somewhat limited with respect to the more recent immigration from post-Second World War Yugoslavia. My own perspective is that of a Canadian historian (my main field of academic interest), and I have attempted to fit the Croatian immigrant experience into a Canadian context, while informing the reader of the main events of Croatian history which bear on it. It is in the latter area of recent Balkan history where this account is thinnest, but there is an ample and growing body of literature of that complex region which is developed elsewhere. If events relating to the Old World experience have been omitted, misstated, or misinterpreted, the intent is neither deliberate nor casuistic. For others still who might have preferred an entirely apolitical book, the author's preference would have been to write an entirely social and cultural history of Croatian community life in Canada, but fortunately or unfortunately, the group's history just didn't happen that way. The European background is therefore important and necessary, but it can only be so insofar as it provides a context for what is happening front stage and centre in Canada. The latter is this particular history's purpose, and hopefully it fulfils its mandate.

Included in this account is mention of many groups and individuals who have played a role in the history of the Croatians in Canada; others of equal significance and importance may appear to have been ignored. Such gaps inevitably occur in a first attempt at a major comprehensive history, which covers the entire span of migration and settlement in Canada. Any such exercise, unfortunately, will miss some and relegate others to the limbo of scholarly footnotes, but I must emphasize that those who have not been mentioned are certainly not omitted intentionally or because their achievements were any less noteworthy. Further, it is my fervent wish that this work will inspire other students to extend this history and to describe in further detail the economic and social process of Croatian migration and adjustment to Canadian society. Even in the relatively brief interval in which this book has been researched and written, several archives, societies, and organizations have been active in the collection of materials and sponsorship of conferences relating to the history of migration from Yugoslavia to Canada. Some that have been active in this respect are the national and provincial archives in Canada, the Immigration Archives at the University of Minnesota in Minneapolis, the Centre for Migration Studies – Zavod za Migracije i Narodnosti – and Matica Iseljenika in Zagreb, the Multicultural History Society of Ontario, and more recently the Croatian Ethnic Institute of Chicago. Some collections, in fact, have been made available only very recently and their materials could not be incorporated into this work. Therefore, the process of defining the Croatian ethnic group's history and place in Canadian history has only just begun. To further this purpose, the author has also deposited the bulk of the research contained in this book at the Public Archives of Canada in Ottawa.

As has been noted above, historians of ethnic history have many intellectual and scholarly debts to acknowledge in writing such history. Not all can be given the credit they fully deserve in such a short space, but some can be given brief mention. Newspaper editors have often acted as the sole repository of ethnic group consciousness in the first phase of settlement: the place of Peter Stanković as editor of the *Croatian Voice* for over four decades from 1929 is a unique one. Although he has recently passed away, he and his newspaper provided me with a valuable continuous record of the Croatian experience in Canada. Other considerable debts are owing to researchers who helped in the collection of documents and data for this book, notably Lorry Felske, George Kokich, and Petr Mirejovsky. Others supplied vital information, photographs, translations, and personal documents and memoirs: Mirko Meheš, Peter Culumović, Dr. Vladimir Markotić, Mladen Giunio-Zorkin, K.N. Beckie, Kae Smiley, A. Miletić, M. Glibota, R.B. Nizich, Fra. Ljubo Krašić, Fra. D. Boban, Alois Graf, W.Shubat, J. Filipovic, M. Matijević, J. Zagar, T. Surluga, M. Prpich, Ian Getty, and many others too numerous to list here. Thanks must also go to the various archives and institutes mentioned above, notably Walter Neutel and Myron Momryk of the National Ethnic Archives in Ottawa, Ivo Baučić of the Centre for Migration Studies at Zagreb, Ivan Čizmić of Matica Iseljenika and T. Telišman and Ivan Marković of the ZAMIN Archives in Zagreb, and R. Vecoli of the Immigration Archives at the University of Minnesota. The support and encouragement of the federal government in this project have been acknowledged by the series editors, but specific thanks are due to Myron Momryk, Steve Jaworsky, Roberta Russell, and Yok Leng Chang of the Department of the Secretary of State, Multiculturalism Directorate, and also to Statistics Canada and to the Department of Manpower and Immigration for their assistance. My deepest thanks and gratitude must go to the patient editors of this series, Howard Palmer and Jean Burnet, for their forbearance and encouragement through every stage of this lengthy process. To the Killam Resident Fellowship Program at the University of Calgary for permitting the time to complete the manuscript, and those who typed and read the several drafts of this work go my heartfelt thanks. Above all, my deepest gratitude goes to my wife, who encouraged this work, and to my children, who patiently awaited the result. Finally, one must add the author's customary and final demur, that despite all of the assistance and encouragement in both the research and writing of this work, any errors and omissions which remain are solely my responsibility.

Anthony W. Rasporich
January 9, 1982

From Croatia: Land, People, and Culture, *vol. II, edited by Francis H. Eterovitch and Christopher Spalatin (Toronto: University of Toronto Press, 1970), p. iii. Reproduced by permission of the University of Toronto Press.*

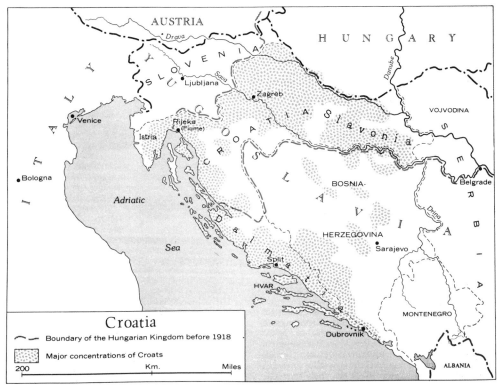

To my parents and grandparents
who came to Canada a half-century ago,
and who taught me the importance of
being Croatian and of becoming Canadian.

Introduction

Croatia is a Balkan and Mediterranean land located in present-day
Yugoslavia. Its historic limits have been the subject of much controversy,
but were in their larger configuration bounded by the Adriatic Sea in the
southwest, the Kupa, Sutla, Drava, and Danube Rivers in the north, and
the Sava and Drina Rivers to the southeast. Croatians have lived along
with other nationalities and ethnic groups in this geographically diverse
region, which can be roughly divided into three parts: the Adriatic
coastal region and island littoral extending from Istria in the north
through Dalmatia to Dubrovnik and Boka Kotorska in the south; directly to the east of this, the Dinaric Alps, a rugged mountainous region
roughly contiguous with the republic of Bosnia-Herzegovina; to the
north, the Pannonian plains stretching from northern Croatia into
Slavonia south to Vojvodina. Because of the varied climate and terrain,
communications have proven difficult historically, and consequently,
geographic isolation imparted regional features to these three maritime,
mountain, and plains societies.[1]

Historically and ethnographically the Croatian peoples were of diverse
origins, and there are various speculations as to their Slavic and Iranian
roots. They were apparently referred to in ancient Persian sources of the
sixth century B.C. and Greek sources of the second century A.D. as
Harahvatish, or Khoroathos.[2] Various layers of history must be pulled
back to uncover the Croatian people from the ancient remains of Illyria
in the Roman Empire forward in time to the invasions of the sixth and
seventh centuries and the barbarian invasions of the Goths, Avars, and
Slavs from the east.[3] The term "Croat" is said by some to have derived
from this later period and from the original location in the Carpathian
Mountains (Karpati, Horvati) and from the names for the inhabitants of
this region (Chrobaten, Hrvati).[4] Brought into the eastern Adriatic
region about 626 A.D. to shore up the failing Roman Empire against the
Avars, the Croatians gradually settled in along with other south Slavic
tribes in the eighth century.[5] Gradually, by a complex series of dynastic

1

wars, a Croatian military-feudal state emerged from the seventh to the eleventh centuries. Within its constantly shifting borders, it contained various peoples – Croatian conquerors, Croatized peoples such as the Latins of the Dalmatian coast, Illyrian remnants on the upper Adriatic, and Avars in the interior. In a sense, the conquerors were also conquered through the impact of Christianity, which spread through southeastern Europe at this time and was complicated in this region by a struggle between the Latin clergy from the West and the old Slavonic liturgy and Bogomil Manicheanism from the East.

Several events and institutions of importance derived from the early medieval period of Croatia. The acceptance of the Croats into Roman Catholic Christianity in 680 A.D. marked the beginning of historic tension between Byzantium and Rome and of cultural tension between Eastern and Western civilization. The beginnings of a Croatian feudal territory linked with the West were evident in the donations of lands, monasteries, and allegiance to Rome by such Croatian dukes and kings as Trpimir, Krešimir, and Zvonimir of Split.[6] Conversely, Pope John X addressed King Tomislav of the Trpimiric dynasty as "Rex Croatorum" in 924 A.D., and he was crowned the following year, according to the traditional custom, before a general assembly. This period also saw the military unification under Tomislav of the three former medieval regions of Pannonian Croatia and "white" and "red" Croatia of the north and south Adriatic coast (both of which were enshrined in the Croatian coat of arms – a red and white chess board). This medieval state reached its peak as a military and naval power strategically placed between East and West in the latter half of the eleventh century under kings Krešimir and Zvonimir. Subsequently, when its bloodline was extinguished the medieval kingdom was absorbed into the Hungarian dynasty in 1102 with the election of King Koloman of the Arpad dynasty. It was this dynastic union with Hungary, with its provision for a separate Croatian viceroy or *ban* and separate *Sabor* (parliament), which was in fact to govern Croatia until World War I.[7]

The next five hundred years saw the Croatian kingdom and its rulers succumbing in succession to the greater empires surrounding it. The brief power vacuum in the West, which had allowed it to emerge during the decline of Rome, was soon filled by the rise of Venice as a powerful state, which held sway over the Dalmatian coast from the fifteenth to the nineteenth centuries. The Croatian kings then threw in their lot with the emergent Hapsburgs and the Holy Roman Empire against the advancing Turks who swept from the south into the Balkans in the fourteenth and fifteenth centuries. Part of Croatia in effect became a military border (Vojna Krajina) against the advancing Turks, with peasants shouldering their muskets as they went into their fields. The subjugation of the Croatian peasantry and aristocracy to the Hapsburg imperial rule was gradual but certain, marked by the futile uprising of the peasant revolutionary, Matija Gubec, in 1573, and by the execution of the two Croatian *bans*,

2

Zrinski and Frankopan, in 1671. Thus, by the seventeenth century, the former medieval Croatian territory was severally partitioned under the divided control of the city-state of Venice, the Ottoman Turks, and the Hapsburgs.

The Croatians continued as a semi-conquered people into the nineteenth century, this time as the Illyrian kingdom under Napoleon, but they were inspired by the French Revolutionary spirit of nationalism that suffused the Napoleonic conquest. Although they continued under Austrian rule, the Croatian intelligentsia became enamoured with nationalism much as did other central and east European peoples such as the Russians, Czechs, Slovaks, and Serbs. The formation of cultural societies such as *Matica Hrvatska* (1842) and the articulation of national poetry and songs such as "Hrvatska Domovina" (Croatian Homeland) and "Još Hrvatska Nij Propala" (Croatia Has Not Yet Perished) were enduring expressions of this Croatian national spirit.[8] The search for a unified South Slav Illyrian literary language was led in the 1830's by the Croatian linguist, Ljudevit Gaj, and the later cultural variant of Illyrianism by Bishop Josip Juraj Strossmayer. Other aristocrats and academicians like Count Janko Drašković and, later, Dr. Ante Starčević were heavily influenced by French liberal and romantic thought and propounded ideas of Croatian self-determination and independence. Thus the articulation of a national ideology was less the product of politicians and statesmen than of poets, philologists, historians, and *philosophes*.[9] The fires that had kindled romantic nationalism needed only the whirlwind of political reaction and oppression to fan them into full flame. This it received in full force during the late nineteenth-century reaction led by the Hungarian nobleman, Count Khuen-Hedervary, who ruled autocratically as "the Iron Ban" of Croatia-Slavonia from 1883-1903. Ultimately the whole Balkan powderkeg exploded into a regional war in 1912-13, then dramatically into World War I when the Serbian nationalist, Gavrilo Princip, assassinated the Austrian Archduke, Francis Ferdinand, at Sarajevo in June of 1914.

The creation of an independent but centralized "Kingdom of the Serbs, Croats, and Slovenes" in December, 1918, did not bring an end to Croatian national aspirations. In 1928 the assassination of Stjepan Radić, the leader of the Croatian Peasant Party, led the Croatian deputies to withdraw from the central Parliament in Belgrade and retire to the old *sabor* (assembly hall) in Zagreb.[10] A year later, King Alexander introduced a dictatorship, changed the name of the state of Yugoslavia, and began a decade of political repression and centralization that forced many Croatians into active and now illegal opposition. Some, like Ante Pavelić, became leaders of the radical-right Ustaša (rebel) faction, and others, including Josip Broz-Tito, continued to promote the Yugoslav-Communist cause of the radical left.[11] Both Pavelić and Tito would eventually form governments: Pavelić the Independent State of Croatia on April 10, 1941, which lasted under German support until Tito's Partisans

3

formed the new government of Yugoslavia in May of 1945. Nor did Croatian dissent and national aspirations end there, for a world community of refugee intellectuals and émigrés actively dissented against the new federal state of Yugoslavia as yet another extension of the pre-war dominance by Belgrade.[12] Also, Marxist socialist dissent continued from within, reflected for example in the journal, *Praxis*, sponsored by the Croatian Philosophical Society until its closure in 1975.[13]

While the message of the latter was more Marxian humanism than nationalism, it still continued to reflect the ethical ideals of human freedom (*sloboda*) and struggle (*borba*),[14] which may also be seen as an expression of cultural environment. The historian Braudel observes on the great passion for freedom in the mountain people of the Dinaric Alps as early as the fifteenth century: "The *Zagorci* were born soldiers, bandits or outlaws, *hajduk* or *uskok* 'nimble as a deer,' their courage was legendary. The mountain terrain lent itself to their surprise attacks, and any number of folk songs, the *pesma* glorify their exploits, the beys they trounced, the caravans they attacked, and the beautiful maidens they carried off."[15] Given similar Croatian heroes like the peasant revolutionary of Zagorje, Matija Gubec, and such popular folk-sayings as "better to drop into a grave than to become a slave," the Croatians' reaction to freedom denied is culturally and historically understandable.

There are many other cultural elements in the ethnic character of Croatians, not all positive. Their peasant character was summed up in the perceptive observations of the Slovenian-American author, Louis Adamic, on his return to the Yugoslavia of the 1930's:

> The Croats are real peasants, slow, plodding, persevering; sad, idealistic, naive, muddled, tragic-minded, not easily articulate, superstitious; always complaining, but in the curious mingling of pagan and Catholic faiths, with their constitutional distrust of everything not of their own making, infinitely patient and quietly strong – in brief full of positive and negative traits.[16]

To the mixture of human frailties may be added a whole list of ethical and moral contradictions identified by the Croatian-American scholar, F.H. Eterovich: humanity and inhumanity; friendship and the law of vengeance; harmony and religious intolerance; brotherhood and anarchy; honour and disgrace; piety and blasphemy.[17] Life itself is considered in the peasant and rural perspective as one of intense struggle and contrast between the ideal and the real – even the final refrain of the national hymn sings of contrasts between sunshine and shadow, and of life and death itself.

Yet another vital element in the rural perspective of Croatians was the communal emphasis upon the extended clan or *zadruga*, which dominated all social relationships. Much like other traditional Mediterranean or East European societies or even the Chinese tongs or the Scottish clans, the family was a complex social web extending well beyond the nuclear family. In Croatia, there were wide regional variations, but in general these extended clans featured strong patriarchy, clear divisions of labour, and little or no private property. The life cycle from birth to death was highly organized and tribal in its prescription, dictating everything from military participation to religious observance. With urbanization and capital penetration of agriculture the *zadruga* declined, but its communal social legacy and moral influence played an important role well into the period of mass migration in the twentieth century.[18]

As in every traditional society custom and folklore were rich, ranging from highly colourful costumes to the *pjesme* or folksongs, sung to the music of the *gusla* (violin-like) and, later, the *tamburitza* (mandolin-like). Regional variations imparted a distinctive flavour to every element of folk art and costume among the similar yet different peoples of the interior plains, the Dinaric mountains, and the Adriatic Coast. The external influences of other contiguous cultures, such as the Turkish, Hungarian, Italian, and German, also had an impact on these regional subcultures. At the same time, however, nearly all adopted some version of the national dance, the *kolo* (circle), which was danced on the village greens of every region.[19] Religious observance of holy days, the celebration of births and marriage, and lamentation of death also followed carefully prescribed ceremonies and rituals. Christmas and Easter were particularly significant in Croatian-Catholic culture, with carefully prescribed calendars of events through the Advent and Lenten seasons. Close attention was paid to the preparation of foods for the Christmas Day feast, such as suckling pig, bread, and *kolaći* (pastries), and to such regional customs as the cutting of the yule log (*badnjak*), the placing of the straw, and the blessing of the herds and flocks.[20] Similarly, at Easter, the colouring and exchange of Easter eggs among the young and the preparation of such special foods as roast lamb, ham, fresh onions, and cakes for Easter Sunday were folk traditions that would be retained even in North America.[21] Also, pagan superstitions and beliefs – the interpretation of dreams, the evil eye, and forecasts of natural disaster so common to agrarian societies – formed part of the people's belief system.[22]

Perhaps the most constant feature of Croatian social life for the last millenium has been the pervasive influence of Catholicism. Despite tensions between the Roman and Slavonic rituals and early difficulties with the papal claims to temporal authority, the historic separation of church and state has persisted for several centuries in Croatia, and "a free state and a free church" has been the general rule.[23] At last official count in 1953, over three-quarters of Croatians were Catholic adherents with minorities of Moslem, Orthodox, Calvinist, and Jewish persuasion, but religious instruction and observance have probably declined since then. There are still powerful evidences of its survival, however. As one observer notes, "The Roman Catholic Church of the Croats and Slovenes is probably more national today in an ethnic sense than ever before in its national history." The substitution of the vernacular for Latin, the creation of two new metropolitan provinces in Rijeka and Split in 1969, and the canonization of the first Croatian Saint, Nikola Tavelić, in 1970 were recent evidence of the durability of the Croatian Catholic tradition in Yugoslavia.[24]

A national language is a further historic issue in the maintenance of an ethnic and national identity among Croatians. Traditionally, Croatian literature had developed in four different dialects with four different orthographies, one in the Zagreb region and hinterland, and others in Dubrovnik, Dalmatia, and Slavonia.[25] Beginning in the nineteenth century with Ljudevit Gaj an attempt was made to adopt a standard Illyrian language and orthography, setting aside some of the other regional dialects such as *Čakavian* and *Kajkavian* in favour of the *Štokavian*. Thereafter, the struggle for linguistic distinctiveness continued between those in the Zagreb school who favoured the unique Croatian linguistic traditions and those who would draw it closer to the Serbian standard language and eastern *Štokavian* dialect.[26] Language policy after World War II was subsequently determined by the Novi Sad agreement of 1954, which aimed at greater linguistic unification in Yugoslavia, stating that Croatian, Serbian, and Montenegrin were one language with two pronunciations (*ekavian* and *ijekavian*) and two alphabets (Latin and Cyrillic).[27] By the mid-sixties this agreement began to come apart, especially in 1967 when many prominent Croatian linguists and writers issued a declaration in favour of a distinct "Croatian literary language" and embarked on a separate orthography, which was printed in 1971 but never appeared in Yugoslavia. The joint dictionary project also begun in the sixties was subsequently abandoned by *Matica Hrvatska* in Croatia, and according to one recent observer, "No monolingual dictionary acceptable to both Croatians and Serbs exists or will be produced in the foreseeable future."[28]

If Croatians shared another characteristic beyond their stubbornness for national survival at home, it was a history of mobility and migration abroad. From the invasion of the Turks in the fifteenth century, they have been a people buffeted about by conquest, wars, and economic crisis. In the last century alone they endured a massive agricultural crisis, devastation of their vineyards, two world wars fought on their soil, a desperate economic crisis in the interwar years, and a difficult post-war economic reconstruction of Yugoslavia after 1945. But where other nationalities often chose to stay, the Croatians more than any of the other nationalities of Yugoslavia emigrated from their homeland. According to some estimates of the recent historic migration from Yugoslavia, the Croatians numbered 1.5 million migrants or three-quarters of all the people of Yugoslavian origin living abroad,[29] despite the fact that in the 1971 census they accounted for just over a quarter of the 20 million people contained in the six constituent republics of Yugoslavia (Slovenia, Croatia, Bosnia-Herzegovina, Serbia, Montenegro, and Macedonia).[30]

And in 1971 alone it was conservatively estimated that there were nearly 261,000 migrant workers from the Croatian republic abroad in Europe, the Americas, and Australasia.[31] Thus, the historical total and the current migration from Croatia have likely produced in combination nearly two million persons of Croatian origin living abroad, most of them in the United States, South America, and Europe.[32] The Canadian share of this total migration has been a modest one, perhaps some 65,000 recent emigrants, and many more if their descendants are added to these. As such, however, this is the fourth largest concentration of permanent migrants in any country outside of Yugoslavia, and the total is proportionally more significant in Canada than Croatian-Americans are within the total population of the United States.

Numbers do not in themselves relate much of the human drama of migration, any more than mortalities relate the true horrors of war or vital statistics the real vitality of a society. For migration also deals with the sum total of human aspirations and hopes as well as the economic calculus of wage differentials and comparative living standards. In some cases, the perception of a better life meant life rather than death or an escape from starvation and abject rural poverty, or more simply, a better material existence which might include comforts rather than necessities. These dreams and hopes were often shattered, for some when cruel misfortune or illness claimed their lives in an alien land, and for others who returned home when Canada did not fulfil the promise of their dreams. In essence, then, the history of immigration is the most intense of human dramas; this history tells of those who, through strength or weakness, fear or hope, boredom or adventure, decided to leave in search of a better life.

NOTES

1. Stephen Gazi, *A History of Croatia* (New York: Philosophical Library, 1973), pp. 1-11.

2. Stanko Guldescu, *History of Medieval Croatia* (The Hague: Mouton, 1964), pp. 29-31.

3. Alexsandar Stipčević, *The Illyrians, History and Culture* (Park Ridge, N.J.: Noyes Press, 1977), pp. 14-77.

4. F. Preveden, "An Outline of a Review of Croatian History (b) Etymology of the names 'Hrvat' and 'Srbin'," *Zajedničar*, 10 January 1940.

5. V. Markotic, "Archaeology," in F.H. Eterovich and C. Spalatin (eds.), *Croatia, Land, People and Culture*, vol. 1 (Toronto: University of Toronto Press, 1970), pp. 20-85; Gazi, *History of Croatia*, p. 11.

6. "Three Medieval Croatian Documents from Split," *British Croatian Review*, no. 16 (June, 1979), pp. 35-45.

7. Guldescu, *History of Medieval Croatia,* pp. 182-4.

8. Eterovich and Spalatin (eds.), *Croatia,* vol. 1, pp. 242-51, 283-7.

9. Hans Kohn, *The Idea of Nationalism,* (New York: Collier Books, 1944), pp. 543-76; Mirjana Gross, "Social Structure and National Movements among the Yugoslav Peoples on the Eve of World War I," unpublished ms. contained in *Yugoslav Historiography 1965-75,* Congress proceedings; and Mirjan Gross, *Povijest Pravaške Ideologije* (Zagreb: University of Zagreb, Institute of Croatian History, 1973).

10. Wesley Gewehr, *The Rise of Nationalism in the Balkans, 1800-1930* (New York: Archon Books, 1967 reprint), p. 107.

11. Ivan Avakumović, *History of the Communist Party of Yugoslavia,* vol. I (Aberdeen: Aberdeen University Press, 1967), pp. 93-173.

12. See N. Dinko Šuljak, *Croatia's Struggle for Independence: A Documentary History* (Arcadia, California: Croatian Information Service, 1977), pp. 201-388.

13. Gerson S. Sher, *Praxis: Marxist Criticism and Dissent in Socialist Yugoslavia* (Bloomington: Indiana University Press, 1977).

14. See Eterovich and Spalatin (eds.), *Croatia,* vol. I, pp. 206-7; M. Spalatin, "Perspectives on the Croatian Concept of Liberty," *Journal of Croatian Studies,* XVII (1976), pp. 3-9.

15. Fernand Braudel, *The Mediterranean and the Mediterranean World in the Age of Philip II,* vol. I (New York: Harper and Row, 1972), p. 57.

16. Louis Adamic, *The Native's Return: An American Immigrant Visits Yugoslavia and Discovers His Old Country,* (New York: Harpers, 1934), pp. 267-8. See also Ruth Trouton, *Peasant Renaissance in Yugoslavia, 1900-50* (London: Routledge and Kegan-Paul, 1952), pp. 24-30.

17. Eterovich and Spalatin (eds.), *Croatia,* vol. I, p. 221. A more recent socio-psychological analysis of Croatian personality is presented in Hrvoje Lorković, "The Dynamic Psychology of Croatian Discord," *Journal of Croatian Studies,* XVIII-XIX (1877-78), pp. 73-85.

18. See Vera St. Erlich, *The Family in Transition: A Study of 300 Yugoslav Villages* (Princeton, N.J.: Princeton University Press, 1966), pp. 3-30; Dinko Tomasic, *Personality and Culture in East European Politics* (New York: G.W. Stewart, 1948); and also Tomasic's "Peasant Movement of Croatia," *Zajedničar,* 30 October, 27 November 1940.

19. See *Fourth Canadian Folklore Festival* (Edmonton: Croatian Folklore Group, Edmonton, and the Croatian Folklore Federation of Canada, 1978).

20. Ante Ostric, "La Structure et Les Moeurs de la Société Croate"(Thesis no. 126, Faculté des Sciences Économiques et Sociales, University of Geneva, 1950), pp. 208-70.

21. Linda Bennett, "Personal Choice in Ethnic Identity Maintenance: Serbs, Croats and Slovenes in Washington, D.C.," (Palo Alto: Ragusan Press, 1978), pp. 112-13.

22. See Lorraine Matko, "The Americanization of Croatian Folklore," Part II, *Zajedničar,* 29 September 1976; see also Stipčević, *The Illyrians,* p. 86.

23. Eterovich and Spalatin (eds.), *Croatia*, vol. I, p. 223.
24. M.B. Petrovich, "Yugoslavia: Religion and the Tensions of a Multinational State," *East European Quarterly,* IV, 1, pp. 118-35.
25. Ivo Frangeš, "Yugoslav Literature: A Review for Foreign Slavists," *East European Quarterly,* VI, 2, pp. 153-76.
26. Christopher Spalatin, "The Rise of the Croatian Standard Language," *Journal of Croatian Studies*, XVI (1975), pp. 3-17.
27. C. Spalatin, "The Language Situation in Croatia Today," *Journal of Croatian Studies,* XIV-XV (1973-74), pp. 3-12. See also George Schöpflin, "The Ideology of Croatian Nationalism," *Survey: A Journal of East-West Studies,* XIX, 1 (Winter, 1973), pp. 123-46.
28. Morton Benson, "Problems of Serbo-Croatian Lexicography," *Canadian Slavonic Papers,* XX, 3 (September, 1978), p. 300; Schöpflin, "Croatian Nationalism," pp. 135-37.
29. Većeslav Holjevac, *Hrvati Izvan Domovine* (Zagreb: Matica Hrvatska, 1968), pp. 350-1. See also Jozo Tomasevich, *Peasants, Politics and Social Change in Yugoslavia* (Stanford: Stanford University Press, 1955), pp. 292-4.
30. See *Nations and Nationalities of Yugoslavia* (Belgrade: Medjunarodna Politika, 1974), p. 20. Estimates by Croatian historians and observers are considerably above the 4.5 million shown in the Yugoslav census of 1971, largely because it counts 1.7 million Moslems as a separate "nationality" in Bosnia. George Prpić, *The Croatian Immigrants in America*, (New York: Philosophical Library, 1971), p. 18, estimates 6 million Croatians.
31. Ivo Baučić, *Radnici u Inozemstvu Prema Popisu Stanovništva Jugoslavije 1971* (Yugoslav Workers Abroad According to the 1971 Yugoslav Census), Studies of the Institute of Geography, University of Zagreb, vol. 12, no. 4 (Zagreb, 1973), pp. 26, 38, 39.
32. Holjevac, *Hrvati Izvan Domovine*, p. 350; Leszek Kosinski, "Yugoslavia and International Migration," *Canadian Slavonic Papers,* XX (September, 1978), pp. 314-38.

ONE

"Kolumbusari" and Ulysses All, 1500-1900

Among many old Croatian immigrants the highest status that might be conferred upon those who came before them was that of "Kolumbusari," those who were old enough to have come with Columbus. This figurative conceit expresses well the gap between the generation of Croatian pioneers who came before 1900 and the mass of those who came later, in the 1920's. But these early migrants, some of whom came not long after Columbus and some as late as 1900, had something in common. They were for the most part highly mobile, single, and male; they sought work and adventure in the New World and often returned as triumphant "Amerikantsi" to their own villages in Croatia. Just as often they would disappear into the great melting pot of American life never to be heard from again. But only in a few instances did they conform to the pattern of the stalwart East European peasant in a sheepskin coat surrounded by a large family and village clan. Few had the intention of settling permanently in North America and fewer still anticipated the prospect of family or communal farming in the vast wheatlands of western Canada. Occupationally they were in classically male categories – soldiers, sailors, fishermen, and miners. Emotionally they were adventurers, men of strong arm and nerve like the ancient Ulysses on a world odyssey full of peril, romance, occasional shipwreck, and always the prospect of a triumphant and often dramatic return home.

Croatian contacts with Canada were understandably few before the nineteenth century. They were limited, in fact, to occasional and sporadic accidents of historical circumstance, and none was to be followed by systematic attempts at colonization. Invariably their story is connected with highly mobile groups, such as military, trading, and exploring expeditions that recruited internationally for skilled personnel. For the most part, permanency in North America resulted only from accidental isolation or death, and the rest returned to Europe to be reabsorbed or lost in the mainstream of human history.

Considerable speculation and guesswork must surround those few

10

early references to Croatians, since they may have variously been referred to in historical records as Venetians, Dalmatians, Germans, Austrians, Hungarians, Sclavonians, or Slavs, and less accurately as nearly every other European nationality from Russian to French. Among the more precise designations, the Venetian results from the maritime hegemony of the Republic of Venice on the Adriatic in the fifteenth century, whence many Croats of the Adriatic littoral were absorbed into the Venetian navy as sailors, artisans, and shipbuilders. Later, this Adriatic nursery of seamen would produce Russian naval officers and seamen for the imperial navies of Peter the Great and Empress Catherine in the seventeenth and eighteenth centuries. And, with the establishment of the Austrian dominance over the northern coastline of the Adriatic in the nineteenth century, it was estimated that the Croatians formed one-half to two-thirds of the naval personnel of the Austro-Hungarian imperial navy.[1]

Independent of these imperial affiliations, Croatians might also be described by their local ethnic or cultural affinities. Hence, a Croat might be inclined to declare himself as a native of Dubrovnik or the flourishing Republic of Ragusa as it was known in the Venetian imperium (whence the English corruption "argosy" describing the spacious carracks that carried cargo from the Mediterranean to England).[2] If he were from the northern coastline he might identify himself as a Primorac (literally "by the sea") or from the southern coast as a Dalmatian, from the former Roman province of Dalmatia. Or he might wish to designate himself a resident of one of the many islands of the Adriatic littoral such as Brač, Hvar, Rab, and Krk or of the coastal towns of Senj, Šibenik, Zadar, or Boka Kotor. Conversely, if he were from more interior locations he might be identified as a "Sclavonian" or native of the region lying between the Sava and Drava Rivers. This region was not to be confused, though it often was, with the territory of Slovenia or Carniola to the northeast or with the cultural designation "Sclav" or "Slav," which became popular with the rise of the Slavic pan-national movements of the nineteenth century.

Both coastal and interior Croats would be mentioned in early accounts of Canadian discovery and colonization. Venetian contacts with the eastern Atlantic Coast prior to Cabot's landfall in 1497 may have substance to them, and it is possible that among the crews of the Zeno brothers' expedition of the late fourteenth century were seamen from the Dalmatian coastline.[3] More positive claims can probably be made for Croatians found in the crew lists of the Cartier-Roberval expedition to Canada in 1542-43. Among the group of some 200 colonists who sailed with Le Sieur de Roberval from La Rochelle to Montreal were two sailors from the Adriatic coastline, one Giovanni Malogrudici (Malogrudic) from Senj and Marino Masalarda from Dubrovnik.[4] Even more positive identification is given some sixty years later to a member of Samuel de Champlain's expedition to Acadia in 1605-1606. Champlain noted in his

11

diary that he was accompanied in his search for precious metals to the mouth of the Saint John River by Sieur de Monts and a miner by the name of Jacques, "a native of Sclavonia, a man well versed in the search for minerals." Champlain further recorded that Jacques (Jakov) explored the coast in the vicinity of the Saint John River for copper and advised him that the mineral matrix was poor and that the rocky overburden and tides prevented easy mining of the metal.[5]

The subsequent history of New France in the seventeenth century was once referred to by an eminent Canadian historian as an armed camp, and significantly those Croats who are mentioned in its history are soldiers and mercenaries. The Croats had earned a fearsome reputation during the Religious Wars in defending the Hapsburg monarchy against the French and the Dutch in the North and the Turks in the South, and the wolf's head banner carried by some of the Croatian regiments bore the slogan "Idem za plinom" (I march for plunder). Their ferocity in combat, or at least an awesome reputation, appears to have carried as far as Montreal with the French Jesuits, who compared the military tactics of the Iroquois besiegers in 1642 to "Goblins" and to "Croats" for their cunning, stealth, and ferocity.[6] Later in the seventeenth century it is apparent that Croatians had actually found their way into French regiments, and Croatian-American historian, Adam Eterovich, has found among the regimental entries in Louisiana a French Acadian, George Mathieu (b. 1685), "Croatian" sergeant of a company of French marines.[7]

Although the process by which such mercenaries found their way into French regiments is unclear, the logic of historical events in the mid-eighteenth century sheds some light on those foreign volunteers raised in Europe for service in French America during the Seven Years' War. In 1757, Maria Theresa of Austria and the rulers of the German principalities became France's ally against England and Prussia. Both would become sources of manpower for the last-ditch defence of French North America as the superior forces of the British army closed the circle around New France in 1758-59. Among the last defenders of Louisbourg against the assaults of Wolfe's army were soldiers from the South German states and from Austria whose names suggest Croatian ancestry. Among the foreign volunteers from the Palatinate, Bavaria, and Swabia were Valentin Butich, Joseph Emich, and Nicholas Vagentac, whose ages ranged from eighteen to twenty-three, and in the Austrian volunteers were Lieut. Konnerad Klic (Klaić?) and Nicholas Vayna.[8]

Croatians may indeed have come with the British conquerors who displaced the French and brought in their train German and south-central European mercenaries and settlers. Among the German settlers recruited for settlement in Nova Scotia in the 1750's were many residents of the Palatinate, Swabia, and Bavaria and a few south Europeans.[9] Equally, there may have been one or two Croatian musicians and artists from Germany and Austria who found their way into the Maritime colonies and the St. Lawrence in the late eighteenth century: among the German mercenary regiments that served in the British army in Canada were many accomplished bandmasters and musicians who brought the music of Handel, Haydn, Mozart, and Beethoven to Canada.[10] Indeed, it is more likely that Croatians would have been found in the ranks of the military regiments themselves, such as the De Meurons Swiss regiments, which were raised in southern Europe and were liberally sprinkled with Italian, Polish, and German volunteers.[11]

Farther to the west, Croatians were in more certain evidence in the naval activities off the Pacific Coast of North America. The imperial rivalry between England, Russia, and Spain for territorial acquisitions in the Pacific Ocean had resulted in numerous reconnaissance and trading adventures by the major European naval powers. Given the ubiquity of Dalmatian sailors in the Russian imperial navies after Peter the Great,[12] it is entirely possible that they were in the international crew of the Vitus Bering expedition that explored the coast of North America from Kamchatka.[13] Recent historical attention has also focused on the Spanish expedition of Bodega y Quadra, which explored the northwest coast in 1779 and is alleged to have had a Croatian sailor named Cosulić aboard. He is purported to have accompanied the Spanish expedition to the southern tip of Vancouver Island and to have returned a decade later with a French ship to explore the fishing potential of the lower Fraser estuary.[14]

In the early nineteenth century, the competition for furs on the Northwest coast was extended to the salmon fisheries. White men gradually began to replace the Indians in the salmon fisheries as the latter dwindled rapidly in numbers from smallpox, which was calculated to have killed off 80 per cent of the Columbia River Indians in the first half of the nineteenth century. Among those who gradually displaced them were whites from California and Louisiana and interspersed among these were a number of Croatian fishermen from Dalmatia.[15] The first of these to appear was a small handful who explored the mouth of the Fraser River in 1800.[16] Gradually, the Hudson's Bay Company empire on the Columbia began to expand, and by 1830 the Company had begun to export fish in significant quantity to the Hawaiian Islands. This liaison was either the cause or result of a visit by another Croat, Captain John Dominis, who came to the Columbia River fisheries in 1829 to put up salted salmon for export to Hawaii near St. Helen's, Oregon.[17] Dominis would later disappear at sea on his way to China, but his son John Owen Dominis would carry on his father's connection with Honolulu and later marry the last Queen of Hawaii in 1862.[18] In Oregon country itself, little residual evidence of Croats remained in the fisheries, however, and permanent settlement would take another generation to be established on the coast of British Columbia.[19]

The next major epoch in Croatian migration to the Pacific Northwest was ushered in by the California gold rush of 1849. Of those Croatians

13

who came to San Francisco and vicinity, the vast majority were Dalmatians by origin, and many considered themselves culturally "Slavonians" or "Illyrians" after the South Slav pan-nationalist movement begun by Ljudevit Gaj in the 1830's and 1840's.[20] Culturally and socially they tended to mix easily with other South Slav groups, such as the Serbians and Montenegrins of Greek Orthodox religious persuasion, and were often involved in common business ventures, mutual benefit organizations, and self-help societies.[21] Economically, an inordinate number of entrepreneurs and "capitalists" was among this group – traders, saloon-keepers, claim speculators, storekeepers, and very few gold miners. They drifted from mining camp to mining town as the gold rush began and petered out during the 1850's in northern California and followed the lure of gold and silver into Nevada, Washington, and British Columbia in the 1860's.

Almost from the beginning of the gold rush into the lower Fraser River, Croats began to drift in with many other nationalities from San Francisco. Among the passengers aboard the steamer *Pacific*, which arrived in Victoria on December 3, 1859, was Sam "Mitlich" [Miletich].[22] He would be followed by other ships, passengers, and crews of South Slavic origin as Victoria expanded within a year from a population of 500 to 25,000 to 30,000. By 1861, a second surge of population entered British Columbia, this time headed for the gold fields of the upper Fraser and Cariboo district at Quesnel Forks. The Harrison River and Lilloet Road were completed to provide land transport by pack train into the interior. But Victoria remained the centre of warehousing, shipping, and commerce for upriver transport to Hope, and in 1861 alone over a thousand ships entered Victoria harbour.[23]

Croats emerged quickly in the shipping trade, which was closely linked to San Francisco. The *British Colonist* of January, 1861, recorded the arrival of two brigs, the *Ivich* and the *Vacorsovich*, from California, and soon chronicled the movements of the schooner *Langley* captained by two possible Croats, Baranovich and Nenovich.[24] The *Langley* was soon plying an active trade between New Westminster and Victoria in the south and Sitka in Russian Alaska to the north.[25] Other Croats also settled into Victoria for the duration of the gold rush in the early sixties. By 1862, Sam Miletich had opened the Adelphi Saloon and Billiard Parlour on the corner of Government and Yates Streets.[26] At a time when a game of billiards sold for a dollar and uncut whiskey cost saloon-keepers fifteen dollars a gallon and sold for a dollar a glass over the counter, Miletich appeared to be on his way to a comfortable fortune. Competition diminished that hope somewhat when, at the height of the gold rush in 1863, a competitor appeared just a block away on the corner of Government and Fort Streets.

Elia Chielovich, a Serb from Boka Kotorska on the Adriatic Coast to the south and east of Dubrovnik, had come to California and established himself as a merchant in the San Francisco area. In 1857 he was a founding member of the Greek-Slavonian Orthodox Church and Benevolent Society. In the same year he married an Irish girl, Jane, and had a daughter by her in 1859.[27] As late as 1862 he owned a saloon on the corner of California Street in San Francisco, but hearing of the riches to be made in Victoria he headed north in 1863. On July 31, 1863, Chielovich announced the grand opening of the Occidental Billiard Saloon, appointed in a style which "is not surpassed in San Francisco." Located in Victoria's prime business district, the Occidental was to have exactly twice as many tables, six of Phelan's finest, as the more modest Adelphi. And it was to have the most modern of amenities offered by Robertson's Brick Block, tasteful carpeting, and handsome appointments, all fully ventilated and illuminated by gaslight.[28]

A friendly competition for public recognition and notoriety typical of frontier societies also seems to have developed between Miletich and Chielovich and between their Adelphi and the Occidental hotels. Both were active in donating to private and public charities, and when Sam Miletich would contribute a dollar to Governor Douglas's special reception fund or to an impoverished widow and her children, Elia Chielovich would respond with a five-dollar donation to the Royal Hospital Fund or give five dollars to the Female Aid Association via Jane Chielovich.[29] Miletich, probably a bachelor, achieved the greatest public scoop, however, when he addressed a get-well card along with a number of his patrons to a saloon singer, "Belle Divine," who was convalescing from an unspecified illness.[30]

In the meantime, a more dramatic story had developed in the gold diggings further up the Fraser in Cariboo country. Thousands of miners, speculators, gamblers, and human beings of every description and nationality swarmed into mining towns such as Williams Creek, Horsefly, Soda Creek, Quesnel, Keithley Creek, and Barkerville. Everyone had one thought in mind, striking it rich on a claim such as the one where "Cariboo" Cameron had hauled out $150 worth of gold in twelve buckets of water.[31] Most, however, were completely unprepared for the poverty, back-breaking labour, hunger, and violence that characterized the gold-diggings. For most it was pick-and-shovel labour at $10-15 per day, with cabbage, beans, and bacon at a dollar a pound and bacon at $1.75, and lodging at $1.50 a night if you could find it. Card games occasionally ended in a gunfight and murder, and despite the sobering presence of the hanging circuit judge, Matthew Baillie Begbie, those who had struck pay dirt could not really be protected against the envy of those who hadn't – such as the two Jews and a French-Canadian who were ambushed on the trail for their gold in the winter of 1862-63.[32]

Unlike many of the overlanders from Canada and the green remittance men from Britain, the Croats came early and stayed late. Most, it seems, did not work for wages on the labour-intensive shafts, holes, and tunnels around Williams Creek, but either operated independent claims or speculated from afar in Victoria. The first recorded claim by South Slavs appears to have been in 1861 at Antler Creek when six claims were recorded below the sawmill by *A. Belisch* (Belich), G. Visa, J. Miller, P. Roberts, *M. Randovich* (Radovich), and S. Bell.[33] By 1862 the Croats were into the more promising claims around Williams Creek, and the mining records indicate that F. Dominis and S. Militisch (Sam Miletich) had filed two claims flanked on the west by the Jeff Davis Co. and on the north by the Bagley Company.[34]

By 1863, it was apparent that the pace and tempo of mining in the Cariboo had shifted to larger operations, with greater capitalization required for the excavation of holes and tunnels and for labour costs in extracting less accessible veins of gold. Larger capital also began to displace smaller operations among the Croats and South Slavs. In the spring of 1863, Edward Radovich, Lazarus Radovich, and Elia Chielovich, all of Boka Kotorska, had bought a number of valuable claims, some in the Steadman Company Tunnel at Williams Creek[35] and some in the vicinity of Black Jack Creek.[36] Dalmatian Croats were evident also in the trading of claims, such as M. Yvancovich and Mitchell Radovich at McCollum's Gulch, and a George Petcovich who purchased seventy-five feet of ground in the same area for the substantial sum of $1,500.[37]

As the gold rush crested in 1864-65 and the Cariboo road was completed as far as Barkerville, Croat and South Slav involvement in mining companies and property trading near Williams Creek reached its peak. Elia Chielovich bought a full claim of 133 feet in the Dixon and Davis Company and in addition purchased and sold a half interest in the Prairie Flower Mining Company for $1,000. At McCollum's Gulch, George Petcovich bought and sold interests in the Hart Company, and Mitchell Radovich in the Dixie Company.[38] The Croat claims also spread further northward and eastward toward new speculative properties in Keithley Creek, Horsefly, and Snow Shoe Creek. Sam Miletich and George Petcovich both bought interests in the Anderson Company at Snow Shoe Creek, and the former bought an interest in a quartz ledge at Little Snow Shoe Mountain in the fall of 1864.[39]

Decline in the Victoria community followed swiftly after 1865. As its population began to contract there were already evidences of Croatian movement outward as letters went uncollected in the Victoria post office or city lots were sold for default of taxes.[40] By 1867 Chielovich had departed for Nevada and Sam Miletich had sold out his interest in the Adelphi; Miletich also left Victoria. Indeed, few remained who were involved in mining speculation, and by 1868 only a trace lingered of the prominent names of the early and mid-sixties. By 1871 the Victoria directory listed but four South Slav names, probably Croat, most of which were involved in some aspect of the import-export or wholesale trade: W. Baranovich, fur trader; M. Maringowitch (Marinkovic), employee of P. Murphy; J. Margotich of the schooner *Favorite*; and John Stanovoitch (Stanojević), miner, who lived at Leach's Building on Yates Street.[41]

In the mining claims of the north, one figure dominated in the 1870's as fortunes of the Cariboo fields in the south declined. He was Mitchell Radovich, perhaps a relative of Edward Radovich, owner of the Adelphi Saloon in the 1860's. In the sixties and early seventies he continued to operate in partnership with F. Dominis and A. Belisch, two Croats with whom he had invested at Antler Creek early in the sixties.[42] Then, in the latter half of the 1870's he concentrated his attention on the "Boneta" and "Barker" companies in the Williams Creek area, buying and selling depleted mineral properties and shares in the two into the mid-1880's.[43] His last serious venture in the late 1870's was the Canadian Company, which purchased and sold claims in the area between Williams Lake and Barkerville, including Willow River, Porcupine Creek, and the aptly named Hardscrabble Creek. He continued to operate with at least one or two Croatian partners, and the Canadian Company included among its cosmopolitan membership O. Darpontigny, Alex Grant, *N. Crmro* (Zrno), A. Eude, *A. Pendola*, and *Frank Petric*.[44] And among the miners themselves at least one miner, William Radovich, probably a relative of Mitchell, remained among the human remnant of the gold rush that eked out an existence at Hardscrabble Creek.[45]

The continuity of Croatian immigration and settlement in Canada thus hung by a few slender threads in the 1870's. A small group of hangers-on in Victoria and a few remaining speculators in the Cariboo country were the most substantial elements of continuity. A few others deserve mention. In the mid-seventies, a few Croatians were isolated on the last gold frontier at Cassiar up the Stikine River in far northern British Columbia. Their number included A. Miletich, B. Rosevich, G. Claich, Peter Cargotich, and Charles Baranovich, a trader.[46] The latter may have been the same Charles Baranovich who was caught in 1875 smuggling Hudson's Bay company goods to the Alaska Indians from his base on Prince of Wales Island.[47] His trading acumen did not, however, match the coup of another possible Croat named Boscovitch (Bošković), who capitalized upon the imminent transfer of Alaska from Russia to the United States in 1867. He acquired the surplus stock of the Russian American Fur Company, 16,000 sealskin pelts, at forty cents each, and disposed of them in Victoria at two to three dollars each! He was subsequently prevented from acquiring the remaining 80,000 pelts by an undoubtedly embarrassed governor of the Russian fur company who soon saw the wisdom of dealing directly with American buyers.

Croatian settlement on the Pacific Coast of Canada was re-established in the 1880's with their reappearance in the salmon fisheries. Again, political and economic changes along the northern Adriatic coastline impelled a new wave of Croatian migrants to America. The control of the region passed to Austrian hands in 1812 and was reaffirmed with the defeat of the Italian navy at the battle of Vis (Bitka kod Visa or Viški Boj) in 1886, and the Austrian merchant marine rapidly grew from 200 steamships in 1875 to double that number by 1905. As a consequence the number of Croatian-owned and -operated sailing ships dropped from

17

nearly 500 to 100 in the period from 1875 to 1895. The displaced man-power was soon conscripted into the Austrian navy for a minimum four-year term, and by 1900 one-half of the 10,000 personnel in the imperial navy were Croats from Dalmatia, Istria, and the Adriatic islands, such as Cres, Krk, and Lošinj. Beyond that there was always the opportunity to serve aboard the Austrian merchant steamers where pay was low and hours were long.[48]

Such conditions in the old country accounted for the appearance of Croatian fishermen at the mouth of the Fraser delta again in 1883. The first to appear in the early 1880's were two Croats, M. Karompona and G. Tolich, who fished between Victoria and Seattle; the latter became established as a fish merchant in Victoria.[49] Perhaps family memories from the salmon fishery in the early nineteenth century brought the next three fishermen from Mali Lošinj (Lussin), an island about ninety miles off the Istrian peninsula south of Trieste. In 1883, Mateo and Dominic Bussanich and Antonio Cosulich came to the Port Guichon-Canoe Pass area at the mouth of the Fraser, which was the terminus of the Great Northern Railway branch line from Colebrook, Washington. They were followed a year later by another fisherman from Fiume (Rijeka), Thomas Vicevich, who was apparently one of the hangers-on from the gold rush era. According to one of this early group, they had come northward to the Fraser delta from the mouth of the Columbia River, and here they found the same favourable fishing conditions that pre-vailed in Oregon. They were soon successful in establishing a small can-nery on Westham Island in 1884.[50] The completion of the transcon-tinental Canadian Pacific Railway line a year later guaranteed economic success to the lower Fraser region and an expanding urban market in Vancouver and New Westminster. By 1886 a substantial Croatian settle-ment had begun at Port Guichon, or Ladner, as it was later called.[51]

The community continued on a very tentative basis until the late 1880's, with the males operating the commercial fishery and gradually bringing in their wives and children. Typical perhaps of the pioneers was Venanzio Martinolich, a widower with a son and daughter who came from Austria to North America in 1885. He stopped briefly in New Orleans, where he married his second wife, Antoinette. After sojourning for a short time in Colorado they went westward to Tacoma, Washing-ton, where Martinolich began fishing with his eldest son, Mario, just as his second son, George (Venanzio, Jr.), was born. Hearing of the good fishing in the vicinity of Ladner, he moved there in 1891 and established himself in the boat-building business with his sons.[52]

Another native of Lošinj, Marco Bussanich, had a more exciting life as an itinerant sailor before coming to settle at Port Guichon in 1890. He first joined the crew of the community-owned sailing vessel, or "carat," at the age of twelve in 1879 and worked in the galley at ten cents an hour during a sixteen-hour working day that began at four a.m. He joined the Austrian merchant marine in the Mediterranean at the age of fourteen and in 1882 served on a vessel that sailed from Marseilles to South America and from there to Baltimore and to Saint John, New Brunswick, where he first caught sight of Canada. He traversed the Atlantic back and forth for the next two years. Marco went home briefly to Istria in 1884 where he took work in a local shipyard. Itching for the open sea, he enlisted again in the merchant marine, this time on modern steamships that plied the Atlantic and brought him once more to the eastern coast of the United States and to Saint John. His odyssey then carried him back to Europe where he spent his earnings and lived "like a millionaire" before going home. Marco married while back in Lošinj in 1889 and decided at that time that Canada presented the best opportunity for a better life, no doubt advised by his relative Mateo Bussanich, who already owned a store in Canoe Pass, B.C. Travelling first to Vancouver, he was joined a year and a half later in 1891 by his wife, Domenica, and their two-year-old daughter.[53]

The Viduliches were a third pioneer family in the Fraser delta. The elder Vidulich, Antonio, sailed around the world to England, then to Ceylon, before coming to Port Guichon in 1886. He fished and built boats there for five or six years before he sent for his son, Marko, who was born in Lošinj in 1879. The son boarded a steamer at Trieste that carried him to Halifax, and from there he travelled by train to Vancouver where he was met by his father, whom he had not seen since the age of six or seven. Two years later the young lad was overcome by homesickness for his mother and his home village and begged his father to send him back. He returned but didn't stay long, as the grinding working conditions and low wages caused him to depart again for Canada, where he would remain for the rest of his life.[54]

The beginnings of a permanent community for these few Croats were made possible by the rapid expansion of the salmon-fishing industry in British Columbia in the late 1880's and early 1890's. The transcontinental railway brought population westward, doubling the population of British Columbia between 1881 and 1891. The eastward-bound trains developed a carrying capacity for frozen fish markets in Calgary, Winnipeg, Toronto, and Montreal. By 1888, one dealer alone, "Dutch Bill" Vianen, was shipping nearly a million pounds of fresh salmon. The expansion this caused in the fisheries and the number of boats employed in the annual salmon catch was dramatic. From 1887 to 1891 the fishing boats increased from a half dozen to forty or fifty and the number of year-round fishermen – Finns, Italians, Greeks, and Croats, in addition to Canadian and British-born fishermen – doubled from 100 to 200.[55]

The Croatians shared in the economic benefits of the buoyant fishing economy. The sockeye salmon were seemingly inexhaustible in numbers. Mike Vidulich recollected in his later years that as a boat-puller he would often hit the salmon with his oars while rowing, and that he netted 12,000 sockeye during a three-week period.[56] Fishing was usually done from a twenty-five-foot rowboat or skiff, which two men operated, one a rower or boat-puller and the other a fisherman. If they worked for wages, they worked twelve-hour shifts and earned $2.25 to $2.50 per day depending on whether one rowed or fished. If he sold independently to the canneries, a fisherman could receive 12¢ per sockeye at the beginning of the run and 5¢ per fish at the height of catch. Of the total salmon catch only the choice sockeye counted, and the coho, chum, pink, and big spring salmon were thrown away![57]

Traces of geographic stability had also developed at Canoe Pass, Port Guichon, and Ladner's Landing. Some of the fishermen's families lived in scow houses, which were moved up and down the waterway to better fishing locations. There were some permanent homes, too, such as the one built by Venanzio Martinolich on River Road that would house three generations of the family.[58] Adjacent to it the elder Martinolich and his three sons operated a boat-building business. Catholic church services, which had formerly been held in the home of Laurent Guichon by the Oblate fathers, were finally transferred to a permanent church in 1891. Built under the direction of Father Iréné Jacob, the Sacred Heart Church was dedicated by Bishop Darieu of New Westminster and subsequently became a vital social and cultural centre of the Croatian community of Port Guichon.[59]

While this fishing community became the nucleus of the first settlement of Croats in Canada, during the remainder of the late nineteenth century they were impermanent and rootless in the mining camps of western Canada. The buoyancy of silver prices in the 1880's accounted for several silver mines, particularly in the Lake Superior country in the region of Thunder Bay. Hundreds of miners in the 1880's clustered into the small community of Prince Arthur's Landing, or Port Arthur as it was later called, worked at the various mines such as Silver Islet, Rabbit Mountain, and Jackfish Lake.[60] Few if any of the active miners were Slavs. As in the Cariboo, a Croat or Slovene would appear, usually further up the economic scale than the average miner, for among the small population of Port Arthur was one Ferdinand Sustersić, "analytical and technical chemist" who acted as metallurgist to the swarm of prospectors who brought in mineral samples for assay.[61]

The bulk of the Slav miners were further west in the base and precious metals mines of British Columbia. They were in the coal mines of Vancouver Island near Nanaimo and in the Crowsnest Pass, and in the gold and silver mines of the Kootenays and the lead and zinc mines of the Rossland-Trail district. Among the miners of North Field, for example, there were a few Croats and South Slavs employed as miners and runners by 1892, among them George Lastic, Victor Mieseck, Bart Setko, and Mack Supina.[62] In the small coal-mining town of Wellington near Nanaimo the Italians formed the bulk of the continental Europeans, but there were a few Croats, too, probably from the Italianized region of Istria.[63] By 1897 a young miner by the name of Daniel Radovich had arrived in Ladysmith and was working in the coal mines in the vicinity.

Born in Croatia in 1875, he may have been of the same enterprising Radovich clan that had come to the Cariboo in the 1860's.[64]

All in all, the occupational composition of the early Croatian community had diversified by the late nineteenth century. Of the old Cariboo gold rush one or two miners remained, such as Antonio Belich, who still worked in the diggings around Lilloet. There were still a few Croatian hotelkeepers, bartenders, and storekeepers sprinkled about the province; Mateo Bussanich in Ladner and Matteo Sedola in Wellington were the two most prominent.[65] In addition to the permanent community of fishermen at Ladner, there were perhaps one or two Croats who had found their way on to the land as farmers,[66] and a few others worked on the CPR as brakemen and maintenance men.[67]

While threads of continuity were being established in the fisheries and mines of British Columbia, the last great gold rush of the nineteenth century occurred further to the north in Alaska and the Yukon. Thousands upon thousands of gold-seekers from all over the world poured into the Klondike from 1898 to 1900. Only a few hundred would become rich in the last of the great gold rushes, and only a few thousand out of the hundred thousand who began the journey would find any gold. Money, if it was to be made at all, was in the supply of that vast human train which made its way from Skagway over the Chilkoot Pass and up the Yukon River on to Dawson City and the Klondike gold fields. The prime location was at Skagway before the hungry miners headed over the pass and the prime business was the restaurant and saloon trade. And there on Broadway Street amid the shacks and tents and makeshift saloons was the Pack Train Restaurant owned and operated by Anton Stanish and Leo Ceovich. Opened in the fall of 1897 in a tent, it became the most successful and permanent of Skagway's fly-by-night restaurants.[68]

"Tony" Stanish and "Louie" Ceovich operated a twenty-four-hour-a-day business in their first two years of operation, the first few months of which were spent in the large tent that served as temporary shelter for their fine Austrian-American cuisine. By the winter of 1898 they had moved to the modest structure that was to house the Pack Train Restaurant and Saloon. The restaurant and saloon were related but separate businesses under separate ownership. Occasionally the interests of the two would merge when a customer wished to wash down a meal with a mug of Budweiser beer at five cents or a bottle of Mumm's champagne at ten cents. Customers might even wish to combine eating and drinking after a gruelling trip to the summit or a hard night on the dance floor. They could and did order such spontaneous concoctions from the proprietors as salmon bellies stewed in champagne or eggs sizzled in beer! For the most part, however, the Pack Train simply offered good food and good service – "Eindt de ham and," ordered by Tony, and served within ten minutes by "Big Louie," who operated as the lone cook for fifteen years. The business lasted longer than any other in Skagway and only ended when the chef quit and the *maître d'* retired to

Oregon to raise the hogs and chickens that had fed many hungry prospectors heading for the Yukon gold fields.[69]

There were other Croatian entrepreneurs who went over the mountains into the Yukon, no doubt prompted by the mercantile success of the partners at Skagway. One was Andrija Juraj Miletić of Ledenik in the province of Lika, who observed that there were few fortunes to be made in the gold-diggings and concentrated on his own trade of bricklaying, carpentry, and general contracting and built several log cabins, houses, and commercial establishments in the burgeoning mining towns of the Yukon. When the Yukon bubble burst he invested the capital he had made in the north and settled in Winnipeg, where he built and operated the Bell Hotel on Main Street.[70] Other Croats hung on longer, such as B. Jelich and Martin Zadielovich, who continued to operate a restaurant in Dawson City until at least 1910.[71]

Many miners from Hungary and the adjacent Croatian province of Slavonia also worked as wage labourers in the mining camps of the Yukon. In the winter of 1898, a passenger agent located in New York wrote to Clifford Sifton, Minister of the Interior, asking for the protection of Hungarian and Slavonian miners who would be entering the Yukon, and was assured by his Deputy, James Smart, that all precautions had been taken to preserve law and order there by the local constabulary of the North West Mounted Police.[72] Indeed, the Mounted Police closely monitored the movements of all miners as they travelled up the Yukon River, noting particularly their nationality, age, height, weight, and manner of dress. Their records indicate that a number of Croats and Hungarians poled and punted their way up the Yukon River in the summer of 1902 and later made their way to Dawson Creek by dog-team and sled in the winter of 1903.[73]

The nineteenth-century period of Croatian migration to Canada had thus ended where it had begun – in British Columbia, the Yukon, and Alaska. It had been a migration borne from the east and south, via the Pacific Ocean or the isthmus of Panama. Few Croats had come into the Atlantic provinces or Ontario since the end of the French regime. Two Slovenian missionaries, Frederik Baraga and Franc Pirc (Pierz), were the sole examples of missionary work emanating from south-central Europe that touched upon central Canadian soil in the nineteenth century. Sponsored by the Leopoldine Society of Vienna, Baraga became Vicar-General of Upper Michigan and was authorized by the Bishops of Toronto and Hamilton to include the Lake Superior region of Canada in his ministry. Both he and Pirc would make substantial contributions to the education and Christianization of the early Indians of the Fort William and Michipicoten districts, and Baraga's translations became standard works for the communication of the Scriptures in Ojibway.[74] Beyond these cultured individuals there were few South Slavs, let alone Croats, who can be traced in central Canadian history in the nineteenth century. The censuses for the city of Toronto, for example, yield many Germans,

Poles, Italians, Jews, and even Swedes, Norwegians, and Portuguese in the 1860's and 1870's, but few Croats are as easily identified.[75] Indeed, the only positive identification that can be made in eastern Canada for this period comes from the port of Quebec. It is there in 1870 that *Le Courrier du Canada* reported among its arrivals the barque *Sansego* sailing out of Marseilles and captained by a Croat named Mircovich.[76] He and other Dalmatian crewmen may well have walked the streets of Quebec, Halifax, and Saint John, but there is little evidence to indicate that their stay in Canada was more lasting than a visit to a local alehouse or tavern.

The Croats of the first generation to come to Canada were thus atypical for the most part in not being poor landless peasants with large families seeking a chance in the prairie West. They were largely men of one maritime frontier bound for another, exchanging the mountainous Adriatic Coast for the Pacific Coast of the United States and Canada. Before 1880, the migrants had been almost entirely from the Dalmatian coast, a region renowned for an extraordinarily versatile type who was neither peasant nor fisherman or sailor, but a combination of all three. And as Emily Balch notes, the Dalmatian was, unlike most Slavs, an excellent trader, since the region essentially produced goods for export – fish, wine, olive oil, and fruit.[77]

These were men of great geographical range, sensing and realizing opportunity on the rapidly changing mining frontier of the Far West. Before 1880 they would rarely stay, but many did thereafter as migration to North America assumed a more economic aspect. The wage-labourers from Istria in the Austrian merchant marine and navy were trying to recapture some of the economic independence they had enjoyed in the days of wood, wind, and sail. The relatively primitive state of the salmon fisheries in British Columbia and the abundance of the catch allowed at least a glimmer of economic opportunity and a refuge from the all-pervasive presence of the Austro-Hungarian military authority in northern Croatia. The competitive economic advantage of wages in the mines of western North America had also begun to operate as a pull factor for Croat miners from the coastal interior and from Slavonia. More and more, migration from Croatia was becoming an economic necessity rather than an economic choice and opportunity.

NOTES

1. W.A. Bachich, "Maritime History of the Eastern Adriatic," in F.H. Eterovich and C. Spalatin (eds.), *Croatia, Land, People and Culture,* vol. 2 (Toronto: University of Toronto Press, 1970), pp. 128-45.

2. Barisa Krekic, *Dubrovnik in the Fourteenth and Fifteenth Centuries* (Norman: University of Oklahoma Press, 1972).

3. F.W. Lucas, *The Annals of the Voyages of the Brothers Nicolo & Antonio Zeno in the North Atlantic About the End of the Fourteenth Cen-*

tury and the Claim Founded Thereon to a Venetian Discovery of North America (London: Stevens and Stiles, 1898).

4. Nedo Pavesković, "Croatians in Canada," in Eterovich and Spalatin (eds.), *Croatia,* II, p. 479. Gilles Gagnon, *Le Sieur de Roberval* (Montreal, 1937), is cited in support of this claim. Some of these names may perhaps reflect Italian ethnicity as do some present-day Croatian surnames such as Gavazzi, Strozzi, and Cosetti. It should also be remembered that Italian-Croatian contact has been close since Roman times and dual nomenclature has persisted among place names such as Split/Spalato, Šibenik/Sebenico, and until World War I, Rijeka/Fiume, later Trst/Trieste.

5. H.P. Biggar (ed.), *The Works of Samuel de Champlain,* vol. 1 (Toronto: Champlain Society, 1922), p. 101. This reference was first noted in Dan Mrkitch, "A History of the Croat Immigration to Canada," unpublished ms., Department of the Secretary of State, Ottawa, 1970, p. 7.

6. R.G. Thwaites (ed.), *The Jesuit Relations and Allied Documents, 1610-1791,* vol. 27, *Hurons, Lower Canada, 1642-45* (New York: Pageant Book Co., reprint), p. 221.

7. Adam Eterovich, "The First Croatian Pioneers in America, 1685-1860," *Zajedničar,* 30 March 1974, p. 2. The source for his reference is *Le Conseil de la Vie Française en Amérique* (Quebec, n.d.).

8. PAC, Archives de la Guerre, Series X, Archives des Corps des Troupes, xc, carton 87, Volontaires Etrangères (microfilm).

9. E.g., Johann Sebastian Nicola, ship's doctor; Francis Bartelo, mercenary volunteer; Vide R. Winthrop Bell, *The Foreign Protestants and the Settlement of Nova Scotia* (Toronto, 1961), pp. 141, 347.

10. Among such musicians prominent German and Italian names were Glackmeyer, Vogeler, Molt, Brauneis, and Barro. See Hellmutt Kallmann, *A History of Music in Canada, 1534-1914* (Toronto, 1969), pp. 50-90 *passim.*

11. E. Valois, "Les Officiers du Regiment des Meurons," *Bull de Rech. Hist.,* IV (1898), pp. 368-9; J.M. Lemoine, "Les Meurons et les Wattevill," *ibid.,* p. 318; G. Malchelosse, "Deux Regiments Suisses au Canada," *Cahiers des Dix,* no. 2 (1937), pp. 261-96.

12. See *Pomorska Encyclopedia,* IV (Zagreb, 1957), pp. 509-10.

13. The crew lists contain a few possibilities, e.g., Marko Golovan [Golovic]; Ivan Stupin [Stupin]; and Zakar Medvedev [Medvedec]. H.H. Bancroft, *History of Alaska* (New York: Antiquarian Press, 1960; reprint of 1886 edition), pp. 93-4.

14. N. Pavesković, "Croatians in Canada," *Slavs in Canada,* vol. 2 (Ottawa, 1968), p. 111. This claim was apparently established by the oral memory of the Cosulić family, which settled in the Ladner area in the 1880's. Crew lists of the Quadra expedition, which may be incomplete, do not reveal his name. See *Expeditions in the Years 1775 and 1779 Towards the West Coast of America by Captain Bodega Y Quadra,*

translated by G.F. Barwick (n.p., 1912). The French explorer named "Buchand" does not appear to have explored the area in 1790, although the Etienne Marchand expedition did appear in 1791-92. E. Marchand, *A Voyage Around the World Performed During the Years 1790-92*, vol. 1 (London, 1801), makes no mention of Cosulić. Two or three names – Car, Lhostis, and Pochic – do, however, appear among the crew lists of the La Pérouse voyages of 1785-88. J.F.G. De La Pérouse, *A Voyage Round the World*, I (London: J. Johnson, 1798), p. 333.

15. See M.M. Vujnovich, *Yugoslavs in Louisiana* (Gretna, La.: Pelican Publishing, 1974), p. 21-33.

16. Mrkitch, "History of Croat Immigration," p. 8.

17. Carlton E. Appelo, *Brookfield – The Joe Megler Story* (Wahkiakum County, Washington) (Deep River, Washington, 1966), p. 12.

18. George J. Prpic, *The Croatian Immigrants in America* (New York: Philosophical Library, 1971), p. 63.

19. Of this Hudson's Bay settlement at Fort Vancouver in Oregon, only one trace seems fruitful. A John Peter Barch [Barich?] was listed as a resident of the Stellamaris Mission in 1854. It is speculated that he may have been an HBC employee or perhaps a demobilized cavalryman. See *Catholic Church Records of the Pacific Northwest, Vancouver and Stellamaris* (St. Paul, Oregon: French Prairie Press, 1972), p. A 5.

20. See among many other studies on Illyrianism, Mirjana Gross, *Povijest Pravaške Ideologije* (Zagreb: Institute of Croatian History, 1973), pp. 15-34; E.M. Despalatovic, "The Illyrian Solution to the Problem of a Modern National Identity for the Croats," and P.J. Adler, "Why did Illyrianism Fail?", *Balkanistica: Occasional Papers in Southeast European Studies*, I (1974), pp. 75-103.

21. The extent and nature of "Slavonian" settlement in California has been exhaustively analysed in Adam Eterovich's many works, e.g., *Croatians from Dalmatia and Montenegrin Serbs in the West and South* (San Francisco: R&E Research Associates, 1971). See also Vjekoslav Meler, *The Slavonic Pioneers of California* (San Francisco, 1932; second edition, R&E Research Associates, 1972).

22. *British Colonist,* 3 December 1859.

23. A summary of the economic effects of the gold rush on British Columbia is contained in Paul Phillips, "Confederation and the Economy of British Columbia," W.G. Shelton, *British Columbia and Confederation* (Victoria: Morris, 1967), pp. 43-66.

24. *British Daily Colonist*, 26 January, 23 April 1861.

25. *Ibid.,* 14 August, 15 September 1862; 21 January, 2 February 1863.

26. *Mallandaine's Victoria Directory,* 1860, lists a "S. Milditch" on Pandora Street, p. 72, and the Adelphi is first listed in the *Colonist*, 30 August 1862.

27. Adam Eterovich, *Croatians and Serbians in the West and South, 1800-1900* (San Francisco: R&E Research Associates, 1971), pp. 108-9.

28. *British Colonist*, 31 July 1863, p. 2, col. 2.

29. *Colonist*, 4 March, 20 April 1864; 3 July, 18 April 1865.
30. *Ibid.*, 16 May 1863.
31. See, e.g., William Rodney, *Kootenai Brown, His Life and Times, 1839-1916* (Sidney, B.C.: Gray's Publishing Co., 1969), pp. 46-53.
32. Details taken from the diary of George Blair, New Westminster, January, 1863, George Blair Papers, PAC, MG 24, H48, pp. 68-129 *passim*.
33. B.C. Provincial Archives, Mining Records, Sales, Transfers, Water Rights, etc., Antler Creek, 1861-64.
34. *Ibid.*, Williams Creek, 1862-63, vol. 1.
35. *Ibid.*, Williams Creek, 1861-96, vol. 1. Entries dated 16 and 25 March, 22 and 25 May, 5 August 1863. For Radovich's connection with Chielovich and the Slavonic Society of 1857 in San Francisco, see Eterovich, *Croats and Serbs*, pp. 11, 108.
36. *Ibid.*, Williams Creek, vol. 2, p. 18: 28 August 1863.
37. *Ibid.*, Williams Creek, vol. 1, p. 286: 3 June 1863; p. 34: 11 September 1863; vol. 2, 26 April 1864.
38. *Ibid.*, Williams Creek, 1861-96, vol. 3, 14 June 1864 to 31 May 1865, pp. 30-308 *passim*; vol. 1, 1864-1908, bills of sale, 2 September 1864 to 20 August 1866, pp. 87-378.
39. *Ibid.*, Keithley Creek Mining Records, 1864-81, 6 July 1864; 23 August 1864.
40. See *British Colonist*, 16 September 1865. Tax defaulters, City of Victoria, A. Milatovich, block V, Lot no. 53, amount $4.00. *British Columbia Gazette*, unclaimed letters, E. Chielovich, V. Baranovich, 10 August 1867.
41. See *Mallandaine's B.C. Directory* (Victoria), 1871, pp. 3, 25, 37, 48, 69.
42. B.C. Mining Records, Antler, Grouse, Canadian, etc. . . . Bills of Sale, 1864-70. Union Co. at Grouse Creek, 17 November 1868; 11 July 1870; Antler, vol. 1, April, 1868-May, 1874, pp. 294-587 *passim,* "Canadian Company," "Cosmopolitan Co."
43. *Ibid.*, Williams Creek, vol. 4, 1861-96 Boneta and Barker Co. refs., 1 August 1873 to 15 November 1883, pp. 216-415 *passim*.
44. *Ibid.*, Keithley Creek, . . . Canadian Company, refs. 31 August 1875; 16 December 1876; 11 August 1879; 9 August 1880; 11 August 1881. Italics the author's.
45. *Williams B.C. Directory*, Barkerville, p. 332.
46. For a general account of the Cassiar gold rush, see R.M. Patterson, *The Trail to the Interior* (Toronto: Macmillan, 1970), pp. 84-5. *Mallandaine's B.C. Directory,* Cassiar, 1874, pp. 53-6, 92. Cargotich is also listed as a barkeeper in Virginia City, Nevada, in 1868 – see A. Eterovich, *Yugoslavs in Nevada, 1859-1900*, p. 222.
47. Bancroft, *Alaska*, p. 635.
48. W.A. Bachich, "Maritime History of the Eastern Adriatic," in Eterovich and Spalatin (eds.), *Croatia,* II, pp. 139-44.
49. *Kanadski Glas,* 2 August 1929: "Naši Ribari u British Columbia."

50. *Ladner Optimist*, Delta Anniversary Issue, 10 November 1954; *ibid.*, November, 1951. Clippings from B.C. Archives, Victoria.
51. *Ibid.*, 14 August 1963. Some of the early fishing pioneers who followed in 1886 were Michel Silek, Antonio Vidulich, Romolo Cosulich, Marco Bussanich, Venancio and Antonio Marinolich, Pasquale Dorotich, Gasparo Nicolich, Guesepe Martinich, John Manderich, Guesepe Marenkovich, John Mariani, Giovani Scopincich, and John Giuricich. The source for these newspaper accounts is a history of the Sacred Heart Church of Ladner compiled by the Augustinian Fathers.
52. The Surrey Delta *Messenger,* 20 September 1973, p. 5.
53. *Ladner Optimist,* 17 May 1951. *Mallandaine's B.C. Directory,* 1887, lists Mateo Bussanivick's general store in Ladner-Delta. It also lists for Victoria: John Medwedrich, fishing boat owner; Antoine Cosulich (New Westminster), fisherman; Apostele Yenasovitch (Surrey), fisherman. *Williams B.C. Directory* lists for 1893-94 in Port Guichon: J. Bussanich, Sr., fisherman; Marco Bussanich, fisherman; John Bussanich, blacksmith; Antonio Cosonlich [Cosulich], boat builder; Romelo Cosonlich, fisherman; Jos. Martinolich, M. Martinolich, fishermen; V. Martinolich, ship carpenter; S. Paveisch, fisherman; Thos. Vicevich, fisherman; A. Vidulich, boat builder; G. Nicolich, ship carpenter.
54. *Jedinstvo,* 15 September 1967: "Marko Vidulić, Iz galerije likova Naših Pionira u Kanadi."
55. H. Keith Ralston, "Fraser River Salmon Fishermen and License Limitation, 1888-92," paper presented to the Canadian Historical Association, Edmonton, 1975, pp. 4-6.
56. Surrey Delta *Messenger,* 24 January 1974, p. 8b: "Pioneer recalls days of plenty in Delta."
57. *The Fisherman,* 3 July 1959, pp. 5-6: "Mike Vidulich – 70 Years a Unionist and a Salmon Gillnetter Since 1892."
58. Surrey Delta *Messenger,* 20 September 1973, p. 5.
59. Ladner *Optimist,* 15 November 1951; 10 November 1954; 14 August 1963.
60. See Elizabeth Arthur, *Thunder Bay District, 1821-92* (Toronto: The Champlain Society, 1973), pp. 142-62; Kevin H. Burley, *The Development of Canada's Staples, 1867-1939, A Documentary Collection* (Toronto: McClelland and Stewart, 1971), T.A. Keefer report on silver mining on the North Shore of Lake Superior, 1845-85, pp. 281-9.
61. From A. Walpole Roland, *Algoma West: Its Mines, Scenery and Industrial Resources* (Toronto, 1887), p. 215. Other possibilities include: John Visick, proprietor of the Continental Hotel in Port Arthur, *Henderson's Directory, Manitoba, Northwestern Ontario and Winnipeg* (Winnipeg, 1886-87); and a "Mr. Zanic" mentioned in Dorothea Mitchell, *Lady Lumberjack* (Vancouver: Mitchell Press, 1967), pp. 45-50.
62. *Henderson's British Columbia Directory*, 1892, p. 16.

63. *Williams British Columbia Directory*, 1895, Wellington, p. 191, e.g. Badovenene [Badovinac?] brothers and Dominic Berto [Berta?].

64. Ladysmith *Chronicle*, 3 October 1947: "Another Ladysmith Pioneer Removed by Death." *Colonist*, 28 September 1947: "Early Resident of Ladysmith Dies."

65. *Williams B.C. Directory*, 1895, vol. 1, pp. 194-5; *ibid.*, p. 687.

66. *Ibid.*, 1895, e.g., Brownsville, John Brodvick, farmer.

67. *Ibid.*, Notch Hill, Jacob Car [Car], brakeman. *Henderson's B.C. Directory*, 1891, CPR Pacific Division employees, car oiler, Vancouver, A. Svencick [Svencich]. *Henderson's B.C. Directory*, 1898, p. 493, J.P. Urich, steamboatman. Several Croats were also listed as guests at the Dominion Hotel in Victoria. Among them were R. Perlich (N.Y.), Petar Milovince (San Francisco), R. Dimich, J. Kapetanich (N.Y.). B.C. Archives, Dominion Hotel Register, 1898.

68. P. Berton, *Klondike: The Last Great Gold Rush, 1896-99* (Toronto: McClelland and Stewart, 1972), p. 139.

69. "Stroller" White, "The Pack Train Restaurant," *Alaska, Magazine of Life on the Last Frontier,* 35 (November, 1969), pp. 20-45.

70. Information supplied to the author by Miletić's grandson, Anthony Miletich, 23 May 1976, Hamilton, Ontario.

71. *Henderson's B.C. and Yukon Directory*, 1910.

72. PAC, Record Group 15 Bl(a), vol. 236, F464066; Henry Barna to the Minister of the Interior, New York, 19 February, 10 March 1898; James Smart, Deputy Minister, to Henry Barna, 25 February 1898, Ottawa.

73. Among these miners were Mike Steverich, J. Wusich, G. Vidas, A. Novack, F. Sunich, D. Chatovich, George Jovanovich, and F. Spelletich. NWMP Register of Travellers on the Yukon River, 1901-03, microfilm, Glenbow-Alberta Archives.

74. See Rudolf P. Čuješ, "Contributions of Slovenes to the Socio-Cultural Development of the Pre-Charter Canadians, The Canadian Indians," in *Slavs in Canada*, vol. II (Ottawa, 1968), 117-26; E. Arthur, *Thunder Bay District*, xxix, xlvii, 61n, 73.

75. A few possibilities include: Charles Zeh [Zec?], German wagon-maker, b. Wurtemburg, age 26, and resident of St. Lawrence Ward, Toronto, 1861; Joseph Stark [Štark?], German labourer, 37, resident of St. Patrick's Ward, Toronto, 1871; Sophia Shuffla [Šuflaj?], f. 71, b. Germany, listed as a Dutch charwoman, St. Lawrence Ward, 1871; Peter Rumohr [Rumora?], m. 30, b. Germany, Christian, butcher, Pickering Twp., 1871; F. Kepor [Capor?], m. 27, b. Germany, farmer, Pickering Twp., 1871. *Census of Canada* (microfilm), PAC.

76. *Le Courrier du Canada*, 18 July 1870. See also *Le Journal de Québec*, 5 September 1870.

77. Emily Balch, *Our Slavic Fellow Citizens* (New York: Charities Publications, 1910; reprint, 1969), pp. 192-3.

TWO

Push and Pull: The Causes of Pre-war Migration, 1900-14

Mass migration from Europe to North America may be likened to the movement of traffic along a major thoroughfare. At a given intersection, the intending emigrant is allowed entry to the main artery of traffic when the appropriate signal to proceed is indicated by his government. The reasons for entry, and the timing of the signal itself, are many and varied. The vast majority of twentieth-century migrants were metaphorically and literally on foot, seeking the barest economic opportunity in the New World. A rare few were impelled by a sense of adventure and discovery, and could figuratively afford to hire a cab to proceed into the mainstream of traffic. But for a large majority even the most crowded form of public transportation was beyond their means, and they had to borrow their fare from their families on the promise of their future prosperity. For the sending government, the mass transfers of population meant the disposal of unwanted numbers and the prospect of returned remittances; for the receiving society, the prospect of cheap labour and economic expansion.

Whatever the motive and whatever the means of the migrants, the mass of European migrants to North America increased phenomenally in the last two decades of the nineteenth century and the first decade of the twentieth. Those thirty years brought nearly twenty million immigrants to the United States alone. Canada lagged behind the United States, and did not share substantially in the flow of immigrants until the 1890's and the opening of the prairie West. Once begun, the flow proved considerable: Canada received nearly three million immigrants from the beginning of the century to World War I. Canada's total population doubled from five to ten million in the first two decades of the century, and its farms and cities, particularly in the West, increased many times over.[1]

The swelling tide of migrants carried in it vast numbers from the polyglot Austro-Hungarian Empire, nearly 5,100 in 1900, 10,000 in 1902, and over 21,000 in 1910.[2] Despite Canada's colonial status and continued

29

dependence upon formal ties of diplomacy and trade with Austria-Hungary, there were long-standing economic ties that involved shipping companies and colonization societies even before the completion of the Canadian Pacific Railway in 1885. Canadian immigration officials were already in touch with a vast and sometimes clandestine organization of nearly 600 agents spread over the area of Austria-Hungary; these agents received bonuses sometimes amounting to five dollars per head to attract settlers to the Dominion.[3] Thus, Croatians knew of the presence of Canada and the agricultural potential of the Northwest from an early date through a vast network of family contacts, emigration agents, and various newspapers printed throughout the Austro-Hungarian Empire.

The tempo of mass migration was also accelerated by the transportation improvements and the rationalization of railway and steamship services in the late nineteenth century. The integration of the railway networks that traversed central Europe and connected it with Mediterranean and Atlantic ports was complete by the late nineteenth century. Increased transatlantic passenger service was evident also in the number of shipping lines authorized by the Austrian authorities to carry their emigrants. From 1885 to 1908, seven foreign lines were authorized to operate in Austria besides the native Austro-Americana lines, the last of which was the Canadian Pacific Railway Company. With the exception of the CPR, each would ultimately receive a portion of the steerage business through the mechanism of rate fixing and distribution of passenger loads among the various lines such as Holland-America, North-German Lloyd, and the Hamburg-America Line. In addition, each of the lines in the North Atlantic consortium controlled a large chain of ticket agents, promoters, emigration associations, and currency exchanges. Beyond these were emigration agencies in the port cities and a large network of local agents spread through the countryside, for the most part well-connected local notables, innkeepers, teachers, and village priests who shared in the spinoff of commissions earned at each level for recruitment. An intending emigrant might earn a commission from his relatives by securing a reduction in his own ticket for each person he persuaded to migrate. Even the ethnic organizations formed in Austria-Hungary for the protection of the immigrant were themselves in the business of promoting migration, with the result that many were discredited in the scandals that followed the contraction of migration in the depressions of 1908 and 1913.[4]

Beyond these factors, which began to pull over 100,000 emigrants from Austria to North America each year, other factors were pushing them from their home country. The overwhelming motive was economic. It is rendered by the old immigrants themselves in such phrases as "stomachs after bread" (*trbuhom za kruhom*), or "the search for a better life" (*za bolji život*). Economic prospects in the homeland were dim, and a whole chain of economic factors conspired after 1880 to drive Croatian emigrants in ever increasing numbers to North America.

THE PUSH: ECONOMIC CRISIS IN CROATIA

The prime factor impelling emigration was a profound agrarian crisis and resulting overpopulation of the marginal soils of northwestern Croatia and the lands bordering on the Adriatic. Ironically, the depression in agricultural commodity prices in the urban marketplaces of Europe was caused by the penetration of American grain into that market, which led to a decline in grain-producing areas of Austria-Hungary and outward migration to North America. The depression in world prices from 1873 to 1895 had disastrous effects upon the small, communal, family farm or *zadruga* in Croatia. At the same time, penetration of European capital, transportation improvements, and the coincident extension of Austro-Hungarian taxing power into Croatia and Bosnia further eroded traditional agriculture. As agricultural prices dropped, the taxes levied on the peasant were tripled, and ordinances broke up the communal system into small private parcels.[5]

The end result was a massive increase in the number of landless peasants and a dramatic increase in agricultural labour, which doubled by 1900. And for those who were not driven off the land, the prospect was often more dismal. In all of the Austro-Hungarian Empire, only Galicia and Bukovina ranked above the Croatian coastline in the number of landless day labourers, and Croatia easily ranked the highest in the percentage of small peasant proprietors on the land (71 per cent).[6] At a time when it was estimated that one and a half acres represented a minimum individual subsistence, the average small landholding in Dalmatia was barely at this level. And in the rocky Lika-Krbava region to the north, according to the census of 1900, the average parcel per individual was three-quarters of an acre to one acre.[7]

Secondary factors promoting emigration and complicating the agrarian crisis were the failure of industrialization and overpopulation. Industrial development was an illusion for Croatia under Austro-Hungarian domination, despite apparently auspicious beginnings. In 1873, a railway link was built connecting Fiume (Rijeka) with Karlstadt (Karlovac), thus offering competition via Budapest to the Vienna-Trieste link with the Adriatic. The result was a modest increase in the forest industry of the lush region of Gorski Kotar between Karlovac and the sea, which expanded its board footage of sawn lumber by ten times.[8] Just as in the agricultural sector, the large landowners who were often foreign to the region were successful in having communal pasture rights eroded in the process of abolishing serfdom. The net result was that the forest was rapidly despoiled as small landowners tried to meet the heavy compensation charges, and this indebtedness ultimately forced the smaller farmer to emigrate in search of employment.[9] The railroad itself even removed jobs it never replaced, for about $15,000 to $20,000 was annually earned by the inhabitants of Gorski Kotar in freighting goods over the mountains, and this income was now lost with no replacement in industrial jobs.[10]

Mining and manufacturing suffered similar underdevelopment in the late nineteenth century. In the metallurgical sector, there were clear difficulties both in the nature and extent of iron, copper, and coal deposits and these were complicated by underdeveloped capitalization, technology, and transportation provided by metropolitan sources in Austria and Hungary. Thus, iron mines in northwestern Croatia at Delnice and Čabar underwent a very modest expansion in the mid-nineteenth century and began to decline by 1880. A similar fate awaited the copper mines at Samobor-Rude near Zagreb and the lignite mines near Karlovac, at Duga Resa and Ogulin. Heavily dependent upon Austrian finance and only underwritten by 5 per cent with Croatian capital, they could not succeed. The same structural difficulties plagued the forest industry in the Gorski Kotar region, which was slow to develop steam and hydroelectric power. The number of workers employed in the small factories in this region after the opening of the Rijeka railway never exceeded 20 to 25 per cent of the region's male labour force. Thus the more promising regional industrial base of the late nineteenth century never employed more than 8 per cent of the population by 1900 and for most of the rest of Croatia, particularly the military frontier, the figure was rarely above $1\frac{1}{2}$ per cent.

While population growth in general was not as great as the end of the nineteenth century as at the beginning,[11] it remained at a steady thirty to thirty-five per one thousand and in some districts over forty per thousand annually. The important factor was not the birth rate, but the declining death rate. In the demilitarization of the frontier, the number of deaths due to war and military service declined substantially, and in many districts improved hygiene and medical practice dramatically cut infant mortality and the deaths of young children.[12] In certain areas such as Herzegovina one-third of the babies still died of exposure and lack of food before the age of two, and the local phrase persisted into the twentieth century that, "Here in our country, if children do not die, they live."[13] But nonetheless, the death rate declined substantially to level off at twenty-five per thousand, and the natural increase in some areas, such as Petrinja and Jastrebarsko, climbed to thirty per thousand, and in Gorski Kotar remained at a steady twenty per thousand for the critical decade at the end of the century. Families rose sharply in size in these districts. It was not uncommon for them to have a dozen and more children and to increase the communal *zadruga* to the breaking point, sometimes fifty in number.

The irony of modernization and industrialization was that migration was produced in heaviest number from areas adjacent to the railroad. Population statistics in western Croatia demonstrate that the percentage of migrants to total population was greatest in Delnice, Vrbovsko, Jastrebarsko, and Karlovac, reaching as high as 35 per cent in the first and diminishing to 20 per cent in the latter. By contrast emigration was less dominant in areas within the more isolated and backward military frontier, in Vrgin Most, Pisarovina, Glina, and Petrinja. Nor does population density entirely explain the choice of emigration as an option, for in many of the latter districts natural increase was higher and surplus population was absorbed by further partition of the lands, use of uneconomical lands, and reduction in the living standard of the *zadruga*. This was particularly characteristic of the Varaždin district to the northeast of Zagreb, which had a higher density of population (209 per square kilometre) than Lika-Krbava (135 per square kilometre). Yet that region far into the interior would not produce such substantial emigration to North America, in the same way that even the more sparsely settled plains of Slavonia would not. The answer, then, is not purely demographic pressure outward but also the proximity of the migratory regions to communication and transportation links with the outside world.

Migration was also tied closely to the prior geographic mobility and to the declining hold of the agrarian community or traditional villages upon their inhabitants. Again, Gorski Kotar of the late nineteenth century serves as a classic example of pre-adaptation for overseas migration. The *gorani* (highlanders or mountaineers) were excellent woodcutters with phenomenal geographic range. They would depart in October and November for the forests of Bosnia and Slavonia where they worked on a piecework system for various lumber-jobbers. They, like the nineteenth-century Irish work gangs, would gather in informal work groups comprised of friends, neighbours, or members of the *zadruga* and would submit to the discipline of a freely elected work captain or foreman. Working from "dark to dark," fourteen or fifteen hours a day with two breaks of three-quarters of an hour each, they would continue through from fall to spring, when they returned to their home villages.

Other seasonal workers in the region migrated for work during the winter into the city of Rijeka about forty miles distant. Young women from Lokve and Delnice often worked as servants in the hotels there until spring and were charmingly designated by local dialect *lastavice* or "sparrows." The men often operated as teamsters and colporteurs in Rijeka or further afield in Vienna and Budapest, and others were colourful *pokućari* – news-hawkers, vendors, and messenger boys in the same cities. Whatever their trade, the young people of the hills had set up a rhythm of migration that carried them further and further afield, and ultimately on to North America.

The heaviest migration to North America was generated along this Karlovac-Rijeka axis, which alone lost some 33,000 people to emigration from 1880-1900. Wholesale depopulation occurred in such towns as Ravna Gora and Lokve, the first of which dropped from 3,192 inhabitants in 1870 to 2,684 in 1900, and the latter from 2,068 to 1,969.[14] In 1910, the Austrian census listed as "absent" in America over 2,000 from the population of Delnice, 1,600 from the jurisdiction of Karlovac, and over 1,100 from the civil district of Vrbovsko. Thus, over a third of the population had gone to North America, totals that exceeded internal migration within Croatia itself.

Other areas, as well, contributed migrants to North America in great number: the hinterland of Agram or Zagreb, Lika-Krbava, and the southern coast of Dalmatia. The country of Zagreb was heavily afflicted with phylloxera, an aphid infestation of the vineyards, which seriously curbed wine production in the region. In 1890, over 5,000 of the population were listed as absent from their homes and over the two decades from 1880 to 1900 over 26,000 were counted absent. Lika-Krbava, a rocky and unyielding region of karstland (limestone plateau with underground caverns and streams) adjacent to the middle Adriatic Coast, lost over 28,000 to migration in the same period, and the Istrian peninsula to the north alone counted over 25,000 emigrants to America before 1900. The Dalmatian coast to the south continued to send hordes of migrants to the United States, exporting 5 per cent of its population, or 31,000 people, from 1890 to 1900. As in other regions, phylloxera, overpopulation, the decline of the *zadruga*, and the opportunity presented by higher wages for male migrants in North America were the prime factors pushing overseas migration.[15]

Thus, emigration was engendered in part by a set of rising aspirations partially induced by the intrusion of the market economy into the local villages via the returned migrant and the remittances others so faithfully sent home. The unsettling effects the returnees had upon Austrian officials were marked, for they suspected the libertarian and republican notions being brought back from America. As the Austrian ambassador to Washington candidly observed of the returnees, "These people are usually saturated with radical, democratic and for the most part republican maxims, and as naturalized American citizens, they are hostilely disposed toward the authority of the native administration."[16] The dangers presented by liberalism were also fuelled by the rising spirit of the Croatian nationalism, which soon began to measure the gap between the lot of the Croatian peasant at home and in America and placed the blame squarely upon the ruling Austro-Hungarian authorities for the underdevelopment of their homeland. This resurgent national spirit was well-captured by the poem by Antun Gustav Matos, himself an emigrant, who wrote in 1906 that "America was the main factor in the creation of Croatian democracy."[17] In 1911, in his poem "The Emigrant" (*Iseljenik*), published in a Zagreb newspaper, Matos issued the call to arms against the Austro-Hungarian feudal oppressors: "From my land I am driven far away/For taxers and usurers/Confiscate even my plow."

Such, then, were the major economic, social, and political forces that pushed Croatian migrants from Austria-Hungary to North America in the early years of the twentieth century. They do not, of course, explain why each individual chose to migrate, but most would admit that the desire for a better life ranked high in their aspirations, at least as high as the negative drives of poor land, excessive taxation debt, and unemployment. Occasionally some were driven by the motive of adventure in seeing new lands; others wished to avoid an unpleasant family situation; and still others simply wished to avoid four years of military service in the Austrian army. Certainly this latter motive would play a much larger role as the Balkan Wars threatened after 1910, but for the time being, hunger and economic opportunity were the primary drives behind migration.

THE TRANSATLANTIC PULL:
WAGES, AGENTS, AND TRANSPORT

Strong economic and social attractions pulled migrants overseas. The foremost for a rootless, unskilled labouring population was the attractiveness of pay scales in North America. A day labourer could expect to earn from ten to thirty cents a day in Croatia, whereas he could earn as much during one hour in the cities, in railway construction, or in the lumber camps and mines of the United States and Canada. Indeed, it had become common practice for the family heads of the *zadruga* to detach one of the males and pay his transportation to America, in order that he might remit funds for the improvement of the communal farm in Croatia. The effect on the villages and farms of the homeland of these carefully accumulated savings in America was dramatic – one author places their value at $10 million in 1903 alone! The money paid for long deferred farm improvements and machinery and for vital local improvements such as roads, water supply, churches and hospitals.

The social and cultural effects of both returning capital and returned migrants were equally destructive to the old agricultural order. A letter from a schoolteacher in the Gračac district in Lika graphically illustrates the effect of money on the pre-war agrarian economy:

> Before the war, a large number of men, particularly married men, went to America whence they sent large sums of money home to their wives. The wives gave up folk costume and began to deck their daughters with ready-made garments and thereby trained the girls away from needlework. The folk custom of the "sewing bee" had meant the girls getting together in this house or that, where two rooms were set aside for embroidering on cloth and open work in linen, but now they get together just for parties, to be joined by the lads with *tamburas*. So long as money flowed in from America, they spent freely, even getting into debt at shops and inns (which rapidly sprang up) but when money ceased to pour in, when they felt the burden of debts, there began dissatisfaction in many households and the splitting up of the married sons.[18]

The returned immigrant was often more vivid and compelling witness to the superiority of the North American economy. First would come the letters from the uncle in America ("stric u Americi") homeward, indicating that he was living well on wages of a dollar and a half a day. Immediately a sensation would be created among the youth of the village as they calculated the immense riches to be earned in the promised land. Then the returned emigrant would appear, an "Amerkanac," overdressed and overblown with a sense of his newly acquired fortune. The scenario of the poor immigrant's triumphant return has been told time and again, by the Slovenian author Louis Adamic in *The Native's Return*, and by the Canadian author Henry Kreisel in *The Rich Man*.[19] In the Croatian context, it is best told by a young Croatian lad, Stjepan Lojen, who describes in a series of reminiscences the feelings of envy and admiration excited by the appearance of a young neighbour who returned one Christmas Day before World War I. He paraded before the local church on Sunday morning dressed in a new suit, fedora, and black patent leather shoes and periodically would check the time of day by ostentatiously drawing from his vest pocket a watch dangling from a heavy silver chain. To complete the overpowering visual effect upon the village peasants, the American dandy punctuated his native tongue with modish English phrases learned in the New World – "Well" and "all right." His young admirer was so impressed that he vowed he, too, must go, to the exclusion of even the larger towns and cities of Croatia, which he felt were so much under the economic control and strangulation of the Austrians, Hungarians, and Germans.[20]

The hope of America was also carefully nurtured by a vast chain of economic enterprise that stretched from Vienna and Paris to London, New York, and Montreal. Bankers, travel agents, steamship companies, railways, and governments all participated in the promotion of emigration, and, they hoped, return as well. The village merchants and bankers, who acquired money at 6 per cent from Austrian sources, were excessively cautious about advancing any money to the peasant for farm improvement at rates any less than 12 to 40 per cent on loans and at specified minimums of $200. Subsidization of emigration was generally a more secure investment since cash flows and remittances from America provided more certainty than the output of a twelve-acre plot, which the banker in any case held as security against the loan.[21] The Austrian government co-operated in encouraging labourers to migrate both to other parts of the Austro-Hungarian empire and abroad. Young men were often issued temporary passports only valid for one year, thus ensuring that a two-way ticket would be bought and that potential draft dodgers would return to complete their military service.[22]

The most active agents in the promotion of emigration were the steamship ticket agents who literally combed the highways, byways, and hillsides of southern Europe selling steerage tickets at $25 one-way to prospective migrants. With the systematic policy of depopulating Croatian landholdings pursued by the governor, *banus* Khuen Hedervary, steamship agents representing American firms were allowed to roam freely over the hill country adjacent to the Karlovac-Rijeka hinterland. Work gangs were herded by the inducement of profitable contracts and high wages into the cities of Rijeka and Trieste where they boarded Austro-American lines sailing for New York. Or, conversely, they might board trains from Split or Dubrovnik for Zagreb and travel further by train to Paris and Le Havre where they might embark aboard a Cunard White Star liner headed for Halifax and New York.[23]

But whether the destination was American or Canadian, and whether the steamship agents worked for Austro-American lines or Cunard and German Lloyd, they were universally suspected by the immigrant of excessive charges, bad advice, and exaggerated accounts of prosperity. In fact, the most blatant of these malpractices by American agents was by a Croatian-American named Frank Zotti, a powerful banker and steamship agent from Chicago, who had over 300 agents recruiting passengers in Europe during peak travel season. In 1908, his empire included a Croatian bank, a fraternal union ("The National Croatian Society"), and a newspaper (*Narodni List*) in addition to his steamship enterprise. When the complex structure collapsed in the depression of that year and defrauded 8,000 depositors of over $500,000, Zotti and other Croatian entrepreneurs of his type brought the reputation of the transatlantic immigration business to a new low.[24]

On the European side of the Atlantic, the Swiss agents in Buchs, Johann Buschel and Viktor Klaus, very ably attracted legal and illegal migrants to come their way from Croatia. The mechanics of that intricate system have been well-described by Johann Chmelar in his study of pre-war Austrian migration. Many immigrants from Zagreb and Rijeka would come via Innsbruck and Feldkirch in Austria to Buchs just inside the Swiss border. Since a special agreement persisted between the Duchy of Liechtenstein and Austria, an effective border patrol could not be maintained on the Austrian side, and once in Buchs the emigrants could no longer be detained by customs officials. They were confronted there by a horde of emigration agents who attempted to direct them to prospective employers and to cheap hotels further on in Basel. The direction of the migrants to and from that point is vividly described in the report of a Swiss consular official in 1913:

> The emigrants from the western countries and from Northern Croatia turn, as a rule, to an agency in Laibach (Ljubljana). The emigration agency "Putnik," located in Agram (Zagreb) is used less and less frequently. The formalities associated with clearance and also the required procurement of a passport, etc., make the people uneasy.
>
> The most effective propaganda is conducted by those people who have already been in America once. They usually collect a number

of emigrants at home and deliver them either to Laibach or to Buchs where they receive a commission for each passenger.

Because of the widespread urge to emigrate, the agents don't find it particularly necessary to advertise continuously. Only in the summer when the flow of migration subsides, do they send by means of the Imperial customs office in Buchs, printed propaganda material into the Monarchy.

Passage occurred only after a medical examination, and fares were not uniform. Sometimes different prices were demanded for the same route and the same class ticket . . . .[25]

Paternal treatment of illiterate migrants was demanded all along the route of travel, from the rural villages of Croatia to western Europe. And the slightest deviance from the prescribed route or mode of travel could result in the total loss of the small capital margin that most immigrants carried with them. Even quasi-legitimate agencies such as Viktor Klaus suggest this vulnerability in the carefulness of their instructions to the Croatian immigrants intending to travel through Switzerland and western Europe. They were counselled to forward their baggage well ahead of departure to avoid the payment of bribes along the way and to display yellow cards in their hats at their destination for purposes of identification. If all of these instructions were followed, Klaus agencies promised a trip without worry or care aboard commodious steamships that crossed the Atlantic in four and one-half days and never more than six or seven days![26] The Croatian immigrants themselves verified the widespread existence and persistence of such European agencies and illegal practices, for some of the immigrants who travelled along the Buchs-Basel route to northern European ports composed a rhyme on their experiences: "Jer agenti varalice Jesu, samo za se napunjaju kesu." (For the agents are surely swindlers, since they are always lining their own pockets.)[27]

A harsh underworld of immigrant culture and experience was created by this system of transport and commerce, and many a tale of human misery told of the detention and deportation of immigrants from North America. In this respect, Canadian and American experiences were different in that few south Europeans would be allowed to enter Canada prior to World War I, whereas American treatment of the immigrant at Ellis Island ("The Isle of Tears") was harsh and democratically direct in its discrimination against the alien. A typical entry, describing a character who drifted between the two countries, may be taken from the deportation records at Ellis Island to demonstrate the brutalizing nature of this exploitative system of immigration and transportation. On October 15, 1909, a male Croatian aged thirty-five arrived with his family at the Port of Quebec and "obtained admission under false pretences, his alleged wife having entered the United States for an immoral purpose without inspection." Close examination by the board of enquiry revealed

VELECENJENI GOSPOD!.

NASLOV ZA BRZOJAVKE: VIKTOR KLAUS, SANKT MARGRETHEN, ŠVICA.

Ker vem, da Vi zavoljo svoje službe imate velik vpliv pri svojih rojakih, zato Vas uljudno vprašam, ali bi ne hoteli v svojem kraju sodelovati za mojo glavno agenturo, namreč tistim ljudem, ki se iz lastnega nagiba za to zanimajo, priporočiti mojo glavno agenturo, obenem pa Vas uljudno opozarjam, da pričujoče pismo ni nikak poziv za izseljevanje, temveč jaz želim le tem, ki hočejo, kakor že veliko Vaših rojakov, zavoljo dela peljati se v Ameriko, pokazati jim priložnost, kako se lahko dobro in po ceni, na hitrih in varnih ladjah morejo peljati v dotične kraje.

Potniki, ki se izročijo v moje varstvo, peljajo se vselej na najbolj hitrih, najbolj dobrih in najbolj varnih parobrodih na svetu, ladje prevozijo progo v Ameriko v 4½—8 dni, kar pa zadeva hrano, pijačo, prenočišče in red, je vse najbolj in najskrbneje urejeno.

Jaz vozim že veliko let Vaše rojake v Ameriko in zraven sem vedno skrbel, da potniki, ki so izročeni v moje varstvo, tudi udobno in varno se peljajo. Da sem vselej ravnal pošteno in pravično, izpričuje število potovalcev, ki se vsako leto bolj množi, ki mi vožnjo preko morja zaupajo.

Poglavitni vzrok, zakaj mi toliko Vaših rojakov zaupa, je pa gotovo ta, ker so pri meni jako zmerne cene, moji skrbi izročeni potovalci plačajo iz Sankt Margrethen v New-York najnižjo ceno, zraven pa nimajo za hrano in prenočišče nobenih stroškov, tako da se odtod vozijo udobno in čisto brezskrbno.

Zraven Vam pošiljam vse potrebne načrte in navodila za vožnjo, zglasilnice ali oglasne listine in listke za klobuk, po katerih jih tukaj spozna moj uslužbenec.

Trdno zaupajoč, da mi bote v tem oziru vspešno pomagali, pričakujem od Vas takojšnji odgovor, prijazno Vas pozdravljam ter bilježim

VIKTOR KLAUS, travel agent at St. Margarethen on the Swiss and Austro-Hungarian border. Advice to intending emigrants going to America, regarding currency required, travel time, food, and accommodation.

SOURCE: Vienna, Staats Archiv, Ministerium des Innern, Kart 322 8/4.

This address card must be worn visibly, only upon arrival at St. Margarethen, either in your hat or carried in your hand.

GENERAL-AGENTUR.
HLAVNÍ JEDNATELSTVÍ
GLAVNA POSLOVNICA.
GLAVNA AGENTURA.
ГЛАВНА ПОСЛОВНИЦА.
AGENZIA GENERALE.

Nur 4½ Tage über den Ocean!
Jen 4½ dne trvá plavba oceánem!
Samo 4½ dana oceanske vožnje!
Vožnja črez ocean traja samo 4½ dneva.
Само 4½ дана оцеанске вожње!
Solo 4 giorni e mezzo sull'Oceano!

VIKTOR KLAUS

Filiale :: Pobočka :: Podružnica :: Podružnica :: Подружница :: Filiale

SANKT MARGRETHEN

(Österr.-schweiz. Grenze). (austr.-švicarska granica). (аустр.-швицар. граница).
(na rak.-švýcar. hranici). (na avstrijsko-švicki meji). (Confini austro - svizzeri).

Beförderung von Passagieren mit Schnelldampfern. :: Doprava cestujících rychloparníky. :: Otprema putnika najbržim parobrodima. :: Popotniki se vozijo po brzih parobrodih. :: Отпрема путника најбржим пароброднма. :: Servizio di passeggieri con piroscafi a grande velocità.

General Agent VICTOR KLAUS Only four and a half day's ocean voyage!

Located in the jurisdiction of St. Margarethen on the Austro-Swiss border

Carrying travellers on the fastest ocean steamers

SOURCE: *Vienna, Staats Archiv, Ministerium des Innern, Kart 322 8/4.*

that the young immigrant had represented a woman with four aliases as his wife while in Montreal and had tried to find employment there as a policeman but could not do so as he was not a British subject. He subsequently drifted across the border from Montreal to New York and Pennsylvania, where he operated for a time as an agent for the infamous Frank Zotti, then went into the business of immigrant intermediary on his own and was charged with embezzlement of funds by Croatian immigrants who claimed to have been defrauded by him in settlement of their overseas estates. Subsequently, his criminal and fraudulent activities forced the American authorities to require a $1,000 bond for his admission to the United States. Failing to raise that amount, he was deported in 1911 and later found his way back into Canada, where he worked once again as a travel agent and intermediary, this time in British Columbia.[28]

Such characters were uncommon, however, in the early history of the Croatians in Canada. There were few ethnic intermediaries among the Croats to rival Antonio Cordasco, the "King of the Italian Labourers" in Montreal.[29] This social fact was less a result of ethnic virtue than from lack of sufficient numbers in major Canadian urban centres. If anything, the Croatians – because of their relatively small numbers – had to depend on the employment services provided by immigrant intermediaries from other ethnic groups. Often a lower order of services was provided in restaurants, hotels, and boardinghouses, much as Croatians had historically operated in the late nineteenth century. Indeed, the lack of Croatian-Canadian institutions, such as the ethnic newspapers and loan agencies that existed in the larger parent community in the United States, meant that the few Croatian immigrants to Canada in the early twentieth century had to rely upon a more familiar and limited clan or village system of obligation and help.

CANADA: THE CLOSED DOOR
AND "THE CANADIAN PACIFIC AFFAIR"

The spillover of abuses into Canada was not widely prevalent before 1910, if only for the reason that mass immigration was initially designed to fill the open spaces of western Canada. Unlike the masses huddled in the urban ghettoes of American cities in "the gilded age," the European immigrants who came to Canada before 1905 were destined for the agricultural frontier. The presiding genius over the settlement of the West was the Liberal Minister of the Interior, Clifford Sifton. His recruitment policies for immigrants were based upon the simple assumption that what Canada needed most was farmers and rural labourers capable of the back-breaking labour to prepare the Prairies for cultivation. The central appeal of his recruiting agents, who swarmed over such distant locations as the Great Plains of the United States and the steppes of eastern Europe, was that the Canadian Northwest abounded in free homesteads and cheaply bought virgin land that offered "a second chance" to the poor of Europe.[30]

But Sifton also thought some immigrants were better than others. American farmers were better than British labourers, northern Europeans were better than southern Europeans, and Asians were no good at all.[31] Croatians, along with Italians, Serbians, Macedonians, Bulgarians, and Romanians, were generally considered racially undesirable and unadaptable as farmers to the harsh environment of the Canadian frontier. Consequently, up to 1905 immigration statistics reveal that during Sifton's tenure only 172 Croatians were admitted to Canada. The greatest percentage of these were in the category of general labour, thus reaffirming the intent of Canadian immigration laws to discourage southern European farmers from entering.[32]

Two events transpired to increase the tempo of central Croatian and south European migration to Canada. The first was Sifton's resignation from the Cabinet in 1905 and his replacement by Frank Oliver as Minister of Interior. The second was the beginning of the government-financed National Transcontinental and the federally subsidized Grand Trunk Pacific in 1904. The government-backed railways were quickly freed from the laws forbidding the importation of contract labour that had dogged the operations of the CPR. When the president of the Grand Trunk Pacific said he needed 20,000 navvies for railway construction, the Laurier government suddenly found the ways and means to admit them in 1906-07. Previously, the immigration officials had encouraged Scandinavian and Galician farmers to work part-time at railway construction during the summer season and then return to harvest their crops in the fall. The railway companies, however, preferred a more stable work force that would be available year-round and be more susceptible to management. In this respect, British railway workers proved to be the most prone to strike and the least amenable to the primitive working conditions in the construction camps. Suddenly, southern European migrant labourers organized under the leadership of a head man, a *padrone* in the case of the Italians and the *bas* or *gospodar* in the case of the Croatians, became desirable aliens from the standpoint of the railways. They worked hard from dawn to dusk and only complained through the straw boss when pay or work grievances surfaced. As former Austrian army veterans, they were also susceptible to military-type discipline and were reputedly impervious to union organization.

The railway lobby thus began in earnest to break down the national restrictions on immigration. The first tactic employed by "labour and lumberman's supply agents," such as M.D. Davis, a contractor for the Grand Trunk, was to work through their legal counsel to influence the immigration officials. Davis began by approaching T.C. Robinette of Toronto, claiming that he could secure 500 to 1,000 Hungarians and Croatians with less than the $500 required to come to Canada as farmers, if he could be allowed to place advertisements in ethnic newspapers such as *Magyarsag* in Winnipeg and the *Hungarian Daily News* in Cleveland.[33] The plea was then made via Robinette to Frank Oliver as Minister of the Interior, but the request was denied.[34] Davis then turned to a contact in London who promised to deliver Serbian, Macedonian, and Bulgarian contract labour on demand. He was promptly reprimanded by the Superintendent of Immigration on the grounds that these nationalities did not make good railroad labourers, but Davis stoutly claimed that he had contracts only for Swedes, Finns, Dutchmen, Hungarians, and Croatians.[35]

Davis and the Grand Trunk then began a running feud with immigration officials throughout 1908 in order to secure admission for track workers from any nation in south-central Europe. The immigration authorities claimed, with some accuracy, that there was a recession in building and that they had to deport considerable numbers of railway navvies who had become dependent on public welfare. The Superintendent of Immigration, W.D. Scott, claimed also that he could provide on a moment's notice at least 500 track workers of Scandinavian, Austrian, or Galician background.[36] In addition, accusations were made by immigration officers that such labour agents as the Grand Trunk was employing were taking on excess labour in order to receive commissions from continental booking agencies. Beyond that, they were not ensuring that the immigrants had sufficient funds ($25) to get back home, nor could they guarantee work to the Hungarians and Croatians once here. Furthermore, Austrian government authorities charged that there was great dissatisfaction on the immigrants' part, for they found after working a few months on such projects as the Toronto and Northern Railway that their pay cheques were considerably less than expected. Such high charges for provisions and transportation were deducted that workers were often left with too little to return home.[37]

Had the depression of 1908 not intervened and allowed the immigration officials to assert their formerly restrictive policies against southern Europeans, there would have been a steady increase in Croatians in the years from 1905-10: 226 Croats and Slovenes entered Canada in 1906; 273 came in 1907; and in 1908 the aggregate diminished to 224. The effect of voluntary return and deportation began to take its toll, and in 1909 only one Croat entered, and in the following year only a slight recovery was apparent with seventy-four new immigrant arrivals.[38] Thus, just as the steamship scandals and bank failures in the United States had surfaced during a period of economic failure and widespread unemployment, the deportations and alleged scandals relating to the exploitation of south European and Croatian construction workers were also symptomatic of larger problems in the Canadian economy.

Pressure to reverse restrictions against southern European construction workers began with economic recovery in 1909-10. Grand Trunk construction, particularly in northwestern British Columbia, was in full swing. One of its contractors, Foley, Welch and Stewart, an American firm that constructed much of the Grand Trunk Pacific trackage, was in a position to employ 3,000 men. Consequently, the partners lobbied vigorously through their counsel, Duncan Ross, to open the border to south European trackworkers from the United States and not to insist on the regulation that each man possess $25. Despite the reluctance of both immigration officials and the Minister of the Interior, Frank Oliver, Austrian immigrants were allowed to enter, but only under certain conditions. They were required to return to the United States after their sojourn in Canada, and even if they were naturalized American citizens they were still required to meet the financial qualification.[39]

The railway lobbies, encouraged by the victory of the Conservative Party in 1911 and the fantastic boom in western Canadian real estate and urban expansion, won further concessions in 1912. Despite a sustained rearguard action by the immigration officials, who were under great public pressure to exclude aliens, the new Minister of the Interior, Robert Rogers, ruled in favour of the railway companies. And in March, 1912, the restrictions against alien trackworkers were all but lifted insofar as Scandinavians, Finns, Poles, and Austrians were concerned. However, subsequent enquiries by shipping agents soon brought out the clarification that the lifting of the moratorium on Austrian trackworkers did not apply to Bulgars who were typed as "such an undesirable class that they have to be palmed off as Austrians or some other nationality."[40] The upshot for Croatian migration was that over the years 1912-14 there was a marked increase in arrivals, from 281 in 1912 to 642 in 1913 and 803 in 1914.[41] (See Table 1.)

The increase seems to have occurred despite official discouragement from both Canada and Austria-Hungary. Canadian immigration officials and the Ministry of the Interior still continued to favour northern Europeans because of their potential as farmers for the Canadian Prairies. Moreover, Mediterranean peoples such as Croats, Serbs, Italians, and Greeks were looked upon with jaundiced eyes because of their tendency to return to their homeland during cycles of economic recession and depression such as had occurred in 1908. On the other hand, the Austrian War Office began to receive support from other sectors of public opinion in the home country concerned about the loss of conscriptable manpower during a period of grave foreign crisis. With war impending in the Balkans and many of its male citizens abroad, the perpetual complaints of the monarchy's military establishment began to tell. In the military muster of Austrian troops in 1913 a shortage of over 100,000 men in the army produced a wave of public consternation. Although such absenteeism was really not much higher than in 1907, times had changed and Austria-Hungary was now vitally concerned for her military security.

The growing xenophobia in Austria-Hungary exploded in an outburst in 1914 that was to include the CPR and the Croats as co-conspirators. "The Canadian Pacific Railway Company Affair" was a scandal to rival

TABLE 1

Immigration from Austria-Hungary, Croatia, Dalmatia, and Serbia, 1899-1916

Year	Dalmatians	Croatians	Austrians	Hungarians	Serbians
1899	41	18	131	276	—
1900	—	36	248	530	23
1901	—	65	228	546	23
1902	—	—	320	1,046	—
1903	—	1	781	2,074	2
1904	—	16	516	1,091	10
1905	4	27	837	981	7
1906	16	226	1,324	739	19
1907	9	273	1,537	850	8
1908	10	224	1,899	1,307	48
1909	1	1	1,830	595	31
1910	11	74	4,195	621	76
1911	24	121	7,891	756	50
1912	38	281	4,871	482	209
1913	155	642	1,050	578	366
1914	182	803	3,147	833	193
1915	24	164	502	218	220
1916	—	—	15	—	6
Totals	515	2,972	31,322	13,523	1,291

NOTES: From the above figures it appears that some 3,487 Croats and Dalmatians entered Canada prior to 1915, although it is not entirely clear how many of these may have been Slovenes since their number was often incorporated into the Croatian total. Nevertheless, this figure is much less than estimates given by the recent commission on bilingualism in Canada, which places the total number of Yugoslavs (Croats, Macedonians, Serbians, and Slovenes) at 17,805 immigrants from 1900-14. (*The Cultural Contribution of Other Ethnic Groups*, vol. IV, pp. 238-9.) Estimating the percentage of Croatians in this Yugoslav total at 65-72 per cent, according to similar percentages in the American figures for this period, the number of Croats should have been 11,000 or 12,000 immigrants before 1914. The disparity between this figure and the lower immigration statistics presented above may be partially accounted for by the number of Croats who might have been hidden in the Austrian and Hungarian statistics. Again, using similar American data for this period when Croats may have counted between 7 and 8 per cent of Austrian and Hungarian immigrants, it is possible that between 3,000 and 3,500 Croatians may have been submerged in the Austrian and Hungarian groups. (See Branko Colaković, *Yugoslav Migrations to America* [San Francisco: R&E Research Associates, 1973], pp. 37, 45.) The total number of Croatians, then, may have been closer to 6,000 or 7,000 immigrants entering Canada prior to 1914, but certainly much less than the estimates indicated in the bilingual commission report, or the even more inflated 40,000 pre-war Yugoslav migrants given in Arthur Benko Grado, *Migraciona Enciklopedija* (Zagreb, 1930), p. 191.

and outdo the Zotti imbroglio of 1908 in the eyes of the outraged Austrian press. The CPR had been permitted to operate legally with shipping agents in Austria since 1908 and had applied in 1912 to establish a direct line between Trieste and Canada. Despite the fact that the CPR shipping line met all of the conditions for operation and was duly approved by the Ministry of the Interior, it soon became involved in a major public scandal. While this one lacked the dramatic political consequences in Canada of the earlier Pacific Scandal of 1873 it provoked a national outburst in Austria-Hungary over the loss of its manhood to North America, and this despite the CPR's rather innocuous position as the fifth largest transporter of emigrants and Canada's similar rank as a receiver of Austro-Hungarian migrants. But the depopulation of one of Austria's favourite recruiting grounds for soldiers in Croatia was enough to initiate the Canada or Canadian Pacific Affair of 1913-14.[42]

The scandal apparently resulted from collusion among the major shipping pool that controlled Atlantic trade, the German newspaper *Reichspost*, and the Austrian army newspaper, which mounted an intense press campaign against the CPR. Because many of its agents employed in Europe were also Jews, the editorials had an anti-Semitic flavour and the impression was given of a vast underworld operation functioning beneath and beyond the law. One need only sample the fantastic accusations published in the *Reichspost* to appreciate the nature of the campaign fabricated against the CPR. The purported letter of a Galician emigrant to Canada was published in August of 1913 to counsel Austro-Hungarian citizens against emigrating to Canada because of bad pay, hard work, and broken promises by the railway and the government. He counselled the peasants that their poverty as compared with Canada was "paradise and splendour" and urged them to "chase away the agents of the Canadian Pacific for they are as dreadful as the plague and foul air."[43] In September, a further editorial claimed that 500,000 men had escaped the draft by illicit emigration, and that this manpower drain had now been increased because of the appearance of the Canadian Pacific. The system of peonage encouraged by the CPR and other colonization companies was denounced in an emotional harangue, which concluded:

> According to this system thousands and thousands of healthy persons, willing to work, the state's most precious asset, are subtracted from the monarchy precisely in those regions in which the future, the fate of the realm will possibly be decided, the remaining are hurled into bitter misery and the beneficiaries of this misery are the Galician and Russian Jews and foreign billionaires.[44]

The immigration scandal subsequently surfaced in the Austrian parliament, and the Austrian Ministry of Trade in charge of emigration came under severe fire. The upshot was that in October of 1913 the CPR's business operations were suspended, and the directors and leading officials of the company in Austria were arrested. British embassy officials who had been responsible in the first place for negotiating the Trieste concessions quickly sided with the CPR over the issue,[45] the Austrian authorities were forced to retreat, and the CPR charter was ultimately restored in mid-1914.[46]

The specific allegations deserve some treatment if only for the half-truths and misrepresentations they contained and the inadvertent glimpses they give of the social history of immigration. The press reports were full of accounts of conspiracies involving men from the highest ministry on down to the lowest customs agent. In the first place, the CPR was accused of liberal distribution of 50,000 kronen ($10,000) to win sole carrying rights of migrants from Trieste to New York. Secondly, an Austrian cabinet minister, Dr. Gustav Frank, was accused of taking bribes from a CPR agent named Zagorac in Agram (Zagreb).[47] The Ministry of Trade was also accused of allowing gross breaches in regulations forbidding the emigration of males of military age after December, 1912.

Several cases were cited from the Thirteenth Corps of Command in Zagreb to demonstrate the wholesale defection encouraged by the CPR from Croatia to North America. One infantryman named Josef Svećnjak purportedly indicated to his superiors that,

> In October of 1912 agents repeatedly approached me in Vienna and urged me to emigrate to America with the Canadian Pacific Railway Company. The condition was that I pay the sum of 115 kronen, out of which 10 kronen went to the agent as his commission, and 105 to cover the passage. I was told that once I paid the money down I would not have to worry about anything, since the company would issue me with a passport and I would get across the border without any problems, and that I would be exempted from military service.[48]

The aggressive recruiting tactics employed by the CPR were documented in several other instances by evidence that was either improbable or simply untrue. One young recruit who had already been to America in 1910-11 as a railway worker in Buffalo claimed that he was approached by three CPR agents at the worksite there and promised a daily wage of seven dollars, which he declined because the CPR had "a bad reputation in America." Another claimed to have been approached in a park in Vienna shortly before induction into the army by an agent who gave as his address, "Grand Trunk Railway, Montreal, Car Department, Canada, Wien IV, Wiedenerhuptstrasse." And a third, Josip Pavleković, who claimed to have been a trackworker on the CPR from 1906-13, confessed that he had signed a declaration whereby he was supposed to assume an obligation to become a Canadian citizen for a fee of ten dollars. He further added that "such hirelings received in private possession from the company a parcel of land of 30 acres, 2 buffaloes [!] and the necessary farm machinery."[49] While there may have been some truth in the perception such prospective migrants had of the activities of CPR agents and the false promises that were doubtlessly made, internal scrutiny of the allegations demonstrates the slender case constructed against the railway company.

The Canada Affair thus slammed shut a door that had just begun to open between south-central Europe and Canada. The CPR had become a pawn in an internal power struggle between the army, the churches, and the Ministry of the Interior within Austria-Hungary. But in 1914 the scandal was quickly resolved with an end to open-door emigration from the Hapsburg Empire. If the termination of the flow had not come from Austria, it would have come soon from Canada because she was experiencing a major depression and oversupply of labour by 1914, and the war itself would soon create massive discrimination against the citizens of the Austrian and German Empires.

Significantly, it was the fringe groups of European society – the Croats, Bulgarians, Serbs, and Romanians – who became the cause of an immigration scandal that marked the end of an era. The Croats were in fact the western European equivalents of the Japanese and East Indians who were met with hostility at the port of Vancouver in 1907 and 1914.[50] The CPR, like all other passenger shippers, had as their sole concern the transport of cheap labour across the Pacific and the Atlantic Oceans, and they directly challenged whatever formal or informal quota systems of emigration or immigration they had to in order to keep that supply moving. Their aggressive business tactics thus brought them into conflict with governments of both friendly and enemy persuasion. Ironically, the only groups with which they won any favour were the immigrant passengers in steerage, for whom the misery and deprivation of a journey halfway around the world meant the opportunity for a lifetime.

NOTES

1. Ramsay Cook and R.C. Brown, *Canada, 1896-1921: A Nation Transformed* (Toronto: McClelland and Stewart, 1974), pp. 49-82.
2. Johann Chmelar, "The Austrian Emigration, 1900-14," in Donald Fleming and Bernard Bailyn, *Perspectives in American History,* vol. VII, *Dislocation and Emigration, The Social Background of American Emigration* (Cambridge, Mass.: Harvard University Press, 1973), pp. 282-3.
3. Andrew A. Marchbin, "The Origin of Migration from South-Eastern Europe to Canada," *Canadian Historical Association Annual Report,* 1934, pp. 110-20.
4. Chmelar, "The Austrian Emigration," pp. 339-46.
5. R. Bičanić, *Agrarna Kriza u Hrvatskoj, 1873-95* (The Agrarian Crisis in Croatia, 1873-1895) (Zagreb, 1937).
6. Tibor Colossa, "The Social Structure of the Peasant Class in Austria

Hungary: Statistical Sources and Methods of Research," *East European Quarterly,* III, 4, pp. 420-37.

7. Gerald Govorchin, *Americans from Yugoslavia* (Gainesville: University of Florida Press, 1961), p. 12; Emily Balch, *Our Slavic Fellow Citizens,* p. 177.
8. André Blanc, *La Croatie Occidentale, Étude de Géographie Humaine* (Paris: Inst. des Etudes Slavs, 1957), pp. 301-3.
9. Marijan Britovsek, "The Process of Individualization of Agriculture in Carniola in the Second Half of the Nineteenth Century," *East European Quarterly,* III, 4, pp. 482-8.
10. Balch, *Our Slavic Fellow Citizens,* p. 175.
11. Dr. F. Mikić, "Natural Movement of the Population in the Village of Jalzabet, 1758-1960," *Sociologija* (Zagreb), IV, 1-2 (1962), summary, pp. 55-6.
12. André Blanc, *La Croatie Occidentale,* pp. 312-14.
13. Quoted in Louis Adamic, *The Native's Return: An American Immigrant Visits Yugoslavia and Discovers His Old Country* (New York: Harpers, 1934), p. 208.
14. Statistics presented in A. Blanc, *La Croatie Occidentale,* pp. 314-19.
15. See George Prpic, *The Croatian Immigrants in America* (New York: Philosophical Library, 1971), pp. 134-6.
16. Ambassador Dumba in Washington, 16 August 1913, cited in J. Chmelar, "The Austrian Emigration," p. 293. See also *ibid.,* p. 335.
17. Prpic, *Croatian Immigrants,* pp. 150, 321.
18. Cited in Vera St. Erlich, *Family in Transition: A Study of 300 Yugoslav Villages* (Princeton: Princeton University Press, 1966), p. 47.
19. Adamic, *The Native's Return,* pp. 24-5; Henry Kreisel, *The Rich Man* (Toronto: McClelland and Stewart, 1948), pp. 60-1.
20. Stjepan Lojen, *Uspomene Jednog Iseljenika* (Zagreb: Znanje, 1963), p. 9.
21. Balch, *Our Slavic Fellow Citizens,* p. 180.
22. Interview, John Susak with George Kokich, Toronto, December, 1974.
23. *Zajedničar,* 3 November 1976: "Kako su naši iseljenici putovali u Ameriku?" Ivo Šiševic.
24. Prpic, *Croatian Immigrants,* pp. 210-13.
25. Cited in Chmelar, "The Austrian Emigration, 1910-14," p. 313. See also ch. 4, *supra.*
26. *Allgemeines Verwaltungsarchiv* (Vienna), Ministerium des Innern, Kart. 321, 8/4 in G.zu 48.870/13. Viktor Klaus Agency, Buchs, 16 May 1913.
27. Interview, Ivan Jurich with George Kokich, Sault Ste. Marie, December, 1974.
28. B.C. Provincial Archives, Victoria, British Columbia Police Papers, Correspondence and Reports, ff. 35, Shawnigan Lake, 1914-17, Evidence taken at a Special Inquiry at Ellis Island, New York Harbour, 6 June 1911, Supplied to U.S. Immigrant Inspector in Charge, Vancouver, B.C., 14 February 1914.

29. See Robert Harney, "The Padrone and the Immigrant," *The Canadian Review of American Studies*, V, 2 (Fall, 1974), p. 111.

30. See David J. Hall, "Clifford Sifton: Immigration and Settlement Policy," in H.D. Palmer, *The Settlement of the West* (Calgary: Comprint, 1977), pp. 60-85; Harold Troper, *Only Farmers Need Apply: Official Canadian Government Encouragement of Immigration from the United States, 1896-1911* (Toronto: Griffin House, 1972).

31. See Donald Avery, "Canadian Immigration Policy and the 'Foreign' Navvy, 1896-1914," *Canadian Historical Association Annual Report* (1972), p. 143.

32. See PAC, RG 76, vols. 97-98, ff. 12681B-parts 1-3. Monthly returns, arrivals and departures, Immigration by Nationalities, 1899-1904.

33. PAC, RG 76, vol. 485750771, M.D. Davis, West Toronto, to T.C. Robinette, 5 December 1907.

34. *Ibid.*, T.C. Robinette to Frank Oliver, Minister of the Interior, 7 December 1907, Toronto.

35. *Ibid.*, W.D. Scott, Supt. of Immigration, to Thos. C. Robinette, Ottawa, 24 December 1907; W.D. Scott to Henry V. Moore (London), 12 May 1908; M.D. Davis to E. Blake Robertson, Toronto, 13 May 1908.

36. PAC, RG 76, W.D. Scott to Fred C. Salter, Grand Trunk Rlwy. System, Liverpool, 4 May 1908, ff. 594511, part II.

37. PAC, RG 76, vol., 485, 485750771, J. Henry Lawford, Dominion Immigration Officer, Montreal, to W.D. Scott, Supt. of Immigration, 31 May 1908; J.H. Lawford to O. Campeau, Chief of Police Montreal, 1 June 1908, Montreal.

38. See Canada, *Sessional Papers*, Annual Reports for the Department of the Interior, Ottawa (1905-10), vols. 29, 41, 42, 43, 45.

39. PAC, RG 76, vol. 407, file 594511, Part II A, J.O. Reddie, Immigration Agent and Medical Inspector, Prince Rupert, to W.D. Scott, 1 April 1910; Duncan Ross, of Foley, Welch and Stewart, Contractors, Prince Rupert, to W.D. Scott, Superintendent of Immigration, 3 May 1910; F. Oliver to W.D. Scott, Ottawa, 13 May 1910, memorandum; J.O. Reddee [sic] to W.D. Scott, telegram to W.D. Scott, 27 May 1910; W.D. Scott to J.O. Reddie, 28 May 1910.

40. *Ibid.*, W. Cory, Deputy Minister of Immigration to W.D. Scott, 26 March 1912; W.D. Scott to Mr. Buskard, 8 May 1912, memorandum.

41. See table opposite, p. 45.

42. This incident is fully described in Johann Chmelar, *Höhepunkte der österreichischen Auswanderung; Die Auswanderung aus den im Reichsrate vertretenen Königreichen und Ländern in den Jahren, 1905-14* (Wien, 1972), pp. 140-53.

43. *Reichspost*, 30 August 1913, no. 407, p. 5.

44. *Ibid.*, 28 September 1913, no. 456, p. 7.

45. PAC, RG 25 A2, vol. 148, File (Canada House Records, C8/6). Fairfax Cartwright to Rt. Hon. Earl Grey, Vienna, 16 July 1913.

46. Chmelar, "The Austrian Emigration, 1910-14," p. 368.

47. *Zajedničar* (Pittsburgh), 11 March 1914: "Vijesti iz hrvatskih zemlja: Skandal u Iseljeničkom Odsjeku." See also *ibid.,* 25 March 1914.

48. *Allgemeines Verwaltungsarchiv* (Vienna), Ministerium des Innern, Kart. 321, 8/4, in G.zu 48.870/13. From reports concerning emigration machinations received the units belonging to the 13th Corps Command in Agram (Zagreb).

49. *Ibid.,* Reports from Vid Par of the 3rd Squadron, k.u.k. Ulan Regiment no. 5; Artillerist Robert Kuster, Field Artillery Regiment no. 39; report of Infantry Regiment no. 96, Josip Pavleković. The author is indebted to the references and translations provided by Petr Mirejovsky of The University of Calgary.

50. See Ken Adachi, *The Enemy that Never Was: A History of Japanese Canadians* (Toronto: McClelland and Stewart, 1976), pp. 63-99 *passim*.

THREE

Migrant Work and the Beginnings of Settlement, 1900-20

From the turn of the century to the end of World War I, the Croatian community in Canada was small and had no common sense of identity or culture. The immigrants were poor, and life in Canada was a brute physical struggle for survival, whether in the mines or forests, on homesteads or in the fisheries, or in urban construction or industry. In this respect, the Croatian immigrants were not unlike other Central or East European groups, which together occupied the bottom rung of Canada's economic and social ladder. They were among the 800,000 or so European peoples of non-British, non-French stock who swelled Canada's population between the censuses of 1901-31.[1] In the cities, they took up shabby, overcrowded dwellings along with other European immigrants in the urban ghettoes of the Ward in Toronto, Winnipeg's North End, and Regina's East End.[2] In the country, they took up homesteads alongside the Scandinavians, Germans, Poles, and Ukrainians who settled on the agricultural frontiers of northern Saskatchewan and Alberta. And on the resource frontier to which most Croats migrated, they worked alongside Italians, Bulgarians, Slovaks, Finns, and others on railway extra gangs, in hardrock mines, and in logging camps.

The signs of civilization in this widely scattered group of 3,000 or so migrants were precariously few. Family and home were unknown to the vast majority, except as a village or farm in the old country. Women were largely absent; theirs was a bachelor society that drifted about from place to place in search of work and wages. For those who were literate, there were no newspapers or magazines in their own language, unless one of the several Croatian-American newspapers should fall into their hands. Cultural organizations were virtually absent except for the lodges of the parent National Croatian Society in the United States, which were only four in number by the outbreak of World War I.[3] As peripheral entities in their day-to-day existence, and cut off from their parent culture or its larger satellites in the United States, the Canadian Croats were exposed to a social melting pot more pervasive than that to the south. Insufficient in numbers to command any preferred status or to raise the necessary social capital for music, culture, or education, the community could remain alive only through informal means. These might be frontier work gangs organized by family kinship circles, villages, and regions from the old country. The urban counterpart was the boardinghouse organized under the village hetman, the *gospodarstvo;* the rural equivalent was the bloc settlement of contiguous farms settled by interlocking family clans. Whatever the occupational or spatial context, the Croats responded with the only cultural tools of survival they had known through centuries, the peasant *zadruga* and its traditions of communal co-operation.

Because of its informal and largely unrecorded character, the historical record of this formative period must be reconstructed by the fragmentary means of oral history, family reminiscence, obituaries, and occasional entries in local histories and town newspapers. In short, the historian must rely on fragile folk memory, which occasionally distorts to negative or positive effect the daily experiences of work, settlement, and survival. Unity often is substituted for division or militancy for submission, but despite these imperfections the human memory yields what is human, and for that reason it must have a place in any history.

For the migrant labourer and railway navvy, bunkhouse life on the frontier was not the romanticized log cabin of North American fiction, nor did it even approach the antiseptic reconstructions of log fortresses for latter-day tourism. The shacks and shanties the navvies and lumberjacks had to live in were leaky and overcrowded, smelling of foul straw and sweat-soaked underwear and penetrated by vermin, mosquitoes, and disease. These physical hardships, in combination with smoke, noise, and occasional violence, were all threats to the sanity, sobriety, and physical health of the immigrant labourer. As Edmund Bradwin observed in his classic work, *The Bunkhouse Man,* such conditions were "perhaps liveable for the man newly arrived from the Balkans, but hardly a wholesome environment for the shaping of a future citizen of Canada."[4] Work on the outside was scarcely the fresh-air life depicted so glowingly in the prospectuses for young Canadian gentlemen in the northern woods. Backbreaking pick and shovel work on the extra gangs, incessant flies, pick and axe wounds that were not dressed properly – all were bearable alternatives to the innumerable construction deaths that dogged every mile of the National Transcontinental and the Grand Trunk Pacific construction. Bradwin tersely observed that back of each work camp on the frontier were crosses up on a hillside – marked by the epithet, "Oh, some Russian is buried there" – which "usually meant some foreign-born worker of Slav or Balkan extraction."[5]

The dynamite accident at Mile 41 of Grand Trunk Pacific construction near Yale, British Columbia, might be taken as typical. Dead were six Swedes and two Croats from an explosion on February 23, 1912, at the camp of J.M. Kullander, a Grand Trunk jobber. A brother of one of the deceased tersely described the accident, which occurred during the building of a railway tunnel at the Miette River:

> My brother, Frank Larson, was loading a hole at top of the cut. An explosion occurred suddenly. I was thrown down and when I got up I saw E. Lindquist and W. Persson lying close to the derrick on the lower slope of the cut. They were not covered by rock or dirt. I heard some one cry from beneath the rocks. I and others began to try and remove the rocks from above the men who we believed were buried. None were got out while I was there. I was hurt and unable to work and returned to camp.
>
> I have seen the bodies of those killed and identify them as W. Persson, Gus Carlson, Mike Postovich [Milo Pastuovich], Mat Postovich [Monte Pastuovich], C. Johnson, E. Lindquist, Frank Larson and Gust Starr.[6]

Further evidence established that Larson, an experienced powder monkey, had somehow detonated the dynamite charge, that he and his partner were literally blown sky-high, and that tons of rock and debris were dumped into the rock-cut ahead, where the other Swedes and Croatians worked.

The proportion of Croatians killed in industrial accidents was no higher than for other immigrant groups, but their numbers added to the high mortality rate incurred in the building of Canada. The injuries and fatalities in the mines of the Far West reveal similar hazards to life and limb. Among minor incidents reported in the mining districts of British Columbia in 1913 were two involving Croats, the first working at the Granby mine in Phoenix and the second at the Mother Lode mine at Greenwood. One B. Spelac, a mucker, was injured about the shoulders after being struck by a motor, and another, Matt Zellinich, was similarly injured by falling rock in a chute. Two others at the Britannia mines on Howe Sound were less fortunate. Emil Siukovich was instantly killed in 1915 when he drilled into a hole packed with dynamite that had not fired, and John Pradovich was killed when his head was crushed by falling rock. And at the Extension Mine near Ladysmith in 1915, another four Croats were fatally injured: Juraj Berdik, "Bill" Keserić, Janko Bulić, and Loje Jurkaš.[7] The Alberta Mines reports reveal the same toll on human lives in the coal mines of the Rocky Mountain range from the Crowsnest coalfields in the south to the Coal Branch mines east of Jasper in the north. Every year at least twenty names of European immigrants would be added to the list of fatalities, and in some years bumps and explosions such as the one at Hillcrest in 1914 claimed hundreds of miners' lives.[8]

For others who survived the experience, the fullness of time diminished the painful memories of the bunkhouses and the hazards of working on the railroad. An old-timer's communication to his grandchildren

some fifty years later gives a Croatian immigrant's affectionate perceptions of his first year in Canada as a navvy near Kenora:

> I was born, 19th December, 1891, in country Croatia in the Village
> of Krizische, Croatian sea shore (Hrvatsko Primorje). Emigrated to
> Canada, month of May, year 1907, when I was just over fifteen year
> old. King Edward VII, was the King of England and King of
> Canada, Sir Wilfrid Laurier was Prime Minister of Canada.
>   Canada population was around seven million. My first job was
> north of Kenora and east of Winnipeg River, on the then Grand
> Trunk Railway, which is now Canadian National (north line), work
> was pick and shovel in small rock cut, ten hours per day, and no
> coffee break, wages was twenty two and one half cents per hour, on
> construction. Sleeping camp was build of log not peeled, floor of
> round pole, no bed springs, no mattress, bunk was made of round
> poles, with little hay on it. We got to have our own blanket. We did
> not have machinery that will do the work, so we can watching it and
> get pay for it (like getting today) all the power we have to work was
> horses and mules, and our arms. (Armstrong power) [sic][9]

Some immigrants nurtured positive if not poetic memories of the
northern bush and snowy winters in northwestern Ontario. One migrant
who later found his way into Minnesota and the Middle West of the
United States fondly reminisced in the 1930's of his days as a lumberjack
near Port Arthur and Fort William during the winter of 1912. He
remembered the camaraderie of "junaki" (strong men) and "hajduks"
(vagabonds), and conjured visions of the imaginary nymph of the forest,
"Vila," who had left the Adriatic shore to accompany them to the
forests of northern Ontario. And although "Vila" was terribly afraid of
the cold winters and deep snowdrifts, he comforted her with the words:
"Don't be afraid as long as you are in the company of Croats, even
though the church should be destroyed and its doors buried." To this she
replied, "Good, good, my love, let us make love then through to mid-
night, and then we'll begin to build our house."

Nor were all of the pre-war immigrants to northern Ontario pick and
shovel labourers. By the canons of their day, some were successful entrepreneurs, acting as small contractors and jobbers for the railways and
timber companies. One old migrant who came to the Sault Ste. Marie
area in 1910 had acquired experience working in Minnesota and Wisconsin logging camps, and upon arriving in Canada he began to supply wood
on a small contract basis to the pulp and paper companies.[10] Other bud-
ding businessmen hired themselves out as cooks to the railway extra
gangs and later became restaurateurs. Yet others soon tired of the heavy
physical labour of trackwork and began to establish themselves in small
businesses, such as boardinghouses, bakeries, and groceries. Inevitably
these men were Dalmatians from the southern Adriatic coastline, from
towns and cities with a strong mercantile tradition.[11]

Ethnic communities had begun in northern Ontario cities where the Croatian labourers settled and worked in the off season, which was usually summer if they were lumberjacks and winter if they were navvies. The city of Sault Ste. Marie became a natural magnet to which Croatian immigrants were attracted, first to live and then to work permanently, once they had broken the cycle of seasonal labour. The city already had a reputation as an important gathering point for migrants in Canada, no doubt because of its location on the Canadian-American border and because work was to be had in abundance there. Family and chain migrations had already begun from villages in Dalmatia, Hrvatsko Primorje, and Herzegovina, nearly always from locations close to the Adriatic coastline. The most common were Slivno in Dalmatia, Drinovci in Herzegovina, Krivi Put in Lika, and Crikvenica and Hreljin in the northern coastal region. One old migrant from Slivno recalled from memory eighteen members of his own clan, the Glibotas, who lived in the Sault before 1914, as well as the names of over eighty other migrants from the three areas mentioned. Most were like himself, related to others by kinship ties or at least by the common geographical familiarity of the village or "selo."[12]

Old migrants in Sault Ste. Marie commonly remembered about twenty Croatians who had settled before 1910, and who were known affectionately as "Kolumbusari." Two names common among the early settlers in the Algoma district were Blaz Pagden (Padjen) of Krivi Put and Marko Soyatt (Šojat) of Senj, a village and a coastal city no more than ten miles apart on the northern Adriatic. Both were identified by Nikola Krmpotić, a ninety-three-year-old immigrant, as "lopovi" (rogues) and "builders."[13] Others were Pavao Crnović (Crnko), a coke-oven operator with Algoma Steel, and Stjepan Polić, a CPR employee, both of whom were thought to have been in the region before 1900. Josip Levar and Marko Pavelić were mentioned as farmers in the hinterland of the Sault before 1910. Yet others, such as Ivan Stilin (Stilinović) and Marko Krpatic, were in construction and bushwork. In common with the other old-timers, all of these seemed to have come from Hrvatsko Primorje or Lika on the northern coastline.[14]

The second wave of post-1910 migrants seemed, on the other hand, to have come largely from the southern Dalmatian coast and adjacent towns in Herzegovina. Common patterns of work were forestry and construction, and after 1912-13 increasing numbers were employed by the Algoma Steel Company.[15] Some Croats, including Rafael Stilin, Dujo Pekanić, Vicko Milošević, and Stipan Majić, were involved in the stone-cutting operations for the construction of the Algoma Central Railway station, which was built in 1912.[16] These Croats not only worked together but lived together in crowded boardinghouses usually located close to their work. A favourite residential location was James Street in the west end, where apparently a hundred Dalmatian men and approximately ten women lived in several closely situated boarding and rooming houses.[17]

These, along with others strung out along Cathcart Street, housed mainly the newer migrants from Dalmatia and Herzegovina, while others in the region of Beverly Street and Hudson housed mainly those Croats from the coastline of the northern Adriatic Sea.[18]

Croatians had also begun to settle sporadically in the mining camps of northern Ontario to the east of Lake Superior. The silver mines at Cobalt, which were staked out in 1906, and the gold mines at Porcupine and Timmins, established between 1909 and 1911, attracted their share of South Slavs from the Balkans. One of the earliest Croatian miners in the Cobalt and Sudbury region was Luka Klemenčić, a native of the town of Sisak who came to Canada in 1905 and worked for a time in the Cobalt mines before moving to the Nickel Belt during World War I.[19] Another was Joseph Kranjević (Šiško), a native of the rocky barrens of Lika, who also came in 1905 and worked in the mining camps of the Porcupine district, which were still in their infancy.[20] Both the Sudbury basin and the Timmins-Kirkland Lake region, however, would await the post-war migration for more substantial numbers of Croatian miners.

The other major pole of attraction in the northern regions of Ontario was the Thunder Bay district, diagonally opposite from Sault Ste. Marie on the western shore of Lake Superior. As in the case of the Sault, Port Arthur and Fort William were initially attractive because of their ease of access to the northern states of Minnesota, Michigan, and Wisconsin. A number of Croats, particularly from the Hrvatsko Primorje district and others from the southern Dalmatian coast, worked with railway extra gangs and lumber crews and used Port Arthur as their home base. Among the earliest migrants who settled in the district were John Polić and John Pavletić, natives of the northern Adriatic: Polić worked as a stevedore in the Canadian Northern freight yards in 1902; Pavletić kept a boardinghouse not too many years after his arrival in 1905. Other Dalmatian migrants tired of the heavy manual labour of the railway frontier and soon looked for opportunities in the city. Typical of these were John Filipovic, a Grand Trunk employee who settled in 1904 and later established a bakery and confectionery, and Nick Miosich, a cook with the CPR who later entered the confectionery business in the city during the First War.[21] Others from Herzegovina were also in Port Arthur by 1907-08 and often worked as stevedores with the Canadian Northern or operated boardinghouses briefly before World War I.[22]

Residential segregation proved more difficult in Port Arthur than in Sault Ste. Marie – Finns, Italians, Slavs, and other minorities were closely crowded into the "foreign quarter" of its south end. Yet, identifiable patterns were beginning to develop, with the Dalmatian and Herzegovinian Croatians settling along the lakeside streets, Manitou and Lake, and those from Hrvatsko Primorje another block farther to the north, along Wilson Street. But the latter group was too impermanent as yet to constitute even a nascent settlement, as they continued in the capacity of transient labour. More than the southern Croats they tended to find their

57

way home to the old country and their home villages before the outbreak of war. Typical of the returned migrant was one Dijać (Dan) Blazina, an old-timer from Hreljin, Primorje, who had come as a young lad of fifteen with his two brothers, Karlo and Luka, in 1903. Working for a time as a domestic, then as a quarry worker, he was forced to return in 1910 to Hreljin as his elder brothers had returned one by one to work on his father's land. A term of military service followed and it was fifteen years before he could re-emigrate to Canada.[23]

More established Croatian communities also were formed in southern Ontario prior to World War I. The Niagara Peninsula witnessed spectacular industrial growth with the development of cheap hydroelectric power generated from Niagara Falls. Factories sprang up in the Crowland district at Welland, Port Colborne, and Port Robinson, including Atlas Steel, Electric Steel Foundry, Page-Hersey Tube, Plymouth Cordage, and Beatty Foundry. A heavy demand was thereby generated for a large industrial labour force to do the heavy foundry work such enterprises entailed, and large numbers of French Canadians from Massachusetts and Italians from New York and Pennsylvania flocked in during the 1905-10 period. Croats, along with Romanians, worked in the first construction phase of the factory buildings, but either from lack of skill or disinclination to work in the foundries, they often worked in "The Yard" and as labourers to avoid the noise and heat of the smelters.[24]

Partly from economic necessity and partly from their peasant background, the Croatians who came to the Welland district also purchased garden plots and acreages upon which they could grow vegetables to supplement their factory wages. Two examples demonstrate the peculiar urban-rural lifestyle that became characteristic of the Welland community. One of the earliest farmers in the area was Stjepan Pihać, who had worked as a labourer's helper in one of the steel mills from 1907-14. He gradually accumulated enough savings over seven years to purchase 128 acres of land at ten dollars an acre. And there were at least five other families from Zagorje north of Zagreb who purchased acreages from established farmers in the environs of Welland.[25] One of these was Stevo Knezić, a native of Oroslvalje who had worked as a young boy in the forest industry of his native District of Zagorje, then as a leatherworker in Zagreb, and finally as a steelworker in the United States after migrating to America in 1906. In 1910 he came to Canada while in his mid-twenties and worked as a steelworker in Welland and Hamilton for the next four years. In 1912 he married Beta (Barbara) Franković of the nearby village of Donja Stubica, and in 1914 he and two other friends purchased some land near the present Welland airport. The Knezićs then began to raise a family of six on their hundred-acre mixed farm, which produced fruit as well as dairy products and vegetables.[26]

The appearance of women from the old country was perhaps the first civilizing element to distinguish the Welland community from the male sojourners' cultures of northern Ontario. Yet another family was completed in 1913, when Kata Milković and her seven-year-old daughter joined her husband Ivan, who worked near Orillia. They then moved to Thorold.[27] With such changes, a sense of community had begun to develop. Already there had been the brief establishment, in 1909, of a lodge of the parent Croatian Fraternal Union, entitled St. Peter and Paul (Sveti Petar i Pavao), which lapsed by 1911-12.[28] But there were more certain signs of cultural awareness by this time, which may be more forcefully related in a reminiscence of one of the early pioneers, Stevo Škvorc:

> In the winter of 1910, when we were young and days were slipping by, we had to do something, at least this was the thinking of Mijo Pavešić of Nova Gradiška, for he constructed out of a small cheese box a *berde* and a small *bugarija* [stringed instruments], and out of a piece of electric cable, he made strings. I and Silvester Hrastović from Stubica bought a *Brač I* and a *Bugarija II*. Jovo Merlović gave a few cents towards the purchase of a *berde*. We taught ourselves to play a few pieces, and we were hurried along by Gajo Vasiljević and his wife who called us over to their place to demonstrate our talents. Eh, it went well, but without practice strumming there was nothing we couldn't learn . . . CGD . . . DCG, but even this went quickly. After some time we admitted into our midst Nikola Baltužić with his violin, and we were talked about by the whole community. Boarding-house boss Vasiljević often invited us over to play at his place, because he was able then to sell more whiskey than a saloon.[29]
>
> But his house proved too small for dancing, and we needed to construct a larger hall. But where? With what? Then we began to take up a collection, to buy a piece of land, and we were joined by several other of our fellow-countrymen. The merchants we approached for money as a large loan to finance the hall. Vasiljević, upon his own recognizance, bought a piece of land as a beginning.
>
> In May of 1911, ours must have been the first home in Canada that had a roof overhead, and constructed on piers so that the water wouldn't rot it! But what was to become of it? What sort of a church or mosque would it be? For we as comrades wished to avoid any trouble. No, let it carry instead a progressive workers' label, so we called it "Slavenski Dom" [Slavic Home], and it would also serve under the same name as a mutual benefit organization, which however did not last long [the Croatian Fraternal Union, Lodge #517, which lasted only from 1915 to 1928].
>
> The first marriage to be celebrated in the new hall was that of Stevo Knezić and Beta Franković, both born in Donja Stubica. They booked tamburitzans from Hamilton: Gaspočić, Gorupić, Bosnar and Brajković. The home was the pride and honour of the colony, and we took great pains to pay for it, for there was a great sense of worry which surrounded its existence. For we were much poorer

D.P.'s than those nowadays. The young people came to it in droves, and the young girls were so few that there was a great struggle over whom would be the first to marry. There were so many of us young people that we had to make our own fun, but to-day it is different.

Hardly any were at that time able to send for a wife. The first children born here: Dolenac, Bilvolčić, and Repar. The first of our people died: Martinić and Ivan Bivol at Port Robinson. We bought lumber, and as God is our witness, we also gathered boards which we found along the railway tracks and made a cross out of them. There the first of our people were born: Čukel, Mučnak, and Toma Škvorc, so in 1915 we had future tamburitzans at Port Robinson.

The Slavic Home served many purposes; the municipality of Crowland had an office there for the magistrate; there was a lock-up; a basic school, our school . . . But it was never free of lingering debt, and later it fell prey to the creditors.[30]

A unique community had thus began to take shape, neither purely urban nor rural, but well-adapted to the local circumstances it faced. It was destined to become one of the most enduring of Croatian communities in Canada, constantly attracting immigrants in subsequent decades.

It was further to the west, however, that Croatians were more successful in establishing rural communities along the co-operative pattern of the ancient *zadruga*. In common with many other groups that settled in bloc settlements on the Prairies between 1880-1914, the Croats found security in numbers just as other groups, such as the Ukrainians, Hungarians, Norwegians, and Icelanders, did.[31] Their basic impulse was to huddle together in close-knit ethnic communities, an urge summed up by one prairie pioneer of Slavic descent in northern Saskatchewan: "We all felt lost . . . we wanted to stay together and help one another, just as we did in the old country. If something happened to me, my neighbours would look after my family."[32]

This spirit prompted the formation of two Croatian settlements in Saskatchewan. Both were situated on the Canadian Northern line, under construction near Saskatoon and Prince Albert in the years 1904-05, one to the south and east of Saskatoon at Kenaston, Hanley, and Bladworth, and the other to the west of the more northerly Prince Albert at Duck Lake and Leask. This latter location was chosen by several copper miners from Calumet, Michigan, who explored the Duck Lake region in 1904 for homestead land. Their trials and tribulations were vividly described by one of the original settlers, G. Lucas [Lisac]:

In the spring of the year 1904, my father and my mother took our four homesteads – 640 acres of land, 25 miles from Duck Lake, Saskatchewan, where the town of Leask is now located. In the fall of the same year, my father and two of his brothers, Blaz and Ivan all came together in order to settle on this land. They bought horses and necessary agricultural implements with which to construct buildings and barns for livestock. In the meantime, however, my father took a terrible cold which inflamed his lungs, and in mid-February 1905, he died at Duck Lake Saskatchewan five days after he was admitted into hospital. His earthly remains were sent back to Calumet, and one of my brothers returned back to Leask and sold the farm and everything on it.[33]

However tragically, the northern region of Saskatchewan was effectively advertised by the returnees to Calumet, and in the next five years nearly fifteen Croatian families came to Duck Lake to farm. One was the family of Joseph Gerich, who brought his wife and nine children with him in 1910. Within two years he had put fifty-seven acres under crop, had broken another twenty-seven acres, and had erected farm buildings in the value of $1,000. In addition, his application for homestead patent indicated that he ran fifteen head of cattle on his quarter-section by 1912. In that same year, his eldest son filed for an adjacent homestead and had cropped twenty-five acres by the end of that year. The family became naturalized Canadians in 1913 and they were firmly launched in the farming business by the outbreak of World War I.[34]

Greater success by force of sheer numbers was achieved by a group of Croatian farmers from Lika, who came via the midwestern United States into central Saskatchewan. In March of 1904, an initial foray into the Kenaston-Hanley area along the Canadian Northern line southeast of Saskatoon was made by four Croats from Lovinac in Lika. Nikola Pavelić, accompanied by half-brother Joseph and two other natives of Lovinac, Paul Tomljenović and Matt Prpić, surveyed the land near Kenaston and built outbuildings to be used as temporary homes in the following year. The following spring they sent for their sweethearts, wives, and young children, and they were soon joined by Marica Mašić, Ana Prpić, Kata Pavelić, and Mara Pavelić. A typical chain migration of families then swelled the numbers of these pioneers to over fifty families in the next decade. Further extensions of the same core families – the Masiches, Sekuliches, Brkiches, Vrkljans, Matoviches, Persiches, Sariches, Zduniches, and Krpans – were gradually added to the clan. All were from the same area of Lika, in the intermountain valley around Lovinac, from such closely contiguous villages as Vagan, Muntenja, Ričice, Sveti Rok, and Bruvno. All were farmers, all were poor, and most were forced to sell their share of the family farm to subsidize their passage across the Atlantic in search for a better life.

The transatlantic experience of the Paveliches, the first of the families into the Kenaston-Hanley area, is vividly recaptured by one of its familial descendants:

Katerina Tomljenović [was born] the oldest daughter of Stipan and Marija Pavičić on March 1, 1884 in Lovinac, Croatia. In those days of large intermingled families, and a mostly illiterate population,

61

birth dates were remembered as being on or near a Church feast-day and . . . she was told she was born "na Gregurovo" on St. Gregory day, March 12th. . . . Grandfather [Josip Pavelić] was in fact born on his presumed birthday of March 19th, 1876 – St. Joseph's day.

As males were preferred because they grew up to be soldiers and received up to four years of schooling, the young ladies of the day were kept at home to do the cooking, weaving, crop-raising, sheep and cattle-herding and the many menial tasks necessitated for lack of material goods. For instance, daily laundry dipping down at the river because they possessed only one change plus the Sunday best – beautifully hand-sewn and embroidered in bright colors on snow-white cloth – eye-catching and hopefully 'beau-catching' for the after-Mass folk dance [kolo] on the green. . . .

Marriage was mostly pre-arranged by the parents. When a girl reached that age she usually married a lad from the same or nearby parish, and so it was that at the age of seventeen . . . she married Josip Pavelić on January 6th 1902, and moved into their family residence. And family it was, where three brothers and their wives all lived under the one roof [zadruga]. Realizing that their small holding could not provide more than adequate return, and wishing to better their lot in life, Nikola, the eldest brother, and Josip left their wives behind and struck out for the promised land of North America. Many a winter evening we youngsters heard Gramps recall how he landed in New York with the equivalent of $25.00 in his pantaloons, unable to speak English, but willing to do any and all manual labor to earn enough to live on and save up enough besides to get established in order to send for wives and families. For a year they worked on railroad section gangs in the mid-western states, and when word reached them that land was available for homesteads in Canada, they made their way northward.

After working out as farm hands to acquire the necessary capital and experience, they filed claims on a homestead in the Briggs district, built a shelter, pooled their meagre savings and sent for their families. . . . It is hard to imagine the weeks of waiting – the length of time it took for arrangements to be made both on this and that side of the Atlantic – the 28 day crossing of the Atlantic, the long over-country train ride from New York – then horror of horrors to discover that one of the children had developed smallpox and had to be in quarantine for a further 26 days in New York. As if that wasn't bad enough, when at last Gram and my mother (the child who got the smallpox), were to arrive at Bonnington (as Kenaston was then called), travelled alone, unable to speak English, they were taken right through to Saskatoon, where they had to spend the night and return the next day. . . .[35]

Other families from the Lovinac area followed soon after the Paveliches' arrival in 1905. A nearby family in Lovinac, the Brkich clan, saw its family numbers rapidly multiply and drive the younger members from the small family farm of forty acres. Both the origins and the pattern of migration of the Brkich family were similar to those of the previous migrants to Kenaston, and are carefully preserved in family memory:

> Simun Brkich [Sam Beckie] married Ika Prpić on April 29, 1901 at St. Mihovila's in Lovinac (both were 19 years old). . . . Before the birth of their first child, Sam left Lovinac (in Austrian Croatia), in 1902 (age 20) for the U.S.A. never to return. His brothers-in-law Mat, Anton and Nick Prpić also went with him. He worked in Arkansas, on a crusher in Oklahoma and Kansas, then a wiremill in Aurora, Illinois. His brother Paul joined him in 1905, and they

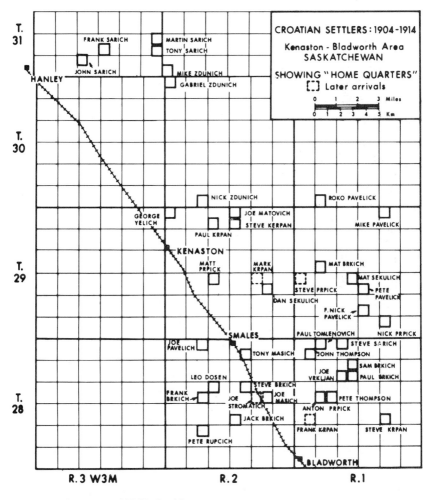

SOURCE: *Courtesy of K.N. Beckie.*

63

boarded together in a house run by a Mrs. Baričević. In March, 1906 he moved to Bladworth where his brothers-in-law had preceded him lured by cheap homestead land.[36]

By 1910, the pull of family chain-migration became stronger, resulting in the attraction of other interlocking families. (See map, p. 63.) The first visible pattern appeared to be prior migration and return to and from the United States, and then to Canada. Generally, these were somewhat younger males in the clans about Lovinac who sought their fortune first in America, returned to Croatia to marry, and then returned to Canada. A typical example of such re-emigration is provided by the Zdunich clan, both younger brothers in their respective family *zadruga*. Mike Zdunich first arrived in 1912 at Hanley after emigrating first to the United States where he worked as a stone quarryman in Oklahoma and took out American citizenship.[37] He was then joined by both a younger and an older brother in 1913 and 1914. The first, Nick Zdunich, migrated directly to Canada with his wife and two children and worked in the coal mines of the Crowsnest Pass at Bellevue before purchasing land in Hanley, a bare half-mile from his brother.[38] Then the eldest brother, Gabriel, who had himself been to the United States and Argentina, arranged to bring his entire family plus portions of others in the troubled year 1914.[39]

In April, a package fare was arranged with a ticket agent, Johann Büchel in Buchs on the Swiss-Austrian border, for the total price of $70.20 (1,310 *kronen*), which covered the journey from Lovinac to Kenaston, Saskatchewan, for two adults and five children! (See illustration opposite.) They were accompanied by fragments of the Brkich family (Paul and Mat) and the Krpans (Steve), who were joining brothers who had migrated before 1910.[40] They loaded their oxcarts and travelled over the craggy Velebit mountain range to the coast, where they boarded a boat from Pag to Fiume (Rijeka). There they boarded a train bound for Le Havre, France, where they embarked on the *Ionian* of the Allan Steamship line and set out for Canada on April 15. Mat Brkich's three-year-old daughter died and had to be buried at sea, and the family itself had to undergo quarantine for suspected scarlet fever. The remainder of the party proceeded ahead and reached Kenaston on May 5, 1914, arriving with a sense of wonderment and despair at the isolation and barrenness of the Canadian West.[41]

Whatever their route and whatever their time of arrival, the fledgling colony of Croatian farmers began to take shape; indeed, among themselves and relatives back in the old country it appears to have become known as Lovinac.[42] And in many basic ways, the material subsistence of the first years in Canada assumed a similar character to that in Croatia. There were the inevitable milk cow, several chickens and pigs, and a varied homegrown diet of hard-wheat bread, cornmeal porridge (*palenta*), salt pork, sauerkraut (*kiseli kupus*), beef soup, and homemade

Auswanderungs=Agentur

von

Johann Büchel in Buchs (Rheintal)

neben Bahnhof beim Gasthof zum „Arlberg".

Patentiert vom schweizer. Bundesrate.

Zürich.

Reise=Vertrag

Zwischen obiger Agentur und den nachstehend verzeichneten Personen ist folgender Vertrag abgeschlossen worden:

Geburts-jahr	Geschlechtsname	Vorname	Alter	Zivilstand (ledig, verheiratet, verwittwet, geschieden)	Heimatort	Letzter Wohnort	Beruf
	Zdunić pl. Gabriel		40	ver	Kroatien		Landarbeit.
"	"	Maria	37	"	"	Lovinac	"
"	"	Dane	11 5 m	led	"	"	"
"	"	Jakov	6 6 m	"	"	"	"
"	"	Joso	4 3 m	"	"	"	"
"	"	Cilika	3	"	"	"	"
"	"	Markos	1 6 m	"	"	"	"

§ 1. Die Agentur übernimmt die sichere Beförderung der vorgenannten Personen.

von **Buchs** den 15 / IV 914 in Dritte-Klasse nach dem Einschiffungshafen,

von Havre den in Dritte-Klasse des Dampfers Jonian

der Allan Linie nach ~~New-York~~ Quebec und von da

nach Kennaston Sask. via **all rail** und es haben sich die Reisenden

den in bei der Agentur einzufinden.

"Emigration Agent, Johann Büchel, travel agreement with Gabriel Zdunić and family for third class travel from Lovinac to Havre and by Allan Steamship, Ionian, *to Quebec, and by rail to Kenaston, Saskatchewan."*

SOURCE: *Courtesy of K.N. Beckie.*

65

cheese. Family formation was also rapid and it was common for families to reach six or seven in number. Clothing was most often homeknit and handsewn, liberally passed from one tier of the family to the next. Wives assisted in the heavy labour of the farm, walking behind the plow, stooking sheaves, planting and hoeing in the vegetable garden, and searching after lost cows.

But there were rapid cultural adaptations as well to the peculiar nature of prairie culture. Children were sometimes boarded out to non-Croatian families in nearby towns such as Bladworth for several months a year, until a school was constructed closer to home in the Briggs school district. And great pride was taken when the children were able to inform the parents of the contents of English-language newspapers. In the earliest pioneering phase, the community of practising Roman Catholics depended on missionary priests; in 1913, the same year the school was built, St. Andrew's Church was constructed in Kenaston, and the families travelled a few miles to and from town in a four-wheeled democrat in summer or in a bobsleigh in winter. The convivial atmosphere of such social gatherings with other nationalities of the same faith was also reinforced by long winter evenings spent in the company of neighbours of Anglo-Saxon, German, Norwegian, and Belgian descent.[43]

Pre-war Croatian settlement in Alberta was neither as concentrated nor as successful as in central Saskatchewan. Compact rural communities failed to materialize in the Far West perhaps because of the occupational inducements offered by coal mining in the period immediately prior to World War I. The opening of mines along the Rocky Mountain divide, at Crowsnest Pass and Coal Branch and in the interior coalfields of the Red Deer and Lethbridge areas, attracted Slavic miners from all parts of southern, central, and eastern Europe. Croats were in evidence in all of these mining regions;[44] indeed, the town of Robb in the Coal Branch district was for a time named Balkan, after the Balkan Coal Company founded by an immigrant from the United States who entered Canada before World War I. Given the great number of Croats subsequently hired by that company, its founder was possibly a Croat as well.[45]

A connection of sorts had begun to suggest itself between coal mine and homestead in early Alberta. Much as the factory worker-farmer was not an untypical combination for immigrant Croatians in the Niagara Peninsula, the rural-urban duality is apparent in pioneer Alberta. Croatian coalminers in the Coal Branch area soon heard of the homesteads opening in the Peace River region and began to drift northwards into farm towns such as Spirit River and Rycroft. One of the earliest arrivals in the Peace, Matt Carr (Čar), recollected his arrival there prior to the First World War, when neither road nor rail existed and he walked 120 miles into his homestead in the bush.[46] Others would follow, as the male sojourners drifted northward and inspected the Peace before going back to the old country to collect their families. And some would have to postpone their dream of a farm of their own, as did one Croatian when his eldest son perished in the sinking of the Titanic in 1912 and the war intervened to interrupt the completion of his family.[47]

Other quasi-rural communities of coalminers were established in southern Alberta as well. One such community is reputed to have existed around 1910 near the ghost village of Steveville in the Drumheller district, although subsequent historical traces of it have been lost.[48] Other individuals, such as Mike Miškulin, a native of Jablanac (Jurkuša) on the Adriatic Coast, migrated to the Lethbridge district by way of the United States prior to World War I. Settling near Groton on the Milk River, Miškulin and his wife, Mary, raised two children on their small homestead while he also worked in the nearby coal mines.[49] A similar cycle of seasonal labour on the farm and winter work in the mines was visible among other South Slav pioneers in southern Alberta. Philip Berkovich, a native of Orese (Orašje?), came to Turner Valley near Calgary in 1908 and worked as a ranch hand and farm labourer near Black Diamond during the summer and as a miner in the soft-coal deposits until after the First World War.[50]

The cases of two bachelor pioneers in Alberta perhaps best summarize the failure of rural communities in that province to provide an economic and cultural matrix for survival prior to 1914. Their brief but colourful biographies demonstrate the contrast with the bloc communities in Saskatchewan. Joseph Trafenic, "an Austrian," arrived on horseback from Benton, Arkansas, in 1909 in the Morrin district of south-central Alberta. He painstakingly built a two-storey stone house from flat river stones over the next seven years while he farmed a small garden plot for subsistence. Perhaps this magnificent farmhouse was to be the home of a family that never came; in any event, he suddenly departed for the United States in 1916 and was never heard from again.[51] The case of "Black John" Karlovich, the hermit of Falun, Alberta, demonstrates the personal costs of survival on the lone prairie. Leaving a wife and family in Austria-Hungary, Karlovich came to the Falun district near Wetaskiwin in 1910 as a homesteader. His lifestyle thereafter centred on his marked aversion of water and his taste for alcohol, which he produced in his homemade still. His drinking was contrived seasonally to place him in warm detention homes during the winter, and during the summer he would happily share his homebrew with all and sundry. Locally, Karlovich became somewhat of a legendary figure – at the local auction sales he collected junk for his log shanty, commenting to the local auctioneer, "No good for you, no good for me, no good for anybody – buy anyhow!"[52]

Further to the west on the coast of British Columbia, Croatian settlement began to assume the more permanent character of the prairie communities in Saskatchewan. In the Port Guichon-Ladner area on the lower Fraser mainland, more than twenty-five family heads were listed as fishermen, boat-builders, ship's captains, and marine engineers by

1910.[53] At least ten of these had applied for and received their fishing licences from the federal Department of Marine and Fisheries.[54] Yet others had abandoned the open sea for less risky and year-round employment in the canneries, as did Marco Bussanich, who took employment repairing nets with the Anglo-British Columbia Packing Company in 1900 after ten years in the salmon fisheries.[55]

Family ties multiplied rapidly in the second generation of this small, tightly knit group from Lošinj. One of the earliest arrivals, Marko [Mike] Vidulich, was the first to marry in Canada when he wed, in 1906, Catherine Bussanich, the daughter of a pioneer Ladner family whom he had known since the early nineties.[56] A robust and exceptionally strong woman, Katy Vidulich bore seven children over the next decade and in addition offered foster care for two others. She assisted as well in the fishing boats and occasionally demonstrated her physical strength at dockside by packing hundred-pound grain sacks under each arm![57] Other marriages followed soon after, and in 1908 a recently arrived young fisherman named Andro Radoslovich married Carolina Martinolich, the daughter of a family resident in the Canoe Pass area since the 1880's.[58] A year later, Radoslovich took out his naturalization papers, joined the Croatian purse-seining fleet, and began to raise another generation of fishermen.

The small community of Croats also began to participate in the wider social life of the Pacific Coast community. For some of the older members of the working force, such as Marko Vidulich, assimilation was expressed in belonging to the early fishermen's unions of the Fraser River. However sporadic their success in organizing the fishermen, Vidulich was always a member of the Fraser River Fishermen's Union, the Grand Lodge of B.C. Fishermen, or the Fishermen's Protective Association. He organized picket committees for the strikes of 1900 and 1901, which were occasionally shot at and often resorted themselves to armed retaliation.[59] Other younger members of the community attended school in Canoe Pass, even if there were often only one or two classmates in their particular grade.[60] For all, there was involvement in the highly developed leisure culture of the coast. Young and middle-aged men alike belonged to bicycle clubs, which pedalled along the picturesque coastline on Sundays and holidays.[61] Others adopted hunting as a pastime or participated in various team sports, such as lacrosse and football, which were popular at the turn of the century.

The Ladner community thus looked confidently on at the outside world of Canadian society and its customs and institutions, impatiently waiting to be initiated and included. In this aspect it resembled the tightly knit agricultural villages of Croatians in Kenaston and Hanley, Saskatchewan, which adapted quickly to the cultural polyglot they found around them of Germans, Anglo-Canadians, and Scandinavians. Common ties of religious, social, and economic association cut through both communities to create maximum exposure to the larger society. The

Roman Catholic Church – the Sacred Heart Church in Ladner and St. Andrew's in Kenaston – created a broad mix of old and new cultures. The fishermen's unions and wheat pools and fishermen's or farmers' co-operatives were common institutions of economic self-defence which also cut across ethnic lines. Marko Vidulich, who was active in the creation of a multinational fishing organization on the Lower Fraser delta, observed that he had many friends among the Japanese Canadians fishing in the area. They had their friendly nicknames for him, "Poppa Mike" and so on, and he had his nicknames for them. There was never any thought in his mind of any split or division between himself, "the Japanese Canadians, the Native Canadians or anyone else."[62]

Such openness, however, was not the case with the Croatian miners of Vancouver Island and the interior of British Columbia. The coal mines of the island were the scene of industrial violence at the turn of the century, and the industry itself was the most strike-ridden in all of Canada, accounting as it did for 42 per cent of all time lost in strikes in Canada from 1900 to 1913.[63] Overall, the coalminers of Vancouver Island were among the lowest paid among the mining fraternity, the most prone to industrial violence, and the most exposed to industrial accidents in the labour force as a whole. Given such unhealthy working and living conditions, the immigrant miners resorted to the traditional means of self-defence perfected by their Croatian brethren in the Pennsylvania anthracite fields. They were among the first in Canada to accept the American international and fraternal unions, in the form of the United Mine Workers of America and the National Croatian Union (later the Croatian Fraternal Union) formed originally in 1894.[64]

Thus it was probably no accident that the first lodge of "Zajednica" or Croatian Fraternal Union was formed at Ladysmith near Nanaimo in 1903, just as the United Mine Workers of America had begun to move into the western coal fields to replace the failing Western Federation of Miners.[65] Formally entitled "Sveti Nikola" (Saint Nicholas), Lodge 268, the Ladysmith local met weekly on Sundays in Nicolson Hall. The executive consisted of Vlaso Keserić, president, and Janko Kuljal, secretary, and the lodge boasted a membership of twenty-eight by 1907. By that time two other lodges had been formed in the interior mining district of British Columbia, one at Trail, entitled "Sveti Ciril i Metod" (St. Cyril and Methodius), Lodge 281 (president Stjepan Butorac), and another in nearby Grand Forks, which adopted the title "Andjeo Čuvar" (Guardian Angel).[66] Each of these had a membership of twenty to thirty miners and performed the valuable function of a mutual benefit insurance society for its members, who were otherwise unprotected against the very real possibilities of serious injuries or death underground. In addition to insurance benefits, the fraternal organization sometimes offered legal advice to the new immigrant as well as other, less tangible benefits of socialization and ethnic solidarity in an alien environment.

The pioneer miners' fraternities also served an important disciplinary function in the coalminers' strikes, such as the violent Nanaimo strikes of 1912-13. The bitterly fought strikes at Ladysmith and Extension pitted the United Mine Workers of America against the forces of Canadian Collieries, Attorney General Bowser's special police, and scab labour. The secretary of Lodge 268 at Ladysmith, Janko Grubačević, described the violent confrontation between the two and left little doubt that the sympathies of the Croatian lodge were with the UMWA:

> What does it matter to our lodge, for we will have as many members after the strike as before. There are only a few of us, but we are united and loyal to one another, and it is better for us that we have more solidarity than if we are disunited with larger numbers. As soon as this strike is over, I am certain that our lodge will progress and flourish as never before. Every comrade of those who have come here are nearly all Žumberčani [a region north of Karlovac], therefore of those of us who went out on strike, not one wished to go back to work, and no one wished to scab either, not until the strike is over and until we accomplish those objectives for which we went out.[67]

Nor was the author hesitant to identify by name those Croatians who had chosen to scab on their fellow countrymen from Žumberak – he identified these as coming largely from Lika, another region to the west. Nor did he spare the grisly details in another letter of one scab, who, when beset by the strikers demonstrating in front of his home, threw a stick of dynamite toward them through an open window but missed and lost his hand before he could make a second attempt.[68] The strike ended badly for the militants, however, and finished with the failure of the United Mine Workers by the middle of 1914.[69]

This strike action was part of a wider struggle among the miners and steelworkers for unionization and for better pay and working conditions. It reached across Canada and the northern United States in 1913-14, and in the latter area resulted in the breaking of the radical miners' strike in Calumet, Michigan, and the consequent dispersal of many of the nearly 10,000 Croats who had settled there.[70] In the end, the UMWA and other radical unions, such as the International Workers of the World, were badly beaten in their attempt to radicalize the immigrant workers of the mines, the forests, and the railroads.[71] And the south and east European immigrants were first to lose their jobs in the mass dismissals that followed.

Whether radical strike action prevailed or not, this was the universal condition of the recently arrived migrant during 1912-14. Local resentment against the immigrant would rise in troubled times, such as these two years before the war with the tumbling values in urban real estate and the general contraction in the economy after the completion of the transcontinental railways. Even such well-established Croatian communities as that at Welland in Ontario felt the ripples of economic unrest and nativist feeling directed at the immigrant. When unemployment threatened the local economy, the Welland Trades and Labour Council protested against foreign workers employed on canal construction.[72] Then a further crisis occurred in May, 1914, when a local force of 200 armed militia confronted a mass of immigrants of Austrian, Italian, and Polish descent, who had not worked for four months and were living in impossibly crowded conditions. Their intention was to force the immigrants from town. By August of 1914, many of the newly arrived foreigners were jailed and deported, and had thereby lost even the small capital they had generated by the sale of a house or their belongings in order to establish themselves in Canada.[73]

Such incidents would become more common as the clouds of war threatened in Europe and economic crisis deepened in North America. The gates of immigration were closing rapidly, and the decision of the Borden government to close British Columbia to any skilled or unskilled workers was prophetic of further restrictions to come.[74] For the recent immigrant the war had thus begun even before the first shots were fired in August of 1914.

NOTES

1. *Canada, Report of the Royal Commission on Bilingualism and Biculturalism*, Book IV (Ottawa, 1969), pp. 22-5.

2. See Robert Harney and Harold Troper, *Immigrants: A Portrait of the Urban Experience, 1890-1930* (Toronto: Van Nostrand, 1975); J.S. Woodsworth, *Strangers within our Gates or Coming Canadians* (Toronto: Missionary Society of the Methodist Church, 1909).

3. See *Zajedničar*, 30 September 1914.

4. Edmund Bradwin, *The Bunkhouse Man, A Study of Work and Pay in the Camps of Canada, 1903-14* (Toronto: University of Toronto Press, reprint, 1972), p. 80.

5. Bradwin, *Bunkhouse Man*, p. 153.

6. B.C. Provincial Archives, Coroners' Inquests, vol. VII, file 1912; W.A. Richardson, Coroner, Yale, B.C., 24 February, 1912. Evidence of Otto V. Larson, Labourer. The names given by the witness for the brothers Postovich were corrected in brackets in the coroner's report.

7. British Columbia Department of Mines, *Annual Report*, 1913, p. 320. *Ibid., 1915*, p. 373. Joso Niksić, "Hrvati u 100-god British Columbia-e," *Hrvatski Glas Kalendar*, XXIX (1959), p. 97.

8. Glenbow-Alberta Archives, G-A-1, United Mineworkers, List of Fatalities in the Coal Mines of Alberta, 1904-64. Among those listed in this report are: John Mudrich, Hillcrest, 1914; James Darzic, International Coke and Coal, 1917; J. Rezac, Greenhill, 1920; Frank Yacubic, CPR, 1920; C. Zomic, Greenhill, 1921.

9. Thomas Surluga [Švrluga] recollections, dated Wawa, 9 November 1972, communicated to the author by Mrs. A. Yozipovic, Thunder Bay,

2 January 1975. Mr. Surluga had a road named after him in Wawa, Ontario, and also a gold mine which he discovered. Sault Ste. Marie *Star*, 4 March 1966.

10. "Hrvatski putnik – Uspomena na Kanadu" (A Croatian traveller remembers Canada), *Hrvatski Glas*, 9 February 1932.

11. Nikola Krmpotić, Sault Ste. Marie, interview with George Kokich, December, 1974. Krmpotić was born in 1881 in the town of Senj on the northern Adriatic Coast.

12. Interview, Milan Glibota with George Kokich, Sault Ste. Marie, December, 1974.

13. Interview, Nikola Krmpotić with George Kokich, Sault Ste. Marie, December, 1974.

14. Interviews, Andrija Polić, Milan Glibota, Josip Čulina with George Kokich, December, 1974.

15. An example of an earlier Croatian migrant from Dalmatia was Nikola Bilić, born 1886 in the village of Ronovići, Imotski district. He came to Canada in 1907 and in 1913 started work with Algoma Steel. *Novosti*, 13 March 1947. See also ref., Joe Grgić, *Novosti*, 7 September 1946.

16. Information supplied to the author by Mr. Milan Glibota, July, 1975.

17. Interview, Mr. Joseph Čulina with George Kokich, December, 1974.

18. Interview, Mr. Andrija Polić with George Kokich, December, 1974. The first of those along Cathcart was apparently operated by Mrs. Ann Nogalo (Glibota interview, 1974). Mr. Čulina (ff. 17) started a boarding home in 1921 and later went into the hotel business in 1935.

19. *Novosti*, 24 June 1947.

20. *Ibid.*, 27 February 1947, obituary. One Jura Perković from Brinje also arrived in 1909 in the Schumacher-Timmins area via the United States and worked for McIntyre-Porcupine Mines for the next thirty-five years. *Zajedničar*, 12 December, 1973, obituary.

21. Interview, John Šušak with George Kokich, December, 1974. Filipovic and Miosich each owned a hotel and restaurant business in the 1930's in Port Arthur.

22. *Ibid.* These included H. Hrkac, F. Šlišković, and B. Šlišković.

23. *Jedinstvo*, 4 December 1964, obituary. The author's paternal grandfather, Petar Rasporich, worked from 1902-1906 on track crews in northern Ontario with fellow Croats from his village, Hreljin, and returned to the old country before World War I. Another itinerant who sojourned in Port Arthur as early as 1901 was Vrban Kružić of nearby Zlobin. He returned to his home village eight times and finally settled in the Lakehead during the 1930's. *Novosti*, 15 July 1947.

24. *Jedinstvo*, 19 April 1963: Stevo Škvorć, "Malo Povijesti iz Života Našeg Naroda."

25. See A. Benko Grado, *Migraciona Enciklopedija,* p. 190. Grado likely overestimated in claiming that Croats owned 3,000 acres, literally "jutara," which translates as "a morning's walk" or *morgen*.

26. See Stevo Knezić obituary, *Jedinstvo,* 16 August 1963; Barbara Knezić

obituary, *Novosti*, 5 June 1948. See also Mirko Čukel obituary, *Novosti*, 14 September 1946; Stevo and Ana Kušan obituary, *Jedinstvo*, 21 April 1955.

27. *Novosti*, 29 January 1947.
28. *Zajedničar,* 1909, no. 49.
29. *Zajedničar,* 30 September 1914.
30. *Jedinstvo,* 19 April 1963.
31. For a discussion of bloc settlements of ethnic groups on the Prairies, see Vladimir J. Kaye, *Early Ukrainian Settlements in Canada, 1895-1900* (Toronto: University of Toronto Press, 1964); M.L. Kovacs, *Esterhazy and Early Hungarian Immigration to Canada* (Regina: Canadian Plains Research Centre, 1974).
32. See Denis Fitzgerald "Pioneer Settlement in Northern Saskatchewan" (Ph.D. thesis, University of Minnesota, 1966), p. 150.
33. "Naši Pioniri u Kanadi," *Kanadski Glas*, 9 May 1929. (Author's translation.)
34. Saskatchewan Archives, Homestead Entries, Joseph Gerich, Skipton, Saskatchewan. #2100218, 11 April 1910; Joseph Gerich, Jr., 27 March 1912, Skipton, Sask., #2643826.
35. Personal reminiscence supplied to the author by Mrs. Kae Smiley (née Došen), Prince Albert, Saskatchewan, dated *circa* 1964.
36. Sam Beckie memoir by K.N. Beckie, Calgary, 8 December 1974.
37. Saskatchewan Archives, Homestead entry, Mike Zdunich, 9 August 1912, #21423.
38. *Ibid.,* Nick Zdunich, April 4, 1913, #23953.
39. Gabriel Zdunich memoir by K.N. Beckie, Calgary, January, 1975.
40. Paul Brkich memoir by K. Beckie, Calgary, December, 1974. Funds amounting to some 6,000 *kronen* or $300 Canadian from the sale of the three brothers' shares in the family farm were used to support relocation in Canada.
41. Steve Sarich interview questionnaire to the author from Davidson, Saskatchewan, September, 1975. Mr. Sarich arrived in 1913 to join a brother and an uncle already farming in Saskatchewan, and the funds were raised through the sale of the family farm.
42. A.B. Grado, *Migraciona Enciklopedija* (1928), mentions such a town, "Lovinac, near Calgary," p. 190.
43. Kae Smiley, Reminiscence, pp. 4-6.
44. See, e.g., Arlene B. Gaal, *Memoirs of Michel-Natal* (n.p.: 1971, printed by the author), pp. 36-7, 114-15.
45. See Mike Krypan reminiscence in Toni Ross, *Oh! The Coal Branch* (Edmonton: D.W. Friesen, 1974), pp. 284-5.
46. *Hrvatski Glas*, 24 March 1930: Matt Carr, "30 Uspjelih Farmera."
47. Author interview with Mr. Bob Stanich, Calgary, August, 1975.
48. This information supplied by Dr. V. Markotić of the University of Calgary, Department of Archaeology.
49. See *Long Shadows: A History of the Shortgrass Country* (1974), p. 249,

information supplied by Joseph Miskulin, Calgary, 1975. Another early settler in the Red Deer district was N. Belić of Penhold: see *Hrvatski Glas*, 17 March 1930, p. 6.

50. Information on Philip Berkovich (1884-1975) supplied by Mr. Gordon Scruggs, Calgary, August, 1975.

51. *Blooming Prairie: A History of Morrin and District* (Altona: D.W. Friesen, 1970), pp. 373-4; "Joseph Trafenic Story."

52. *Freeway West: Falun and District* (Altona: D.W. Frieson, 1974), p. 868.

53. *Henderson's Gazeteer and Directory,* British Columbia, 1910.

54. PAC, RG 23, vol. 362, ff. 3185, Part I. Statement of Fishery Licenses Issued May and July, 1908.

55. Ladner *Optimist*, 17 May 1951.

56. Surrey-Delta *Messenger*, 24 January 1974.

57. *Ibid.,* 28 February 1944.

58. *Ibid.,* 20 September 1973: Vi Radoslovich, "I've Always Felt Liberated."

59. *The Fisherman*, 3 May 1963: "Marko Vidulich – 70 Years a Unionist and a Salmon Gillnetter since 1892."

60. Surrey Delta *Messenger,* 28 February 1974.

61. *Ibid.*, 24 January 1974.

62. *The Fisherman,* 3 May 1963.

63. Stuart M. Jamieson, *Times of Trouble: Labour Unrest and Industrial Conflict in Canada, 1900-66* (Ottawa: Queen's Printer, 1968), pp. 95-100.

64. Paul Phillips, *No Power Greater: A Century of Labour in B.C.* (Vancouver, 1967), p. 41.

65. See *Zajedničar,* 19 December 1973, pp. 5, 10. Also Nanaimo *Daily Free Press*, 15 October 1963.

66. *Zajedničar*, 1907, no. 29; 1909, no. 48; 14 February 1912. See also *Upoznajte Hrvatsku Bratsku Zajednicu* (Zagreb: Matica Iseljenika Hrvatske, 1974), pp. 30-1.

67. *Zajedničar,* 1 April 1914.

68. *Ibid.,* 22 October 1913.

69. Phillips, *No Power Greater,* pp. 55-61.

70. See Prpic, *Croatian Immigrants in America,* pp. 120-1. See William Ivey, " 'The 1913 Disaster': Michigan Loca! Legend," *Folklore Forum*, 3 (1970), pp. 100-14, for an oral-historical study of the Calumet strike and its impact on the community.

71. Jamieson, *Times of Trouble,* pp. 122-6, 143-6.

72. Rev. Fern Sayles, *Welland Workers Make History* (Welland, 1963), pp. 59-63, 191.

73. *Jedinstvo,* 3 July 1964: Ivo Braut, "U Wellandu."

74. D. Avery, "Dominion Control over the Recruitment and Placement of Immigrant Industrial Workers in Canada, 1890-1918," unpublished ms. delivered to McGill Conference on "Late Nineteenth Century Society," 18 January 1975, p. 30.

FOUR

Enemy Aliens in World War One

The darkening war clouds over Europe in 1914 had complicated and obscured the future of the Canadian Croats. Ironically, the war began near their home soil with the assassination of the Austrian Archduke at Sarajevo by a young Serbian patriot, Gavrilo Princip, on June 28, 1914. This pistol shot triggered a complex snare of alliances and counter-alliances in the diplomatic courts of Europe. When the smoke of the first offensive cleared, Great Britain lurched indecisively into battle on the side of the Low Countries and France and thereby became a committed ally to Serbia and Russia in eastern and south-central Europe. Since Canada was automatically involved in the war as a colony of Great Britain, German minorities within Canada were placed in jeopardy as potentially hostile enemy aliens. Canada's fledgling Croatian communities were also caught on the wrong side, as were other minorities of the Austro-Hungarian Empire: the Bohemians, Ruthenians, Hungarians, and Slovaks.

Public reaction against citizens of Germany and Austria was swift and harsh. The foreigner, who had been the object of mixed feelings before the war, suddenly became universally suspect. The rather benign racial stereotypes held by J.S. Woodsworth or Ralph Connor of the Austrian Slavs as "simple sluggish people" or as "strong, phlegmatic and slow to anger" were replaced by much more virulent prejudice.[1] Contemporary intellectuals such as Stephen Leacock noted that pro-German newspapers were still circulating in the Canadian mails, and the demand soon came from the press to dispossess German and Austrian nationals of their property.[2] Prominent German-born citizens were dismissed from public office, and Baron Alvo von Alvensleben was refused entry back to Vancouver and was forced to liquidate a fortune in stocks and bonds. On a lower level, Austrian miners were looked upon suspiciously in the at Cobalt, and others were shot at by militia patrols in the Welland district. War hysteria gripped Canadians. The plight of the Austrian enemy alien was not helped by the fact that just before the war, in July of 1914, the Austrian consul at Montreal had reminded his fellow subjects that neither the German nor the Hapsburg government recognized Canadian naturalization, and that both considered allegiance and military service as irrevocable and permanent conditions of Austrian and German citizenship. Austrian reservists were reminded that any general call to service extended to North America.[3] Then, on August 3, a day before war was formally declared by Great Britain, the Austrian-educated Uniate bishop of Winnipeg issued a pastoral letter supporting "the peace loving Emperor Franz Joseph" and called upon Austrian reservists, mainly of his Ruthenian flock, to return and defend "the endangered fatherland." His retraction a few days later, which came in the form of a command for absolute loyalty to the British Empire, did little to erase the negative impression made by his first letter. And, in fact, Austrian and German consular officials still worked covertly to expedite the flow of Austrian reservists from Canada back through the United States to Europe.[4]

The reaction of the Canadian government was natural in view of the official and unofficial activities of the Austrian and German governments, and also in view of the threat posed by the presence of some 80,000 non-naturalized aliens born in countries at war with Great Britain. In addition to the 45,000 males in this alien category, there were the larger numbers of naturalized foreign-born Germans (39,577) and Austrians (121,430) whose loyalties were in some question. The Austrians, with whom the Croat minority were counted, were most heavily concentrated in the Prairie Provinces and in British Columbia, with over 100,000 of their number in the West. A particular hotbed of aliens, in government eyes at least, was north Winnipeg, with its 5,000 adult Austrian- and German-born males and influential ethnic publications such as the German-language *Nordwesten,* the Hungarian *Magyarsag,* and *Ukrainsky Golos* and *Kanadski Farmer*, both of which spoke to Winnipeg's Ukrainian population.[5]

The British and Canadian governments reacted quickly by instituting measures to contain this perceived threat to national and imperial security. The first proclamation on August 7 announced that German officers or reservists attempting to leave Canada were liable to arrest by the militia and Austrians were subject to surveillance. This warning was accompanied by assurances that those who refrained from aiding and abetting the enemy powers would not be interfered with. Further powers were given the following week to the Dominion Police and the North-West Mounted Police to arrest departing reservists and anyone else whose departure could be construed as actively contributing to espionage. The continuing distinction that those who co-operated were immune to forcible detention was made in a further proclamation of September 2, but the iron fist was only thinly veiled in the glove of the law. For those who could read and decipher the many Orders-in-Council, their meaning was entirely clear: no one was above arbitrary arrest if he should travel or send and receive monies in the mails, and migrant workers and visitors were forced to curtail any plans they had for return to Europe.[6]

The effect of this legislation on Austrian nationals in western Canada is apparent in the desperate circumstances of Mike Orlich, probably a Croat, who was apprehended in September, 1914, as he attempted to leave Canada. The informant in the case tells the graphic story that preceded Orlich's arrest and internment for the duration of the war in British Columbia:

> About 9 am on Tuesday 15th September 14 [sic], an Austrian Mike Orlich, by name came up to me on the streets of Sidney [B.C.] and asked me if I knew where he could hire a boat. He seemed excited at the time and was a foreigner. I guessed that he wanted to get out of the country, so I told him that I had a boat myself and would hire it to him, and I asked him where he wanted to go. He said he wanted to go a long way, and asked where my boat was and how big it was. I took him down to the breakwater & showed him a large boat moored there & said it was mine.
>
> He asked me when I could go, and I said right away and again asked him where he wanted to go, and he said "to the other side" [presumably the United States]. He said there was 18 of them altogether wanted to go; I told him I would take them across for twenty dollars. He agreed to the price & offered me 5 dollars extra, but I said 20 was enough.
>
> He said I was to be ready to start at 6 pm. as the men were in Victoria and were coming out on the train due Sidney at 6 o'clock.
>
> I told him that 9 of them ought to come out on the B.C.E.R. [British Columbia Electric Railway] and nine on the V&S [Victoria and Sidney] Railway. As soon as he left me I told Prov. Const. Macdonald, and came into Victoria on the noon train. Orlich was on the same train, but did not see me. When I got to Victoria, I pointed Orlich out to Const. Owens.[7]

Despite the apparent efficiency of police operations in this instance, considerable numbers of Austrian and German aliens escaped via small launches to Anacortes, Washington, and disappeared into American society. Combined operations involving the provincial police and the customs collector at Victoria were suggested and new tactics of apprehension employed, but their success in containing reservist escapees is unclear.[8]

The greater problem related to the vast majority who stayed and wanted work in Canada. Canada had been in an economic depression since 1913, which only deepened with the outbreak of war. The foreigners were the first to be laid off, particularly if they were members of an enemy nation, and they were the first to be suspected of criminal intent and espionage as they congregated in the crowds of unemployed that walked the streets of Canadian cities. The choice presented to the Canadian government was either to allow the unemployed to mount in number and swell the municipal relief rolls or to allow them to drift south in search of work. Prime Minister Robert Borden preferred the latter tactic but was prevented from employing it by the parent government in Great Britain, which feared that once in the United States Germans and Austrians would drift onto the Western front. The compromise solution was then to require, by Order-in-Council in October, 1914, that enemy aliens register at designated centres and later report on a monthly basis to the local police station. Only those who were considered of no value to the enemy were to be allowed exit passes. The administration of such a clause could be interpreted liberally by certain officers, but the local registrars could intern any alien upon suspicion, and the police could similarly detain any alien who did not report or who contravened any regulation.

The search for Austrian aliens began in earnest, but the authorities appeared at a loss where to begin or where to look, beyond the obviously unemployed who congregated in the cities. The Lakehead cities of Port Arthur and Fort William used the opportunity presented by the internment legislation to gather together 800 or so Austrians and dumped them in the lap of the federal Militia Department and General William Otter, who organized the internment operation. Faced by municipalities that simply wished to avoid the relief costs of unemployed construction and bushworkers, Otter was inclined to be lenient in releasing Austrians in particular for work elsewhere. The others considered a threat were to be confined to the experimental farm set up at Kapuskasing in the clay belt of northern Ontario.

Of the Croatian pioneers in northern Ontario, it appeared that those in the Port Arthur-Fort William area were the most susceptible, because of unemployment, to internment at Kapuskasing. Consequently, the relatively open border of the frontier invited some to search for work in Minnesota and Wisconsin. Some would return later, during the war and after, as economic conditions improved in the lumber and construction camps, but in the meantime, the fear of unemployment and forced labour had driven them out of Canada.[9] In Sault Ste. Marie, by contrast, where the demand for wartime steel production was high, Croatians had the secure prospect of employment at Algoma Steel for the duration of the war. Some unemployed Croats west of the lake even travelled eastward to secure employment in the steel mills.[10] And for the most part, the threat of internment and occasional harassment by local militia officials appeared to be the maximum extent of punishment meted out to Croatian and other Austrian aliens.

Those Croatians involved in vital industrial and agricultural production in other areas of Canada were left relatively undisturbed by the war. The quasi-agricultural communities in the Niagara Peninsula and the farmers farther to the west in Saskatchewan and Alberta were generally subject only to the normal sting of anti-German prejudice and nativist feeling. On the forestry, fishing, and mining frontier of British Columbia, however, anti-alien activity seemed to be more intense. Here even long-established communities of Croats came under police surveillance. And many Austro-German nationals suffered retribution for their activities in the radical unions of the western frontier and the violent strike activities of the IWW (International Workers of the World) immediately prior to World War I.

The drive to identify all aliens began in the fall of 1914. Croats were clearly among the groups that concerned the authorities on Vancouver Island, for the superintendent of provincial police in Victoria attempted to secure the services of a Serbian informer but admitted the difficulty "to get a Serbian even to take up the work and point out hostile aliens."[11] Even the city engineer's department, perhaps fearful of the poisoning of the city water supply, was actively pursuing Austrians near the reservoir and in the local hotels.[12] The police dragnet in Victoria yielded a number of Croats in September and October of 1914, among them Joseph Uremovich, Joseph Hecimovich, Sam Ansjelich (Dalmatia), John Uzelac (Smilyin), S. Babich (Kropa, Bosnia), George Vicich (Crkivenica), M. Perich (Mostar), and Joe Sagnain (Fiume). The first two were bound over to the Militia Department for further confinement, and the rest were required to sign an undertaking and take an oath of allegiance to Great Britain and Canada and to report monthly to the provincial police office in Victoria.[13]

For the remainder of 1914, and indeed for the rest of the war, the Croatians of British Columbia were required to report their occupations and addresses to the authorities. Hundreds of male Croats, many of whom had been resident in British Columbia for years as fishermen and miners, were required to report their whereabouts each month. The geographic distribution of those aliens is in itself a good reflection of the occupational and settlement pattern of Croats in British Columbia.[14] The police records reveal, for example, that there were many miners in the Nanaimo, Ladysmith, and Wellington area on Vancouver Island, and some of these who had been in the country for several years and were naturalized citizens were required to report along with those single men who had recently left their Austrian regiments and were still considered reservists by Austrian and Canadian authorities.[15] Another heavy concentration of Croats – to the north in the Granby Mines at Anyox near Prince Rupert – was also closely watched during the war and for the most part reported faithfully until 1916. In one specific instance, two Croats, Miller (sic) and Seculich, were indicated as collecting money for the Central Powers. Others were under surveillance for receiving the Croatian newspaper Adriatic from San Francisco, which warned Croats in Canada and the United States not to collect money for the Red Cross, since it would find its way into the hands of the Central Powers for use against the South Slavs.[16]

NOTICE

All German's or Austrian's resident in the Boundary Police District, whether naturalized or not naturalized are hereby notified to report at once to the nearest Provincial Police Office, to the Constable in charge.

JOHN SIMPSON,
CHIEF CONSTABLE,
Greenwood, B.C.,   Boundary Police District.
June 16th, 1915.

UNDERTAKING.

I, _J Sagnain_ at present of _Albert Head Quarry Victoria_ in the Province of _B.C._ in the Dominion of Canada, do hereby declare that I am ~~a German~~ an Austro-Hungarian subject; I now in consideration of my exemption from detention as a subject of ~~Germany~~ Austria-Hungary, do hereby undertake and promise that I will report to such official and upon such terms as the Canadian Authorities may from time to time prescribe; that I will carefully observe the laws of the United Kingdom of Great Britain and Ireland and of Canada and such rules as may be specially laid down for my conduct; that I will strictly abstain from taking up arms and from doing any act of hostility towards the Government of this Country, and that, except with the permission of the officer under whose surveillance I may bè placed, I will strictly abstain from communicating to anyone whomsoever any information respecting the existing war or the movements of troops, or the military preparations which the authorities of Canada or Great Britain may make, or as respects the resources of Canada, and that I will do no act that might be of injury to the Dominion of Canada or the United Kingdom of Great Britain and Ireland and Dominions and possessions thereof.

Dated _9th_ day of _October_ 1914.

WITNESS:

R B Culverwell.   _Sagnain Joe_

Born at _Fiume Austria_ in _____

on the _23rd_ day of _November_ 1874

P. O. Address _Albert Head Victoria_ Occupation _Laborer_

Required to report monthly, on the _last Saturday_ day of each

and every month until the termination of the war, to

Prov. Police, Victoria

SOURCE: *Provincial Archives of British Columbia, Provincial Police, Superintendent's Correspondence, 1912-22: GR 57, Box 24, ff. 1355-7; Box 20, Victoria District.*

Further into the southern interior, another prominent minority of Croats in base metal mines at Princeton and Greenwood and in the Trail-Castlegar region reported on a monthly basis to the police for the duration of the war. As the police superintendent at Greenwood observed, the miners were almost entirely foreigners, "principally Austrians with a few Montenegrins, Italians and Serbs," and most earned between three and four dollars a day given the buoyant prices that metals earned in the wartime economy. Although a local constable labelled most of the aliens as "Austrian Serbs who left the country to escape military duty," there were many Croats from locations such as Dalmatia, Gospić, and Severin. The constable's principal observations were that they contributed generously to the Canadian Patriotic Fund and the Red Cross and that, "From a police point of view, there has been much less trouble amongst them since the beginning of the war than previously, the fact that several of them were sent to the internment camp at the beginning of the war seemed to have a good effect on the remainder."[17]

From a personal standpoint, however, the impact of such arrests and detentions was felt with varying degrees of severity by those who were detained in internment camps and prisons. A relatively mild incident occurred with the arrest of four young Croatian railway labourers, who were detained at Lytton in the British Columbia interior and held in the jail there for a week in the summer of 1915.[18] Others were held at the Edgewood internment camp on Vancouver Island at the same time and then released to work in the collieries at Nanaimo, South Wellington, and Ladysmith or as relief workers in the same towns, where some had lived for several years before the war.[19]

Perhaps the most poignant account of the indignities visited upon some of the new immigrants was given by a young immigrant, Peter Stimac, who was bundled off to Jasper Park in the Rockies. He posted an eloquent letter of protest from Edmonton to the Austro-Hungarian consulate in Winnipeg, but the letter was intercepted, opened, and translated in Ottawa by a government interpreter. His poignant plea began:

> In the month of July [1916] I was arrested without any reason, and for 15 days I was feed [sic] on bread and water. After that they sent me to Jasper Park, where I was tortured and beaten without cause for same. On order from my inspector, I was treated like a tramp, and beaten and locked up in a dark cell without a matrass [sic] or a cover. It was a cold place. I was not permitted to wash for several days, and was fed on bread and water only, so that I am scarcely alive. Since my arrest I have been so sick and weak that I can hardly stand on my feet. They call me a "Black Hand" etc. I really do not know what to think about such a system in a new country. It seems to me as if my life were like what one would read in a book. I am liberated at last, and enjoy God's freedom. I look like a ghost walking from one city to another on foot. I am sure the silly

newspapers published the news about me. I never expected to meet such absurdity in Canada in the twentieth century.[20]

The internment of Croatians during the early part of the war was soon brought to the attention of the National Croatian Society (Hrvatska Bratska Zajednica) in the United States.[21] By the early summer of 1915, the editor of *Zajedničar* in Pittsburgh, Joseph Marohnich, had applied to the Serbian consul in New York, Dr. Michael Pupin, to make representation to the British embassy in Washington to enter Canada. The stated purpose of the visiting commission was to identify "Croatians and members of other non-Austrian races amongst the prisoners of war in Canada."[22] The petition of the National Croatian Society to the British ambassador stressed the loyalty of the 35,000 Croats in the Society to their adopted countries, the United States and Canada, and noted also their "orderly and thrifty" character. The Croatians had no sympathy with Germany or Austria, which had oppressed them for centuries, and merely wished like their kinsmen in New Zealand, South Africa, and Australia to pursue their vocations with full freedom of movement and immunity from arbitrary arrest.[23] Permission was granted on June 3 by the Minister of Justice, who contacted Major-General Otter, the chief of internment operations, to comply with request.[24] Subsequently the three commissioners, Joseph Marohnich representing the Croats, Matija Godzid the Slovaks, and Frank Sakser the Slovenes, crossed the Niagara frontier at Buffalo in early June and proceeded to Ottawa to meet with General Otter.

The commissioners were most impressed with Otter's commanding presence and the respectful treatment he accorded the delegation. They were then directed to the several camps in Ontario where the enemy aliens had been interned, first to Fort Henry in Kingston, then to Camp Petawawa at Pembroke, and finally on to Kapuskasing in northern Ontario. At Fort Henry, the commissioners were allowed into the heavily armed fortress overlooking the St. Lawrence, and after careful examination of the internment lists were only able to find one prisoner of Croat background, a Slavonian, Mladen Budišin. The delegation then proceeded to Petawawa, 150 miles to the north. Among the 600 or so inmates there, Marohnich was able, with the assistance of the camp commandant, to identify two dozen Croatians. Of these, a few had come via the United States, from Ohio and Pennsylvania to Canada. Their surprise and welcome of a fellow countryman concerned for their welfare was warm and spontaneous. Marohnich asked,

"Where are you from Polić?" I asked him – "From here [Hrvatsko Primorje], and you?" he replied laughingly. "Where are you from, – go on!" he replied. In a few moments, I found out that his grandfather was blood brother to my elderly mother. Polić worked with Stjepan Toić from Vrba in greater Istria. They were all enlisted as soldiers at a young age, they spoke English fluently and gathered round and told me that they had come here a year ago and had tried everything to gain their freedom. Toić was a sailor, then was transported from a Canadian port to the concentration camp.[25]

The commission then returned to Ottawa, and on June 13 proceeded 500 miles northward by rail to Kapuskasing. There, in the isolated wilderness of northern Ontario, they discovered another fifty or so Croats, Slovenes, Montenegrins, and Serbs who had been interned since the beginning of the war. Of these, some three dozen were identified as Croats: for example, Anton Salopek (Ogulin), Nikola Paunović (Bjelovar), Franjo Kružić (Hreljin), and Anton Krmpotić (Senj). Marohnich explained to them that the parent Croatian Society would do everything in its power to help them, particularly those who were members of the American fraternal organization.

Upon the commissioners' return, the Croat internees were circularized with typed questionnaires enquiring after every detail of their status, work, and institutional affiliation in North America. When the forms were completed and sent on to the parent organization in the United States and verified, the members of the Croatian Society were to be set free. By October, several Croats were released on the recognizance of the Society, and contact was established with relatives and acquaintances in Canadian and American towns and cities who could act as sponsors. Further requests were made on behalf of two dozen more internees upon whom insufficient information had been forthcoming, and who might be released if representations could be made on their behalf.[26] Precisely how many were actually freed from the internment camps is not known, but the actions of the National Croatian Society had at least secured the release of its own members and had alerted the Canadian authorities to the fact that representations would continue to be made upon behalf of those Croats whose civil liberties were endangered by arbitrary action.

Coincident with the harassment and detention of Austrian aliens during the early part of the war was the resolute vigilance toward the ethnic press of the Chief Press Censor of Canada. Since the Canadian Croats had no indigenous press, as did such other alien minorities as the Hungarians and Germans, the imported newspaper became the sole source of potential treason and sedition. In September, 1915, the chief of internment operations in the Niagara district, Lt. Col. W.H. Ptolemy, called attention to the circulation of a number of copies of *Narodni List*, a New York paper published by Frank Zotti. The editorials were identified as pro-Austrian and tending to "keep the Austrian element here in a more or less beligerent [*sic*] state of mind." The intercepted paper, it was noted, belonged to a John Bosak, a naturalized Canadian who owned a prosperous business and several thousand dollars worth of real estate.[27] The newspaper was subsequently circulated to special agents in the employ of the government as translators. One of them, Agent #208 in Vancouver, commented in disgust:

I, as a born Croatian, am ashamed of this publication printed in the Croatian language, and Austrian thru and thru in spirit. This paper would do must [sic] anything for the Austrian government and is responsible for the big fights daily all over the States between loyal Croatians, who aim the Yugoslavia [sic] and those in favour of the miserable government rule and governed by the biggest enemy of the Southern Slavs with its Headquarters in Berlin.[28]

Despite later claims by other interpreters that *Narodni List* was not seditious in content, the government continued to monitor its content during the war.[29]

Other newspapers of American origin were censored at the insistence of the British Colonial Secretary, Bonar Law, who secretly instructed the Governor General in Canada in 1915 to exclude particular Croatian publications from Canada because of their anti-British attitude. The newspapers in question were *Domovina* (New York), *Hrvatski Svijet* (New York), *Rodoljub* (Calumet), and *Radnička Obrana* (Duluth and Salt Lake City).[30] They must have had a limited or a very clandestine circulation in Canada, for it took some time for the censors to locate copies for their translators. Ultimately, their contents were confirmed as pro-German and Austrian in sentiment, and further analysis of the Croatian-American press revealed that of a total of twenty-two publications, six favoured the German and Austrian cause and three of these had begun publication since the beginning of the war. Pro-German statements such as, "Should you not recognize the divine work of the German people for a world civilization?" and evidence of solicitation for Austrian War Loans were enough to bar the newspaper *Domovina* from the mails in Canada. Further solicitation of information regarding munitions workers in the United States had serious implications in view of the fact that many Austro-Hungarians in Canada were "steel workers in different plants and have been given work as naturalized Canadians."[31] While the censor and Postmaster General were alerted to the contents of these papers, it appears that several copies were still being delivered in 1916 to the Croats in Welland, for several copies were seized by the chief of the enemy internment operations in the Niagara district.

Whether coincidental or not, the attitude of the Canadian military authorities began by 1916 to moderate toward the Croats and other Austro-Hungarian minorities. A significant factor in this alteration was the anomalous position of the Canadian government vis-à-vis that of the United States, where the immigrant experienced far fewer restrictions on his liberties particularly in the neutral phase of American foreign policy before 1917. Another factor may have been the realization that there was a potential pool of military recruits not only in the Serbian opponents to Austria, but also in the dissident ethnic groups whose aspirations toward nationality had been frustrated by centuries of Hapsburg rule. This growing awareness was readily apparent in the zealous recruiting activities of Canada's irrepressible Minister of the Militia and National Defence, Sam Hughes. In March, 1915, Hughes received a letter from Prince Lazarovich Hrebeljanovich, a Serbian nationalist and military strategist from New York, who explained the military potential of South Slav minorities in North America to the British government. Hughes was quick to grasp the recruiting implications of the Prince's letter,

> In which you state that about one-hundred thousand men, of which four to six thousand are now in our concentration camps, are anxious to fight against the Hapsburg enemy; and your desire to ascertain if means can be found to have these men concentrated in Canada, equipped, organized into fighting units, and transported to the war zone to fight against either Austria-Hungary or the Turk.[32]

What Hughes failed to appreciate, in much the same way he refused to understand the peculiar national aspirations of the French Canadians, were the intricate political questions that lay behind auspicious estimates of South Slav manpower. Notwithstanding the obvious difficulty that most of these men would have to be recruited and transported largely from a neutral country, the United States, there was the additional difficulty that not all the South Slavs to be recruited were Serbians. The letter from Prince Hrebeljanovich was over-optimistic in its claim that among those anxious to fight against the hated Hapsburgs were men "though belonging to the same race, and speaking the same language with slight differences of dialect, [who] are designated by reason of local or artificially created territorial divisions, – Serbo-Croats, Croats, Slovenes, Bosnians, Herzegovinians and Dalmatians."[33] Further to this, the letter went on to explain that the creation of the Jugoslavenski Odbor (Yugoslav Committee) in London at the outbreak of the war was to promote the idea of a greater South Slav state. While this idea had some currency with the Serbian premier, Nikola Pašić, there were tensions between his government and the Yugoslav Committee in 1915, and these were not fully resolved until the collapse of Serbia before the Austrian and Bulgarian offensive of 1915 gained further support for the Yugoslav union in allied councils.[34] By April, 1916, both Pašić and Prince Alexander stated their unequivocal support of the idea in London, thereby immensely strengthening the hand of the Yugoslav Committee. By 1917, the Committee had sent a manifesto to the representatives of the British Dominions, which was forwarded to the prime ministers of Australia, Canada, New Zealand, and South Africa.[35]

As a result of the activities of the Yugoslav Committee in London and Pašić's search for Serbian allies, the net was cast further for support in the emigrant colonies in North America. Following directly upon appeals by both groups for support in October of 1915, Milan Pribičević was named Commander in Chief of the Serbian military mission in America to search for Yugoslav volunteers.[36] The relative ease of recruiting volunteers in the United States versus Canada was graphically described in a letter Pribičević wrote to the Canadian Under-Secretary of State for External Affairs, Sir Joseph Pope:

> In the Dominion of Canada there are about 15,000 Serbs, Croats and Slovenes [Southern or Yugo-Slavs] from Austria-Hungary. Although the subjects of the latter country, they stand with their sentiments to Serbia and her Allies. Being of the same race as the people of Serbia, they claim their deliverance from the Austro-Hungarian yoke and their union with Serbia.
>
> The Yugoslavs in the United States have an especially privileged position. The authorities don't consider them as alien enemies, but as members of a friendly nation. On the contrary, the Canadian Yugoslavs are likely enemy subjects obliged to present themselves every week to the authorities.
>
> This obligation is felt by them as a great injustice to their pro-Allied sentiments. They don't cease to ask my intervention in order to get the right of free movement.
>
> I have the honour to present and to recommend you [sic] most vigorously the request of my countrymen. Its fulfilment would be of the greatest advantage to my campaign of enlisting Yugoslav volunteers in Canada. Now they don't answer to my appeal to join the Serbian Army. They don't see the necessity of sacrificing their lives for Serbia and the Allies' cause, the latter treating them as enemies and Serbia not being able to protect them.[37]

Pribičević then began the difficult task of negotiating through the maze of inter-ethnic rivalries in order to recruit South Slavs to the Serbian cause. Although his recruiting was based in New York, his agents scoured the western states, Canada, and Alaska for volunteers. Pribičević appointed an agent in Winnipeg, Spiro Hutalarovich, who would meet Yugoslav volunteers passing through to mobilization camps in eastern Canada.[38] While the initial camp was established at Sussex, New Brunswick, to receive and train 400 men as horse attendants, it was moved after April, 1917, to Lévis, Quebec. Since there was also some political sensitivity in the recruitment of quasi-aliens from a neutral country, the military authorities were careful not to publicize the activities of the mobilization camps or the methods of recruitment.[39] It was carefully stipulated that their travel expenses and training would be absorbed by the Serbian government, while their transportation overseas would be at British expense. While controversies inevitably developed over the quality of the supplies delivered to the troops, camp sanitation, and the jurisdiction of Canadian versus Serbian officers, 5,899 "Serbian" recruits were processed through the Canadian camps by the fall of 1918.[40]

While the official title given to the mobilization camps was the "Serbian Mobilization Camp,'' the Commandant, Major J. Hamilton, scrupulously noted in his reports that the men originally came from Serbia, Bosnia, Croatia, Dalmatia, Lika, Montenegro, and Herzegovina.[41] The actual number of Croats among the 2,500 men trained and transported from Canada in 1917 may be established from the muster rolls of training camps and the steamship lists at between 5 and 10 per cent of the total.[42] Later, another 1,200 horse attendants were trained at the Sussex camp, but the number of South Slavs who enlisted is more difficult to estimate because the camp became a general regimental one into which a number of Serbians were intermixed, and because conscription in Canada netted a small number of draftees from within Canada.[43]

That 300 to 500 Croats in Canada and the United States had chosen to declare a Serbian or Yugoslav affiliation to enlist in the Allied cause was perhaps indicative of a positive spirit of commitment. But several other incidents involving Austrians of Croat, Czech, and Slovak background indicate that their claim to Yugoslav status may have been to avoid Austrian alien status and possibly to gain access to the United States. One Vancouver Croat, for example, was accused by police authorities of organizing upon behalf of the Yugoslav Commitee an association "among the Austrians of British Columbia for the purpose of trying to convince the authorities that these Austrians were Serbians, so that they would not have to report to the police, having joined this society, named the 'Yugoslav Society.' '' The police detractors insisted that the purpose of the organization was to levy a tribute payment of two to three dollars per month, whereby a member mistakenly believed in his immunity from arrest as an Austrian alien.[44]

Indeed, it is also apparent that the Serbian National League was itself anxious to admit as many members as it could by interpreting the "Yugoslav" designation liberally, for the Serbian consul in Montreal, Captain A.V. Seferovitch, was upbraided in 1918-19 by the Canadian authorities for admitting Czechs and other aliens too freely into the fold. The consul was particularly eloquent in his pleas immediately after the war to allow Yugoslav status and passports to the 2,500 or so South Slavs in the Niagara Peninsula. Arguing that they were now unemployed, Seferovitch insisted that they be assisted either by exemptions as Serbians or with passports to find work in the United States. To this request, the Chief Commissioner of Police in Canada promptly replied that each request for change in nationality was inspired "by individuals who are not the Yugoslavs who volunteered to serve the Allied cause in Europe, but are already deriving some benefit from the loyal actions of their compatriots." He cynically concluded that the number of Yugoslavs was increasing daily since the conclusion of the war, "but it is doubtful that so many would have been in evidence if the result had been different."[45]

The hostile attitude of the Canadian press censors and police authorities toward the Austrian alien continued for the duration of the war. Newspapers of the American Croat and Slovene groups, particularly of the radical socialist variety such as the Slovene paper *Proletarec*, were closely watched. With the rise of working-class protest within Canada toward the end of the war, the Chief Press Censor was more convinced than ever that "we [Anglo-Saxons] cannot possibly fathom the subleties [*sic*] of the foreign mind." Even the Serbian daily press, which was critical of the Yugoslav cause, came under the censorious eye of the government because of its critical posture to the war and the creation of a new Yugoslav state. As a result, the importation of *Srbski Dnevnik* from New York was legally prohibited in 1918, and the possession of offending copies was considered a criminal offence.[46]

As the war drew to a close the main political issue for the Croats and other South Slavs in the United States was whether or not Yugoslavia would become an independent state at the Paris Peace Conference. But, given the lack of a daily or even a weekly press among the Canadian Croats, it is impossible to determine what perceptions or attitudes they held of these events. The Canadian South Slavic minorities were likely much less involved than their American counterparts in the overtures of Woodrow Wilson at Versailles to have his Fourteen Points accepted and thereby allow self-determination for oppressed national minorities under the old Austro-Hungarian order. Without a middle class or intelligentsia to vocalize their feelings on this issue, they could not have participated, if they had wanted to, in that great debate.[47]

Overall, their concerns were more basic and elemental in Canada, such as the search for work in a highly inflated economy which now had to undergo the painful process of demobilization and re-absorption of war veterans. The anger and resentment of the returned soldier toward the enemy alien who had taken his job was deep, as was graphically demonstrated during the Winnipeg General Strike of 1919. The explosion of native sentiment over the assault by some Austrian strikers on Sergeant F.G. Coppins, a Victoria Cross war hero, was typical of the ugly turn that Canadian public opinion had taken in 1919.[48] The workers were characterized as terrorizing Winnipeg's "white people" and of being Red Bolsheviks and German sympathizers and at the same time they absorbed such epithets as "Hairy Bolshevists," "Prussian curs," and "cowardly Huns." If the attitude of English Canadians had been a qualified negative prior to the war, it became hostile and reactionary after the war.

For Croats, as for Germans, Austrians, and others, this was a dark time indeed to be an alien abroad in Canadian society. The nativist reaction that gripped Canadian society after the war was profound, and this nativism would result for a time in the closing of doors to undesirable nationalities.[49] Typical of the reaction Croats could expect in the post-war period was an RCMP investigation of a report on German war veterans in the employ of the Dominion Coal Company's mines at the Cape Breton collieries in 1920. The miners claimed to be Serbians and Yugoslavs who had been in Germany during the war and forced to wear the German army uniform, and who, thin on clothing in coming to Canada, had decided the uniforms were good enough for work in the mines![50] While no deportation orders seem to have been issued, the incident demonstrated the sensitivity of Canadians and newly arrived British miners to the presence of the enemy within so soon after the bloodiest war in history, and in direct contravention of the laws excluding German immigration, which would last until 1923.

NOTES

1. See J.S. Woodsworth, *Strangers within our Gates* (Toronto: Missionary Society of the Methodist Church, 1909), p. 149; Ralph Connor, *The Foreigner* (Toronto: Westminster, 1909), pp. 88-90, 100-1.
2. *Canadian Annual Review,* 1914, pp. 282-6.
3. Desmond Morton, "Sir William Otter and Internment Operations in Canada during the First World War," *Canadian Historical Review*, LV, 1 (March, 1974), pp. 33-4.
4. J.A. Boudreau, "Interning Canada's 'Enemy Aliens,' 1914-19," *Canada: An Historical Magazine,* II, 1 (September, 1974).
5. See R.H. Coats, "The Alien Enemy in Canada: Internment Operations," in *Canada in the Great World War*, vol. II (Toronto: United Publishers of Canada, 1919-21), pp. 144-61, for a reflection of contemporary feeling of the German and Austrian threat. German newspapers were a particular source of worry and were monitored very closely; e.g., Agent #208, Vancouver, B.C., to Malcolm R.J. Reid, Chief Dominion Immigration Inspector for British Columbia, Sept. 9, 1915, Re: "Foreign News-Papers not Favorably [*sic*] to the Allied Cause," PAC, Record Group 6, E.1, vol. 42, ff. 182, n. 2, n. 3. See also W. Entz, "The Suppression of the German Language Press in September 1918," *Canadian Ethnic Studies*, VIII, 2 (1976), pp. 56-67.
6. See T.D. Regehr (ed.), *The Possibilities of Canada are Truly Great, Memoirs, 1906-24, by Martin Nordegg* (Toronto: Macmillan of Canada, 1971), pp. 201-40.
7. B.C. Provincial Archives, B.C. Police, Alien Enemies Correspondence & Reports (1914-1918), ff. 1-22. H.A. Tietz's statement to the Superintendent of Provincial Police re: arrest of Austrian reservists at Sidney, 15 September 1914.
8. *Ibid.,* Anonymous of Provincial Police, B.C., to John C. Newberry, Collector of Customs, Victoria, B.C., 23 November 1914. There were reportedly 10,000 reservists who had been confined or had taken the oath of allegiance by October, 1914. Morton, "Sir William Otter," p. 37.
9. Thomas Surluga interview with George Kokich, December, 1974. Surluga was absent from 1915-17 in Minnesota and Wisconsin.
10. John Šušak interview with George Kokich, Toronto, December, 1974.
11. B.C. Archives, B.C. Police Papers, ff. 15, Colwood and Parson's

Bridge, C. Campbell, Supt. of Prov. Police, Victoria, to C.H. Rust, City Engineer and Water Commissioner, 10 November 1914, Victoria.

12. *Ibid.,* C.H. Rust to Colin Campbell, 9 November 1914, Victoria.

13. B.C. Provincial Archives, B.C. Police Papers, Victoria file (misc. 1914-17) #3, dated Victoria, 19 October 1914.

14. *Ibid.,* B.C. Police Internment Files, 1355-56, vols. 1-6.

15. *Ibid.,* B.C. Police Papers, Entries, Pt. Guichon, Wellington, Nanaimo, 3 March 1915; "Alien Subjects Living at Ladysmith, 18 May 1915," ff. Nanaimo, 1355.

16. PAC, Record Group 6, E-1 (Secretary of State Chief Press Censor, 1915-20), vol. 41, File 182-A-2, 182-B-1. Agent #208, to Malcolm Reid, Dominion Immigration Inspector for B.C., Vancouver, 22 September 1915. "Re: Austrian at Granby Smelter Taking up Collections for Alien Enemies."

17. B.C. Provincial Archives, B.C. Police Papers, Constable John Simpson, Greenwood, B.C., to Colin S. Campbell, Supt. Prov. Police, Victoria, 26 January 1916, ff. 1355, 7-15, vol. 2.

18. *Ibid.,* Lytton, Colin Cameron, Chief Constable Yale Police District, 28 July 1915.

19. *Ibid.,* B.C. Internment Files, 1355-56, 1-6. Nanaimo District, 18 May 1915. See also *ibid.,* B.C. Police Papers, Correspondence and Reports, 57-100, Britannia Mines, 1916, ff. 1264-94. Re: Detention and release of two Austrians, Mitro Papovich and Mat Katalinich, 1 May 1916.

20. *Ibid.,* Correspondence and Reports, 101-145; ff. Peter Štimac, 1916-17, #1264-117. Letter dated Ottawa, 6 November 1916 (translator F. Macka), original letter posted Edmonton, Alberta, 27 October 1916.

21. *Zajedničar,* 17 February 1915.

22. PAC, RG 13 A 2, vol. 195, ff. 1216.19.5. Cecil Spring Rice to the Duke of Connaught, Washington, 26 May 1915.

23. PAC, RG 13 A 2, vol. 192, ff. 397/1915. J. Marohnich, Supreme Pres., National Croatian Society, to Cecil Spring Rice, British Embassy, Pittsburgh, 16 February 1915.

24. *Ibid.,* vol. 195, ff. 1216,19.5. Deputy Minister of Justice to Major Gen. Otter, Ottawa, 3 June 1915.

25. A full description of the tour is contained in *Zajedničar,* 30 June 1915.

26. *Zajedničar,* 20 October 1915.

27. PAC, RG 6 E 1, vol. 42, ff. 182-N-2 N.3. Lt. Col. W.H. Ptolemy to the Chief Commissioner of Dominion Police, Welland, 8 September 1915.

28. *Ibid.,* Agent #208 to M.J. Reid, Chief Dominion Inspector for Immigration in B.C., Vancouver, 9 September 1915. The style and syntax of the letter suggest that the author of the letter was Stefan E. Raymer. See below ff. 5.

29. *Ibid.,* A.J. Shumiatcher to E.J. Chambers, Chief Press Censor, Calgary, 15 April 1918.

30. *Ibid.,* Bonar Law to the Governor General of Canada, London, 3 September 1915.

31. *Ibid.,* vol. 41, ff. 182-D-1. Agent #208 to M.J. Reid, Chief Dom. Inspector of Immigration for B.C., Vancouver, 14 December 1915.
32. *Ibid.,* RG 24, vol. 2523, ff. 1562, pts. 1-2. Dept. of National Defense – Army Services; General Sam Hughes to Prince Lazarovich Hrebeljanovich, Ottawa, 10 March 1915.
33. *Ibid.,* Prince Lazarovich Hrebeljanovich to Sam Hughes, New York, 3 March 1915.
34. Ivo J. Lederer, *Yugoslavia at the Paris Peace Conference* (New Haven: Yale University Press, 1963), pp. 3-35. For a different view supporting Pašič's consistent Yugoslavism, see Alex. N. Dragnich, *Serbia, Nikola Pašić and Yugoslavia* (New Brunswick, N.J.: Rutgers University Press, 1974), ch. 7.
35. *Sessional Papers,* House of Commons, RG 14D2, vol. 25, ff. 228. Forwarded by George Perley to Robert Borden, London, 28 June 1917.
36. Ivan Čizmić, *Jugoslavenski Iseljenićki Pokret u SAD i Stvaranje Jugoslavenske Države, 1918* (Zagreb, 1974), pp. 299-304.
37. PAC, RG 24, vol. 97, ff. 1895, Col. M. Pribičevich to Joseph Pope, Ottawa, 12 November 1917.
38. *Ibid.,* Pribičević to Maj. Gen. W. Gwatkin, 30 October, 12 November 1917.
39. *Ibid.,* vol. 4581, ff. 35A-1-9, Maj. Gen. Gwatkin to G.O.C., Halifax, Ottawa, 22 February 1917.
40. *Ibid.,* vol. 441, File HQ 54-21-1-159A, Maj. J. Hamilton to the Director General of Supply and Transport, Ottawa, 20 December 1918, Kingston, Ont.
41. *Ibid.,* vol. 425, ff. HQ 54-21-1-48, pts. 1-2-3, Maj. J. Hamilton to Adj. Gen. Militia Headquarters, Ottawa, dated Kingston, Ont., 18 January 1919.
42. *Ibid.,* vol. 4576, ff. 3-37-1, Same to same, Kingston, 20 December 1918.
43. B.C. Provincial Archives, B.C. Police Papers, ff. 35. H.S. Wood to Deputy-Attorney General, 10 February 1917.
44. *Ibid.,* "Rex v. Bozo Rasata and Others"; T.G. Wynn to Colin S. Campbell, Vancouver, 19 February 1917.
45. PAC, RG 25 G-1, vol. 1238, Supt. of External Affairs, ff. 116-19. Status of Czechs and Yugoslavians, 1919.
46. *Ibid.,* RG 6 E 1, Secretary of State, Chief Press Censor, 1915-20, vol. 134, ff. 363, E.J. Chambers, Censorship Notice, Ottawa, 23 July 1919; Rev. Auto M. Jaksitch to Sir Joseph Pope, Hamilton, 17 September 1919.
47. Ivan Čizmić, *Jugoslavenski Pokret . . .,* pp. 299-304. Dragan Zivojinović, *America, Italy and the Birth of Yugoslavia* (Boulder: East European Quarterly, 1972).
48. J.E. Rea (ed.), *The Winnipeg General Strike* (Toronto: Holt, Rinehart & Winston, 1973), pp. 38, 39, 81, 87, 91.
49. H. Palmer, *Land of the Second Chance: A History of Ethnic Groups in Southern Alberta* (Lethbridge Herald, 1972), pp. 186-8; Palmer,

"Nativism and Ethnic Tolerance in Alberta, 1920-72," Ph.D. thesis, York University, 1973.
50.   PAC, RG 76, vol. 498, ff. 775789, part II, Dominion Coal Company, Glace Bay. Re: German Labourers Imported by Dominion Coal Company.

FIVE

The Twenties:
The Opening Door and
the Expanding Community

Odlazak U Kanadu

Evo ide šesta godinica
što su nam se pogledala
u Zagrebu naša mlada lica.
Sakupi se naša raja
u Zagrebu gradu,
agent reče: "ajte momci
vidjeti Kanadu!"
Bilo toga, što se kaže,
ko u gori lista,
pitali su puno novac –
do dolara dvista.
Neko uzme putni trošak
od svojega kuma,
računa mu i kamate –
velike je suma.
Neki opet uzme trošak
od svojega tetka,
povrati mu cijelu svotu
do Božića svetka.
Neko opet uze trošak
iz kase – blagajne,
založio i imetak
na kamate trajne.
Neko opet prodao je
što kod kuće ima,
nadajuć se da će opet
pomoć svojim svima.
Akent kaže, kuf're [sic] slaže:
"Pakujte se momci,

Departure for Canada

Here have six years past
Since we last saw each other's
Young faces in Zagreb.
Our gang gathered
In the city of Zagreb
The agent said, "Let's go boys
To see Canada!"
We were many, as they say,
As the leaves in the forest,
They were asking a lot of money –
Up to two hundred dollars.
One obtained a loan
From his godfather,
The toll mounts, and with interest –
The sum is great.
Another took a loan from his uncle,
To return the whole amount
Before the Christmas holidays.
Another loaned it from
The treasury of the company
And had to mortgage his property
At perpetual interest.
And still another sold
Whatever he had at home,
Hoping to help
All his family.
The agent says, as he sorts suitcases:
"Get ready, boys,
Because 'trains' do not wait

jer "trenovi" već čekaju
i čuju se zvonci."
Evo za čas punog vlaka
te zaplače svaka majka:
"Ajte sinci, zdravi bili
i živi se povratili!"
A i žena svoga muža
tobož na njeg' ruke pruža:
"Ajde mužu, ostani duže,
jer tamo se pare služe" . . .
Medju rajom nastala je bajka,
teško ide od svog sina majka:
Sine, kad češ natrag doći,
mene ne češ više živu naće".
Zadnji časak žena kod muža,
ali nakon dvaju sata
drži drugog oko vrata . . .
Za kratko vrijeme
ne čuju se zvonci,
prodjoše nam svi
mladjahni momci.
Iza brda i velikih planina
izgubila majka mladog sina,
a i žena bez svojega muža,
tekar sada rascvala s'ko ruža,
Broji dane jel će novac doći,
jel ce moći u birtiju poći. –

Spjevao: M. Barkovic, Arvida.

And the bell has sounded."
And in a moment the train was full
With every mother crying,
"Go my sons, be healthy,
And come back alive!"
And the wife with her man
Reaching after him:
"Go my husband, stay longer,
For money is made over there."
Amidst the crowd the mother started,
For she cannot part from her dear son:
"My son, when you return,
You will no longer find me alive. . ."
Until the last, the wife remains with
    her husband,
But after two hours,
She holds another at the door . . .
In a short time
The bells are silent,
And all our young lads
Are gone.
Over the hills and mountains.
Mother has lost her young son,
And a wife her husband,
Deserted to flourish like a rose,
Counting the days for the money
    to come
So she may go to the tavern . . .[1]

M. Barkovic, Arvida.

ENTER "THE DARKER RACES," AND THE VANISHING FARMER

The 1920's was a decade of rapid change, one of extremes and contrasts. American economic penetration was poised against a dying British Empire, and the popular culture of the new American aspirin age challenged the outworn Victorian social order. Cities struggled with the country for supremacy, and Canada's population teetered on the brink of modern industrialism, with a population that hovered between 50 per cent rural and urban in 1921. A decade later, the balance had shifted decisively in the direction of urban life and would never look backward. Symbolic of the rapid change that occurred in the twenties were the decline of prohibition by the mid-decade and the onset of the signs of prosperity–booze, stock-speculation, political corruption, bribery, and scandal.[2]

94

Canadian immigration policy toward Croats would also shift to accommodate the rapidly changing character of Canadian society. Wartime hostility against enemy aliens combined with the post-war economic slump to sustain a closed-door policy to immigration until 1923.[3] Then a dramatic change in American immigration policy profoundly altered the direction of southern European immigrants seeking a home in America. The United States, which had previously admitted the masses of southern and eastern Europe that Canada had never seen fit to allow entry en masse, began closing her doors with a series of restrictive quotas. By 1924, the doors were all but closed to those immigrants by the Johnson-Reed Act.[4] Canada would now be the beneficiary of the displaced flow of migrants to North America if she chose to have them, and not surprisingly, she began to lift the restrictions previously imposed against the undesirable races of southern and eastern Europe: the rapid expansion of Canadian industry in the mid-twenties necessitated a large surplus of unskilled labour to increase the output of its mines, forest industries, and factories.[5]

Canadian immigration laws during the twenties were governed by distinction between "preferred" and "non-preferred" immigrants according to race and country of origin. Asians were virtually excluded from entering, southern Europeans found considerable difficulty placed in their paths, and northern Europeans and British subjects experienced the least difficulty of all. As had been the case before the war, the two transcontinental railways were most active in the recruitment of immigrants, and by 1923 they had founded the Canada Colonization Association in co-operation with the federal Department of Immigration.[6] By 1924 the CNR had gone its own way with its own internal colonization department, completing a process begun the year previously when Dr. W.J. Black, the former federal Deputy Minister for Immigration, was appointed Manager of Colonization and Development for the Canadian National.[7]

Both railway companies established recruiting offices in London and in central Europe, and the CPR alone carried 58,000 immigrants aboard its steamships in 1923. Within two years, under Black's able hand, the CNR could claim that over 30,000 settlers had been attracted from Europe to agricultural and domestic occupations, and over 60,000 had proceeded to their destinations over CN tracks.[8] The strong recruiting role played by the central European offices of the two railways was acknowledged by the federal government when it announced in September, 1925, that the railways would be allowed to solicit, transport, and settle agricultural workers from both preferred and non-preferred countries, provided that they would return all those who refused to engage in agricultural pursuits and who had become public charges.[9] Because of difficulties in holding the railways to the terms of the agreement, it was further relaxed in May, 1927, when the government entered a three-year agreement with the railways, giving them virtually a free hand in bringing out inexperienced agricultural migrants from southern Europe. Under the new policy, the federal government continued to monitor the health and moral character of the migrants, but made the significant concession of allowing the railways as colonizing agents to certify immigrants independently, provided they could guarantee employment to them in Canada.[10] As a result, the annual immigration, which had been below 140,000 per year in the early twenties, suddenly rose to 160,000 for the years 1927-29. More significantly for the Croats, the effective limits upon Yugoslav migration were removed, and the annual intake doubled from 2,000 to 4,000 during the 1924-28 period. Thus, in the five-year interval of the late twenties, probably over 10,000 Croats out of a total of 16,000 Yugoslavs had migrated to Canada. (See Table 2.)

TABLE 2

Croatian Immigrants to Canada, 1921-31,
As a Percentage of Total Migration from Yugoslavia to Canada

Year	Yugoslavs	Croats	% C/Y	Return/Y	Return/C	Net/Y	Net/C
1921	87	—	—	—	—	—	—
1922	179	(93)	(51.7)	—	—	179	(93)
1923	717	(371)	(51.7)	31	(21)	686	(350)
1924	1,976	(1,021)	(51.7)	130	(88)	1,846	(933)
1925	2,487	(1,286)	(51.7)	106	(72)	2,381	(1,214)
1926	4,998	2,719	55.2	253	(172)	4,745	(2,466)
1927	4,656	2,142	46.1	418	(284)	4,238	(1,858)
1928	5,921	3,423	57.8	673	(458)	5,428	(2,965)
1929	4,030	1,682	41.7	783	(532)	3,247	(1,150)
1930	2,745	1,576	57.8	1,115	771	1,630	805
1931	604	(315)	51.7	1,265	861	−661	(−546)
Totals	28,400	(14,628)	(51.7)	4,774	(3,259)	25,041	(12,380)

SOURCE: Annual Returns reported to Canada, Department of Immigration from Iseljenički Komesariat, Zagreb; contained in PAC, RG 76, vol. 623, ff. 938332, Parts II and III.
NOTES: Estimated figures appear in parentheses where statistics are unavailable. Estimates are taken as average actual figures in that category for the decade. The number of Croatians who remained in Canada by 1931 with the effective closing of Canadian doors to migrants from "non-preferred' countries is open to some question given the figures presented in the 1931 census. The total number of Yugoslavs declared in that census were 17,110 of whom 12,674 were males and 4,436 were females. Given the net migration of some 25,000 Yugoslavs in the decennial period since 1921, and adding to these the approximately 2,000 Yugoslavs listed in 1921, there were theoretically 27,000 Yugoslavs in 1931 in Canada, some 10,000 more than the actual number declared. Leaving aside those who returned to Yugoslavia or migrated elsewhere it appears at minimum that Croats could be counted at 52 per cent of the total 17,110, or 8,845. If one were to count as Croats the number of Roman Catholics declared in the 1931 census, the percentage of Croats would be higher, at 77 per cent or 13,141 Croats, a figure which closely approximates the above projection of Croatian immigrants entering in the ten-year period prior to 1931. Source: Canada, *Dominion Census* (Ottawa: King's Printer, 1936), vol. 1.

Indicative of the efforts made by railways in attracting migrants was the organization of the continental division of the CNR under W.J. Black. In 1924, he recruited a young Canadian social scientist, Robert England, to his staff, as well as two experts on central European agriculture, Dr. F.W. Baumgartner and Dr. Hoffman. England related that his two able assistants, "with their specialized knowledge of Slovonia [sic] and the Banat, Western Galicia and Bukovina, Bessarabia, Dobrudja and Croatia succeeded in aiding many German, Ukrainian, Croatian and Slovak families to migrate from territory not too congenial to these minorities, and the new governments were not unwilling to grant passports . . . ."[11]

The sophistication of these colonization agents, compared with the simplistic racial imperative that governed Canadian immigration policy, is evident in Baumgartner's eloquent treatises on the complex ethnography of Yugoslavia to his superior, England. Faced with instructions that categorically denied entry to Canada of southern Europeans of a "darker race," Baumgartner constructed elaborate anthropological defences for issuing emigration certificates to Croats and Slovenes, as opposed to Macedonians, Dalmatians, and Montenegrins. A typical rationalization included the legitimization of the Croats, Slovenes, and Serbs as Aryans and the abandonment of the others to the "darker" category:

> The pure Slav, Serb, Croat and Slovene can fairly well be recognized as fair skinned, and by other features, but they themselves are not uniformly blond and fair, and in addition there are all degrees of blends to which this centuries' long mixtures of races has led, and it is not always easy to decide just where to draw the line, the less as this line does by no means always correspond with agricultural fitness and other qualifications of Canadian immigrants.[12]

Canadian immigration officials thus had the intending immigrant from Yugoslavia caught on the horns of a dilemma. Large numbers of potential immigrants had simply substituted Canada for the United States as their country of first destination after 1923. To be sure, a great number still preferred the more congenial Mediterranean climates of Argentina or Australia, but the force of kinship and the economic lure of higher wages were stronger attractions for many Croats to Canada as a lesser version of the American dream. There was the additional hope for many that they might eventually be able to migrate via Canada to the United States when the golden door of opportunity opened once again.

The anticipation of these basic economic drives led to an attitude of distrust and suspicion among Canadian immigration officials. Their most pervasive and immediate fear was that the South Slav migrants would use Canada as an illegal back door to the cities of the northern United States. As early as 1921, immigration officials in Ottawa were alerted to the clandestine movement of Romanian and Hungarian labourers from boardinghouses in Montreal across the Vermont and New York borders.[13] By 1923 and the opening of Canada to a limited number of Yugoslavs, their suspicions were realized, and in mid-1923 six Yugoslavs were to be deported from the United States for illegal entry through Canada.[14] Warnings were issued to the Yugoslav Consul-General in Montreal, A.V. Seferovitch, that Canadian-American relations might be severely damaged by such action.[15] Reports continued through 1926, however, that such activities were conducted on a large scale across the Niagara and Windsor-Detroit frontiers, operating out of smuggling rings centred in Toronto boardinghouses located on Western Avenue.[16] Counter-measures were soon effected with the co-operation of American authorities, and by early 1927 some thirty Yugoslav immigrants to Canada were deported from the United States to their homeland for illegal entry to the United States.[17] While some of these were Montenegrins and Macedonians, unwanted as members of the "darker races" in Canada, a large number were Croats attempting to improve their economic position in the New World and to join their relatives and friends south of the border.

The monitoring of racial purity among the South Slavic immigrants entering Canada became the second obsession of a nervous immigration department, well attuned to the nostrums of pseudo-scientific social theory and eugenics retailed by such respectable authorities as J.S. Woodsworth and the Protestant churches.[18] Unsophisticated laments on the impending deluge of Slavic darkness were bandied about immigration offices in Europe and in Canada. A wild flutter of interdepartmental memos was occasioned by this overseas early warning emanating from Canadian House in Trafalgar Square, London:

> In a conversation with our Mr. Mitchell at Antwerp the other day I gathered that 75% of the Yugo-Slavia emigrants brought forward through this office were not of the class that are readily assimilated into Canadian conditions. He advised me that transportation companies at his port presented Macedonians as Serbs, who are really Turks in origin and customs: Yugoslavs from the Banat district, who were originally Roumanians, and so-called Croatians recruited on the Dlamation [sic] border, and consequently really Dalmatians of the dark type; as well as a considerable sprinkling of Bosnian, Hersegovinian [sic] and Montenegrins.
>
> These emigrants are all of the dark type, and not by any means desirable for Canada. They are themselves willing workers, but leave the hard tasks for their wives while they sit at home and smoke and rest themselves.[19]

Immigration agents throughout Canada and Europe were then alerted to look out for immigrants of the "dark type" from these regions and those who were clearly unfit for agricultural occupations. Immediately, a memo appeared from the official at Antwerp confirming the worst, that the Yugoslav government was indeed conspiring to unload undesirable non-agricultural migrants upon Canada, and that "there is even talk of including Dalmatians of the dark type from the West coast, who are anything but desirable for our Dominion."[20]

Lists of undesirable aliens in immigration files dating back one year were brought forward to demonstrate the wholesale deception by the CPR certification officer in Zagreb, Dr. Ivan Shvegel. Carefully documented files demonstrated that 142 Dalmatians, 127 Herzegovinians, 150 Macedonians, 59 Serbians, 45 Romanians, 63 Montenegrins, and one Bosnian had been issued visas by the CPR and were now in Canada, likely in non-farming occupations.[21] Further, male migrants who were clearly Croats were identified collectively as "All of the Serbian race and Turkish origin; therefore not adaptable to the conditions in Canada."[22]

Supporting evidence was soon produced within Canada of deception practised by the Yugoslav migrants in conjuction with the steamship agents and the railways. The agents were accused of their traditional practice of securing deposits in advance from the prospective immigrants to ensure the necessary documents for emigration. They thus deprived the immigrants of as much as $200 or $300 each, which otherwise would have been spent in Canada, according to Canadian immigration officials' reasoning.[23] More than this, Yugoslav agents in the employ of the CPR in Montreal were conspiring with agents in Zagreb to furnish affidavits at $200 each, which indicated the agricultural destination to which the immigrant would go.

Immigration officials and employers in Canada then lodged vigorous complaints that the supposed agricultural immigrants from Yugoslavia had come under false pretences, and that they were intent upon securing more lucrative construction and navvy wage labour. According to one official in the federal government's land settlement branch in Calgary, this deception was obvious: "We offered to find work for these men [nine Yugoslavs] at from $5.00 to $10.00 per month and their board. All but one declined to accept this. They cannot speak English and are difficult to please as a result, besides which they know nothing of Canadian farming methods."[24] The CPR, which had hired these immigrants, was chastised for taking on navvies so late in the season and not allowing for the contingency that they would be unemployed over the winter.[25] Nor was the railway's case made any more palatable to a suspicious immigration department when it was revealed that the Yugoslav migrants indicated that they had been promised railway work upon coming to Canada. The government consequently insisted that the CPR make a greater effort to guarantee year-round employment to immigrants.[26]

Further reports from Vancouver and the West Coast demonstrated that the CNR's colonization agents, too, had not been wholly scrupulous in applying government policy. The Department of Immigration noted that several Yugoslavs had come to Canada under CN certificates in five different vessels destined for the Canadian Natural Resources Building in

Winnipeg, but had not been placed in agricultural occupations. Instead, they had proceeded to Vancouver where they hoped to join their country-men in the fishing industry or to take up labour on construction crews or in the lumber camps. The Yugoslav vice-consul in Vancouver reported that sixty-two unemployed men had applied for work to him, although none were really farm labourers but had rather been forced into that category by steamship agents in order to qualify for immigrant status.[27] By the spring of 1927, the unemployment situation had worsened con-siderably, with south European immigrants swelling the immigration hall in Winnipeg and other western cities.[28] In June, the government applied the brakes to further entry under the Railways Agreement by refusing to grant entry visas unless the continental immigration officers could be convinced that they had a farming background and that they were proceeding directly to a relative's farm in Canada.[29]

In July, 1927, the discriminatory policy toward the "darker races" of Yugoslavia took a bizarre turn in the port of Montreal. Captain Sefero-vitch, the Yugoslav consul-general in Montreal, had conversations with F.C. Blair, the Acting Deputy Minister of Immigration in Ottawa, over the delicate subject of the racist policy pursued by the Canadian govern-ment. He subsequently refuted the government's attitude in a masterly theatrical stroke at the docksides of Montreal where the Yugoslav ship, the *Alexander I*, was moored. He invited E.C. Moquin, Montreal agent for the government, to inspect the crew of the ship, all Dalmatians. Mo-quin candidly reported to his superior in Ottawa that he was "very favourably impressed with the appearance of these men, about thirty in number, who were mustered on the deck, and none of them could be called 'dark'; in fact, only two men had dark eyes, and the rest of them all had blue eyes and more or less fair and light brown hair, and all of them were of good physical appearance and good-natured looking." To drive his point home, Seferovitch further indicated that the very best farmers were Dalmatians from the interior, and that should Canada want some of these, immigration officials should not be under the im-pression that they were "a colored people."[30]

The great pigment debate was on, and further memoranda were gener-ated from as far away as the CNR offices in Zagreb to demonstrate that since April, 1927, "*absolutely no passenger had been given a certificate from any part of Southern Serbia or Dalmatia, or of in a slight degree of dark shade.*"[31] To complicate the issue further, the head of the CNR Department of Colonization, W.J. Black, cannily admitted to the Dep-uty Minister of Immigration that the degree of dark skin would have to be precisely defined, since it was possible to find dark-skinned people "not only in southern Serbia, but also in Carniolia [sic], Croatia, and in-deed in many parts of Hungary and Austria. In the examination of these immigrants it is sometimes necessary to inspect the skin underneath the clothing as in many cases the arms, neck and face are somewhat dark owing to exposure in a more or less sunnier climate than that obtaining in the Northern parts."[32] The immigration department rather sheepishly acknowledged the receipt of this additional evidence, and the issue was laid to rest, not to be raised again.

Sensing an advantage, the Yugoslav officialdom pressed the Canadian Department of Immigration to define further the limits of Canadian immigration laws. The Department, for its part, resolutely defended its objective treatment of all Yugoslav immigrants without exception.[33] The Yugoslav authorities conversely urged greater concessions in the agriculturist restrictions now in force and urged the revamping of the cumbersome and often unfair medical inspection in Canada. To demonstrate their good faith, they made considerable efforts to inform the Canada-bound immigrants about what to expect upon arrival. The immigrants were also warned to beware of unscrupulous agents, who would inveigle them into non-farming occupations, and were advised that agricultural jobs were more rewarding from the point of view of year-round security of employment.[34] Each emigrant was additionally required to sign a register or control book acknowledging a mandatory copy of emigration instructions. In this way, none could complain as they had earlier that they had been wrongly advised or deceived in their occupational expectations upon coming to Canada.[35]

For the time being it appeared that the barriers of race had been dismantled, and the economy had recovered enough in 1928 to absorb a record number of migrants for the interwar period. Over 4,000 entered according to Canadian statistics and 5,921 by Yugoslav records, of which there were over 700 returnees to the homeland.[36] Approximately 3,000 Croats entered in the freest year of entry before the onset of the Great Depression. There were low grumblings from the Canadian daily press about the excessive numbers of central Europeans now entering Canada, but few complaints were on the scale of those registered in 1926-27 against railway corruption and Yugoslav deception. A few minor complaints surfaced in British Columbia that the Yugoslav consul there was recruiting farmers at $7.50 each to sign applications for the admission of Yugoslavs whom they would not have to employ as farm labourers, since they would not appear for work in any case. Thus, the elaborate safeguards erected to prevent non-farm labour from coming into Canada were apparently as penetrable in 1928 as they had been two and three years before.[37]

The additional factor explaining the lesser public outcry against south European immigration was that the government had already indicated its determination to cut back on continental immigration late in 1928. Accordingly, it announced in January, 1929, that it would reduce central European migration to 30 per cent of its previous levels, precisely because of the problem of single male migrant workers drifting into non-farm labour and depriving Canadians or British immigrants of these jobs. The restrictions, however, would not apply to domestic servants, family migrants, or wives and children rejoining a family already settled in Canada.[38] The grounds for migration had been reduced to compassionate family reasons, and the decade to follow would be essentially one of restoring a female balance to a vastly overbalanced male society.

The failure of completed family migration among the Croats had been quite uniform during the twenties. Beginning in 1924, several schemes for family migration had been launched, but these had not attracted the numbers anticipated by the immigration department. Their expectation had been to persuade rural families with a minimum of $500 capital to migrate to the West; later in 1925 this figure was lowered to $300 in view of the less than twenty agricultural families that came.[39] Given the loss of capital and the remittances posed by such family migration, the process was generally discouraged by Yugoslavia and other continental nations. But with the opening of the door to non-rural migrants in 1926-27, a greater number of Yugoslav families migrated under the modified continental family scheme controlled by the two railways. In 1927, several families were allocated for immigration from Bosnia to the Abitibi district in northern Quebec under the Railways Agreement, either as farm workers or domestics, and it also appears that a few Bosnian families worked as tobacco growers in the Okanagan Valley in 1927.[40] It is difficult to find positive evidence of their persistence as farmers, however. Generally, the same pattern was found as with the single male migrants, that is, that families allocated as rural farm workers in western Canada soon disappeared. For example, several Croats and Yugoslavs placed on farms near Sifton and Dysart, Saskatchewan, either disappeared or sold out and went to settle among the Croats in Welland, Ontario, or in other Croatian communities in the West.[41] Thus, with the single possible exception of the German-speaking Yugoslavs from Vojvodina (the Banat), who occasionally succeeded in Canada, few completed families migrated as a whole from Yugoslavia in the 1920's.

Family completion had to wait until the males had earned or saved enough to send for their wives and families or to return to Yugoslavia to find a wife. For the time being the Croatians would remain a subculture largely composed of single males employed in seasonal labour on Canada's frontiers. An index of the sex imbalance in this rootless population was that males composed 73 per cent of the total Croat population,[42] and the surplus of males was exceeded only by the Chinese.[43]

Measured statistically, the Croatian community of some 10,450 in Canada in 1931 was composed largely of migrants who had arrived since 1921 (approximately 67 per cent), with very few (20 per cent) who were born in Canada. Indeed, of all the ethnic groups in Canada, only the Chinese had fewer Canadian-born children. Yet the population gap was narrowing, since Croatian women recorded the highest number of live births (21.2 per 1,000) of all groups in Canada during 1930. The Croats were also predominantly urban (55 per cent urban, that is, in towns and villages of 1,000 or more). But the proportion (27 per cent) settled in small towns was only exceeded by two other ethnic groups, the Finns and the Italians, and equalled by the Chinese and the Greeks. Demographically, of the native population groups, the Croats most resembled the French Canadians. Croats were, as the French Canadians described themselves to be, "hewers of wood" and "drawers of water" for the rest of Canada.

The migrant male labourers of no fixed address, who numbered over 1,000 in the late twenties, were vastly outnumbered by resident settlements of Croats across Canada, which included some 8,000 or 9,000 in total. According to some generous estimates prepared by Yugoslav authorities, there were over 150 communities of varying size across Canada.[44] Half of the Croats were located in Ontario, 17 per cent in British Columbia, another 17 per cent in Alberta and Saskatchewan, and 10 per cent in Quebec. Few settled in Canada's largest cities, for Toronto, Montreal, Vancouver, and Winnipeg only contained 20 per cent of the entire group.[45] In fact, the larger and more specialized manufacturing centres in Ontario, such as Hamilton, Welland, Kitchener, Windsor (Ford City), Sault Ste. Marie, and Port Arthur, contained as many as the largest metropolitan centres.

The mining towns of northern Ontario and Quebec – Timmins, Schumacher, Sudbury, and Rouyn-Noranda – accounted for at least 700 residents; the interior of British Columbia and Vancouver Island towns such as Nanaimo and Ladysmith, Britannia, Princeton, and Nelson counted well over 1,000; the Alberta mining regions of Coal Branch, Drumheller, and the Crowsnest Pass accounted for 200 or 300 more Croat miners and their families. Thus, the mining frontier alone accounted for as many as the metropolitan centres or smaller manufacturing cities, and, if the single migrant labourers were added to resource-town populations, their accumulated total would be roughly equal to all urban concentrations of 30,000 or over.[46] Thus, by the late twenties the Croatians were evenly dispersed through city, town, and country, and with the exception of the Maritimes were more evenly distributed across Canada than the pre-war communities had been.

EASTERN CANADIAN COMMUNITIES: NEW AND OLD

The only population of any significance in the Maritimes was located in the Cape Breton mining communities of Glace Bay and New Waterford and in the mainland towns of Springhill and Stellarton. The steel smelters of British Empire Steel Corporation, later Dominion Steel, began to attract workers to the Sydney steel plant, particularly after the long and bitter BESCO strike of 1925, which had driven out some of the English-speaking militants.[47] In all, there were about 130 Croatians; the vast majority (92 per cent) were men, who gradually built up their savings to bring out their wives and families.

One such miner was Anthony Shelleby (Anton Šelebaj) from Kostel on the Croat-Slovene border in the mining region of Delnice and Čabar,

103

who arrived in 1927 after mining in northern Quebec, Ontario, and Cape Breton before settling in Stellarton.[48] Another miner, an early resident of New Waterford, was John Raćki, also of Delnice in Gorski Kotar, who came to Nova Scotia via Sudbury in 1928. Both took an active part in the promotion of musical activity among the Croats in Nova Scotia, building upon their previous involvement in glee club and tamburitsa orchestras in Croatia.[49] They would be joined by others from the Gorski Kotar and Lika regions who came to work in the Cape Breton coalfields in the late twenties.[50] By 1928, there was a lodge of the Croatian Fraternal Union formed in Springhill (Cvijet Sloga), and another in New Waterford (Triglav). The traditions of mutual help soon flowered, and collections were regularly taken to assist unemployed workers and incapacitated brethren.[51]

Further to the west in Quebec, a community that was more Yugoslav than Croatian in character had already begun to form in Montreal. The approximately fifty residents who had lived there prior to World War I had dramatically expanded to 600 by 1930. This settlement was predominantly Serbian and Romanian ethnically, and its cultural and social organizations were formally Yugoslav in name and were headed by the Yugoslav consular representative in Montreal, George Sigmund. The bulk of this mixed Yugoslav community, some 200 in number, lived in the area bounded by de Bleury and St. Denis, and by Prince Arthur and Craig. A substantial number of Croats, however, lived outside this predominantly Serbian urban core, especially on the periphery of Montreal in Lasalle and Beauharnois, where many of them already owned their own homes. As a group, they participated in musicals, glee clubs, picnics, and other social activities sponsored by the majority Yugoslav cultural groups, Jugoslavensko Prosvetno Drustvo and Jugoslavenski Zbor, formed in 1929.[52]

Farther to the north in Quebec, the Croats congregated in the gold mining camps of Rouyn-Noranda and Val d'Or (Bourlamaque) and in the mill town of Arvida. The three areas had in common their recent development of production in 1926-27 and a shortage of industrial labour for the initial construction phase and for first efforts at production.[53] A hundred or more Croatian miners came into the Noranda goldfields, among them several permanent residents from Herzegovina such as Ilija Juričič from Mostar.[54] Others, like M. Barković of Arvida, were less happy with their domestic life in their first years in Canada and lamented bitterly their isolation from their loved ones in the old country and their loneliness, as suggested in the poem which heads this chapter.

The perils of mining as an occupation were ever present, as illustrated in the death of Jure Čuvalo, an immigrant to Noranda. The brother of two Toronto Croats from Ljubuški in Herzegovina, Stipe (father of the yet unborn George Chuvalo) and Ante Čuvalo, he died in Noranda hospital in 1932 of a mining accident.[55] The cruelty of such hazardous working conditions to men of agrarian background, thousands of miles from home and family in isolated northern work camps, was often the subject of lament in their first years in Canada. One forlorn voice from northern Quebec echoed the sentiments of a generation of dispirited immigrants in the free folk verse common to his native land:

Mili Bože Kako Raja Strada

Braćo moja teške nami muke,
Kad dodjemo u tudjinske ruke!
Posal težak, govorit neznamo,
Pa da vidiš kako nastradamo!
Klete "šuflje" i "piki" al' rade,
Vražje ti je tu brale parade . . .

Jedni šute u dubokoj jami,
Iznad galava dereki im sami
Tu se stavija sedam derekova,
Kao crnih sedam gavranova.
Tu se kopa jama, al'duboka,
Izmjerit je nemožeš od oka.
Tu ti radi čovjek do čovjeka,
Iznad glave derek do derska . . .

"Počinimo", vele tada ljudi,
"Sjedmo malo, nek s'odmore
    udi!"
"Al' za minut eto "working
    basa",
Ide k njima, drži se za pasa,
Muči, čika, pljuje, al' ne psuje,

Gleda na njih ko na bjesne kuje.
Pita momke ak' je kebl "redi",
Sve ih redom ostrim okom gledi.
"Jeser, mister, finis – kebl is
    gut" . . .
A kebl se trese ko mokar prut.
Working bas je baš Skačman
    pravi,
Ogleda kebl i seče s' po travi.
Visok je i tanak, ni brkova nema,
Uvijek lulu puši, nigdje mira
    nema . . .

Svaki radi za te male pare,
U kraj mora mnogo da pošalje.
Novac šalje svojoj vjernoj ljubi,
Da mu ona za sve doma skrbi
Ima dobrih žena, a bome i loši,
Kojoj ne tvornica ne bi smogla
    groši
Mnoge žene doma švalere imadu,
A muževi im ovdje muče se u
    smradu . . .

My God How the Lowly Suffer

My brothers, great is our
    suffering,
When we have fallen into
    foreigners' hands!
Heavy work, we cannot speak the
    language,
And you should see how we
    suffer!
Damned picks and shovels, but
    they work,
This my brothers is a devil's
    parade . . .

Some are silent in the deep hole,
Over their heads only derricks to
    be seen,
Here stand seven hoists,
Like seven black ravens,
Here a hole is dug, but so deep.
It cannot be measured with the
    eye,
Here men work shoulder to
    shoulder,
And above, hoist beside hoist . . .

"Let's rest," say the people,
"Let's sit down, let's take a
  rest,"
But in a minute, the foreman is
  here,
He moves towards the men,
  hands upon his belt,
Silent, defiant, spitting but not
  cursing,
Looking upon them as on mad
  bitches.
He asks the boys if the cable is
  ready
Gazing upon all with a fearsome
  eye
"Jeser, mister, finis – kebl is
  gut". . .
But the cable shakes like a wet
  pole,
The straw boss is a true Scotsman
Inspecting the cable, striding over
  the ground,

tall and thin, not even a
  moustache,
Always puffing that pipe, no
  peace anywhere . . .

Everyone works for these few
  pennies,
to send many more across the
  sea
He sends money to his faithful
  wife
So that she could take care of
  home.
There are good wives, by God
  and bad ones too
For which even a factory could
  not supply enough cash
Many women have lovers at
  home
While their husbands here suffer
  in the stench . . .[56]

F. Berdik, Rapide Blanc,
Quebec

Just across the Ontario border, in the goldfields of Kirkland Lake, Timmins, and Schumacher, the Croats had at least overcome the problem of numbers, for in Schumacher the core of the largest frontier settlement of Croats was established in the 1920's. The first Croat miners to come to these northern mining camps had come as early as 1907 and 1908, particularly from Lika and Gorski Kotar. In 1923, they had become great enough in number to form a mutual benefit lodge of the Croatian Fraternal Union, "Radnička Grana," under its officers Ivan Krančević, Nikola Zubrinčić, Anton Pataran, and Tona Gomerčić.[57] By 1928-29 the Schumacher Croatian community had grown to some 400, most of them from the Žumberak region near Karlovac and the nearby region of Brinje in the Kapela range. Many of the new migrants lived along First, Second, and Third Avenues, close enough to the Hollinger and Dome mines to walk to work. Others lived in nearby Timmins on Second and Algonquin Streets, within walking distance of the McIntyre mines. A large number owned their own homes and there were some eight Croatian boardinghouses and hotels for single Croatian men.

In 1928 the Croatian Roman Catholics had already invited a young priest, Rev. Z. Mandurić, to establish a Croatian parish in Timmins and also to initiate an immigrants' library and reading room.[58] There was general elation at his arrival at the local railway station (Evo nam našega popa! – Here at last is our priest!), but the celebration proved premature. The young priest felt that there was not enough of a Croatian population base nor enough social capital in the poor congregation of fifty or so families to sustain a parish. A visit to the Roman Catholic bishop in Sudbury confirmed that a separate parish was unwarranted, and that the single English-speaking church would have to do for the time being.[59] The same sorry tale of poverty and insufficient numbers would plague Mandurich's further efforts to establish a parish in other Ontario towns and cities, for nowhere could the magic number of 1,000 souls and eighty families be found to begin a parish.

Disappointed in this venture, the Croatian residents of Schumacher and Timmins began to collect funds in 1929 for the building of a Croatian hall. By April, 1929, $245 had been collected, and by 1932 the young community held the grand opening of their cultural centre, built by their own efforts.[60] The extension of mutual assistance from the Croats to their fellow countrymen caught the attention of residents in Timmins-Schumacher, and the local newspaper complimented them on their support of an injured workman who had been disabled for two years. In addition, the Croatian Fraternal society had become more active in the late twenties in support of injured miners and their bereaved families.[61] Accidental death was the bitter legacy of mining towns, and this was driven home yet again in the Hollinger mine explosion and fire which claimed thirty-nine lives early in 1928.[62] The ethnic communities of Schumacher as a whole were so incensed by this disaster that they united to protest the negligence of the mine owners and inspectors. Their spokesmen were so volatile in their denunciation of the capitalistic system that it was no surprise when they ultimately invoked the three most radical of Canadian miners' unions to represent their united front on this issue – the IWW (Wobblies), the OBU (One Big Union), and the Communist Mine Workers' Union of Canada.[63]

Assimilation proceeded rapidly in the cultural isolation of this northern mining town. Without a church or school of their own, the Croats adapted quickly to the dominant English-language cultural institutions. Marriages were celebrated in the regular local parish or perhaps, if the bride happened to come from the older communities to the south, in Welland or Sault Ste. Marie.[64] The lower grades of the Schumacher Public School began to fill up with children of the Croatian mining families, and such youngsters as Madeline Ostovich and Tom Holgovich appeared on the honour roll in 1926-27. By 1930 the Croatian children were evident in virtually every grade, occasionally dominating a particular classroom but generally intermixed among a school population of ethnic backgrounds ranging from English and French to Finnish and Ukrainian.

By the spring of 1927 the Croatians of Schumacher had formed a Croatian tamburitsa orchestra, which gave performances at benefit charities in the town and at various band concerts, dances, and music festivals. The string group was strongly promoted by the local entrepreneur and hotel-owner, Ivan Krankovich, and burst into sudden prominence with its orchestral benefit for the local Children's Aid Shelter Fund.[65] The tamburitsans, directed by Peter Samtlick, included a dozen or so musicians, among them Joso Begović (first brač), Sam Marich (berda), Nick Ostović (kontrašica), and Frank Gerović (second bugaria). The group travelled to a folk music festival in Montreal, advertised as a Yugoslav ensemble for local consumption, and it placed second in a competition that attracted several professional entertainers. The wildly enthusiastic Montreal audience appeared unable to believe that such a hastily assembled group of amateur musicians, who in reality were hardrock miners, could have delivered such a polished performance.[66] As a consequence of its success, the group was roundly applauded on its return to Schumacher, where it continued to captivate local audiences.[67]

Sports traditions were also fostered in the isolated northern mining towns and were actively promoted by the company management, which was itself cut off from metropolitan amusements. Young Croats participated widely in the innocent and unsophisticated entertainment sponsored by the local community associations, such as box socials, dances, and even beard-growing contests for the older males.[68] The ebullient promoter, Ivan Krankovich, was expected as owner of the Schumacher Hotel to provide occasional free meals for victorious local sporting clubs.[69] It was some time, however, before the sons and daughters of the miners became participants in the competitive team and individual sports, which would eventually produce such hockey greats as the Mahovlich brothers. For the time being, only in the one area of brute strength could the recent immigrant make his mark, and in boxing a young Croat attained some local prominence. He was Spaso Kalember, a native of Lika and resident of nearby Kirkland Lake. He gained local notoriety for a quick decision in 1930 over the visiting "Russian Kid," Belzimar, who dissolved in tears of defeat after one punch to the heart by the mighty Croat![70]

While the new Croatian communities of Schumacher-Timmins, Kirkland Lake, and Rouyn-Noranda began to flex their young muscles, the gristle of youth in the larger settlements of Sault Ste. Marie and Sudbury, with its satellite towns of Levack and Creighton Mines, had begun to harden into the bones of maturity by the late 1920's. These smelter and mill towns both had populations of 500 Croats. The "Soo" had continued to pull Croatian immigrants to its steel mills even during the troubled war years, and this trickle gradually increased during the twenties into a steady stream of Croatian migrants from Slivno, Krivi Put, Sisak, and Drinovci in Herzegovina.[71] In this instance the process of migration served to fill out the existing population primarily with relatives of the first generation who had come prior to World War I. A secondary process of migration was the pull of the Sault for the frontier migrants of northern Ontario, who found the more established community there more congenial than the new communities on the mining and forest frontier.

Unfamiliar with the language and dependent upon the assistance of their families and relatives, they invariably settled into the west-end Dalmatian community, which by this time had begun to assume the shape of an ethnic "quarter." Women were now less scarce than they had been, and gradually large family dwellings with the inevitable boarders and lodgers were acquired by the new immigrants. But there was still sufficient demand as well for the larger commercial boardinghouses for single males: one of the earlier ones was established on St. James Street by Mijo Majić and Joe Čulina in 1921 and became the basis of a life-long partnership in the hotel business.

The vital signs of community were now strongly in evidence in this northern steel town. The young Dalmatian Croats who had just arrived were pleased to have jobs with Algoma Steel and were prepared to endure the perils of foundry work for the steady wages and relative job security. Industrial accidents were still common and claimed lives occasionally, but not with the frequency of mining accidents in the north.[72] Some of the Croats of the first generation had also begun to move out into the timber hinterland of the Sault as jobbers supplying local sawmills and paper mills. In fact, some of the older migrants such as Krmpotić, Prpić, and Kaich had become logging contractors, often supervising as many as a hundred men in their camps, many of them recent Croatian arrivals.[73] The success of their enterprise had even become an object of social concern to the local branch of the Croatian Fraternal Union, which was having to establish accident insurance and other benefits to cover workers employed by these small independent operators.

Across Lake Superior, the Croatian community of Port Arthur had achieved a similar maturity. Its essential difference from the new mining towns of northern Ontario was that, although its total population was still less than two hundred, the number of completed families was about thirty.[74] As in Sault Ste. Marie, the signs of stable community were well in evidence by the 1920's. Women domestics were not employed for long in Port Arthur before they were betrothed.[75] Often the males were thirty years of age and well-established employees in local industrial firms. Other new migrants were already in a position to bring their wives with them, and often settled in suburban fringes of the city, such as Current River to the northeast, a full three miles from the more established ethnic quarter in the city's south end. Many of the recent migrants in Current River were from Gorski Kotar and were employed in the two lakeside paper mills within walking distance of their homes. Among these were such families as the Belobrajdiches, the Grguriches, and the Kendas.[76] Soon they were able, by stringent saving, to take advantage of the collapsed real estate market on the exterior fringes of the city where urban services were poor and lots were plentiful. Small houses on double and triple lots were often purchased with ample land about them to raise vegetables to feed growing families.

Children of school age were still few, but family formation was rapid in the prosperous late twenties. A few young children were now enrolled in the junior grades of the Catholic and public elementary schools, St. Andrew's and Cornwall in the south end and St. Theresa's in the northern suburb of Current River. Many had been born in the old country, but they were rapidly learning their new second language in the schoolroom, schoolyards, and streets of Port Arthur. The lessons did not come easily at first since the language of their homes was Croatian, with various village dialects within that mother tongue. But the ethnic polyglot of Port Arthur, composed of Finns, Ukrainains, and Italians, made the transition easier, since it seemed that everyone was learning the English language afresh.

A series of informal institutions appeared to characterize this small community. Mutual help was often organized upon a satisfactory basis where need was demonstrated, and often was done by local subscription.[77] A formal lodge of the Croatian Fraternal Union appeared in 1929 under the name "Sveti Nikola," with Petar Marohnić and Ivan Dominović as president and secretary.[78] But it appeared that there would be no possibility of a Croatian Catholic parish here, despite the enthusiastic reception given to Father Mandurić, who made an early visit to affirm the faith of his brethren. Croats melded into the local English-speaking congregation in Port Arthur as they had in Schumacher and Sault Ste. Marie. Equally, the social capital for cultural activities was not well enough developed among the striving young families to provide for formal orchestral, choral, and dance groups. Able volunteers from the adult ranks of the community supplied the music and dancing for weddings or infant christenings. Further development of cultural institutions would have to await the thirties and the maturing of the children of the first generation. For the time being, life was ordered about work, the acquisition of homes, and tending the young in the cramped quarters of their small homes and boardinghouses.

Similar but deeper social forces were at work changing the social landscape of the Croatian immigrant communities of southern Ontario. There it was clear that urban migrants shared in the economic advantages that factory labour brought in wages, but they shared also in the social dislocation brought on by city life. The urban ghetto which had suggested itself in the northern Ontario cities of Sault Ste. Marie, Sudbury, and Port Arthur was clearly in evidence in the larger cities of the south: Hamilton, Windsor, and Toronto. Here settlement patterns had long dictated the segregation of certain areas as ethnic and working-class as early as the nineteenth century. Much as the Yugoslav community of Montreal was confined to a small area, so the Croatian and Yugoslav settlements of Windsor, Welland, Hamilton, and Toronto were clearly identifiable spatially and socially.[79]

The Toronto settlement of South Slavs had been traditionally dominated by Serbian and Macedonian migrants from the pre-war period.
Thus, it grew in proportion to its mixed South Slav predecessors, just as
its sister community in Montreal had, and by the late twenties stood at
approximately 900 Serbs, Slovenes, and Croats, and 2,000 Macedonians.
The Croats numbered perhaps some 400 in the total. Most of them had
come after 1924 and were mixed in with groups from Primorje, Dalmatia, Herzegovina, Lika, Žumberak, and Slavonia. But their numerical
strength was clearly submerged in a larger cosmopolitan community and
a superstructure of government-sponsored Yugoslav clubs and agencies.
Indicative of this minority position, the small lodge of the Croatian
Fraternal Union was perpetually frustrated at its low membership of
seventy or so members.[80] Despite its size its activities were diverse, ranging from the sponsorship of choral societies such as the "Hrvatski Pje-
vački Zbor" to a separate cultural club, "Prosvjetni Klub-Hrvatsko
Bratstvo."[81] Other Croats were absorbed into the Communist Jugoslavenski Prosvjetni Klub (Yugoslav Cultural Society) founded in 1927,
which sponsored plays, orchestral recitals, and picnics for its members.[82]
Yet others were attracted to the more conservative social activities of the
Slovene Catholic organization or to the Serbian-dominated cultural
organization, "Plavi Jadran."[83]

The reasons for such group interaction were social and economic.
First, intermarriage between South Slavic groups was common because
of the extreme scarcity of women, and Croatian men were forced to
marry outside their own ethnic group. Second, economic power resided
with the previous generation of Serbian and Montenegrin pre-war migrants. This group controlled the majority of boardinghouses and restaurants in east Toronto on King Street, and also controlled entry into the
factory jobs to which every new Croatian immigrant aspired.[84] Among
this earlier generation were Pera Borojevic from upper Bosnia, who
owned a music shop and restaurant, and Franjo and Sofia Benk(o) from
Slavonija, who owned a boardinghouse on Mariposa Street.[85] Others
who owned boardinghouses in Toronto by the late twenties were Marijan
Filipovic and Nick Brozović on Osler Street, and Peter Lovrić and Ivan
Lasić on Schumacher Street.[86] By the late twenties, the Momčilović
brothers, well-known goldsmiths in Yugoslavia and the United States for
twenty years, opened a jewellery establishment in Toronto to make the
unique filigree jewellery and ornaments of their homeland.[87]

The unique, intermixed character of the Toronto community is suggested by mutual co-operation in religious rituals and celebrations of the
late twenties and early thirties. Funerals were sometimes the occasion for
common lament by individuals whose family and clan relationships ran
across two or more groups. This phenomenon was apparent in the fatal
injury to Vojin Jokanović of Trebinje in Herzegovina, who was killed by
a train near Milton in 1929.[88] Both the "Plavi Jadran" Serbian organization and the Croatian Fraternal Union offered their condolences and

111

took up the customary collection to cover funeral expenses.[89] The unique position of the Croats of Herzegovina was that they could interact successfully with other South Slavs, in celebration as well as in grief. In the former vein, a native of Ljubuški, A. Mišetić, penned a poem titled "An Expatriated Croatian," on a public parade and celebration of Roman Catholic mass in Toronto. The poem spoke in glowing terms of the public procession through the streets of Toronto by Croats and "brother Macedonians," of the blessing of Croatian flags by a visiting priest, and of the placing of wreaths dedicated to fallen Croatian heroes.[90]

The Hamilton community of Croats, like that of Toronto, grew up in the shade of the more established Serbian pre-war settlement. The Serbs by 1914 had constructed their own church, "Sveti Nikola" (St. Nicholas), and by 1927 had built beside it a large hall to accommodate wider cultural activities.[91] Thus, the several hundred Croats from Primorje and Žumberak who crowded into Hamilton, seeking work in the steel mills or construction work in the nearby Welland Canal project, had relatively few contacts with long-standing citizens of Croatian origin.[92] A recently arrived immigrant intermediary was the boardinghouse owner, Stjepan Tomljenović, who often arranged affidavits from nearby farmers in the Niagara Peninsula that they would hire incoming Croats as agricultural labourers. His boardinghouse on Avondale Avenue operated as a clearing house for employment in canal construction nearby and also as an organizational centre for the Croats, for it was here that the local chapter of the Croatian Fraternal Union, Matija Gubec, was located.[93]

By the late twenties there were probably fifty Croatian families in Hamilton, and the community appeared to take shape very rapidly, no doubt because of the relatively high wages earned by steelworkers.[94] Within a short time these residents had organized a choral society, orchestra, and kolo dance group. Under the leadership of Stjepan Bradica, a new arrival, the local activities of the Croatian Fraternal Union, of which he was president, were tied into the cultural clubs and societies which were later sponsored by the Croatian Peasant Party.[95] It was partly his leadership and partly the spirit of competition with the more established Serbian community which inspired the building in Hamilton of the first Croatian hall in Canada by common subscription and collective effort.[96]

The nearby community in Welland on the Niagara Peninsula began to flourish with the industrial expansion occasioned by the boom of the twenties. Although nearly 1,700 foreign workers had returned to their homelands in the post-war economic crisis in 1919, gradual economic recovery was apparent by 1924.[97] Industrial growth occasioned by the deepening of the Welland Canal caused further growth in such local firms as Page-Hersey Tube, Plymouth Cordage, Empire Cotton Mills, and Canadian Rubber. Many of the new migrants who entered directly into these expanding industries were from the Karlovac hinterland and such villages as Ribnik and Barilović. They usually took up employment with Page-Hersey or Union Carbide, often a year or two after their arrival and after a brief period of apprenticeship in the seasonal industries on the northern Ontario frontier.[98]

The seasonal construction industry also absorbed much unskilled labour and resulted in spin-off settlements of Croats in Chippawa and Port Colborne. In fact, it appeared that many of the agricultural immigrants of 1926-27 made Welland their final destination and were prepared to forfeit their $400 deposit in order to enter lucrative construction work rather than take the $25 a month that farm labour promised.[99] Several workers took seasonal construction work in Welland and environs in 1926 rather than farm labour either in southern Ontario or western Canada. Others, mainly of German-Yugoslav background who had taken up farms in western Manitoba, also left occasionally for Welland to take up farming, industrial work, or a combination of the two.[100] In doing so, they fell into the same occupational mixture and lifestyle characteristic of the first Croatian migrants who had come to the Welland area before 1914.

The Welland community was able to absorb this rapid increase in numbers to some 500 precisely because of the stable pre-war element of leadership and a solid Canadian-born nucleus of sixty Croatian Canadians. The institutions that had been set in place and fallen into disuse during the unstable war years were revived. The Croatian Fraternal Union lodge, "Hrvatski Sinovi" (Sons of Croatia), was reorganized in January, 1924, with some forty members on its rolls.[101] A cultural arm was soon attached to it with an active children's organization and orchestral ensemble that performed at group gatherings. The lodge also set up a building committee to enquire into the prospect of building a cultural home to house their activities.[102] Soon, capital was forthcoming from the more established sectors of the community, from merchants and from boardinghouse owners, to begin the project.

Despite its advantages as an older community, there were still hardships and difficulties. From the American side of the border came accusations of phantom employment agencies in Welland defrauding Croatian-American immigrants who intended to take up jobs in Canada.[103] Internally, the community leaders had to remind their members of their duty to seek work for their fellow countrymen and to assist them in adjusting to their new surroundings in Canada.[104] Practical advice was dispensed to new immigrants that factory jobs were not easily come by and had to be secured through "pull" by a friend or relative. Once gained, such jobs were not to be easily given up, for in the phrase of local workers, "When you lose your job, you have to wait till someone else gets killed to get another one." Counsel was also given to new immigrants about housing, indicating that many homes and lots were available because of the depressed real estate market resulting from workers migrating across the border to the United States. But the newcomers were cautioned against assuming the outstanding mortgage debts attached to these properties, in view of the fact that a worker's maximum salary was only $80 a month.[105]

As might be expected, the bleakest tales to come from the new immigrants were less from such established communities with concerned leaders than from cities in southwestern Ontario. The most pitiful laments on the single migrant's miserable life, without wife and family in an alien land, came from two wandering urban migrants in the western Ontario cities and towns between Hamilton and Windsor just at the beginning of the Great Depression. One from Woodstock appeared in the *Croatian Voice*. It was an endless tale of misery, fraud, deception, and exploitation at the hands of the "burdingbos" in one city after another from Guelph to Windsor.[106] Another, by a canal worker near Port Colborne, was a classic tale of the forlorn husband who has learned of his wife's infidelity in their home village. It offered the traditional solution, "I loved a wanton until I found a better one, and when I found a better one, I lost my passion for her." Great thankfulness was expressed to the new land of Canada, which provided a refuge where a man could "calm his heart and look for another wife."[107]

The border city of Windsor provided the last urban refuge against the problem of economic survival for the new Croatian immigrant. A massive surge in the Canadian automobile industry during the early twenties resulted in the expansion of Ford Motor plants in Windsor and the building of a new six-million dollar plant at Ford City in east Windsor.[108] The further increase of ancillary machine industries such as the nearby Canadian Bridge Company and Canadian Forge and Stamping at Walkerville, in addition to the building of the Hydro Electric railway, created a large industrial complex in the border cities demanding a vastly increased labour force. The subtle combination of circumstances, which ever so slightly shifted the balance in favour of Windsor over Detroit for Croatian immigrants, was that the United States had just begun to impose quotas on its southern European immigrants in 1923-24 and Canada had lifted her restrictions against the former territories of Austria-Hungary in 1923.

These shifts in policy brought the first Croatian immigrants to Windsor in 1923-24. Prior acquaintance with the United States and familial connections across the border were typical of other early Croatian migrants to Windsor. Many came from Gorski Kotar, or the Gospić district in Lika, from villages with a window on the Adriatic Sea. Typical of the chain migrations which brought families were the peregrinations of Andrija Šuper.[109] He came to Detroit in the early twenties, returned to Vaganac in Lika, then came to Windsor in 1923 where he worked as a machinist for Ford Motor Company. In 1924, he paid for the fare of his brother-in-law, Matt Prpich, who came directly to Windsor and eventually worked into a machinist's job with Ford. Gradually, their families were completed, and within two or three years their wives and children were brought out to Canada.[110]

Most of these early immigrants to Windsor, some 200 in total, settled into the eastern section of Windsor known as Ford City, which was within walking distance of the automobile plant. Many bought homes along Drouillard Road and Charles and Cadillac Streets, and soon they and their wives were in the boardinghouse business. In the words of one of these enterprising women, "It was *essential* to keep boarders because women couldn't find much work, and their husbands only made a few dollars."[111] Soon, the indicators of a more permanent community emerged with such services as Croatian-owned restaurants, grills, barbershops, and real estate firms stretched out along Drouillard and Hickory Roads.[112] A mutual benefit society of some fifty members, Lodge 635 of the H.B.Z., "U Slogi je Spas - In Unity There is Salvation," was formed in the mid-twenties with Joseph Raćki [Ratchky] as its first president, and Jure Šaban as his successor.[113] It was later accompanied by a choral society and tamburitza group, and a few Croats also participated in the new Yugoslav athletic club, "Soko" (Falcons), located in Walkerville.[114]

The re-creation of the peasant village in an urban society – as had been done by the Ličani in Windsor, the Žumberčani and Karlovčani in Welland, Toronto, Hamilton, and Schumacher, the Dalmatians, Primorci, and Herzegovci in Port Arthur and Sault Ste. Marie – was a common pattern of ethnic settlement in the North American city. The semi-segregated colonies were essential to economic and social survival, but they were not inward-looking ghettoes isolated from the outside world and dedicated to the preservation of Old World values. Rather, despite their newness and strangeness to their neighbours, they represented a necessary halfway house in the assimilation and integration of the immigrant. The English-speaking Catholic churches and schools, both public and separate, had started their assimilative work upon the women and children. The marketplace and factory had begun an equally effective transformation upon the male work force.

The rapid transformation of language had already begun with the injection of anglicisms into their native language and with the adaptions of personal names. Among the older migrants "ch" or "c" was being substituted for the inflected "č" and "ć"; thus, the example, Raćki was soon transformed into the more phonetic "Ratchky," "Šuper" to simpler "Super," "Canjar" to "Kanjer." Similarly, given names were rapidly simplified to short anglicized versions, Božo to Bob, Andrija to Andrew or Andy, Ivan to John, Valentin to Walter, Šime to Sam, and Mile to Emil or Mike. While the changes were often not as dramatic as those made to American Slavic surnames, as noted by the Slovene author Louis Adamic and the American linguist H.L. Mencken, they were nevertheless a major step in the direction of assimilation.[115]

The new urban immigrants of the twenties had not yet become so assimilated as to adopt the heavily Americanized Croatian slang satirized by Louis Adamic in 1927.[116] The experience of the immigrants to

115

Canada, with perhaps the exception of the Windsor group, was too recent for the melting pot to have done its work. Radios were still too scarce and newspapers too expensive for the urban popular culture of North America to have made its inroads on Old World language in Canada. Literacy was also such a hard-bought and recent victory in the home villages that the immigrants were not yet prepared to yield its valuable lessons. Most would have subscribed to one of the popular folk sayings in their native tongue, "A people without school is a people without a future." They were thus prepared to consign their young children fully and unreservedly to the urban school systems of their adopted country.

THE TWENTIES IN WESTERN CANADA

On the Prairies, there were fewer urban Croats than in central Canada, largely because of the less industrial character of the western region. The choice of town and country over the larger city was not a willing one, however, since many an immigrant abandoned an agricultural job for which he was destined to try his luck in Winnipeg and other larger urban centres. But it also appeared that Winnipeg, Regina, Calgary, Edmonton, and Vancouver were perhaps less open occupationally to Croatian immigrants than to others with more saleable industrial and commercial skills. In Winnipeg the new immigrant met with a chilly reception by immigration officials and city police who deterred him from remaining there for very long.[117] Since Winnipeg also served as a deportation point for those immigrants who were unable to prove their ability to survive in a tight employment market and to remain off the urban welfare rolls, it had a reputation as a city to avoid in the late twenties.[118]

Thus fewer than a hundred Croatians had settled permanently in Winnipeg and its environs by 1930, although it served as a temporary stopping-off point for many navvies, lumberjacks, and miners headed for the northern frontier of Manitoba, perhaps to work in The Pas or on the Hudson Bay Railway. A small number of Croats apparently did settle near the main CPR shops in the town of Transcona to the northeast of Winnipeg. Several had worked there since the First World War on piecework production of rolling stock at thirty-five cents an hour or ten dollars per week. In order to supplement these meagre incomes, others bought small farms or lots to grow vegetables for their growing families.[119] But the Croats were far too few in southeastern Manitoba to resist the pressures of assimilation, and they melted into the more substantial Polish and Ukrainian communities. They thereby assumed a larger and more pluralistic Slavic or eastern European identity characteristic of the Winnipeg hinterland.

In the city of Winnipeg itself, several Croatians were employed in the hotel and boardinghouse trade, serving the considerable immigrant traffic through the north end of the city. Characteristic of these was the Bell

Hotel of North Main, owned and operated by the ex-hotelkeeper of the Yukon, Andrija Miletić, who had come "down south" to north Winnipeg after a sojourn in Austria-Hungary during the war.[120] The north end had also become the permanent home in 1929 of *Hrvatski Glas (Croatian Voice)*. Titled for the first few years of its operation *Kanadski Glas (Canadian Voice)* in order to avoid confusion with a Croatian-American newspaper based in Chicago called *Hrvatski Glasnik*, this publication, the first Croatian newspaper in the British Commonwealth, emanated from King Street. Its first editor, Petar Stanković, was a young Croatian journalist from Zagreb who had been educated in a classical college in Karlovac. A migrant to the United States prior to World War I, he had acquired journalistic experience in the lively and radical Croatian-American pioneer press. As a returned migrant to Zagreb, he was encouraged in the later twenties by the leader of the Croatian Peasant Party to begin a newspaper in Canada to carry the message of Croatian nationalism to Canadian immigrants.[121] In 1928, he was also urged by the CPR's colonization director, who had visited Zagreb, to establish such an information service in Winnipeg to the Croatian immigrants in Canada, informing them about the customs and laws of their new country.[122] Stanković had been discouraged by events in his native land, which saw the harassment and imprisonment of young Croatian radicals and nationalist intellectuals under the political regime of King Alexander. Coincidentally with Stanković's migration to Canada came the assassination of the charismatic Croatian Peasant Party leader and parliamentarian, Stjepan Radić, and later, the murder of the Croatian intellectual, Dr. Milan Šuflaj, a Croatian professor of history, in February, 1931.[123] These events would impart an early and consistent thread to Stanković's criticism of the dictatorship in Yugoslavia and its repressive tactics against the nationalist aspirations of all groups, but particularly the vocal Croats.[124]

Less serious but regular information services provided by the *Voice* were sports, social, and entertainment features, relating the exploits of the Croats to their readership. One story in 1930 concerned the travelling Elias tamburitza orchestra from Racine, Wisconsin, which was touring the West with the Chatauqua educational and entertainment program. As the small Croatian band barnstormed through small prairie towns, Stanković regularly printed the itinerary for his readers. On the sports front, he would occasionally enliven his heavy political columns with interviews featuring Croatian personalities such as the boxer, M. Pavičić from Lovinac, who had acquired a reputation in the small-town fight circuit in western Canada.[125] Other services were the *Voice's* advertisements concerning the whereabouts of itinerant migrants with whom relatives and friends had lost contact. Often, debts could be retrieved or the news of bereavement conveyed in no other way than by a general notice in the language of the immigrants. At times, Stanković acted as an amateur physician dispensing folk nostrums for the treatment of rheumatism and arthritis or whatever other ills his readers confronted him with. Obituaries, marriage notices, and other social events were regularly reported to a readership that grew rapidly to some 5,000 by the early thirties. Its folksy small-town flavour, which included everything from folk humour to home remedies and strongly nationalistic editorials, soon made the *Voice* the most powerful news instrument in Croatian homes from coast to coast.

The newspaper also filled a vital regional role in providing colonization news and land advertisements for the Prairies. Coming as it did from the central nervous system of the grain companies, wheat board, and immigration capital of the West at Winnipeg, the *Voice* carried farm news to both established and prospective farmers on the Prairies. Croatian farmers, mainly from central Saskatchewan, southern Alberta, and the Peace River country submitted regular reports on the state of farming in the West, both the opportunities for acquiring land and the climatic and soil problems that would face prospective farmers. Indeed, the noun "farmer[a]" had itself come to displace "seljak" (peasant), as effectively as the entire New World terminology of plains farming displaced Old World notions of subsistent peasant agriculture. Such units of measure as "bušela," "akera," and "milja" displaced hectares, kilometres, and the more traditional "jutara" (morgen). And new mechanical terms such as "mašina" (machinery), "bander" (binder), "brekanje" (breaking sod), and "grener" (thresher) were introduced to the language since there were few equivalents which could be imported from Croatian peasant agriculture. Thus, the material culture of the Prairies and the grain economy were at least as powerful a force for assimilation as were the paved streets of the eastern Canadian city, and perhaps even more so because of the dispersed nature of Croatian settlement on the Prairies.

It appears that rural communities of Croats were less developed in Manitoba than in other western provinces because of the absence of pre-war migrants. The high capital qualifications for continental families created additional and more permanent barriers to settlement in Manitoba, where only the relatively wealthy German-speaking "Schwabian" farmers from Slavonia and the Banat could come.[126] Often, they settled under the CNR's colonization scheme and enjoyed the sponsorship of the German Catholic Association for settlement in such locations in western Manitoba as Ogilvie, and Dysart in eastern Saskatchewan. But their contribution to the mosaic of Canadian life was largely as German-speaking Canadians rather than Croats, Serbs, or South Slavs. As such they would participate in the wider range of cultural and social benefits accruing from membership in this much larger and more significant cultural minority in western Canada.

It was in central Saskatchewan in the pre-war settlements of Kenaston, Bladworth, and Hanley that the Croats began to melt into the wider mainstream of the Canadian community. In material terms, these fifty farmers had already accumulated some 15,000 acres of land near the three towns and had purchased ten automobiles and an equal number of threshing machines costing $3,000 each by the late twenties.[127] Great pride was also taken in private ownership of homes and farm buildings built on their farms. One settler, Steve Krpan, eloquently phrased the Croatian version of "Home Sweet Home" to the editor of the Croatian Canadian *Voice* in 1930:

Kučica je svakom mila	Home is to everyone dear
Makar ona kakva bila	No matter how humble it might be
Još kad u njoj baka sedi	Moreso with grandma sitting within
I na djela mila gledi	Looking on benignly at the work about her[128]

But he was also careful to point out that it was the communal practice of agriculture, not individual enterprise, which was necessary to successful farming in western Canada. According to him, the communal traditions of the *zadruga* applied well to the pooling of mechanical resources, the common dwelling of sons and their wives with their fathers, and concentration of buildings at the centre of four converging blocs of land. Such co-operation, he maintained, was essential to economic survival on the Prairies.[129]

An interesting facet of the social life of these small prairie communities was the rapid assimilation of entire families, both the Canadian-born children and the first generation of migrants. They were too assimilated by the late twenties to be much affected by the urban cultural institutions and societies spawned by the new wave of migration. The children of the pre-war migrants had already passed through the greatest cultural melting pot of its day, the little white schoolhouse on the prairie.[130] While Croatian was the language of the home, English was firmly and unquestionably the language of the schoolhouse. Parents and grandparents occasionally were challenged enough by their children's schooling and their own illiterate and semi-literate upbringing to improve their own mother tongue or to learn some elementary English. This was the case with at least one of the eldest members of the Kenaston settlement, Katarina Pavelić, who was tutored by a kindly neighbour, Stanley Persick, so that she might correspond with her children as they left home and write letters to her kinfolk in her homeland.[131]

The older Croats also participated actively in the co-operative movement, and the elder Rock Pavelić was an early member of the United Grain Growers, and subsequently of the Saskatchewan Wheat Pool and the Bladworth and Kenaston Co-operative Associations. Imbued by the characteristic spirit of co-operation that swept through rural Saskatchewan, Pavelić also served as a church trustee of St. Andrew's Roman Catholic Church in Kenaston and was one of the first organizers of the Gopherdale school district. He sat on its first school board, which constructed a rural school a more comfortable distance from the family farm. Too late to be of direct benefit to his own family, he would take pride in bringing an education closer to home for the population of the district.[132] As the sons and daughters of the first generation came of working age, some did not quit school but went on to further training at the secondary level. Daughters were also encouraged in school, and aspired to secretarial training and to the teaching and nursing professions.[133]

Domestic life assumed the natural cycle of prairie pioneer folk, and is vividly recollected in the memories of a child of the twenties:

> As the children got older and more settlers arrived, visits to the other houses introduced different ways to prepare foods, and the Blue Ribbon cook book and the Watkins and Rawleigh's spices were soon to be found in every kitchen. Advent and lenten regulations then had three fish days a week for the four and six week period, so before Christmas a hundred pound barrel of frozen fish from the North was ordered through an ad in the *Western Producer*, and heaven help us if Easter was late and a thaw came before the fish was consumed! Dried beans and home-made cheese and eggs were protein producers between meat seasons. Without refrigeration, butchering was done just before the threshing crew arrived in the fall, and again after freezing temperatures arrived to stay. Smoke houses resembling another privy from the outside were used to cure the pork and smoke the home-made sausages. Turkeys and chickens were raised – some marketed in the fall and chickens were canned for summer uses or for unexpected guests. . . . Pioneer life was hard but one was thankful for the gains made each year, for food and the joys a family can bring. Highlights of the year were the school Christmas concerts in which all the pupils participated; the Agricultural fair in Bladworth where Gram often took prizes for her canning, butter and handiwork; the annual Church bazaar and chicken supper; and Homemakers' meetings. As the children grew older, there were weddings, usually after a fall's work was done and never-ending Christenings at all times of the year.[134]

The rituals, games, and amusements of this society had thus assumed a Canadian, but more particularly a plainsfolk, shape. The funeral of a neighbour, whatever his nationality, was the cause for great mourning, since few people more than prairie farmers valued the presence of a helpful "susjed" (neighbour) on the adjacent quarter.[135] On the lighter side, the music most often to be heard among these Saskatchewan Croats was just as likely to be played on the harmonica and fiddle as on the tamburitsa so popular among urban migrants. Great interest was also taken by the men and boys in boxing, and gloves were kept in store for the exuberant physical outbursts demanded by trim bodies hardened by farm labour. Considerable spectator enthusiasm was generated in this sport when the young visiting heavyweight from their own town, Pavičić from

Lovinac, put away the Saskatchewan champion, Kid McCoy, in three rounds in 1929.[136]

The Kenaston-Hanley Croats thus looked confidently on at the outside world on the eve of the Great Depression. Many had already been naturalized. Their children's given names had already begun to take on an Anglo-Saxon flavour, and even some surnames had been substituted, like Thompson for Tomljenović.[137] Some had moved from their farms to the city to make their fortune. Paul Brkić sold out in 1923 and moved to Winnipeg to play the grain futures while his wife worked in a pickle factory. But they, like many who moved off the farm in the roaring twenties, would soon return to the security of the farm and rural community life in the desperate times that followed the crash of 1929.[138] As it did for the central character, Sandor Hunyadi of John Marlyn's novel, *Under the Ribs of Death*, the belief in unparalleled prosperity and progress in the twenties often sacrificed ethnic identity itself.[139]

Elswhere in Saskatchewan, Serbian settlements were more dominant than Croatian both in the eastern urban sector of Regina and in the smaller rural communities such as Shaunavon, Bethune, Wood Mountain, and Weyburn. A dozen or so Croatian farmers, the most notable of whom was Nikola Kasun, still farmed the northland near Leask, and several others were concentrated around the towns of Avonlea and Truax.[140] A far larger and faceless number of migrant farm labourers and navvies worked on the Kenaston and Hanley farms during the summer, then spent their winters in Saskatoon or moved on to work in the northern woods or mines. Sometimes they would drift eastward to The Pas in northern Manitoba and sometimes westward to the Coal Branch region in northern Alberta, in a seasonal cycle of labour that would usually last two or three years until some more permanent work materialized.[141]

A migration chain along the CNR had, in fact, begun to connect firmly the northern Saskatchewan communities to the mining area of Coal Branch in northern Alberta beyond Edmonton. As elsewhere on the frontier, the economic expansion of primary industries was responsible for attracting further settlement to towns such as Brule, Luscar, Mountain Park, Robb, and Mercoal. A typical migrant who pulled along this railway axis was Mike Krypan. He was an Austrian army veteran who came in 1924 to his uncle's farm in Kenaston because he could no longer migrate to the United States. His uncle sponsored him, paid his ticket and travel expenses, and on arrival put him to work at thirty dollars plus room and board. But after the harvest he could no longer afford to pay his wages, so the younger lad headed off for the Coal Branch where wages ran as high as ten dollars a day in the winter season. He joined the Balkan Coal Company where he worked with many of his countrymen, such as John Minerich, Peter Stanich, Mane Marjan, John Štimac, and Alex Šušnar. Some of the latter apparently had been expelled from university back in Yugoslavia for advocating Croatian nationalism. The new arrivals fitted quickly into the small miners' fraternity, a consolation for the loneliness they would experience for the first few years away from their families for whom they were yet unable to afford transportation to North America.[142]

Elsewhere in the Coal Branch the Croats were employed in various seasonal industries, particularly in the Edson and Jasper region where several were employed partly as miners and partly as timber cutters in the summer months.[143] The colourful "Black Frank" Knežević of Lovett was a trapper, and tramped the mountainous region in search of fur pelts and big game until his mysterious disappearance some thirty years later in the Rocky Mountain range.[144] Yet other Croats worked near the town of Luscar on small farms to supplement their uncertain income from the mines. By the late twenties, there were still too few women present in the area to exercise much influence on the seasonal bachelor culture of the mountains. But when women did appear they would lend a distinctive feminine character both to the nature of the radical protest in the dirty thirties, and to the close community life of the Coal Branch district.[145]

In the nearby Peace River region, the Croats had expanded their numbers in the late twenties to an assortment of thirty farm families from Primorje, Lika, Dalmatia, and Bosnia.[146] The lands of the Peace around the town of Rycroft were still advertised to a second generation of homesteaders willing to try the hardships of pioneering. The virtues of its prime agricultural land, which could be had for a ten-dollar filing fee for 160 acres, were lauded by the *Croatian Voice* in Winnipeg. And its extreme northerly location was played down in eyewitness accounts of homesteading in the Peace from Croatian and Slovak farmers in the region.[147] Soon, several migrant workers drifted north from the mines, forests, and even farms of Alberta and Saskatchewan to file for homestead patents. As early as 1926 the local Peace River *Record* noted that eleven Yugoslavs had come to work at McRae's camp at Driftpile and observed that a similar number had come last year and were farming successfully in the High Prairie area.[148] Thus, by 1930 a diverse mix of pre-war and post-war settlers dotted the small farms of the Peace River frontier. The Ličani from Lovinac were there in force – the Krpans, Šeginas, Sariches, Prpiches, and Sekuliches.[149] There were some natives of Primorje at High Prairie – men like Frank Kučan and his father-in-law Andrew Šubat, the latter of whom had farmed unsuc-cessfully in the Calgary area and was now trying his luck on the new frontier.[150]

In southern Alberta, a similar cycle of seasonal work had developed about the sugar-beet fields, factories, and mines of the Lethbridge district. With the expansion of the sugar-beet industry in the prosperous twenties, a greater demand resulted for cheap immigrant labour to work in the fields during the summer months. In the winter, work might be secured at the nearby sugar factory or perhaps at the soft coal mines in Picture Butte or to the west at the Crowsnest Pass. Wages for the backbreaking field work might run an attractive ten dollars per acre with the possibility of further bonuses for high productivity in harvesting the large sugar beets.[151] Such were the prospects that attracted several hundred Croatian immigrants into the southern Alberta towns of Raymond, Wayne, and Taber in the later 1920's. Only the obvious economic benefits enabled them to endure the living accommodations offered to them on the farms – old granaries, chicken coops, and tumble-down shanties. Sometimes at a dozen in a shack of twelve by fourteen feet, they endured the heat and noise of overcrowding at night in addition to the blistering summer heat of day-labour under the blazing prairie sun.

Yet the incentive to work was there, as it obviously was to Peter Boras who left a wife and three sons in the old country in 1928 and would not see them again unless his industry afforded the opportunity for a reunion. Working during the summer in the fields, and in the Knight sugar-beet factory in Raymond and for the CPR during the winter, he accumulated enough within five years to bring his family to Alberta.[152] Lesser men, who had also left to earn enough for a triumphant return to the homeland, soon became locked into the cycle of seasonal labour, gambling, and drinking. Boras himself took an active role in attempting to diminish this sense of rootlessness in spearheading the drive for the first Croatian mutual benefit organization in southern Alberta at Raymond.[153] Other organizations sprang up as well in nearby Wayne and Taber, the latter of which by 1928 had its first "Tamburaški Zbor," and had established a committee to look into the building of a Yugoslav hall to house cultural and social activities.[154]

The temptations of the city were considerable in Alberta in the twenties, and immigrants were drawn to the two largest urban centres, Edmonton and Calgary. For some reason Edmonton attracted a greater number of Serbians, and Calgary more Croats and Slovenes, but mixed populations of South Slavs resulted in both cities.[155] The growing petrochemical industry of Calgary, based on the buoyant Turner Valley boom, attracted approximately fifty Croats who worked on the rigs in the field as well as in the oil refineries of east Calgary.[156] The Croats sensed a strong need to organize among themselves, and by 1928 had a local of the Croatian Fraternal Union of America headed by Nick Badovinac. The traditions of mutual help were strongly in evidence in their contributions to the families of fatally injured workmen, such as Miško Miškulin who died in Calgary in 1929.[157]

An interesting assimilative development within this urban organization was its initial difficulty in attracting members, and the suggestion by one of its members that the lodge conduct its business in English and thereby make an attempt to recruit and involve the younger Croatian Canadians.[158] The Calgary community also appeared in its beginning to take on a broader South Slav and even larger Slavic identity because of its difficulty in attracting members to a cohesive Croatian group.[159] Great delight was taken in a co-operative Slavic concert and festival organized for Christmas of 1929; it was noted that this should be an example for the Croats to follow.[160] Considerable local pride was also taken in the wrestling activities of the "modern Samson" from Lika, Marijan Matijević, who before a local Ukrainian athletic club successfully wrested the championship from the "Russian" champion of Alberta, Alick Lee, for a purse of $1,000 in 1930.[161]

Further west, in British Columbia, the large pre-war community of over 1,000 was decimated by the unpleasant experiences of the war and by emigration to the United States and to the homeland. A large number also succumbed to the Spanish influenza epidemic which swept through western Canada in the fall of 1918.[162] But the new wave of immigration from Yugoslavia after 1924 rapidly replenished the depleted numbers of Croats, so that by 1928 their population had reached 1,500. They were spread nearly evenly at 500 in each of Vancouver, Vancouver Island, and the northern coast and interior. For the most part, the immigrants worked in the seasonal labour economy of British Columbia – in the logging camps, urban construction, highway and railroad construction, and the mines and metals industries of the interior.[163]

The Croats in Vancouver and vicinity were largely involved in the construction of the city's major building projects in the 1920's. They were variously engaged in the digging of the harbours and canal improvements and the erection of the Georgia Hotel and the federal government building. Others were involved in logging activities within reach of Vancouver or in farming on the lower mainland.[164] Some of the larger farms in the lower mainland, owned by Stjepan Čepuran, Mato Vinski, and Josip Špiro, reached a size of 500 to 1,000 acres and were valued at $20,000-$30,000 in the late twenties.[165] New fishermen, principally from the northern and southern Adriatic coastline, were also recruited into the rapidly expanding fishing industry.[166] The continued prominence of the Croats in the hazardous life of the sea was reflected in the continuous disasters which befell the fishing boats. For example, in July of 1928, the *Nippon Current* owned by Lorwin Fisheries exploded and burned up off the Pacific Coast 250 miles from Vancouver, entailing losses of over a quarter of a million dollars. The Croat captain and crew, composed of Jakov Fiamengo, Perić Krušelj, Pavle Vojković, and Stjepan Juho, narrowly escaped with their lives, some of them suffering serious burns that required hospitalization at Port Alice. Fortunately, financial help was forthcoming from the Dalmatian community in Vancouver, and further pleas for help by the Croatian Fraternal Union resulted in some assistance to the injured.[167]

Social leadership within the Vancouver community developed along similar lines to those in Toronto and Montreal. Because of the concentration of at least 500 Serbs in the Vancouver area, there inevitably tended to develop a wider South Slav identity and tone to community politics and social activities. Since capital concentration, mercantile establishments, and boardinghouses were more often in the hands of the Serbs or

Montenegrins, social institutions for the Croats were often absorbed into these. Indicative of this trend were the activities of the local consular representative of the Yugoslav government, Stjepan E. Raymer, who had done much to promote the Yugoslav cause during the First World War in the Vancouver area. Raymer himself was descended from a prominent Zagreb family and had become a typical immigrant community leader, variously involved in real estate, notarial, and journalistic activities directed to serving the larger South Slavic community in Vancouver.[168] Thus, when such issues as the construction of a community hall were raised, it was inevitably a Yugoslav rather than Croatian enterprise.[169] Equally inevitably, such projects necessitated the co-operation with a Serbian element in the leadership and funding and became the objects of hot dispute, despite the representation of Croats on the building committee.[170]

On Vancouver Island, the Croatian communities were more continuously isolated from the upheavals which had shaken and partially dispersed the mainland settlements. The older pre-war settlers at Nanaimo and Ladysmith had come early enough in the 1900's that their families had been clearly shaken by the earlier mine disaster at Extension Mines in 1915.[171] But others, such as the Popovićs, Pojes, Grubačevićs, and Nikšićs, had formed the core of a stable and enduring community of over 300 miners from Žumberak and Lika.[172] By the twenties, they had the traditional defence mechanisms of the Croatian ethnic group well in place and smoothly functioning. Croatian Fraternal Union lodges were operative and active in Nanaimo and Ladysmith, and musical societies already were formed in both. In addition to these tightly knit mining settlements, several Croats were scattered throughout the island as farmers and loggers. The farmers were operating small dairy farms of twenty or so acres near South Wellington and Chemainus, and the loggers and pulp workers were located near Campbell River and Port Alberni.[173]

Up the coast of the B.C. mainland were scattered yet another 400 or so miners from Britannia Beach on the south, to Alice Arm, Stewart, and Anyox in the north. Of these, the largest single concentration was that at Anyox, where there were almost 200 miners from Lika, Herzegovina, and Montenegro in a total work force of 2,500 men. Intermixed with the Serbs, Slovenes, and other European nationalities were over a hundred Croats bearing such names as Marjerić, Žitko, Mikelli (Mikulčić), Kružić, Barić, and Božic.[174] Stjepan Raymer, the Vancouver entrepreneur, travelled to Anyox in the late twenties and noted that most of the young Croats with families had comfortable homes provided by the company, but they were unable to grow vegetable gardens because of the noxious pollutants given off by Granby Consolidated Smelter. He noted also that several of the miners had saved a considerable portion of their daily pay of five dollars and had already accumulated savings of $1,000 or more each.[175]

The interior mining towns and lumber camps of British Columbia were

125

also well-populated by Croatians. The closest in from Vancouver were the base metals mines of Copper Mountain, Princeton, Blackburn, and Allenby near the American border, situated in a countryside reminiscent of the Gorski Kotar region of northwestern Croatia. Approximately one-half of the 300 miners were from Lovinac, Lika, and the other half were from Hrvatsko Primorje. The Lovinčani were so numerous that one of the Croatian Fraternal Union lodges in Princeton was named "Bratstvo Lovinac" (Fraternity of Lovinac), and its executive was dominated by them.[176] The Croats in the Princeton area were so well-organized that their lodge of seventy members approached mine management for some reading matter in their own language to be placed in the miners' library to which they contributed a monthly deduction from their pay cheques. They were firmly told to "mind their own business" but continued in their efforts by approaching the parent body of the Fraternal Union in the United States.[177]

The Croats in nearby Copper Mountain numbered approximately 120 and were generally well off by their terms, living in houses provided by the company. Thus, the wages of $4.50 per day were scrupulously saved, and two or three men had already purchased automobiles as symbols of their newly acquired riches. Among community leaders were Milan Cvetković and Jack Pešut, who assumed executive positions of the local chapter of the Croatian Fraternal Union.[178] The radical miners' movement was also active in Copper Mountain and was promoted during the late twenties and early thirties by such Lovinčani as Joso Šarić. He had originally been a migrant to the United States in 1912 and had been active in the Wobblies, fleeing from town to town before the authorities. Finally he had returned to his homeland in 1920, where he was pursued for his involvement in the radical movement and was finally jailed in 1922. After his release, he returned to Canada in 1925 to work for Granby Consolidated in both Anyox and Copper Mountain, and became heavily involved in the radicalization of the miners as an organizer for the Communist Mine Workers' Union of Canada.[179]

Although smaller, the Croatian colony in Trail, some 200 miles to the east, was more firmly established. It had a larger percentage of pre-war Austrian migrants and married couples and a solid core of more than thirty Canadian-born children. One of the prominent leaders of this small community was "Mike" Butorac, a longstanding resident of Trail and a well-known local merchant and entrepreneur. Indeed, Butorac was one of the earliest immigrants to arrive in the district by virtue of his migration northward from Portland, Oregon, to Rossland in 1895. He had worked for a time in the mines at Trail but in 1908 became a hotelkeeper for the Union Hotel, and later still in the twenties a dealer for Buick automobiles.[180] Because of their long residence in the community, Butorac and other Dalmatian Croats came to be identified by the mine management of the town as conservative Austrians. These were not to be confused, in management terms at least, with the new arrivals

126

from Primorje and Lika who were promoting radical ideas and organization among the mining fraternity.

Further into the Kootenay district, the Croats were often employed as seasonal construction workers in the South Slocan hydroelectric station and related railway construction in that area. Others were engaged in timber work in the Nelson district, some of them having been established in the town for a number of years. One of them was Petar ("Pio") Fuček, a skilful powder monkey who had survived several major construction projects in the B.C. interior dating back to the pre-war years. Like many of the early migrants, Fuček had participated in the radical miners' strikes, including the violent action at Nanaimo in 1912, and had been interned in Ontario during World War I as an enemy alien.[181] Other families, such as those of Ivan and Joso Strižić, Josip Stepančić, Ivan Maras, and Nikola Karuk, formed the core of the South Slav settlement in Nelson and participated actively in the formation of the first Croatian Fraternal Union Lodge in 1930.[182]

Tragic death and injury haunted the early immigrant communities of these interior mining towns, and for this reason the fraternal union lodges and the miners' unions were a necessity. In 1929 and 1930 the list of fatalities among the Croatians alone was lengthy. Two Croats were killed in Copper Mountain in 1929, two more in logging accidents near Vancouver, and a further seventeen in the Princeton mine explosion of 1930.[183] These deaths were persistent, grim reminders that the pall of uncertainty had not yet been lifted from the working life of the immigrant on the British Columbia frontier.

Farther into the interior the Croats had also settled into somewhat safer patterns of agricultural occupation. Several Croats and natives of Bosnia and Herzegovina settled into the Okanagan region, where some had first come as migrant agricultural labourers and as fieldworkers and pickers on the fruit and tobacco farms.[184] Some of these and others purchased small farms in the Okanagan Valley. At Penticton were located several small landholders, several more at Oliver, and another handful at Summerland.[185] And in the distant northern interior, several small farmers located at Smithers and Prince George (Šintić, Jelić, Grgurić, and Mešić).

The woods and minerals industries near Prince George attracted greater numbers of immigrant Croats from Primorje and Lika, in addition to a larger number from Serbia and Montenegro. One of the most prominent members of this pluralistic Slavic community was a Montenegrin, Petar Pavić, who was a local fur and leather merchant. As an early resident of Prince George he had established himself as a leader of the mixed community of 150 South Slavs. Croats who had attained some local notoriety and wealth in real estate were Petar Duralo and Martin Zadjelović. The latter was a Dalmatian from Gruž who had pioneered as an entrepreneur in the Yukon gold rush and had reputedly become one of the wealthiest Croats in Canada by virtue of his real estate holdings in Vancouver and Prince George.[186] Because of their wealth and breadth of interests, such individuals were less interested in the typical first institutions of ethnic self-defence. Instead, by 1930 they had subscribed several hundred dollars for the purchase of a small reading room, where newspapers and books might be read by the immigrants for their self-improvement and intellectual growth.[187]

The more northerly locations in British Columbia thus conformed to the earlier patterns of enterprise on the northern frontier. The towns of Prince George and Prince Rupert contained the customary social ingredients of nineteenth-century migration – Dalmatian and Montenegrin hotelkeepers and a sprinkling of miners from Lika and fishermen from the Adriatic Coast. Duralo and Zadjelović of Prince George had their counterparts in Prince Rupert, like the merchant Nikola Gjurgević of Boka Kotorska. Precisely the same social mixture was apparent in small Yukon communities like Dawson and China City, where the Croats were either hotelkeepers, restaurateurs, or merchants, or, lower down the scale, miners who drifted about the northland.[188] A typical but tragic case of the latter was a seasonal migrant miner named Ivan Butković from Gospić in Lika. Previously, he had worked in the Copper Mountain mines of southern B.C. from 1923-28 until he had accumulated enough capital to return home to Lika to claim his wife and family. They would not return with him, and he drifted back to Canada and to Dawson, where his health was broken by a fall through the winter ice with his sled and dogs. He soon died, after a lung operation in a Vancouver hospital.[189]

The Croatians had come a long distance in the brief half-decade from 1925 to 1930. Their numbers had multiplied several fold to over 10,000, and their settlements now approached 200 in number. They had tasted the fruits of prosperity, both in human and material terms. The rapid expansion of their families was clearly visible in the soaring birth rate, and their material prosperity was visible in the numbers of homes, automobiles, and consumer goods owned by the new immigrants. The optimism of the roaring twenties had indeed been infectious for the Croats as it was for native Canadians.

The new immigrants from Yugoslavia and the pre-war Austrian generation united in this honeymoon of rising expectations. It appeared as if the golden door of opportunity had been opened to the Canadian promised land, just as its American counterpart had been slammed shut. Both the new and the older immigrants experienced an advance in their fortunes in the twenties, the old because they and their children had shed the bitter memories of wartime persecution as aliens, and the new because they had escaped the tentacles of rural poverty in the developing dictatorship of King Alexander's Yugoslavia. The promise of a better life seemed as capable of realization in Canada as it had formerly been in the United States. To be sure, some yearned to be closer to their relatives in

America and would take the first opportunity to be with them if the opportunity to re-emigrate presented itself. But the conviction was growing among many new immigrants that they had escaped by the skin of their teeth, and that was enough to be thankful for.

There was also much to be anxious about as the decade closed. The stock market crash of 1929, the tumbling mining stocks of the Toronto exchange, and the plummet of the grain futures on the Winnipeg exchange all indicated trouble on a clouded economic horizon. Many of the newly arrived immigrants also had gambled heavily on their own future. Wives and families in Yugoslavia sustained by remittances and the hopes of reuniting with their spouses would now have to wait until more prosperous times returned. Others whose nostalgia led them to hope for one last visit to their homeland had now to resign themselves to never seeing their loved ones again. And some, particularly the last single male arrivals in 1929, knew by their empty pockets that they had gambled and lost as the door of opportunity closed with the Great Depression.

NOTES

1. *Kanadski Glas*, 31 March 1932.
2. See James H. Gray, *The Roar of the Twenties* (Toronto: Macmillan, 1975); Susan M. Trofimenkoff, *The Twenties in Western Canada* (Ottawa: National Museum of Man, 1972).
3. *Report of the Royal Commission on Bilingualism and Biculturalism*, Book IV (Ottawa, 1970), p. 25.
4. Prpic, *The Croatian Immigrants in America*, p. 253.
5. H.V. Nelles, *The Politics of Development: Forests, Mines and Hydroelectric Power in Ontario 1849-1941* (Toronto: Macmillan, 1975), ch. 10.
6. *Canadian Annual Review*, 1924-25, p. 198.
7. *Ibid.*, 1923, pp. 351-63.
8. *Ibid.*, 1926, pp. 186-7.
9. PAC, RG 76, vol. 263, ff. 216, 882. Joint Agreement Between C.N.R. and C.P.R. and Immigration Department; Memorandum by Robert Forke, 18 January 1927, re: Railways' Agreement.
10. *Canadian Annual Review*, 1926-27, p. 187.
11. Robert England, "Ethnic Settlers in Western Canada: Reminiscences of a Pioneer," *Canadian Ethnic Studies*, VIII, 2 (1976), p. 24.
12. PAC, RG 76, vol. 623, ff. 938, 332, pt. 3. F. Baumgartner [*sic*] to Robert England, Zagreb, 22 July 1927, Re: Macedonians and Dalmatians; F. Baumgartner, "Central European Immigration," *Queen's Quarterly* (Winter, 1930), pp. 186-8. See also, PAC, RG 76, vol. 631, ff. 963866, A.V. Seferovitch, Consul-General for the Kingdom of the Serbs, Croats and Slovenes in Canada, to W.J. Egan, Deputy-Minister of Immigration and Colonization, Montreal, 12 January 1927.

13. PAC, RG 76, vol. 81, ff. 8051, John H. Clark to the Commissioner of Immigration, W.C. Blair, Montreal, 18 October 1921.
14. *Ibid.*, Commissioner of Immigration to Immigration Inspector Gosmer, Prescott, Ontario, 31 August 1923.
15. *Ibid.*, Assistant-Deputy Minister to Captain A.V. Seferovitch, Ottawa, 11 July 1924.
16. *Ibid.*, "O" Division, Western District Report Re: Smuggling of Aliens from Ontario to the United States, Toronto, 26 April 1926, contained in Cortland Starnes, Commissioner of the R.C.M.P., to Assistant-Deputy Minister of Immigration, Ottawa, 29 April 1926.
17. *Zajedničar*, 20 July 1927.
18. See Ian H. Clarke, "Public Provisions for the Mentally Ill in Alberta, 1907-36," Master's thesis, University of Calgary, 1974, ch. 3.
19. PAC, RG 76, vol. 145, ff. 342744, J. Bruce Walker, Director, European Immigration, to W.J. Egan, Deputy-Minister of Colonization and Immigration, London, 12 November 1926.
20. *Ibid.*, vol. 263, ff. 216882, pt. 3, J.A. Mitchell to J. Bruce Walker, Antwerp, Belgium, 23 November 1926.
21. *Ibid.*, J. Bruce Walker to W.J. Egan, London, 21 December 1926.
22. *Ibid.*, J.A. Mitchell to J.B. Walker, Ottawa, 17 March 1926.
23. *Ibid.*, D.J. Footman, British Vice-Consul, Skoplje to J.B. Walker, 21 December 1926. See also *ibid.*, F.C. Black to Col. Dennis, 8 June 1927; RG 26 (External Affairs), vol. 189, ff. Colonial Office 21/17, A. Monck Mason, British Vice-Consul, Skoplje, 25 February 1924.
24. *Ibid.*, W.S. Woods to Major John Barnett, Calgary, 30 November 1926.
25. *Ibid.*, A.L. Jolliffe, Comm. of Immigration to Col. J.S. Dennis, Ottawa, 7 December 1926; Asst. Comm. J.N.E. Macalister to A.L. Jolliffe, 17 December 1926.
26. *Ibid.*, John S. Barnett to W.J. Egan, Ottawa, 4 January 1927.
27. *Ibid.*, A.L. Jolliffe to Robert Forke, Re: Railways' Agreement, 17 January 1927.
28. *Ibid.*, F.C. Blair, Assistant-Deputy Minister, File memo, 13 May 1926.
29. *Ibid.*, Division Commissioner Memorandum to all Immigration Inspectors, 8 June 1927.
30. *Ibid.*, vol. 623, ff. 938332, pt. 3, E.C. Moquin to J.C. Fraser, Montreal, 21 July 1927.
31. *Ibid.*, F.C. Baumbartner [*sic*] to Robert England, Zagreb, 22 July 1927.
32. *Ibid.*, W.J. Black to F.C. Blair, Acting Deputy-Minister, Montreal, 6 September 1927.
33. *Ibid.*, O.D. Skelton for the Secretary of State for External Affairs to Lt. Col. L.S. Amery, Ottawa, 15 November 1927.
34. *Ibid.*, Dr. Fedor Aranički, "To All Those Who Intend to Emigrate to Canada: Rates of Wages Paid on Farms." Issued by the Board of Emigration of the Kingdom of Serbs, Croats and Slovenes, No. 3592, 1928.
35. A.B. Grado, *Migraciona Enciklopedija, Kanada* (Zagreb, 1930); [M.

Bartulica], *Iseljenička Konferencija u Splitu* (Zagreb, 1929); M. Bartulica, *Iseljenička Politika* (Zagreb, 1929), Pamphlets contained in University of Minnesota Immigration History Research Centre.

36. Grado, *Migraciona Enciklopedija*, 3: PAC, RG 76, ff. 938332, *Quarterly Review of Yugoslav Migrations*, IV, 1 (January-March, 1930); Dr. F. Aranički, Annual Returns Reported to Canada Dept. of Immigration Komesarijat.

37. PAC, RG 76, vol. 264, ff. 216882, parts 8 & 10, 1928. Dr. Fedor Aranički to W.J. Egan, Deputy-Minister, Immigration, Zagreb, 14 March 1928, and to Robert Forke, Minister of Immigration, Zagreb, 6 June 1929.

38. *Canadian Annual Review*, 1928-29, pp. 229-60.

39. PAC, RG 76, vol. 253, ff. 193745 pt. 1, "Movements of Continental Families"; RG 76, vol. 254, ff. 193745, pt. 6 "Continental Family Settlement – Western Canada – 1928."

40. *Ibid.*, vol. 255, ff. 194628; Glenbow Archives, CPR Colonization Papers, Box 82, ff. 659-60.

41. PAC, RG 76, vol. 253, ff. 193745, part II, 1926-27.

42. *Census of Canada*, 1931 (Ottawa, 1942), vol. XIII, Monographs, "Racial Origins and Nativity of the Canadian People." p. 594.

43. *Ibid.*, p. 563.

44. Grado, *Migraciona Enciklopedija*, pp. 198-202.

45. *Census of Canada*, 1931, vol. XIII, pp. 522-3.

46. *Ibid.*, vol. 1, pp. 456-514; vol. II, pp. 494-500.

47. See D. MacGillivray, "Industrial Unrest in Cape Breton, 1919-25," Master's thesis, University of New Brunswick, 1971.

48. *Zajedničar*, 25 July 1973.

49. *Ibid.*, 28 May 1975; *Kanadski Glas* 18 August 1930.

50. Interview, M. Matijčevich with George Kokich, December, 1974.

51. *Zajedničar*, 17 December 1930.

52. *Glas Kanade* (Toronto), 28 October 1937: "Istorija Jugoslavenske Kolonije u Montrealu."

53. See Leslie Roberts, *Noranda* (Toronto: Clarke Irwin, 1956).

54. *Zajedničar*, 5 May 1926 (Ilija Jukić). See also *ibid.*, 13 June 1973 (Joksan Prpić), 14 August 1928; 20 February, 15 May 1929. *Kanadski Glas*, 31 March 1932. *Jedinstvo*, 2 May 1952 [Markotić].

55. *Kanadski Glas*, 22 December 1932.

56. *Ibid.*, 20 November 1930.

57. *Zajedničar*, 8 August 1923.

58. Grado, *Migraciona Enciklopedija*, pp. 228-30.

59. *Kanadski Glas*, 29 July 1929.

60. *Ibid.*, 6 April 1929. *Spomenica na Dvadeset Godina Hrvatskih Seljačkih Organizacija u Kanadi* (Winnipeg, 1952), pp. 146-47.

61. *Zajedničar*, 10 March 1926; 10 April 1926; 27 April 1927; 23 June 1927.

62. *Ibid.*, 22 February 1928.

63. Porcupine *Advance*, 16 February 1928.

64. See, e.g., Mile Badovinčić and Anka Bilić, *Hrvatski Glas*, 8 February 1934.

65. Porcupine *Advance*, 3 July, 6 November 1930.
66. *Ibid.*, 24 March 1927.
67. *Ibid.*, 19 May, 23 June, 8 September 1927.
68. *Ibid.*, 4, 11 November 1926.
69. *Ibid.*, 1 July 1927.
70. *Kanadski Glas*, 11 August 1920.
71. Interviews, Milan Glibota, Steve Sarich, Mate Yakusović, Mrs. Matija Sanko, Mrs. Filomena Kokich, A. Marinovich with George Kokich, Sault Ste. Marie, December, 1974.
72. *Zajedničar*, 26 December 1928.
73. *Ibid.*, 12 October 1927.
74. *Kanadski Glas*, 11 November 1929: "Kod Braće u P.A."
75. Interview, Zora Domineck with George Kokich, Thunder Bay, December, 1974.
76. See obit., Marija Belobrajdić, *Zajedničar*, 16 January 1974.
77. *Kanadski Glas*, 28 October 1929: "Pomoč Obitelj pok Vidasa."
78. *Ibid.*, 20 September 1929: "Dopisi iz Port Arthura."
79. For a general discussion of spatial segregation among immigrants, see David Ward, *Cities and Immigrants* (New York: Oxford University Press, 1971), pp. 105-23.
80. *Zajedničar*, 27 June 1927: "Naši u Torontu."
81. Grado, *Migraciona Enciklopedija*, pp. 229-31.
82. *Kanadski Glas*, 3 June 1929.
83. *Glas Kanade*, 21, 28 April 1938: "Istorija Jugoslavenske Kolonije u Torontu."
84. *Ibid.*, 7 April 1938.
85. *Ibid.*, 13 January 1938.
86. Grado, *Migraciona Enciklopedija*, pp. 205-6.
87. *Kanadski Glas*, 10 June 1929.
88. *Ibid.*, 28 October 1929.
89. *Zajedničar*, 2 March, 2 November 1927.
90. *Kanadski Glas*, 25 February 1932: "Pjesma Iseljenog Hrvata."
91. Grado, *Migraciona Enciklopedija*, p. 206.
92. *Jedinstvo*, 5 January 1960. (August Rozić, obituary.)
93. Grado, *Enciklopedija*, p. 206.
94. See obit. Louis Škuranec, *Zajedničar*, 10 April 1974; Ivan Brkanac, *Hrvatski Glas*, 21 February 1935.
95. *Spomenica . . . U Kanadi*, p. 119. *Zajedničar*, 29 October 1930.
96. *Kanadski Glas*, 20 October 1930.
97. Sayles, *Welland Workers Make History*, p. 191.
98. See, e.g., *Zajedničar*, I. Barković and L. Franković obituaries, 31 December 1974, 1 September 1976.
99. PAC, RG 76, vol. 263, ff. 216882, pt. 3. Memo of J.A. Mitchell, Antwerp, Belgium, 17 March 1926.
100. *Ibid.*, vol. 253, ff. 193745, pt. II, "Movement of Continental Families."

101. *Zajedničar*, 16 January 1924.
102. *Ibid.*, 25 February 1925.
103. *Ibid.*, 5 October 1927. See also PAC, RG 76, vol. 264, ff. 216882, part 8, 1928. F. Aranički to W.J. Egan, Zagreb, 14 March 1928.
104. *Zajedničar*, 18 May 1927.
105. *Ibid.*, 23 February 1927; "Stevo Škvorc iz Wellanda."
106. See *Kanadski Glas*, 18 August 1930: "Slike iz Prošlosti"; 25 August 1930: "Velika Besposlica."
107. *Ibid.*, 5 May 1930.
108. *Canadian Annual Review*, 1922-23, pp. 513.
109. Interview, Andrija Šuper with George Kokich, Windsor, December, 1974. Other Windsor interviewees were Joseph Ratchky and Mile Surlović.
110. *Zajedničar*, 11 August 1976.
111. Interview, Mrs. J. Bunčić with George Kokich, Windsor, December, 1974.
112. Grado, *Enciklopedija*, p. 208.
113. *Zajedničar*, 22 December 1926.
114. Grado, *Enciklopedija*, p. 231. See also interview, A. Graf with George Kokich, Sudbury, December, 1975. Graf had attended a *gymnasia* in Yugoslavia and was active in early cultural and sporting activities in Windsor.
115. H.L. Mencken, *The American Language: An Inquiry into the Development of English in the United States* (New York: Knopf, 1937).
116. Louis Adamic, "The Yugoslav Speech in America," *American Mercury* (November, 1927), cited in *ibid.*, pp. 667-9.
    See *Zajedničar*, 31 August, 27 July 1927: Mark Vinski on "Work and School" and "Croatian Halls." *Ibid.*, 27 November 1926: "Slot Mašine i Munšajn."
117. Stjepan Bradica memoir in *Spomenica . . . u Kanadi*, pp. 34-42; translation, *Canadian Ethnic Studies*, VIII, 2 (1976), pp. 99-102.
118. *Kanadski Glas*, 26 August, 9 September 1929.
119. See M. Opalić obituary, *Jedinstvo*, 2 May 1958. Grado, *Enciklopedija*, p. 210, ref. to M. Vuković and J. Tomac. See also obituary, Andrija Simon, *Kanadski Glas*, 24 November 1936.
120. Letter to author from A. Miletić, Hamilton, 14 April 1976.
121. P. Stankovic memoir in *Spomenica . . . u Kanadi*, p. 80.
122. P. Stankovic manuscript, provided to author, August, 1975.
123. See Charles A. Beard, "Autobiography of Stephen Raditch," *Current History*, 28 October 1928. Pamphlet reprint by *Croatian Voice*, 1976.
124. See opening editorials, *Kanadski Glas*, 18 March 1929.
125. *Ibid.*, April, 1929, *passim*.
126. PAC, RG 76, vol. 253, ff. 193745, pt. II. "Movement of Continental Families"; also *ibid.*, vol. 241, ff. 148405, pt. II, Association of German Canadian Catholics (V.D.C.K.), 1926-27.
127. K. Beckie, memoir provided to author, Calgary, January, 1975.

128. *Kanadski Glas*, 17 March 1930.
129. *Ibid.*, 29 April 1930.
130. B. Broadfoot, *The Pioneer Years, 1895-1914: Memories of Settlers Who Opened The West* (Toronto: Doubleday, 1976), pp. 283-304.
131. Mrs. Kae Smiley, memoir to author, Prince Albert, 1975.
132. *Ibid.*
133. S. Sarich, interview questionnaire, Davidson, Saskatchewan, 1976.
134. Mrs. K. Smiley, memoir.
135. Frank Sarić, letter to editor, *Kanadski Glas*, 11 August 1930.
136. *Ibid.*, 8 April 1929.
137. Mrs. K. Smiley, memoir to author, 1975.
138. K.N. Beckie, memoir to author, January, 1975.
139. See John Marlyn, *Under the Ribs of Death* (Toronto: McClelland and Stewart, 1957).
140. Grado, *Enciklopedija*, p. 212.
141. Interview, M. Železnjak with George Kokich, Sudbury, December, 1974.
142. M. Krypan, memoir in Toni Ross, *O! The Coal Branch* (Edmonton, 1974), pp. 284-9.
143. Grado, *Enciklopedija*, p. 215.
144. Toni Ross, *O! The Coal Branch*, pp. 168-70.
145. *Ibid.*, pp. 287, 308-15.
146. *Kanadski Glas*, 24 March 1930.
147. See "Mi Kanadske Farme," *ibid.*, 20 January, 10, 24 March 1930.
148. *Peace River Record*, 25 March 1926.
149. J. Sekulich, response to interview questionnaire, 24 October 1975; *Kanadski Glas*, 26 August 1929.
150. Interview, M. Rasporich with author, 26 October, 1975.
151. *Kanadski Glas*, 2 December 1929.
152. Walter V. Boras, "Era of European Immigration," in *Coyote Flats, Historical Review, 1905-65* (Lethbridge: So. Printing Co., 1967), pp. 230-5.
153. See Howard Palmer, *Land of the Second Chance* (Lethbridge Herald, 1972), pp. 313-14.
154. Grado, *Enciklopedija*, p. 232.
155. *Ibid.*, p. 213.
156. *Kanadski Glas*, 3 June 1929.
157. *Ibid.*, 26 August, 4 November 1929.
158. *Zajedničar*, 20 November 1928.
159. *Kanadski Glas*, 24 February, 14 April, 22 July 1929.
160. *Ibid.*, 2 December 1929.
161. *Ibid.*, 13 October 1930.
162. Joso Nikšić, "Hrvati u 100 god. B.C.," in *Hrvatski Glas Kalendar*, XXIX (1959), p. 98.
163. Grado, *Enciklopedija*, pp. 200-1.
164. Nikšić, "Hrvati u 100 god. B.C.," p. 100.

165. *Kanadski Glas*, 22 July 1929.
166. See obituaries of Baldigaria, Šulina, Marinovich, and Antić in: *The Fisherman*, 5 July 1949, 11 May 1950; *Zajedničar*, 30 January 1929; *Jedinstvo*, 18 April 1958; *Novosti*, 6 May 1944.
167. *Zajedničar*, August, 1928.
168. *Kanadski Glas*, 16 June 1930: "Naši U Kanadi." See also PAC, RG 76, vol. 264, ff. 216882, re. "Jugo-Slavia Farm Labourers," in Chilliwack, B.C.
169. *Zajedničar*, 20 June, 19 September, 1928.
170. *Kanadski Glas*, 31 March, 12 May, 16 June 1930.
171. See chapter 3, ff. 7.
172. *Zajedničar*, 8 January 1930: "Pismo iz Kanade."
173. Grado, *Migraciona Enciklopedija*, pp. 216-19.
174. *Zajedničar*, 8 January 1930: "Pismo iz Kanade." *Hrvatski Iseljenik* (Zagreb), br. 3/40, 12.3.1940 in *Zavod za Migracije i Narodnosti Kanade*. 138. II 142. c. British Columbia, 1928-30.
175. *Zajedničar*, 14 January 1930.
176. *Ibid.*, 15 May, 14 September 1926.
177. *Hrvatski Iseljenik*, 29 December 1927, 16 March 1938, "Pisma iz Vancouver, B.C., St. Raymer," in *Zavod Za Migracije i Narodnosti*, Zagreb, 138, II. 142, c. British Columbia, 1928-30.
178. *Zajedničar*, 3 May 1927.
179. *Novosti*, 20 February 1947.
180. *Zajedničar*, 17 November 1926.
181. *Hrvatski Glasnik*, 29 December 1927. Also *Novosti*, 19 March 1946.
182. *Zajedničar*, 24 December 1930.
183. *Kanadski Glas*, 2 December 1929, 14 September 1930.
184. Glenbow Archives, CPR Colonization Papers, Box 82, ff. 649-50.
185. Nikšić, "Hrvati u 100 god. B.C.," p. 100.
186. Grado, *Migraciona Enciklopedija*, p. 191.
187. *Zajedničar*, 15 January 1930.
188. Grado, *Migraciona Enciklopedija*, p. 220.
189. *Zajedničar*, 9 October 1929. See also *ibid.*, 21 November 1928; PAC, RG 76, vol. 254, ff. 193745, pt. 5. memorandum, 22 March 1929.

SIX

The Depression: Two Cultures

In July of 1930, a drilling barge loaded with dynamite exploded while improving the St. Lawrence canals near Brockville, Ontario.[1] Aboard the ill-fated craft were a dozen men from the single village of Hreljin, Primorje, located in northwestern Croatia. Most of the young men had gone to school together and were working together in the customary work gang common to immigrant labourers. Their traditional means of economic self-defence had thus cruelly backfired into one of the worst industrial accidents to befall the Croatians in Canada. Scarcely a month later, eight more Croats were killed in a coal mine explosion at the Coalmont Collieries near Princeton, British Columbia, which claimed over forty lives.[2] Once again, the close-knit nature of Croatian work gangs, and in this case, Montenegrins and Serbians as well, was to result in disastrous consequences.

These two tragic accidents were also related to a larger, more universal disaster of the 1930's – the Great Depression. For what the depression created in Canada, particularly western Canada, was a society composed of haves and have nots. A vast army of unemployed men, over one million in number, came to constitute a society of dispossessed within the larger Canadian society.[3] The essential difference between the itinerant migrant of the twenties and his counterpart in the thirties was that the former was driven by positive choices between varieties of work and wage differentials, while the latter was driven by negative choices between unemployment and relief, and between subsistence wages and no wages at all. And while the migrant labourer of the twenties could occasionally choose to ride in third-class passenger cars, the immigrant hobo of the thirties could choose only between the inside or the outside of a boxcar, and often the underside, on the rods.

For immigrants of fixed addresses life was not luxurious during the depression. Hardships were suffered by the working poor in the cities, by the poor farmers on the Prairies, and by the miners and industrial workers on a short work week. Their plight has been grimly portrayed in literary works which describe the worry and despair of the thirties, of cramped and overcrowded rooms, of pinching hunger and cold in winter. Thus, any one of Hugh Garner's *Cabbagetown*, Gabrielle Roy's *Tin Flute*, or John Marlyn's *Under the Ribs of Death* might be taken to describe the human toll the depression wrought upon urban families. Their problems were, however, of a different order than those of the single migrant worker, who had but his own miseries to consider and not those of a family.

Protest and revolt against the economic conditions of the thirties were more likely to be radical, militant, and violent from those on the margin of society, on the mining and forest frontier, than from those in the cities. The risks of deportation and possible injury or imprisonment were worth taking for men without a country and without a job or even the prospect of one. But those immigrants who had already made a new start in Canada toward a better life had made an essential commitment upon which they knew they could never go back. Thus the depression created an ever increasing rift among the new Croatian immigrants in Canada, between those desperate single men with nothing to lose and those poor immigrant families with apparently everything to lose. The difference was largely in their perceptions of the grim realities about them, but these were nonetheless different enough to constitute two immigrant cultures with competing systems of belief, identity, and behaviour.

FRONTIER MIGRANTS AND MARGINAL MEN, 1930-35

Leaving aside for a moment the settled communities of immigrants, one is left with a residual culture of marginal men. While it is difficult to estimate its size accurately, a core group of several hundred itinerant labourers in the mid-twenties had expanded to nearly 25,000 by the early thirties. How it arrived and how it moved and survived is largely a mystery enshrouded by the folk memories of the depression years. By its very nature, it was a nomadic masculine culture on the move, from construction and work camps to single men's relief projects, and therefore it remains elusive. Some record of its existence does remain in the oral recollections of survivors of that era, and occasionally in the papers of Frontier College, whose peripatetic schoolhouses on wheels were organized during the thirties by Principal Edmund Bradwin.[4]

It appears from these contemporary accounts that Croatians counted for the vast majority of the single male workers who were entered as Yugoslavs by their instructors.[5] The Yugoslavs and Croats numbered from 10 to 20 per cent of the camp population. Occasionally, the concentrations were much higher, as indicated by a young Dr. Benjamin Spock, who went as a student from Yale University to join a railway extra gang in northern Ontario during the late twenties. He was confronted by a track crew which was almost entirely Croatian and which had little inclination to learn English from its beleaguered teacher.[6] Reports by the

Croats themselves often indicate that their absolute numbers ran very high, and one oral account places their number at 1,000 out of 1,400 workers on a highway project near Smiths Falls in the early thirties.

The Croat migrant labourers were highly mobile and organized themselves into work gangs, which suddenly would pull out of camp to take employment on another project. Very often such informal work parties were organized in quasi-military fashion under a natural leader, often one who could speak English with some fluency and who would secure work for an entire gang of otherwise inarticulate labourers.[7] They tended to be drawn from the same village, town, or region in their homeland, in the same way that the Irish railway navvies of the nineteenth century banded together for self-protection.[8] Their almost military discipline is perhaps attributable to the fact that several of the older migrant labourers were veterans of World War I. One instructor observed in this regard during the mid-twenties that a western track crew in Saskatchewan was "all in the Austrian army and wounded in the war."[9]

The crucial determinants in decisions to move on were usually the declining prospects of work and wages as the depression began to settle in. Wages which had been as high as six or seven dollars a day for construction workers, navvies, and lumberjacks in the late 1920's dropped rapidly with the decline in industrial activity during the early thirties. By 1932, if work was available at all, the choice would often be between the federal relief camps established by the Bennett administration, which paid twenty cents per day or five dollars per month, or the more limited private sector where contract work netted the labourer thirty-five or forty cents per hour minus board, or $1.50 per diem.[10]

For Croats in the relief camps, conditions were often more severe than in the lumber and mining camps of the private sector. One critic lamented that, "What was formerly a period of boredom and loneliness which only its briefness made sufferable has now become a more or less permanent state. No amount of recreational or educational facilities, radio or material comforts can take the place of wholesome female companionship in the life of a man." While the same observer and indeed other oral recollections of the depression commented upon the low incidence of "perversion" in the camps there was also evident "a decadence of ambition and intellect, and excessive drunkenness where alcohol was obtainable. . . . Poker and other forms of gambling flourish to pass away the time that seems to the men to be valueless anyway."[11]

As a rule, the incapacity of the Croats in the English language forced them to band together and to delegate one of their number as a spokesman. He would then act as a go-between or intermediary in language classes, where one instructor observed that all immigrant groups of one nationality would sit together and the first to understand would translate for his compatriots. They would then nod in concert and sonorously respond in unison, "We understand."[12] The intermediary would also act as employment agent, rental agent, and amateur lawyer, if necessary, for the group as a whole. One such group leader or "gospodar" (boss) related in reminiscing about his experience on railway gangs in northern Ontario that he was called upon to provide such service for his friends in the late twenties after they had proceeded to a work contract in Winnipeg. First he secured funds from relatives in the United States, then purchased rail tickets to Port Arthur, where he had to secure lodgings for his friends. Next he secured extra-gang work at Armstrong for them at the local employment office. This then began a string of favours on the job, including defending them verbally against racist insults in the cook shack and appealing for their severance pay upon their sudden leaving of that job. It was not until Toronto that the group finally separated several months later, and the more able among them sought work in the factories of the Toronto-Hamilton area.[13]

A rather typical odyssey for a Croatian day-labourer in the early thirties was that of an enterprising young man, Božo Nizich, who emerged as the leader of construction gang labour by the mid-thirties.[14] Before the depression he had worked in isolated railway construction camps in British Columbia, Alberta, and Manitoba. After 1930, he moved eastward in search of work, to Nova Scotia (New Glasgow and Antigonish), New Brunswick (Moncton), and Quebec (Laval and Montreal), and then to northern Ontario (James Bay, Cochrane, and Timmins). After a brief sojourn at a power project at Masson, Quebec, he gravitated to more lucrative Ontario highways projects in 1932. Interim work was provided by the federal air-base construction at Trenton in 1933, and for the next fifteen months he was able to earn very little but alternatively occupied himself with learning English at the Frontier College facility.[15] Then, with little notice, he and several compatriots from his native city of Mostar in Herzegovina departed from a new highways project in the Muskoka district. It was probably this group that another Frontier College instructor at Bracebridge commented upon in 1934: "On arrival I was assigned to this hut and have seven Croatians as roommates. They are very fine bright fellows anxious to improve their English."[16]

This comment points up the apparent willingness of the highly mobile immigrants to assimilate to the host society, at least in the learning of the English language and in applications for citizenship.[17] The numbers of Croats and other Yugoslavs who took an active interest in the English-language instruction offered by Frontier College were generally above average, according to instructors' accounts. Many were mature men in their thirties, and many were married with wives and children in the old country. Often, one of the Croats would emerge as a "brilliant" or "star" pupil and was consequently asked to inscribe his comments in the teacher's ledger either in his native or adopted language.

In general, these comments reveal an eager predisposition to learn English as *the* language of Canada and North America, and they also

139

reveal a considerable deference to their mentors. One of the comments is particularly revealing: *Kao dobar Hrvat, ljubim Hrvatsku, poštivam Canadu, a osobito se interesiram za Engleski jezik kao svjetski, jer isti mi je potrebam u mojoj budućnosti."* (Like a good Croatian, I love Croatia and I respect Canada, and am particularly interested in the English language as a language, because the same is necessary to me in my future.) One Charlie Majhanovich, a naturalized Canadian, wrote quietly but exultantly in his newly acquired language, "I am glad to have learned the language of my new country." Yet others were deeply appreciative of the efforts made by the College's instructors, even if the results were not always perfect, as in the case of Tony Susich, who professed, "I like this teacher. He is greatly good." Another Croat, John Perich, who worked on road construction north of Port Arthur, fervently proclaimed, "With my teacher's help, I have learned more English in five months than I have in six years without help."[18]

The perspective of assimilation and the acculturative process from the single immigrant's standpoint is more difficult to ascertain. Some immigrants on the frontier were of course never exposed to Frontier College nor to formal schooling of any kind. They learned the English language mainly through contact with their fellow workers of other nationalities, and also through reading daily newspapers that were passed from hand to hand in the frontier work camps. Indeed, it seems from the high level of political consciousness among the Croats that they must have had a great deal of exposure to an active ethnic press as well as to Canadian dailies.[19] This certainly appears to have been the case in at least one of the northern Ontario road camps serviced by the College, for the instructor commented, "We had: 'The Toronto Daily Star' – 'The Montreal Star' – 'Port Arthur News Chronicle' – 'Fort William Daily Times Journal'– 'Winnipeg Prarie [sic] Farmer' and a few Finnish and Yugoslavian papers."[20]

The new Croatian migrants were exposed through these latter papers to a welter of competing interests and ideologies in the language of their native and adopted countries. Each could and did offer, under different times and circumstances in the thirties, vital service and information to the immigrant. The official Yugoslav network of consular officials and news service (*Glas Kanade, 1934-43*) served as important intermediaries in the process of immigration and settlement, particularly in deciphering immigration regulations and laws emerging from the major centres such as Montreal, Toronto, Ottawa, and Vancouver.[21] The small-town connection was provided by *Hrvatski Glas* (The Croatian Voice), the patriotic Peasant Party newspaper to which the settled Croats on or near the small urban frontier responded positively. Local news and information was provided by Peter Stanković, the energetic founding editor of the Winnipeg-based journal. Dependent upon generating news, subscriptions by local solicitation, and advertising from small northern communities such as Schumacher, Port Arthur, and Sudbury, Stanković and the Peasant Party won a readership of 4,000 or 5,000 by the mid-thirties.[22]

For those of no fixed address, the male migrant workers, the more clandestine network of the Communist Party provided yet another level of ideology and information through its newspaper, *Borba* (The Struggle), founded in 1931. The worry of relief camp supervisors and instructors who had to compete against these radical foreign-language newspapers was that the immigrants' desperate experience closely conformed with radical ideology's diagnosis and its prescriptions. As the Great Depression deepened, optimistic talk of prosperity around the corner or the revival of industry were received with hostile contempt among the relief-camp workers. Another more persuasive news system appeared to have won many hearts and minds. As one Frontier College instructor in northwestern Ontario observed, "The men get their own papers with all the current news as often as we do, and their attitudes towards the head of all countries at present, are decidedly communistic – Mr. Bennett especially."[23] Yet another analysis of the condition in the camps poignantly acknowledged the futility of persuading the workers otherwise: "They see their useful years passing, and are impatient, thinking that radical change offers them more chance of betterment than patient waiting. Considering them as despairing human beings, can you blame them for their attitudes?"[24]

The radicalism of the frontier Croats and Yugoslavs was naturally most evident on the periphery of Canada's northern frontier. Militancy and radicalism had been a long-standing tradition in western Canada, which had seen the growth and decline of several radical unions from 1900 to 1930, such as the Western Federation of Miners, the IWW, the OBU, and the Mineworkers' Union of Canada.[25] The penetration of the latter into the Coal Branch region of northwestern Alberta radicalized the Croats and other South Slavs of that region into an uncharacteristic outburst of violence in 1930. It was vividly remembered by one of the Croatian participants for the police reaction and deportations that it engendered:

> In 1930 there was trouble at Mercoal. The majority of men joined the Mineworkers of Canada, but the company favoured the United Mineworkers of America. The local union was asked to send miners to Mercoal to protest and picket. One day we were on the ridge facing south to the mine entrance. Some RCMP were escorting some men, about ten or twelve to work. We were shouting Scabs go back. One man by the name of Peter Maticevich and another in a brown leather coat jumped between the police and the scabs. A commotion started and we thundered "Hura-Hura" and started pushing, fist fighting, throwing rocks. Even some of our men got hurt. How we got separated I do not know but they did not start work for some time. One day we got news from Coalspur. Two passenger cars ar-

141

rived with RCMP and Alberta Police and Special Police. They sent a section man from Coalspur to go ahead of the train because somebody was told the Communists set dynamite on the railway. We were told to go home to our camps. In a few days the police started to round up the suspects. They arrested Pete Maticevich, Jack Tomicich, Tony Botrkof and Louis Matonovich. Meticevich [sic] and Tomicich were deported and Matonovich and Botrkof served prison and were released. Funny thing, Matonovich was not in this last push, but someone else was wearing his brown leather coat. If Matonovich told who was wearing his coat he would only put another man in the same spot.[26]

The acute political consciousness of the radical left resulted in the deportation of at least seven more Yugoslavs from 1930-34, and over 200 were deported ostensibly for health reasons or for legal technicalities that contravened immigration department regulations.[27] Many fewer Croats were deported as "public charges" under Section 40 of the Immigration Act, which provided for deportation of non-citizens on relief. Those few who could speak English were by far the majority of such public-charge deportations, for the rest had little sense of their legal rights or access to the means of public welfare. Fewer still would have been acceptable even as initial recipients of public charity, and were summarily told before judges of the court when apprehended as vagrants "to get out of town in twenty-four hours."[28]

Two strikes of the mid-depression years suffice to demonstrate both the sustained and militant quality of radical protest among the South Slavs and the harsh response of the mineowners to a radicalized work force. Although there was a bitter strike at Flin Flon, the two main radical theatres of action were the Anyox strike in northern British Columbia in 1933 and the Rouyn-Noranda strike of 1935. Both revealed the degree to which the Communist Mineworkers' Union of Canada had penetrated labour and ethnic groups abandoned by the international unions or the management-inspired company unions.

The Anyox copper mine, located some ninety miles up the Portland Canal from Prince Rupert, was operated by the American-owned Granby Consolidated Mining Company for some thirty years prior to the depression. It had attracted even prior to World War I many South Slavs, and among those who came to Anyox were particularly heavy concentrations of miners from Lika, Herzegovina, and Montenegro.[29] Working through the war as suspect Austrian aliens, their numbers were increased by the migration of the twenties, and by 1930 they probably counted in total some 170 out of a total labour force of 1,000. In February, 1933, the Mineworkers' local went out on strike for increased wages of fifty cents per day and a reduction in living costs charged by the mineowners. An extremely bitter confrontation ensued, complete with police action against the militant miners, many of whom left for Vancouver. Several, however, were bound over for trial on charges of unlawful assembly in Prince Rupert, and among these were several South Slavs, including Joe Servich, Matt Yurgevich (Jergovich), and John Rodoman. When these were successfully acquitted, the Workers' Unity League carried the battle to the docks of Vancouver where they forcibly attempted to prevent strikebreakers from boarding the steamer *Catala* bound for Prince Rupert. Although the Communists appear to have won the battle for increased wages by 1934, they and the miners lost the war when the Granby interests sold the mine to CPR Consolidated of Trail. The mine was gradually dismantled for scrap metal from 1934 to 1942, despite a reputed fifty million pounds of extractable copper still in the ground.[30]

Radical Croats were the more direct object of discrimination in the case of the anti-foreigners ("Fros") strike of 1934 in Rouyn-Noranda. Here, the Workers' Unity League made a particular effort to organize the Croatians, who numbered about 400 in the labour force in the Noranda district. Radicalized by the decline in wages and deteriorating working conditions, they were at the forefront of the miners' unions for improved conditions. Nine members of the mineworkers' negotiating committee of twelve, which precipitated the strike of 1934, were Croats. However, their attempts to achieve a 10 per cent wage hike, a "dry house" for the muckers, and recognition for the Workers' Unity League met with strong resistance from management.[31]

After a violent confrontation between the militia and the strikers in June, 1935, sixteen Croatians were arrested and charged with unlawful assembly and inciting riot. They were sentenced to prison for two years and were later transferred to St. Vincent de Paul prison in Montreal, where further investigations were conducted by the Department of Labour and Immigration into their possible deportation. While none of the Canadian leaders of the Workers' League were imprisoned, the ethnic elite and rank and file suffered heavily. It was reported in the American Croatian newspaper, *Zajedničar*, that some 350 of the Croatians left Noranda shortly thereafter, and about 100 others were deported to Yugoslavia for their part in the strike.[32] The local Noranda press proudly reported the number of jobs lost by "Yugoslavs" to English and French Canadians and the drop in their numbers from 150 miners before to forty-three after the bitter strike.[33]

Ironically, the sixteen leaders who had been imprisoned were the belated object of a concerted effort for their liberation by the American-based Croatian Fraternal Union, itself heavily supported by Pennsylvania coalminers and the militant United Mine Workers union headed by John L. Lewis. After several visits by its executive officers to prison officials, to the Minister of Justice, and to the newly elected prime minister, Mackenzie King, the sixteen were freed by June, 1936.[34] The wholesale deportation of hundreds of ethnic radicals during the early thirties had thus come to an official end with the Liberal victory in 1935.

Mackenzie King was more inclined than R.B. Bennett to listen to the voices of industry and labour from south of the border, and the more substantial voice of ethnic groups in the AFL and CIO had sharply reduced the forced exodus of labour radicals.

The next displacement of radical Yugoslavs from Canada in the late thirties was the voluntary exile of a few in support of the Republican cause in the Spanish Civil War. When the Canadian Spanish Aid Committee began to agitate for funds in 1936, it found physical and moral support among Canada's radical ethnic communities. Yugoslavs, many of Croatian background, would play an important role both in the leadership and in the rank and file of the International Brigade raised to assist the Republicans. The expatriate newspaper editors, Tomo Čačić and Peter Žapkar, who had been deported from Canada in 1933-34 for their Communist activities, continued to wage an international propaganda effort against dictatorship and fascism in their native Yugoslavia and in Europe.[35] Čačić had been involved in the radical miners' unions of the western American frontier and in the syndicalist agitation of the International Workers of the World prior to World War I. He returned to Canada in 1924, after a brief sojourn in Soviet Russia and a Yugoslav concentration camp, and became involved in the Communist Party and the organization of miners and lumberworkers in western Canada. His propagandist activities formally began with the editing of *Bilten Nezaposlenih*, a mimeographed bulletin for the unemployed in Vancouver, and in 1931 he began a more ambitious fortnightly newspaper, *Borba*, based in Toronto. The editing of this radical newspaper resulted in his arrest under Section 98 as a Communist agitator late in 1931, and culminated, after two years' imprisonment in Kingston Penitentiary, with his deportation from Canada in December, 1933.[36] Another to join was the Mineworkers' organizer, Edo Jardas, who had edited *Borba* for the years 1932-36 and had participated actively in the Anyox strike and later in the radicalization of the gold miners in the Timmins-Schumacher and Rouyn-Noranda fields. Jardas was one of the first to enlist in the George Washington Battalion raised in the United States early in 1937, and he actively promoted the idea of a distinctly Canadian unit, the "Mackenzie-Papineaus."[37]

By late 1937, approximately 1,300 Yugoslavs from Europe and North America had joined the brigade and its national units, and of these some seventy were from Canada. Of the Canadian Mackenzie-Papineau battalion, ten chose to list their nationality as Croatian on their identity cards, the only ethnic group apart from the Ukrainians to insist on their ethnic origin.[38] Those Croats from Canada who served in Spain might be identified more closely, for at least eighteen of them who served in the larger brigade were from the province of Lika, a rugged intermountain karstland region bordering on the northern Adriatic Coast. Occupationally, most were miners in Canada, although many were originally of rural and semi-rural background around the towns of Gospić and

144

Perušić in Lika.[39] What distinguished them from their contemporaries who had emigrated to northern Europe and to Latin America was that most of the Canadian Croatians had been resident in their adopted country for a longer period of time, many for as long as ten years. This commitment was reflected in the fact that many opted to return to Canada when the opportunity for repatriation came in 1939 for those who were already naturalized citizens.[40]

Whether or not the small number of Croats from Canada who participated in the Spanish conflict is interpreted as a significant radical commitment is open to debate. Certainly statistics provided by the Communist "Yugoslav" leadership imply that there were between 1,100 and 1,800 members in the Communist Party of Canada (CPC) and 650 subscribers to their radical newspapers, *Borba*, and its successor, *Slobodna Misao*.[41] Thus the Yugoslav membership within the CPC was certainly substantial, at 10 per cent of the total membership for Canada.[42] But a much larger number certainly was either neutral or hostile to this significant and militant minority among the Croats during the thirties. Participation rates in radical causes were doubtlessly high, measured by other ethnic groups' involvement, and significantly they were high among the Croats because of the tenuous position that they and other minorities like the Finns, Czechs, and Slovaks held at the bottom of a depressed social order. Thus the Spanish interlude in the history of the Yugoslav and Croat minorities in Canada must be seen as a desperate bid to overcome the acute sense of desperation and *anomie* which gripped the single immigrant. Essentially men without a country, they had to weigh the prospect of death in a noble cause against the numbing degradation of poverty, want, and despair in Canadian work camps.

The universal appreciation of their marginal existence may be observed in a poignant poem that appeared in 1930, not in the press of the radical left but in the more conservative *Croatian Voice*. A virtually unknown but eloquent poet from the gold-mining district of Schumacher in northern Ontario lamented the lot of the miner in his native tongue:

Sad, na primjer, u mislima hajte,	And now let your thoughts go,
I prizore čudne pogledajte,	And let them see the sights
Gdje pod zemljom u rupama vrve	Of the underground, where in
Ljudska bića i pećine i mrve.	holes stir
I to crvi kroz tunele gmizu,	Like worms through tunnels they
Težak kamen na b'jel danak	crawl.
dižu.	And heavy rocks pull up to the
Za života kopaju si raku,	daily sun.
Sav im život prolazi u mraku.	During their life they dig their
	grave,
	Passing their entire life in
	darkness.

145

Malo ko za jadnu raju mari,	No one cares for the poor people,
Pogotovo kad su to rudari,	Especially when they are miners.
Tek kad koji i glave pogube,	Only when someone loses his life,
Malo o njim' novice tad trube.	The newspapers make a little
Al' se slegne i to malo graje,	noise.
Ko sve ljudsko kad se tice raje.	But everything subsides, and so
A sto ono udovica placnih,	does this lament,
Broje trupla iz rovora mracnih,	As does anything human
Za to malo koga boli glava,	pertaining to the poor.
Te sviet opet ide mirno – spava.	And when crying widows
	Count the bodies lifted from dark
	caverns,
	For this no one's head aches
	And the world sleeps quietly as
	before.[43]

Under such harsh and compelling circumstances, militancy was a condition of survival, and radicalism offered but one means toward securing it. Desperate men in desperate circumstances – some chose to revolt, others to endure, and yet others to leave. The responses were limited and often resulted in bitter recriminations between one faction and another in regard to the best means of group survival. Yet, ranks closed when there was a fatally injured worker's family to assist, or a home, church, or cultural centre to build through co-operative effort. Each group ultimately recognized the precariousness of its marginal existence in Canadian society, and this recognition served often to blunt internecine conflict under the severe conditions of the Great Depression.

TOWARD A SETTLED SOCIETY, 1935-40

I met a fellow from Europe the other day – a Croat or Chick or a Slick, or something. Where was it he said he came from? Toschen or Poschen, anyway, somewhere. And he seemed all right, a nice little fellow. So they all do.

How often do you hear people say, 'I met a German and he seemed all right,' 'I met a New Zealander and he seemed fine,' 'I met a Norwegian and I couldn't see anything wrong with him.' Of course not. There's nothing wrong with any of them.

All the people of the world, taken by and large, are mighty fine people, with energy and kindness and love, valuing just the things we do, with the same care for their children and their friends, and their home town. All these things we value, they value.[44]

Stephen Leacock, *Funny Pieces* (1936)

The above quotation dispels two myths, the first that Stephen Leacock remained the racist he had been during World War I toward German and Austrian minorities, and the second that all Croats were an un-assimilable radical lump in the national digestive tract. The truth was that the first generation of pre-World War I migrants was now coming of age. Indeed, elements of intergenerational conflict had begun to develop between the more settled, long-standing, and conservative communities and the rootless wandering migrants of the early thirties. Those who had brought their families or who had begun them in Canada could ill afford the militant protest of the angry young men who rode the rails. For many the depression meant a shortened work week, a shrinking pay cheque, and the fear and uncertainty of lay-offs and illness to the breadwinner of the family. To these families a rapid assimilation into the mainstream of Canadian life was a highly desirable social goal, now reinforced by hard economic circumstances.

The mid-thirties also witnessed some imperceptible but significant changes in the Canadian economy. The bitter winter of 1935, one of the worst on record in western Canada, marked a turning point toward a warmer climate and gradual economic recovery in the latter half of the decade. Perhaps the most important factor in this economic equation was the stirring of the American giant to the south and the resultant demand for Canadian natural resources in the United States, which provoked gradual recovery on the resource frontier. There were, for the first time in over five years, jobs to be had in the mining and forest industries and on public works projects, such as airport construction and the improvement of Canada's national railway system.[45] At the same time, the automobile, steel, and paper industries began to increase production and the overall productivity of the Canadian economy rose by 12 per cent in 1936-37.[46]

The improvement of economic conditions, however slight, began to work subtle changes in the demographic character of the Croatian community in Canada. The first and most obvious change was the decline in numbers of migrant labourers and their gradual absorption into the mining and pulp and paper and manufacturing centres from 1935 onwards. In five years' time the migrants dwindled to an imperceptible number. With steadier jobs, wives and children who had long waited in the old country would now be brought over; in fact, female immigrants of all ages exceeded males by 60 per cent in the latter half of the thirties.[47] Girls who came as domestics with a view to finding a husband reduced the number of surplus males by nearly 100 per cent in the thirties.[48] But despite an overall decline, Croats had a male surplus only exceeded, among ethnic groups in Canada, by the Chinese, Greeks, and Bulgarians, with men over 200 per cent in excess of women. The first effect was to induce the Croatian bachelors, in a period of low net migration and rising economic expectations, to seek brides primarily in other ethnic groups and thereby produce in the late thirties a relatively high rate of exogamous marriage. The second effect was to increase the rate of intermarriage and assimilation to the population of British origins, although the rate of intermarriage was still only about one-third of that of all other European ethnic groups.[49] (Conversely, it appears that while the most characteristic form of intermarriage would have been between a Croatian male and a woman of Slavic origins, there was also an observable increase in the rate of intermarriage between women of Croat or South Slav origins and men of British background.) The intense isolation or segregation of the Croatian groups, nearly fourth highest in all of Canada, had thus begun to break down as a result of this new trend toward ethnic intermarriage.

Another dramatic result of increased prosperity and length of residence in Canada among the large number of immigrants who had come between 1926-31 was the sharp upswing in naturalization and linguistic assimilation. The numbers of naturalized Croats increased from 19 per cent in 1931 to 66 per cent in 1941. Among all ethnic groups in Canada this rate of naturalization represented the greatest percentage increase of citizenship acquisition during the 1930's.[50] Approximately 50 per cent of the total "Yugoslav" population group of 17,416, probably over 8,000 of which were Croatians, were naturalized in the depression decade.[51] Linguistically it is difficult to measure their rate of acquisition of either English or French during this period, except to say that it was overwhelmingly in favour of the English language at 96 per cent.[52] Only in Montreal was there any significant deviation downward in this nearly universal preference for English, with the remainder almost totally bilingual.[53] The Croats, like all other foreign-born immigrants, thus showed a marked and persistent tendency to acquire English both formally and informally as the predominant language of North America.[54]

Another significant impetus toward the greater absorption of the Croats into Canadian society was the 5,000 or so Croatian Canadians born in Canada, who represented almost a third of the entire community of nearly 15,000 by 1941.[55] This native-born element provided an anchorweight to the larger proportion of foreign-born immigrants and undeniably drew the latter more quickly to assimilation and acculturation. Of the recent immigrants, 30 per cent had less than five years of schooling. The Canadian-born population soon outstripped these new arrivals in educational attainments.[56] As often is the case among immigrant families, parents were educated in the language, as well as in the manners and customs of their new country, by their children. Exposure to the English language occurred on a broader front as well, for the language of work and the marketplace soon forced the Croatian immigrants, like nearly every immigrant group in North America, to adapt English terms to their native language and fuse them into a bastardized composite language.[57] In addition, the Croatian-American newspaper, the *Zajedničar,* instructed its Croatian-Canadian members in the English language through its bilingual reporting of news, sports, and cultural activities.[58]

One of the distinct services offered in bilingual form to the Croatian-

Canadian readership in the mid- to late 1930's by the Croatian Fraternal Union newspaper was a series of profiles of the various communities spread throughout Canada. These articles were indicators of a developing awareness among the Croatians of the length and breadth of their social existence within Canada. Their first series resulted from an extended report in late 1936 by the president of the CFU, John D. Butković, who undertook a railroad tour and membership drive through the Croatian settlements in Ontario and Quebec.[59] What followed was the first discussion in the English language of the northern Ontario communities in the Timmins-Kirkland Lake region, then farther to the south Port Arthur, Sault Ste. Marie, and Sudbury, and finally the southern urban centres such as Montreal, Hamilton, Welland, Toronto, and Windsor. Apart from its obvious uses as an organizational document, the reporting of the social and cultural activities of its membership gives a composite picture of Croatian community life in central Canada.[60] What it reveals of the CFU at least was a growing emphasis on recruitment of younger membership in English-speaking youth organizations, particularly in older centres like Sault Ste. Marie and Welland.

The series must have proved popular for it resulted in similar annual bilingual reports of Canadian activities within the organization each year thereafter until the onset of World War II.[61] These reports culminated in 1938 with an English-language series entitled "Croatians in Canada in the Fields of Precious Metals," devoted to the mining communities of northern Ontario and Quebec. This first attempt by Mr. J. Horvath at an historical and social profile of Croatians emphasized the fragmentary nature of the account and hoped that "Some day, perhaps, a book will be written in which the Croatian immigrant's adventure into the gold-mining districts will be told as in a novel. Tales of adventure, heroism, fear, failure, happiness, tragedy, and death will make it a kind of epic of new progress made in Canadian territory." As a primitive social record, it succeeded in conveying a sense of their bleak physical surroundings and of the hardship endured by the Croatian miners and their families prior to and during the depression years. A few extracts are printed here to recapture the liveliness of Horvath's social portrayal:

> . . . Schumacher, with a population of about six or seven thousand people, is the largest of three Croatian communities in that section of Northern Ontario, although it is not the largest town. Nearby is Timmins, a city which has been built in slightly more than twenty-five years into a comfortable modern town, in which more than twenty thousand people make their homes.
>   . . . The best available information has it that there are approximately three thousand Croatians in Schumacher (men, women and children). The growth of the town has paralleled that of the entire gold-mining area. Although Schumacher is similar to other nearby towns, it is much closer to bed-rock of the mining country. Outcrops

of rock are to be seen on almost every street and the foundations of many buildings, including the Croatian Home, are set solidly in the ancient formations from which the gold mines sprang.

Drawn from the four corners of the earth, the people living there have made this a truly cosmopolitan community. Not long ago, Indians were the chief inhabitants of the area. The native dress of Finland, Norway, Sweden, Denmark, Russia and Italy and the central Europeans, added to the colorful costumes of Croatians, Serbs and Slovenians, though seldom seen on the streets today, nevertheless turn up at many social functions and public affairs. England, Scotland and Ireland have contributed families to the town, Anglo-Canadians and French-Canadians make up the balance of the population.

The roster of societies and churches reads like a roll call of the League of Nations. It seems however, that everyone enters into the life of the community and it is a rare case indeed, so we were told, in which families from outside Canada set themselves apart, refusing to become one with the rest. Those racial prejudices over which most European wars have been fought – and may again be fought – seem to disappear under the friendly influence of the North.

Croatians are the largest so-called 'foreign' group in the town. They boast of the largest organizations, the one and only hall – the "Croatian Home," situated on the main street and in the very heart of the town. It is used by all the many nationalistic groups, school and town officials. Graduating exercises and high school playletts are all staged in the Croatian Home. Constructed only five years ago at a cost of approximately $23,000 it will be free of debt within the year.

. . . From the log cabins of pioneer days and many hundreds of these can be seen throughout the isolated countryside of Northern Ontario – with their rough tables, hard chairs, crude kitchens and very few if any comforts, have come the finest types of homes to be found anywhere in the United States or the 'States' (Croatian: 'Steć'), which is their name for the neighboring country. Many Croatian families, more so in Schumacher than in either Timmins or South Porcupine, are proud possessors of their own homes dotting in most instances the main street of the community. Commercial enterprises as well as modern hotels are owned and operated by our own people. . . .[62]

Let us say at the outset, however, that it would be a grave error to say that Croatians living in Canada today are that many years 'behind us.' It can be said, however, and without casting any reflections, that they do live in a manner that was all the rage in the United States some quarter of a century and more years ago. . . .

. . . Most of the men – Croatians of course – are young, sturdy

TOP LEFT *Edward Radovitch, owner Adelphi Saloon, Victoria, B.C., ca. 1870. (Courtesy Provincial Archives of British Columbia, 6934)*

TOP RIGHT *Adelphi Saloon, corner Government and Yates Streets, ca. 1910. (Courtesy Provincial Archives of British Columbia, 8712)*

Three generations of Croatian settlers, Kenaston, Saskatchewan, ca. 1910. (Courtesy C11760/Public Archives Canada)

Vancouver office of the Yugoslav Consulate and Information Bureau, 1926.
(Courtesy Vancouver Public Library, 12629)

Prairie home orchestra, Kenaston/Hanley, Saskatchewan, 1920's.
(Courtesy K.N. Beckie, Calgary)

Prisoner of war and alien train en route to Kapuskasing Internment Camp, Hearst, Ontario, 1915. (Courtesy Glenbow-Alberta Institute, Calgary, NA 1098-19)

Enemy internees at Castle Mountain Camp, Alberta, 1915.
(Courtesy Glenbow-Alberta Institute, Calgary, NA 1870-6)

Railway extra gang in northern Manitoba, 1929.
(Courtesy Robert Bozo Nizich, seated on car at right, Toronto)

Grain threshing gang, Kenaston/Hanley, Saskatchewan, 1920's.
(Courtesy K.N. Beckie, Calgary)

*Frontier College labourers, Abitibi
Pulp and Paper, Smooth Rock
Falls, Ontario.
(Courtesy C64844/Public Archives
Canada)*

*Northern Ontario gold miners,
McKenzie Gold Mines, 1935.
(Courtesy John Zagar, Thunder
Bay)*

Music at Home Celebration, Port Arthur, Ontario, 1930's. (Courtesy William Subat, Thunder Bay)

Amateur soccer players, Windsor, Ontario, 1930. (Courtesy Alois Graf, right, Sudbury)

Ford machine plant autoworker, Windsor, Ontario, 1929.
(Courtesy Matt Prpich, right, Windsor)

Salmon Purse Seiners' strike, Alert Bay, B.C., 1938.
(Courtesy The Fisherman, *Vancouver, B.C.)*

Anton Stancic, Captain, salmon-seiner,
"Reel Fisher," Vancouver, 1945.
(Courtesy PA 129263/Public Archives Canada)

Fishermen unionists (UFAWU),
"Mike" Vidulich (left),
Homer Stevens (centre), Vancouver, 1960.
(Courtesy The Fisherman, *Vancouver)*

Mrs. Rubic and friends at home,
Schumacher, Ontario, 1920's.
(Courtesy Multicultural History Society
of Ontario, MSR 9872-5)

Opening of Croatian Hall, Port Arthur, Ontario, 1935. (Courtesy Nick Filipovic, Thunder Bay)

A Croatian wedding, Port Arthur, Ontario, 1938. (Courtesy Milan Rasporich, Thunder Bay)

Ship "Radnik" (Worker), carrier of "Povratnici" back to Yugoslavia after World War II. (Courtesy The Fisherman, *Vancouver)*

Croatian women packing clothes for war torn Yugoslavia, Sudbury Croatian Hall, 1946. *(Courtesy Rose Matijević, Sudbury)*

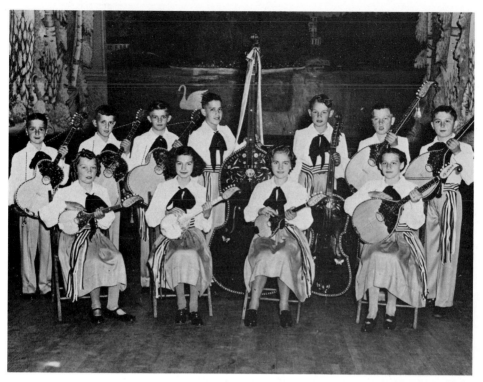

Croatian children's Tamburitza Orchestra, Schumacher, Ontario, ca. 1950.
(Courtesy Multicultural History Society of Ontario, MSR 9879-1)

First Canadian citizenship ceremony, Supreme Court of Canada, Ottawa, January 1, 1947.
Anton Justinić (far right, front row).
(Courtesy PA 129262/Public Archives Canada)

*"Adria" soccer club, winner of Centennial Cup, Sudbury, 1967.
(Courtesy Alois Graf, Sudbury)*

Folk dance group, Edmonton Folklore Festival, 1978. (Courtesy Fra. D. Boban, Calgary)

Canadian visit of
Archbishop F. Kuharić of Zagreb,
Calgary, 1976.
(Courtesy Fra. D. Boban, Calgary)

Calgary Croatian Church,
first communion class, 1979.
(Courtesy Fra. D. Boban, Calgary)

George Chuvalo, Canadian heavyweight boxing champion, 1965. (Courtesy 66-6639/National Film Board of Canada)

Frank Mahovlich checking Bobby Hull, N.H.L. action, 1960's. (Courtesy C29554/Public Archives Canada)

men, almost all of them in their early thirties. The greater number of them are unmarried, while others have wives living in the 'old country.' It is not unusual to find as many as ten, fifteen and twenty in some places, living in a single home – a boarding house, seemingly none too pleasant nor too comfortable when compared to the more modern homes wherein our people live in the country.

The scarcity of women makes it necessary for the 'boarding boss' to employ a man cook, with a helper perhaps, both of whom do all the house chores from day to day.

This will easily lead our readers to the conclusion that there is a noticeable scarcity of women – of girls – among our people in Canada. That, of course, is true, and it becomes more evident as you meet a Croatian who is married to a French-Canadian girl, and then note other marriages that have culminated between our younger men and Roumanian, Ukrainian, Polish and Slovak girls.

Of the Croatian children, most of them have come to Canada from the old country. They speak the mother tongue fluently of course, and we have met several of them varying in ages from ten to fifteen years, who are now trying to master the first reader in the English language . . .

. . . There is, however, some difference as far as the boarding houses of old are concerned. In nearly all Croatian communities one or more of our prosperous Croatians are operating hotels that house as many as thirty and forty such 'boarders.' They are truly modern structures, with individual rooms, comparable in every particular to a modern hotel building. A dining room, as neat as can be found anywhere, where meals are served at stipulated hours, reception rooms, halls, etc., all these seem to speak volumes for the progressive trend of our people in Canada, when compared to the Croatian colonies of old, in the United States in the early days of immigration. There is evident improvement in dress, habits and customs of our people, and a complete absence of any hesitancy, fear or whatever else one may call it, when it comes to meeting new and strange faces. The newcomer, so it seems, becomes more easily and more quickly 'Canadianized.'[63]

Subsequently, the CFU executives undertook more extensive membership drives through the Canadian West in 1938, and again through the prospering northern Ontario mining towns in 1939. Its president, John Butković, undertook an intensive tour of Alberta and British Columbia in July and August of 1938,[64] and the editor of *Zajedničar*, Milan Petrak, recorded his observations of several visits to northern Ontario in the summer of 1939 in a Croatian-language series entitled "Kroz Ontario" ("Across Ontario").[65] The consciousness of the Croatian Fraternalists regarding their own communities in Canada was broadened further by several English-language articles on the subject of Croatian history by

151

Professor Francis Preveden of Duquesne University, who was commissioned to write a more ambitious history of the Croatian people in the English language.[66] Following upon Preveden's learned disquisitions into the complex ethnography of the Balkans, the Croatian-Canadian readers would sample in English other political histories such as Dr. Dinko Tomašić's "Peasant Movement of Croatia" and "Croatia's Role in the Democratization of the Balkans."[67] Both of these Croatian-American scholars thus gave the first rendering of Croatian history, politics, and anthropology to a newly emerging and highly literate second generation of American Croatians. The Croatian-Canadian community was then the secondary beneficiary of an assimilative process already underway south of the border.

A microcosm of the advancing assimilation of the Croatian Canadians in the late 1930's was the oldest established community on the west coast, the colony of Dalmatian fishermen of British Columbia. This colony was already well into its second generation of life and work in the Pacific fishery and had expanded from the original group of less than 100 to 300 in number. Most families owned their houses outright and many of the older immigrants owned their own purse-seiner fishing boats as well. The entire community's capital assets in its fishing fleet ran to a total of $500,000 by 1938, and its annual catch equalled approximately $1.2 million in value.[68] Some of the larger vessels owned by the mainland Croatians were Walter Carr's *Adriatic Star*, Tom Fiamengo's *Bacalhao*, Ivan Radil's *Good Partners*, Alfonso Veljačić's *Ryno II*, and Martin Stojčić's *Sea Ranger*, all of which had a book value of $30,000-$40,000.

Beyond their material achievements and brightening prospects with the gradual recovery of the Canadian economy in the late thirties, several Croatian fishermen were also actively involved in the radical labour movement, particularly in the push of the Congress of Industrial Organizations (CIO) into British Columbia. In 1931 the Fishermen's Industrial Union was formed, and three years later this was enlarged into the Fishermen and Cannery Workers' Industrial Union.[69] Several Croats also participated in the River's Inlet strike of 1936 and the militant fishermen's strike of the spring of 1938 in Vancouver. Beyond this direct strike action, there were attempts in the fall of 1938 to tie local unions like the Salmon Purse Seiners' Union into larger CIO affiliates like the United Fishermen's Union of the Pacific and the Federated Fishermen's Council of the West Coast.[70] For the next two years preceding the war, the Croats continued to play an active role in the expanding international industrial union movement in Canada and the United States, which resulted in the formation of the conglomerate United Fishermen and Allied Workers Union.[71]

The radical Croatian fishermen were also active in the promotion of cultural activities and launched their own Croatian Educational Alliance in June, 1938. Later, in November, they proceeded with raising $14,000 for the erection of a Croatian Educational Home on Campbell Avenue in

Vancouver.[72] This hall soon became the focal point for the union activities of the United Fishermen and for an internationally oriented cultural program.[73] The social committee of Local 44 organized, in the spring of 1940, a multicultural entertainment that included, among other groups in the Canadian mosaic, the Templeton Boy's Pipe Band, the Croatian String Orchestra, Ukrainian Boy Dancers, the Bavarian Alpine Club, and various performers ranging from a Serbian vocalist and an Italian accordionist to a Swedish tenor![74]

Such ethnic interaction was typical of the fishing communities in greater Vancouver and in the Fraser delta. In the latter area intermarriage between the Italian and Croatian Canadians and cultural exchange of music, food, and entertainment were common.[75] At the same time, assimilation often occurred into the pioneer English-Canadian families in the case of those younger Croatian Canadians born in Canada. The case of Edward Vidulich was not untypical of this second generation. Born in Canada in 1914, he was educated at the Canoe Pass and Ladner elementary schools and King George High. Then, after a year at the University of British Columbia and some technical training in aircraft technology in the United States, he settled in the Vancouver area and married Irene Smith, the daughter of a local Fraser delta pioneer, in December, 1939.[76] Thus, from the beginning of the First War to the beginning of the Second, a generation of Canadian-born Croatians had become largely assimilated into Canadian society.

The broad assimilation of the large community of Vancouver Croats, who numbered approximately 4,000 by the outbreak of World War II, was also evident in their diverse economic activities ranging from the service sector to the woods-related industries and agriculture in the Fraser delta.[77] They were also involved in hotel-keeping, a commercial tradition in their past history within British Columbia, and the first of many hotels to be owned by the Croats was started up by Martin Stipac and John Popović in 1940. Even more important for group leadership was Stephen Raymer, who as justice of the peace, notary public, and journalist spoke for the Croatian community and continued to play a vital role as legal intermediary and interlocutor for the group. Often he had to intercede on behalf of individuals caught between various governmental jurisdictions in Canada and their parallel agencies and institutions in Yugoslavia.

It was Raymer's grim task to have to report to the Croatian-language press in Canada and Yugoslavia a tragedy that struck the Croatian fishermen of Vancouver in the fall of 1940.[78] The Vancouver dailies and the union newspaper, *The Fisherman*, also related the wreck of the purse-seiner *Liberty* in the heavy seas off the west coast of Vancouver Island at Useless Inlet.[79] Five of the predominantly Croatian crew survived with the skipper Walter Carr, but two others, including his brother Augustine and Gjuro Stilinović, perished. The tragic overtones of assimilation were not missed in the Croatian-language report of the incident, for the *Liberty* was a very powerful fishing boat purchased to supersede *Adriatic Star* ("Jadranska Zvijezda") as the flag ship of the Carr fishing fleet just a few months before.[80] But, according to reports neither the *Adriatic Star* nor the other smaller tender, *Gospak*, had been able to save the larger *Liberty* and its heavy catch from the rocks. The lessons of providence to those imbued with the acquisitive Anglo-Saxon ethic were mutely implied in the mere contrast of the ships' names.

Settlement and assimilation were, however, inevitable, and this also proved to be true on the Prairies, where the signs of domestication and settlement were evident on farms and in the towns. Economic conditions were often desperate, but with the addition of wives and children from the old country, family life began to assume a normal pace by the mid-thirties. A not untypical case was the Boras family near Lethbridge, which was reunited in 1933 after five years of enforced separation. With the arrival of the wife and three boys the elder Boras soon became a farmer, first leasing land from Knight Sugar Company and then purchasing a nearby acreage in the Raymond district. One of the children recollected his early days of schooling, work, and leisure:

> The immigrant's children were considered different because of their customs, language barrier and possibly their dress. When they were in school they provided a constant source of laughter and ridicule. However, this situation soon disappeared as the new pupils mastered the new language. These children were needed at home to supplement the family income during the peak work periods. This made it much more difficult for the teachers to carry on with these children in their studies. The public schools became a powerful means of preparing the newcomers for the Canadian way of life. Many parents gained their knowledge of the language from the children.
>
> As the depression progressed the conditions worsened, and the resentment of the immigrants became more obvious and tensions ran high. The communities that these people were moving into felt that the newcomers were just adding to the unemployed and competing for the jobs that were available. There was ample evidence of this when in 1935 a labour strike was staged. Anti-social slogans such as "Go home hunkies," and "the only good bohunk is a dead bohunk," among many others, were repeated.
>
> The immigrants who arrived here first and owned their farms continued to supply the necessary labour for agricultural needs by sponsoring relatives in Europe for immigration into Canada. This cycle supplied the necessary labour until 1938 [*sic*] when the war ended all immigration into Canada.
>
> To provide some social life in which a great gap had developed these immigrants organized Sunday picnics which almost always featured barbecued lamb or pork and music from their homeland. House parties were frequently a form of entertainment also.

"Harvest dances" were held in the fall which were symbolic of the gathering in of the fruit – a thanksgiving – in their native land. These events served to introduce the second generation to some of the traditions of the "old Country" and were equally enjoyed by young and old.[81]

Similar experiences were related by other Croatian-Canadian children in Alberta. A memoir by a young arrival in Mercoal, Alberta, with her mother in the darkest year of the depression, 1931, depicts the 1930's in terms of poverty, fear, and isolation. And like young Brian in W.O. Mitchell's *Who Has Seen the Wind*, her earliest memories were of anguish at serious family illnesses, which often required travel to the Mayo Clinic in Rochester for medical treatment. She endured as well the sense of being an outcast "bohunk" at school, and recalls that "When I was growing up I suffered. At times I hated to go to school." She was not allowed, like many immigrant girls from Europe, to take part in sporting and leisure activities but was taught to cook, sew, and help with the housework. School days ended abruptly at grade eight, with marriage to a young Croatian Canadian at the tender age of fifteen in 1941.[82]

Faced with pressures to assimilate, the Croatians responded ambivalently with public acquiescence and private resistance. Within the larger Canadian society in the 1930's, the idea of the melting pot took hold in the "unhyphenated" Canadianism of John Diefenbaker, J.W. Dafoe, and John Ewart.[83] But the contrary mosaic concept of nationality was articulated by such western Canadian intellectuals as Watson Kirkconnell, who saw the Canadian nation as a composite of plural ethnic identities derived from Europe and other continents.[84] This renewed emphasis upon European cultural traditions was paralleled by resistance among the ethnic groups themselves to the pressures of assimilation. Thus drawn at one time by the school, the workplace, and the marketplace to the customs and language of the larger society, minority groups like the Croatians were driven in the other direction of preserving their cultural heritage under the approving eye of another segment of Canadian society.

This cultural resistance largely took forms which had been in place by the early thirties, with the singular difference that they now were applied more broadly to incorporate all elements of the social group. A much broader base of participation, which now included women and children, was pursued and achieved during the late thirties. The formalization and separation of functions was the central difference from the earlier informal institutions for the retention of culture within family and clan. Thus, men's organizations like the Sokol (Falcons) took root more firmly in cities like Sudbury prior to World War II and provided a formal club atmosphere for gymnastic, musical, and patriotic activities of the Croatian men.[85] On the other hand, women were now consciously included in separate organizations by the Croatian Peasant Party, in particular

155

because of their belief in the maternal principle as the central conservator of culture and as the fountainhead of culture, language, and custom.[86] The Croatian women consequently organized auxiliaries attached to the Croatian national homes and conducted their own separate meetings, cultural programs, and entertainment.[87]

A separate cultural offensive seemed to be reserved for orchestral tamburitsa groups for children and juveniles. These were formed across the country in locations as far distant as Vancouver Island and Cape Breton, and they often resulted in co-operation between several organizations. Where the population base was sufficient, as it was in Toronto, the Croatian Peasant Party formed a separate youth orchestra that entertained local audiences.[88] Where it was not, as in Sydney, Nova Scotia, there had to be co-operation between two local lodges of the Peasant Party and the Fraternal Union to secure a director from far away Cooksville in Ontario and then to drum up support among the coalminers from as far as Stellarton on the mainland some 200 miles away.[89] Additional problems of finding a local home in which to practise and store expensive imported instruments and ethnic costumes all had to be overcome before the "Atlantic Croatian Tamburitsa Orchestra" could find a performing stage in October, 1939.[90]

Since all of these cultural activities required a physical base, several more building campaigns were generated and buildings dedicated as Croatian national homes appeared during the late depression years. Occasionally these were the result of co-operative endeavours, as was the building in Vancouver in 1935 that soon became the object of controversy between the contending factions of Communist and Peasant Party groups for its control and finally closed after the war.[91] Others built in the mid- to late thirties in northern Ontario towns like Sudbury (1935), Port Arthur (1935), and Kirkland Lake (1937) were Croatian Peasant Party initiatives combined with those of private individuals.[92] In almost every case, it was apparent that the Croatians wished to cultivate community goodwill by inviting local dignitaries to the opening of these cultural centres. A typical gathering that attempted to explain the Croatian culture to their visitors was held in Schumacher in 1935 on the visit of Dr. Krnjević, a Croatian Peasant Party deputy abroad. To a packed audience of 400 in a three-year-old hall, a typically bilingual celebration was orchestrated for the visiting English-speaking dignitaries. Music was provided by a tamburitsa orchestra, which began with "O! Canada" and the Croatian national anthem "Lijepa Naša Domovina" (Our Beautiful Homeland), and a sumptuous banquet featuring various Croatian dishes was served. The guests, composed of mine managers, local professionals, and priest responded generously to the work of the Croatians in the gold mines and in the local community. The Croatian people were congratulated largely for their assimilative virtues, for being "honest, industrious, kindly and hospitable" and for enjoying "the respect of their fellow Canadians." Additionally, J.M. Douglas of the Hollinger Mines

156

spoke of the necessity for tolerance of each other's languages and feelings, and the editor of the Porcupine *Advance*, G.A. Macdonald, praised the young Croatian children present for their orderly and respectful presence at an adult evening gathering.[93]

At a similar gathering with an entirely different ideological thrust, it may be seen that the Croatians of a pro-Yugoslav persuasion were much less accepted and integrated into the fabric of larger urban life in Montreal. In 1938, the Yugoslav-Canadian Association of Montreal met to celebrate the formation of the Kingdom of the Serbs, Croats, and Slovenes in 1918. This occasion, which was widely reported in the Montreal *Star*, had elements of Anglo-Saxon condescension reminiscent of the pre-war days of British imperialism and Ralph Connor's *The Foreigner*. The reporter commented upon the gathering of 300 at the St. Lawrence Boulevard hall as a near orgy, "Swaying to a gay, wild, madly fiddled Slav dance [Kolo], eating double portions of meat Yugoslav style, and drinking huge drafts to King Peter of Yugoslavia and King George of Britain . . . with spontaneous singing, wonderful minor notes mixing with impromptu whoops, and then there would be a dive into the pockets for another dollar bill, and more beer and then more song."[94] While the stress upon the common features of the Yugoslav and Canadian federal systems by the Yugoslav consul-general, George Sigmund, would not have sat well with Croatian nationalists elsewhere in Canada, the Yugoslav celebration was common witness to an attempt by Croatian Canadians to include the host society more and more in their social and cultural events.

The increasing public visibility of the Croatians suggested that they were amenable to yet another form of assimilation – the quest for the "ethnic vote." The political awareness of the new immigrants and their newspapers had risen above a sole concern about immigration laws and wage disparities across the country and had turned to the Canadian political parties themselves and their platforms. The federal campaign of 1935 caused some considerable if bemused commentary from the *Croatian Voice*, which betrayed a considerable familiarity with the process and its participants.[95] Conversely, the political parties themselves, like the unions, began to realize the potential of courting the immigrant vote as more and more of the immigrants of the late twenties became naturalized Canadian citizens. And by contrast to the largely anglophone appeal of the Tories and even the emergent CCF,[96] the Liberal Party proved astute in seeking out the Croatian vote in the provincial elections in Ontario in 1934 and in the federal election of 1935. Indeed, the Liberals proved in certain northern Ontario ridings that a North American style of immigrant recruitment and politicization could work in Canada.

A classic expression of the machine politics of the American Democratic Party exported to Canada was that practised by "Charlie" Cox, mayor of Port Arthur and simultaneously Liberal member of the provincial legislature from 1934-43.[97] Cox was a superb political boss, much loved by the Italian, Ukrainian, Finn, and Croatian immigrants who as often as not had been in his employ as lumberjacks in the lean depression years.[98] Immigrant loyalties were confirmed by prospects of jobs and nebulous political favours and shrewdly combined with immigrant vote-getting issues, such as low streetcar fares and reduction in property taxes (through reduction in municipal services such as sewers and roads). Consequently, the loyalty of the Croatians and of nearly every other immigrant group swung dramatically to the Liberals and Cox, and stayed there for the next two decades. Nor was it any surprise that when the Croatian Hall (Hrvatski Dom) first opened its doors on Pearl Street in the south end immigrant ward in 1935, the seat of honour was reserved for "Call Me Charlie" Cox.[99] That evening in November, 1935, which followed closely upon yet another federal sweep by C.D. Howe and the Liberals in Port Arthur, marked the beginning of an unswerving loyalty by the Port Arthur Croatians that would last until the advent of John Diefenbaker's "unhyphenated Canadian" appeal in the late fifties. Port Arthur in this period deservedly earned its local sobriquet "Chicago of the North," less because of any economic similarity to that American giant than because of the similarities of Liberal political bosses like Cox to Democratic machine counterparts like Anton Cermak and Richard Daley.[100]

The attachment of the Croatians to the Liberal Party was not universal, for there was often a factionalism and internal division dictated by Old World differences in ideology. Internecine conflict among the left, right, and centre began to develop during the depression years and hardened in the war and post-war period. The central element of conflict was most often a three-cornered debate involving the newspaper, *Glas Kanade (Voice of Canada)*, which represented the views of the government of Yugoslavia and the Yugoslav-Canadian Association; the pro-Catholic and republican Croatian Peasant Party and its central organ, *Hrvatski Glas (Croatian Voice)*; and the left-wing Communist Yugoslav faction represented by its newspaper, *Borba (The Struggle)*, and its successor, *Slobodna Misao (Free Thought)*. The latter two factions constantly attacked the Yugoslav *Glas Kanade*, because the Yugoslav organ was a mouthpiece of the Serbian dictatorship in Yugoslavia, responsible for the imprisonment of both Maček and his Peasant Party followers and the suppression and execution of Communist party members.[101] This common cause against the Yugoslav "dictatorship" did not, however, prevent the Peasant Party and Communists from having their own differences. These proved legion over the decade and ranged over the democratic nature of the Soviet state, a viable social and economic program for Canadian workers and farmers, and the means of achieving social progress.[102]

One of the issues that united the Peasant Party and Communist factions in varying degrees of opposition was the rise of fascism in Europe, in particular the aggressive territorial ambitions of Hitler and Mussolini. Despite the characterization by the Yugoslav Communist press of the Peasant Party as a right-wing fascist organization, the fact was that the *Croatian Voice* mistook Hitler for a pacifist only briefly in 1933,[103] and already it had suspicions on Mussolini's expansionist designs against the Dalmatian coastline.[104] By 1935, Stanković had clear suspicions of German and Italian designs on the Tyrol and anticipated the Axis alignment and schemes for southern and central Europe. The slaughter of the Loyalist forces at Malaga in 1937 and a reprint of Dr. Norman Bethune's account of these events also marked the *Voice's* sympathies with the anti-fascist forces in Spain.[105] But a parallel concern with the totalitarian government of Stalin and the declaration of the Molotov-Ribbentrop Pact threw the *Voice* into unequivocal opposition to the Soviet-German alignment.[106] Then, at the crucial juncture of August and September, 1939, two events created mixed feelings of joy and frustration among Peasant Party followers. The first was created by a power vacuum in 1939 in south central Europe, which prevented an Italian or German invasion of Yugoslavia and allowed, for the first time in eleven years, the participation of the Croats and particularly Vladko Maček in the Belgrade government.[107] Then, just as the realization of these Croatian political ambitions seemed imminent, the Germans invaded Poland and precipitated the entry of Britain, France, and then Canada on behalf of the conquered Poles. The Peasant Party news organ and its editor, Peter Stanković, reacted with mixed joy and sorrow to these events:[108]

> At this moment it is evident that Hitler has, in keeping with his long cherished ambition, plunged Europe into War. Today his hordes have bombed cities, towns and harbours in Poland. His peace proposals could not be accepted by any self-respecting Nation, and the guilt of War with all its horrors definitely and eternally rests upon him.
>
> He has put into operation, wanton aggression, wantonly directed against a people whose only fault was a righteous determination to keep their country from being dismembered and ravished.
>
> Herr Hitler, fortified by his recent pact with Communistic Russia, has drawn the sword against all the freedom loving people of the world.
>
> This newspaper, speaking in the name of the Croatian population of Canada, advises its readers to face whatever issues may arise with calm and confidence. Among Poland's allies in its desperate struggle to retain its independence are the great democracies of France and Britain. It is well for us to understand clearly that when Britain is at War, so is Canada. In this Dominion, our people have found a land of privilege, opportunity and security, affording them at all times every scope for their material development and freedom to retain and enhance their cultural life. No people will appreciate the situa-

tion better than the Croats, both here and in their dear old Motherland. Quite recently they themselves emerged from a position that was little less than serfdom.

Now the ideas promulgated by that great Patriot, Dr. Vladko Matchek, have succeeded. The accord between ourselves and our racial brothers, the Serbs, was consummated on August 26th and a dictatorial Senate and Parliament have given way to a free Assembly of the people's representatives. The Concentration Government was organized with six Croats in the Cabinet with Dr. Matchek as Vice-President. Thus does the march of Freedom carry on despite dictators.

A new world has opened up for our people and well do they deserve their peaceful victory. The duty of every Canadian Croat, while rejoicing in the good fortune of his Motherland, is to give unqualified allegiance to Canada, the land of his adoption and help those in authority in whatever capacity and in every way he can.

The civilization of the world and the freedom of its people is worth striving for at this troubled hour, yes and worth fighting for unless we are prepared to spend our days under the tyrant's heel. No nation is safe that permits the monster of dictatorship to gain a footing on its soil. We have steadfast confidence that right will prevail however great the sacrifice. So again we say to ourselves and our readers—be calm, strong and ready for all eventualities and always worthy of "the rock from whence we were hewn".

The Communists, for their part, were critical of the Peasant Party as pro-fascist collaborators prepared to use Hitler's threats of aggression to force the hand of the Belgrade government on Croatian representation in the ministry. They were perceived as little better than the overtly pro-German leaders like Premier Stojadanović and Ante Pavelić, who were purportedly prepared as early as 1938 to co-operate with Hitler in the establishment of five puppet regimes in Yugoslavia.[109] Claiming at the outbreak of war some 2,000 members in the Croatian wing of the party *(Hrvatski Prosvjetni Savez)* and a further 3,000 readers of its newspaper, *Slobodna Misao*, the Yugoslav-Canadian Communists anticipated the war against the Axis powers in a mood of vindication. But it was not until the invasion of Russia by Hitler in 1941 and Stalin's appeals to partisans in occupied Europe to assist the Soviet Union that this sense of conviction was elevated into moral certainty.[110]

The Peasant Party in the meantime continued during 1939-40 to advocate a workable constitutional monarchy in Yugoslavia, and at the same time demonstrated its support for the English-speaking democracies now at war. The principal officers of the party in Canada, Zvonimir Restek and Ivan Skaćan, issued an appeal to all naturalized and unnaturalized Croatians in Canada to demonstrate their allegiance to Canada and to Great Britain during the darkest hours of the Battle of

Britain. Characteristically, they also denounced totalitarian governments of every kind and issued a call to "crush Nazism, Fascism, Communism and all subversive elements which are attempting to undermine and overthrow our government by force and violence." On the positive side, Croats were encouraged to co-operate with the Serbs and Slovenes to collect funds for distribution to the Canadian Red Cross. The Canadian government immediately replied through Prime Minister King's private secretary that he and his colleagues appreciated greatly "this expression of loyalty and support of the war effort in which our country is engaged."[111]

Thus, the Croatians in Canada, despite their considerable and deep division during the thirties, were curiously united on the brink of war. Although they continued to differ as to the means to improve the ills of Canadian society and of Europe, they were nearly agreed by 1940 upon the end to be achieved – the destruction of fascism. The radical left had been embittered by the harsh circumstances and repression of the early thirties, but the latter half of the decade had been somewhat kinder to those who had neither been deported nor gone to Spain. The prospect of a job, a fixed address, and even marriage and a family were the first glimmers of hope in nearly a decade of wandering and hand-to-mouth existence. For these men, the prospect of a war in combination with Soviet Russia against the fascist enemy in Europe was seen as ideological retribution for the multitude of indignities they had endured.

For those who had managed to secure a foothold in Canada before the Great Depression descended, life had not been without struggle, for death and disease from the ravages of tuberculosis and industrial accidents still haunted the immigrant communities. Yet their life held promise. Children were in the process of their education, and despite the deep hurts inflicted by prejudice, they were firmly on the path to becoming integrated into Canadian society. By 1940, many Croatian Canadians had a growing stake in their adopted country, and were closer than ever before to realizing the better life they had come for. For them, the *via media* of Mackenzie King, their attachment to the Crown as demonstrated in their enthusiastic response to the Royal Visit of 1939,[112] and their deep attachment to their Roman Catholic faith were symbols of security and stability in a world gone mad. That the Old World they had left was once again in the throes of total war was some comfort that their decision, or the decision of their parents, to migrate had been a wise one.

NOTES

1. *Kanadski Glas*, 7 July 1930.
2. *Ibid.*, 26 August 1930.
3. See M. Braithwaite, *The Hungry Thirties* (Toronto: McClelland and Stewart, 1977).

4. See E. Bradwin, *The Bunkhouse Man* (Toronto: University of Toronto Press reprint, 1972).

5. PAC, MG 28, I, T24, Frontier College Papers, Instructors' Registers, vol. 152. Toronto and Northern Railway Extension, Moose Factory, July, 1931. The instructor, J.C. Fair, lists 130-165 men of whom 25 per cent were Yugoslavs; a high proportion were identifiable as Croats. The preponderance of Croatians in this generation of Yugoslav immigrants is also corroborated in an interview with Robert England, author of "The Central European Immigrant in Canada" in *Canadian Ethnic Studies*, VIII, 2 (1976), pp. 18-33. See also the definitive work of Većeslav Holjevac, *Hrvati Izvan Domovine* (Zagreb, 1968), pp. 175-7.

6. Toronto *Globe and Mail*, 3 October 1973, p. 16. Copy courtesy of H.V. Herman of Guelph University, who has authored a recent book on Macedonians in Toronto: *Men in White Aprons: A Study of Ethnicity and Occupation* (Toronto: Peter Martin Associates, 1978).

7. An excellent narrative by one such group leader is by S. Bradica, "Odkriće Kanade," in S. Gaza (ed.), *Spomenica na Dvadeset Godina Hrvatskih Seljačkih Organizacija U Kanadi* (Winnipeg, 1952), pp. 34-42; translated and reprinted in *Canadian Ethnic Studies*, VIII, 2, (1976), 99-102.

8. See Kenneth Duncan, "Irish Famine Immigration and the Social Structure of Canada West," *Canadian Review of Sociology and Anthropology*, II (1965), 19-40.

9. PAC, MG 28, I, 124, vol. 148, SF 1924, D.M. Angevine, dated Strong, Hanley, Dundurn, Saskatchewan, June, 1924.

10. Work rates as established in *ibid.*, vol. 198, 1934-36.

11. *Ibid.*, letter by A.G. Graham to the members of the Rigg Commission, Shoreacres, B.C., 28 December 1935. The Rigg Commission was composed of R.A. Rigg, Humphrey Mitchell, and E.W. Bradwin, and was appointed to investigate conditions in the relief camps for the single unemployed.

12. *Ibid.*, vol. 149. File 1925. Ian Munro, Sudbury, August, 1925.

13. See S. Bradica, "Odkriće Kanade," translated by A.W. Rasporich in *Canadian Ethnic Studies*, VIII, 2 (1976), pp. 99-102.

14. See PAC, MG 28, I, 124, vol. 153, ff. 1933. Hugh Fraser, Trenton, 1933.

15. R.B. Nizich to author, 30 March 1975.

16. PAC, MG 28, I, 124, vol. 64. A.H. Fraser, Trenton Air Camp, May, 1933.

17. See *Census of Canada*, 1931, vol. IV, p. 1010. The illiteracy rate was slightly below that for Poles (13 per cent) and Italians (11 per cent). Most declared Serbo-Croatian as their mother tongue (62 per cent by 1941) but a substantial number declared English (83 per cent) as the major language of usage.

18. PAC, MG 28, I, 124, vol. 152. F. Kinnaird, Hydro, Ontario, July, 1929, pupil E. Ruckmeyer; vol. 155, Camp Dorset, R.R. Gordon, instructor,

entry by C. Majhanovich; vol. 62, Kenora, Ontario, D.S. Wood, instructor, student, M. Kotovich.

19. *Ibid.*, vol. 64, H. Fraser, Trenton Airbase Camp, May, 1933; vol. 152, J.C.S. Fair, Moose Factory, July, 1931.
20. *Ibid.*, vol. 153, ff. 1932, George Lantz, Ouimet Camp, 12 April 1933.
21. The official organ of the Yugoslav government was *Glas Kanade*, which the National Library in Ottawa lists as a "Serbian" newspaper, but it also contained news in the Latin alphabet for Croatian and Slovene readers. "National Library holdings of Newspapers of Canadian Cultural Communities," October, 1973.
22. The newspaper ran under the title *Kanadski Glas* from 1929-31 and then changed its title to *Hrvatski Glas*, 14 March 1939: "Kratki Historijat Hrvatskog Glasa."
23. PAC, MG 28, I, 124, vol. 64, ff. 1933, Vern R. Hawkins to Dr. W.E. Baldwin, Pearl, Ontario, 6 May 1933. See also vol. 71, Principal Bradwin to Allan McColl (DND Project 13, Kowkash), [n.d.] 1935.
24. *Ibid.*, vol. 198, A.E. Graham to the Rigg Commission, 28 December 1935.
25. See D.J. Bercuson, *Fools and Wise Men: The Rise and Fall of the One Big Union* (Toronto: McGraw-Hill-Ryerson, 1978).
26. Reminiscence by Mike Krypan in Toni Ross, *Oh! The Coal Branch* (Edmonton: D.W. Freisen, 1974), p. 287.
27. PAC, RG 76, vol. 16. File re: "Communist Agitators Deported from Canada, 1931-37."
28. Interview, Milan Rasporich, July, 1976, Thunder Bay, Ontario.
29. Grado, *Migraciona Enciklopedija*, p. 217. See also S. Raymer article re: British Columbia on 9 April 1930, *Pucka Prosvjeta* clipping, located at *Zavod za Migracije i Narodnosti* in Zagreb, vol. 138, ff. II, 142c, "British Columbia 1928-30."
30. Oswald Hutchings, "History of Anyox (Hidden Creek) Mining District" (n.p., typescript, 1966), located at U.B.C. Special Collections; *Borba*, 16 August 1935.
31. See Evelyn Dumas, *The Bitter Thirties in Quebec* (Montreal: Black Rose, 1975), pp. 28-42; *Borba*, 29 October 1934, 6 December 1924, 4 January, 30 April 1935. For general discussion of the CIO and radicalism on the northern Ontario frontier, see Irving Abella, *Nationalism, Communism and Canadian Labour* (Toronto: University of Toronto Press, 1973), pp. 1-22.
32. *Zajedničar*, 4 December 1935. John D. Butkovich, Pres. CFU, "My Trip To Canada."
33. Typical deportation entries for this group read: "S.P., Yugoslav, arrived in Canada July 4, 1926 . . . deported aboard Ansonia, Oct. 28, 1933, from Quebec", convicted of unlawful assembly, Royn [*sic*] Quebec." PAC, RG 76, vol. 16.
34. *Zajedničar*, 15 July, 26 October 1936. *Borba*, 30 June, 11 August 1936.

35. *Jedinstvo*, 26 October 1956, 28 January 1957. See also *20 Godina Kratki Pregled Historije Naprednog Pokreta Jugoslavenskih Iseljenika u Kanadi* (Toronto, 1950), microfiche.
36. PAC, Remission File 47424, vol. 1266, ff. Thomas Čačić, dormant file, National Parole Board, Ottawa. See also A.W. Rasporich, "Tomo Čačić: Rebel Without a Country," *Canadian Ethnic Studies*, X, 2 (1978), pp. 86-94.
37. *Hrvatski Narodni Kalendar* (Toronto, 1938), pp. 63-99; *Borba*, 29 October 1934, 4 January 1935.
38. Victor Hoar, *The Mackenzie-Papineau Battalion* (Toronto: Copp Clark, 1969), p. 32.
39. Branimir Gusić, *Lika u Prošlosti i Sadašnjosti* (Karlovac, 1973), pp. 259-63.
40. *Jedinstvo*, 15 May 1970: Ivan Štimac, "Sječanja iz Španije."
41. *20 Godina, Kratki Pregled . . .*, pp. 35-6, 44-5.
42. Ivan Avakumovic, *The Communist Party of Canada* (Toronto: McClelland and Stewart, 1975), p. 121.
43. *Hrvatski Glas*, 25 August 1930: Poem, "Seljak i Radnik," by S. Mahovlić, Schumacher, Ontario, translation by M. Meheš and the author.
44. S. Leacock, *Funny Pieces* (New York: Dodd, Mead, 1936), p. 171. Quotation supplied to author by Beverly Rasporich.
45. *Canadian Annual Review*, 1935-36, pp. 616-60.
46. *Ibid.*, pp. 548-615.
47. *Census of Canada,* 1941, IV, p. 692.
48. W.B. Hurd, "Ethnic Origin and Nativity of the Canadian People," *Census Monograph, 1941*, p. 75.
49. *Ibid.*, pp. 96-103.
50. *Ibid.*, p. 117.
51. *Census of Canada*, 1941, IV, p. 795.
52. *Ibid.*, IV, p. 798.
53. *Ibid.*, IV, p. 842.
54. S. Lieberson, *Language and Ethnic Relations in Canada* (New York: John Wiley, 1970), pp. 31-76.
55. Hurd, *Census Monograph*, IV, p. 210.
56. *Ibid.*, pp. 132-43.
57. See, e.g., C.S. Mihanovich, "Americanization of the Croats in Saint Louis, Missouri During the Past Thirty Years," Master's thesis, St. Louis, University, 1936 (San Francisco: R.&E. Research Assoc., 1970), pp. 21-25.
58. *Zajedničar*, 23 December 1936, 17 August 1938, 7, 14, 21, 28 June 1939, 29 May 1940.
59. *Ibid.*, 6 November 1935.
60. *Ibid.*, 13, 20, 27 November, 4, 11, 18, 25 December 1936.
61. *Ibid.*, 8, 23 June 1938.
62. *Ibid.*, 13 July 1938.

63. *Ibid.*, 27 July 1938.
64. *Ibid.*, 20, 27 July, 10, 17, 24, 31 August, 7 September 1938.
65. *Ibid.*, 21, 28 June 1939, 5, 19 July 1938.
66. *Ibid.*, 19, 26 July 1939, 10 January 1940.
67. *Ibid.*, 30 October, 27 November, 25 December 1940.
68. *Zavod za Migracije i Narodnosti* (Zagreb), 136, II, 12.2; 12, VIII, 1938, I.F. Lupis-Vukić, "Nàsi Iseljenici Ribari," reference to article in *Vancouver Sun*, 7 May 1938.
69. *Ibid.*, reference to *Naš Kalendar* (1956), p. 98.
70. *The Fisherman*, 22 November 1938.
71. *Ibid.*, 3 January 1939, 12 March 1940.
72. *Ibid.*, 20 June, 22 November 1938.
73. *Ibid.*, 29 March 1940.
74. *Ibid.*, 9 April 1940.
75. *Surrey Delta Messenger*, 28 February 1974, 20 September 1975.
76. *Ibid.*, 24 January 1974.
77. Joso Nikšić, "Hrvati i 100 - God. B.C. -e," *Hrvatski Glas Kalendar* (1959), p. 104.
78. *Hrvatski Glas*, 19 November 1940, ZAMIN, 136 II, 12.2. "Ribari, 1929-40."
79. *The Fisherman*, 19 November 1940.
80. *Hrvatski Glas*, 19 November 1940.
81. W.V. Boras, "Era of European Immigration," in *Coyote Flats Historical Review* (Lethbridge, 1967), pp. 233-4.
82. Toni Ross, *Oh! The Coal Branch*, pp. 308-14, Mrs. Robert Spanach reminiscence.
83. H.D. Palmer, "Mosaic Versus Melting Pot?: Immigration and Ethnicity in Canada and the United States," *International Journal*, XXXI, 3 (Summer, 1976), pp. 502-9.
84. N.F. Dreisziger, "Watson Kirkconnell and the Cultural Credibility Gap Between Immigrants and the Native Born in Canada," in M.L. Kovacs (ed.), *Ethnic Canadians, Culture and Education* (Regina: Canadian Plains Research Center, 1978), pp. 87-96.
85. *Hrvatski Glas*, 4 December 1937.
86. *Ibid.*, 21 March 1935.
87. *Ibid.*, 30 August 1934, 4 April 1934, 20 April 1937; *Spomenica Na Dvadeset Godina Hrvatskih Seljačkih Organizacija*, pp. 102-5.
88. *Hrvatski Glas*, 8 June 1937.
89. *Ibid.*, 20 April, 30 November 1937.
90. *Ibid.*, 15 July, 5 December 1939.
91. John Norris, *Strangers Entertained* (Vancouver, 1971), p. 177. See also *Borba*, 1 February 1933, 29 October 1934, 17 September, 24 December 1935.
92. *Hrvatski Glas*, 15 December 1932, 24 January, 5, 26 November 1935, 21 December 1937.
93. *Ibid.*, 8 October 1935.

94. Montreal *Daily Star*, 28 November 1938, clipping from ZAMIN file 132-8-29.
95. *Hrvatski Glas*, 15 October 1935: "Sličice iz izborne kampanje u Kanadi."
96. Ivan Avakumovic, *Socialism in Canada, A Study of the C.C.F. - N.D.P. in Federal and Provincial Politics* (Toronto: McClelland and Stewart, 1978), pp. 91-2.
97. Port Arthur *News Chronicle*, 30 April 1934.
98. See A.W. Rasporich, "Faction and Class in Modern Lakehead Politics," *Lakehead University Review*, VII, 1 (Summer, 1974), pp. 42-51; *Hrvatski Glas*, 27 June 1935.
99. *Hrvatski Glas*, 5, 26 November 1935.
100. See A. Gottfried, *Boss Cermak of Chicago; A Study of Political Leadership* (Seattle: University of Washington Press, 1962).
101. See, e.g., *Hrvatski Glas*, 25 May, 7 December 1933, 14 January 1935. *Borba*, 14, 28 December 1932, 4, 11, 18 January, 1, 8, 22 February, 29 March, 9 August, 1, 15 November 1933.
102. See, e.g., *Hrvatski Glas*, 14, 21 January, 9 June 1936, 18 May, 8 June, 23 November 1937, 18 July, 19 September 1939. *Borba*, 7, 21, 28 December 1932, 18, 25 January, 1 February, 15 March, 5, 26 April, 3, 23 May, 7 June, 5, 19 July 1933, 31 January, 1934.
103. *Hrvatski Glas*, 14 December 1933.
104. *Ibid.*, 7 March 1935.
105. *Ibid.*, 23 February, 6 April 1937.
106. *Ibid.*, 7 March 1939.
107. Ilija Jukić, *The Fall of Yugoslavia* (New York: Harcourt Brace Jovanovich, 1974), p. 99.
108. *Hrvatski Glas*, 19 July 1940.
109. *20 Godina, Kratki Pregled . . .* (Toronto, 1950), p. 42.
110. Ilija Jukić, *The Fall of Yugoslavia*, p. 99. See also Ivan Avakumovic, *The History of the Communist Party of Yugoslavia*, vol. 1 (Aberdeen: Aberdeen University Press, 1967), pp. 174-84.
111. *Hrvatski Glas*, 9 July 1940.
112. For commentary on the royal visit of 1939, see *ibid.*, 10 May 1939. Also *Hrvatski Dnevnik*, Zagreb, 10 June 1939, in clippings file. *Zavod za Migracije i Narodnosti*, 126.2a. H.R.S.S., 1939. *Zajedničar*, 19 July 1939: Milan Petrak, "Kroz Ontario."

SEVEN

World War Two and Aftermath: Co-operation and Conflict

The decade beginning in 1940 was a troubled and turbulent one for Canadian Croatians. The tensions of the war years and the Cold War which followed, difficult for all Canadians, were exacerbated for the Croats by the turmoil within their homeland, which was wracked by bloody civil conflict and Nazi occupation at the same time. In the domestic aspect they were in a far better position in Canada than they had been in World War I when they were aligned with the German enemy as citizens of the Austro-Hungarian Empire and even as recruits to her armed forces. The sympathies of the vast majority of Canada's 15,000 or so Croatians in 1941 were, for various reasons, clearly against the Axis powers, and the internal expectations were that they would contribute to the Allied war effort. The great majority were already naturalized citizens and the Canadian sons of the first generation of migrants were already coming of military age. In addition, the Canadian government was now clearly in control of its own foreign and domestic relations and thus was less vulnerable to the external pressures that had prevailed in World War I. The government was prepared to acknowedge and encourage the wartime contributions of the Croatians, and they were prepared for their part to take seriously their obligations to their adopted country.

The post-war period, however, saw the escalation of anti-Soviet feelings in the West after the Iron Curtain speech by Winston Churchill in Fulton, Missouri, in 1946. The ensuing Cold War witnessed the resurgence of tensions similar to those that had wracked western European and North American society after World War I in the "Red Scare." The effects upon intra-ethnic group relations were disastrous, since the fragile détente that had existed during the thirties and the war years against fascist dictatorships in Europe was irredeemably ended. Factional tensions, which had lain dormant for the war years, erupted with some force in the Cold War as the search for the new enemy alien subversives in North America, the "Communists and fellow travellers," began in earnest with the Kefauver Committee on un-American activities in 1947 and the Gouzenko spy affair in Canada that same year. Friendships and family relations of nearly a decade in duration were suddenly cooler and even hostile as left polarized firmly against centre and right. The only saving grace for the former was that pro-Titoist sympathies on the left were at least halfway acceptable in these troubled times because of the dramatic break of Yugoslavia with Stalin and the Cominform from 1948-53. But that subtlety was to be lost by many in the heated and often irrational rhetoric of McCarthyism in the Korean War years.

An additional and complicating factor was the polarization of intra-ethnic factions among the Croatians after World War II. Generational tensions began to fracture the loose sense of ethnic co-operation that persisted among the immigrants who had come before 1940. Ideological tensions between factions were now complicated by a complete network of social, class, and kinship ties. In the return to "normalcy" and stability after the war, the strain between immigrant parents and assimilated children often became unbearable and degenerated into delinquency or indifference on the part of the upcoming generation. Exogamous marriages of the pre-war and the war periods also produced strains in in-group/out-group relations. Equally, the influx of a rootless generation of refugees from war-torn Europe introduced a new category of displaced persons into the complex web of institutions and established family relationships. Thus, widely variant group experiences were thrown together for good or ill: former Austro-Hungarian veterans and citizens, former political and economic migrants from royalist Yugoslavia, refugees from war-torn Yugoslavia in Italian and Austrian displaced persons' camps, and children who were fully assimilated Canadians, almost entirely ignorant of their parents' language and culture. The result was a highly volatile mix, ready to explode into violent conflict at ethnic gatherings where occasionally the powderkeg was touched off.

THE WAR YEARS, 1939-45

The Croatians in Canada, like their American cousins, were faced with the difficult decisions posed by the war and its effect upon their former homeland. The only difference was that they had to face the hard choices earlier, since the cushion of formal neutrality at least offered the American Croats nearly until 1942 to establish their position. By the early declaration of loyalty to Canada and against fascist aggression, the members of the Croatian Peasant Party were firmly committed, and were followed by the Croats of the Yugoslav Communist Party, who first opposed the war and did not support it fully until Hitler's invasions of the Soviet Union in 1941. The greater indecision that characterized the American community and the isolationist attitude it adopted was a luxury the Canadian Croats could ill afford.[1] While they may have wished, as a Canadian Senator once said, "to live in a fire proof house," they could not accept the Christmas message of the Croatian Fraternal Union president in Pittsburgh in 1940 that "here in our new home we can live without fear from war's grenades, cannons, bombs and poison gas, and thus celebrate Christmas."

In the first instance, there were the official ties between the Croatian Peasant Party and the Royal Yugoslav government-in-exile in London, through its official representative, Dr. Juraj Krnjević.[2] Thus the representatives of this government, such as Dr. Ivan Šubašić, the exiled ban of Croatia, were warmly welcomed on their visit to Canada in November, 1941. A particularly enthusiastic greeting awaited him in Schumacher where he pledged his support to the British cause and his country's determination to continue the fight against Hitler until Croatia regained her independence.[3] At the same time the Peasant Party newspaper, the *Voice*, carried extended editorials denouncing the Ustaša regime of Ante Pavelić as "the puppets of he [sic] German Gestapo" and the fact that "Thousands of Croats were in concentration camps."[4]

Yet it appears that despite the warm and often polite receptions tendered to the Royal Yugoslav government abroad, there was relatively little interest by the Canadian Croats in serving under their flag during the war. This resistance became particularly apparent after 1942 when it was reorganized under the Serbian leadership of Slobodan Jovanović and the Četnik general, Draža Mihajlović, who was promoted to Minister of War in the reconstituted cabinet.[5] The recruiting fortunes of the royalist émigré government were quite dismal thereafter, despite the efforts of Colonel Savitch of the Yugoslav military mission in Canada. The universal preference of the Canadian "Yugoslavs" appeared to be for service with the Canadian Forces and also, according to one confidential source, Yugoslav recruiting was semi-farcical, "Everybody is just marking time and drawing a fat salary. The good old Yugoslav way! . . ."[6] Thus the entire attempt at recruitment and training in the Windsor area was abandoned as hopeless by Colonel Savitch, who in the summer of 1943 discharged the pitiful dozen recruits who had enlisted in the Yugoslav Armed Forces.[7]

Rather more successful were the early efforts of the Croatian Peasant Party and the Communists in raising funds for the support of the Canadian Red Cross in 1940-41. In well-organized subscription efforts reminiscent of successful hospital and charity drives of the thirties, the thirty-six branches of the Peasant Party in Canada raised $800 in November, 1940, as evidence of their support for the humanitarian efforts of the Red Cross, their pride in their Canadian citizenship, and their interest in "crushing the agressor [sic] who seeks to destroy the liberty and culture of all the free peoples of the world."[8] After Hitler's invasion of the USSR in 1941, the Committee for the Medical Aid of the Soviet Union was formed by the radical-left group for the Freedom of the

Old Homeland. By January, 1942, over $600 was raised and over $2,000 more pledged, so that a total of nearly $3,000 was turned over to the Red Cross in this first drive.[9]

External events then appeared to cement further these parallel efforts into a common Yugoslav-Canadian cause for the rest of the war. The first was the heroic resistance of the Russians to the advance of Hitler's divisions in 1942 and the turning of the tide at Stalingrad in 1943. The second was the increasingly stiff resistance by the Yugoslav Partisans to the German occupation and offensive of 1943, and the gradual emergence of Tito's National Army of Liberation as a more viable alternative to Mihajlović's Četniks. As a result, attitudes within the United States and particularly among the American Croatians began to shift more markedly in favour of Tito's Partisans and of Soviet Russia. The All Slavic Congress held in Detroit in 1942 was the first manifestation of this growing sense of the development of a larger pan-Slav unity among the South Slavs. At this time the American Croatians and Slovenes began to unite their propaganda efforts against the attempts by the Yugoslav governments abroad to smear these groups as pro-Nazi and pro-Pavelić, and they shifted their support to Tito's anti-fascist Council of National Liberation.[10] The culmination of this process was the formation of the Congress of American Croatians on February 20, 1943, which brought together nearly 1,000 delegates from across the United States and Canada. The upshot of the Congress was to endorse strongly Stalin and Tito as allies and to urge in the name of a million American Croats, that all Croatians, Serbians, and Slovenians unite against "foreign occupiers and native traitors."[11]

The Canadian Croatians had already begun to swing markedly in this direction early in 1943 by supporting the Canadian Aid to Russia Fund, which was collected by Communist and Peasant Party organizers alike. Nearly every community on the northern mining frontier subscribed $1,000 each and a total of $18,000 was raised in Canada and sent from Vancouver to Vladivostok in March of 1943.[12] Subscriptions continued to the Canadian Red Cross, which raised another $37,000 in a sustained subscription drive among the Croatians, Serbs, and Slovenes.[13] Congratulations also went to the Congress of American Croatians in Chicago from Peter Stanković of the *Croatian Voice* in Winnipeg, impressing on them his desire for "a better understanding and closer fellowship between Croats, wherever they are located and also to our neighbour Slovenes, Serbs and Bulgars."[14] His newspaper followed up on this plea for Slavic unity by carrying further lead articles by Bogdan Raditsa praising the heroic efforts of Tito's Partisans, and by others congratulating the Committee of American South Slavs (Jugoslavenski Američki Odbor) for its efforts in support of the National Liberation Front.[15]

This new leftward re-orientation of the Croatians to a South Slav posture in 1943 produced a significant disturbance in extra-group relations with the Serbian Nationalist group supporters of Mihajlović and the Royal Yugoslav government. In essence, the latter government saw its ethnic base narrow to the Serbian group from the more powerful Yugoslav-Canadian Association of pre-war years. Its newspaper arm *Glas Kanade* suffered increasing competition from new Yugoslav Communist publications such as the Serbian *Herald (Srpski Glasnik)* and the Croatian *News (Novosti)*, which were created during the war.[16] At the same time increasing competition occurred from 1943 on between the Montreal-based Canadian Friends of Yugoslavia, which sought to raise funds for support of war-torn Yugoslavia, and the Toronto-centred Council of Canadian South Slavs to Aid Free Yugoslavia, which represented the new coalition of pro-Titoist forces. The first organization was composed of prominent English and French-Canadian citizens in Montreal and had on its board and executive churchmen, businessmen, politicians, and academicians ranging from Samuel Bronfman to Charles Dunning and Watson Kirkconnell. Yet by the very fact that it had as its patroness Queen Marie of Yugoslavia and one of its principal organizers was a Russian count with Montenegrin background, it was perceived by the Croats and Slovenes in Toronto, in particular, as a front for pro-Serbian hegemony and pro-Mihajlović fund-raising.[17] Complaints of their lack of representation on the CFY Yugoslav Relief Fund were lodged by the federated groups composing the Tito-oriented Council of Canadian South Slavs and sent to Ottawa.[18] While attempts at mediation were made throughout 1943-44, significant blockages developed in the delivery of clothing, medicine, and other supplies to Yugoslavia.[19] One exasperated politician from the northern Ontario riding of Porcupine, J.A. Bradette, brought the matter to the attention of the Minister of National War Services in Ottawa, observing that the Yugoslav immigrants in Canada had collected $230,000 and sixty tons of used clothing, but could not secure permits from the Yugoslav Fund to forward supplies to the needy and suffering in Yugoslavia. Reducing the entire matter to human terms, he observed that "these Canadian Yugoslavs, who have always been very faithful in all their war activities . . . do not understand the present situation in Canada, nor do they know of the regular contribution Canada is making to Yugoslavia, but the day will come when they will realize this."[20] Faced by the blockages in wartime supply transport and legal authorization, the Council of Canadian South Slavs and other organizations like the Croatian Peasant Party sought various unilateral means to expedite the delivery of clothing and supplies. Two approaches taken by the Council with the approval of the Wartime Prices and Trade Board were either to send funds to the Red Cross or to send them directly to Italy, whence medical supplies worth $50,000 were distributed in Yugoslavia.[21] The uneasy relationship of the Council with the Canadian Friends of Yugoslavia continued to the end of the war and beyond, with the result that nearly $500,000 were collected by 1945 and sent by various means to Yugoslavia through the Toronto-based Council of Canadian South Slavs.[22]

171

The military contributions of the Croatian Canadians to the Canadian Armed Forces during World War II cannot be accurately determined. In the United States it was estimated that 14,000 or 23 per cent of the entire membership of the American Croatian Fraternal Union enlisted.[23] While no similar statistic can at this point be derived for Canada, the honour roll and the nominal rolls of regimental histories in Canada indicate that the enlistment rates must have been significant.[24] Numerous citations of enlistments in the armed services were printed in the various Croatian-language publications during the war. One article, for example, in the radical newspaper, *Novosti*, referred to the sending of Christmas parcels by the League of Canadian Croatians to forty-four "Canadian boys of Yugoslav origin at present overseas with the Canadian armed forces."[25] From Kirkland Lake alone there were seven enlistments to the three services announced on December 14, 1943, in the *Croatian Voice*.[26] Other regular announcements were made of military decorations and of those killed in action, particularly after the invasions of Italy and Normandy in 1944-45.[27] Several Croats also chose to serve in the armed forces of other Allied nations during the war. The American services sometimes attracted Croatian Canadians, perhaps because of special opportunities or kinship relationships south of the border.[28]

Other Croatian Canadians served in Tito's Partisans during the latter part of the war for the liberation of Yugoslavia.[29] One of these was Tomo Čačić, who had been deported from Canada in 1933 and had served in the Spanish Civil War in 1937-38. In 1942 he returned to his Nazi-occupied homeland, joined the Partisans, and served in the hardened Primorje and Lika brigade of his native region until 1944. Debilitation from wounds and tuberculosis forced him to retire to an Italian military hospital in Bari where he lost a heavily infected leg to surgical amputation.[30] Among others who served in the Partisans was Peter Erdeljac, a Yugoslav-Canadian radical who was parachuted into Lika in the British supported airdrop to assist the Partisans. He later became a political commissar in the Karlovac brigade, which had also attracted several other Canadians to its service.[31] How many Canadians actually served with the Partisans is unclear, but it is estimated that close to forty Canadian paratroopers were recruited for the British airdrop into Yugoslavia and eight of them were killed in action.[32]

While the Croatian-Canadian contributions of manpower were not nearly as heavy as the Croatian-American contributions, it must be remembered that the community in Canada was much smaller and younger. Since the bulk of the 20,000 or so Yugoslavs in Canada by 1941 had been in Canada less than fifteen years, the Canadian sons of military age were few and compulsory military service only a recent introduction to Canada in 1944. The predisposition of the older migrants was less toward military service than to financial contributions to assist their war-torn homeland. And by comparison to the American contribution of $3 million to the Yugoslav Relief Fund, the $500,000 from the Canadian community some twenty times smaller was impressive. This united affirmation of support for the homeland was fortuitously combined with a similar concern for Canadian volunteer efforts, and Croatians' contributions to war bond drives and Red Cross blood donor efforts were substantial during the war.[33] Often underestimated also was their work in wartime industries – in munitions and heavy factories such as Canada Car and Stelco, the shipbuilding industries on the Great Lakes, and the mining industries of the northern interior. All told, their war effort was creditable indeed for a group of new Canadians with scarcely two decades in their adopted country by the end of the war.

POST-WAR REFUGEES AND RETURNEES (POVRATNICI)

The war had left deep scars on Yugoslavia, some it appeared irreparable. Military and civilian casualties ran to nearly two million (11 per cent of the total population) and property losses nearly $50 billion.[34] The post-war recovery of the economy thus demanded enormous infusions of capital and volunteer work in reconstruction, some of which was provided through the United Nations Relief and Reconstruction Administration and some by Soviet technical assistance and trade agreements. The resulting post-war reconstruction in the ensuing five years was dramatic and a tribute to the resilience of the peoples of Yugoslavia.

But the war, like all wars, was to have its winners and its losers, and among the latter were those displaced by the victory of the Partisans and the establishment of a Communist Yugoslavia in 1945.[35] The living remnant were 15,000 refugees who were living in displaced persons camps in Austria, Italy, and Germany.[36] There were many – exactly how many is not determined – who perished during the war and its bloody aftermath. The toll included, by various estimates ranging from tens of thousands to 250,000, Croatian soldiers and civilians near Bleiburg in May, 1945.[37] Thus, almost immediately the uneasy alliance that had operated during the war ruptured as the Croatian immigrants abroad began to take a critical posture toward the political oppression of the Croats in the war's aftermath. By August, 1945, both the president of the Croatian Fraternal Union in the United States, John Butković, and the president of the Croatian Peasant Party in Canada, Stephen Bradica, dissociated themselves from Communist Yugoslavia.[38] The latter, in an open letter addressed to Prime Minister King, delineated the historical evolution of the Croatian people and deplored the political oppression of the Peasant Party in Yugoslavia by "Tito's Communists," and further stated the intention of the party in Canada to support "those Croats who, during Italian occupation were interned in Italy and today do not want to return to Communist Yugoslavia." Bradica further demanded "the guarantee of life" to refugees in Europe so that they might be permitted to migrate to other lands until the atmosphere of human rights and liberties in their homeland was improved.

173

Political pressure for the acceptance of refugees from Italy and Austria was initiated in 1946 by the Peasant Society and the Roman Catholic Church. This action created an immediate rift with the Canadian Council of South Slavs, which argued that relief activities should be directed, as before, at the needy half-million war orphans within Yugoslavia.[39] But the Croatian patriotic societies vigorously defended their concern with the European refugees and found some support among the Canadian Friends of Yugoslavia, which had directed the efforts of the Yugoslav Relief Fund during the war. As one of their officers put it in a letter to the Canadian Red Cross, "I may say that not only small children but many boys and girls of tender age that are suffering in Europe and some of their parents should be brought to Canada so that in this free and democratic country they could start a new life."[40]

Both the Croatian and Yugoslav groups continued in their efforts to relieve human misery both within Yugoslavia and without. The Yugoslav nationals for their part continued to collect funds in 1946 for Yugoslav Relief and transmitted another $15,000 to the Yugoslav Red Cross.[41] At the same time the Canadian Council of South Slavs pledged itself to closer co-operation with the Canadian Friends of Yugoslavia and collected $67,000 by December, 1946, for hospitals, schools, and railways in the old country.[42] For their part, the officials of the Croatian Peasant Party addressed themselves to the refugee problem and persistently petitioned Ottawa for assistance in expediting the passage of displaced Croatians to Canada.[43] They were subsequently assured that the Canadian government was assisting in refugee settlement, but that the admission of displaced persons was not restricted "to any particular race or races," and hence displaced persons of Croatian origin would have to meet "the requirements of health, character, etc. as required by the regulations."[44]

The ideological divisions between Croatians and Yugoslavs deepened further in the next two years. The Yugoslav Communists in Canada became more imbued than ever with the pan-Slavic movement and congress which swept through Europe and North America in the mid-forties.[45] They participated actively in the Third All-American Slav Congress held in New York on September 20-22, 1946, and sent four delegates to a similar demonstration of pan-Slavic unity at Belgrade in November.[46] Even before the left-wing congress met, the anti-Communist Croats had begun to form their own organization, the United Croatians of America and Canada, which was founded in the spring of 1946 in Cleveland. The founding organizations included six national organizations of a fraternal, Catholic, and cultural orientation, and they agreed to meet in Chicago in early September. This organization was soundly endorsed by two affiliated Canadian organizations, the Croatian Peasant Party and the Croatian Fraternal Union, and it roundly denounced the activities of the parallel pro-Communist congresses being held in New York and Belgrade.[47] Thus, on the one hand the leftists vigorously denounced in New York the American anti-Communist foreign policy and their refusal to allow entry to Tito's Yugoslav delegates, and on the other the anti-Communist coalition denounced Yugoslavia's trial and sentencing of Archbishop Stepinac and the denial of freedom of the press to foreign news agencies such as Reuters.[48] In the Canadian context, the debate became particularly heated when Dr. Vladko Maček, leader of the Croatian Peasant Party in exile, came to Hamilton in November of 1946 to address a party-sponsored banquet in that city. The occasion followed a visit to Ottawa by Maček and was celebrated by the issuance of the new Canadian naturalization papers by the federal Liberal MP for Hamilton, T.H. Rose, to a new Canadian of Croatian descent. Mr. Rose took the opportunity to respond to leftist hecklers outside the hall and suggested that a collection be taken up for the hecklers' transportation back to dictatorial Yugoslavia.[49] He also promised Maček and his supporters that as of the New Year the Canadian government would "open her doors for Croatian refugees in Austria and Italy." The left-wing Croatian *Novosti (News)* was driven into a verbal fury over the whole affair and denounced the politicians who represented Hamilton for appearing to support Maček and "his bosses" in Washington and London and the immigration of further "fascist murderers and bandits" into Canada.[50]

A more sustained and heated issue was inserted into the left-wing combat in the fall of 1946, when the Canadian Council of South Slavs officially endorsed a policy of repatriation to Yugoslavia.[51] This policy of transportation of people, tools, and machinery back to Yugoslavia initiated the *"povratnici"* (returnees) movement, which became a hotly debated issue in the South Slav communites across Canada for the next five years. The motivation for the back-to-Yugoslavia movement was complex but initially appeared as an extension of the Yugoslavia relief measures of the war years and another means of direct contribution to the reconstruction of the homeland.[52] By mid-November, the reconstruction group had over two dozen contributory members and a total subscription of $10,900. By mid-December, the idea had caught hold; the Vancouver colony had promised to invest a half-million dollars in machinery, and the first group of repatriates was slated to sail in the spring of 1947.[53]

By January, 1947, the Canadian Council of South Slavs had collected $337,105 of the $2 million quota that had been established as their objective.[54] More significant perhaps than the resounding success of the fund drive was the sentiment generated in the radical left for the return to Yugoslavia. The enthusiastic tales of the returnees who had served with the Partisans and delegates to the various pan-Slav congresses fuelled a utopian nostalgia of unprecedented dimension. To a generation of immigrants cut off from their homeland by two decades of depression and war, the prospect of contributing to the socialist reconstruction of a society they had been forced to leave seemed overpowering. The idea of

175

work with a purpose among people whose language was their own and among faces which were becoming by now a dim memory was a dream come true for many.

The transportation of the first group of returned migrants from Vancouver was aboard a ship, the *Radnik* (Worker), expressly purchased for this purpose by the Yugoslav government. Originally an old ocean freighter that had plied the waters of the Pacific as a troop carrier for the United States in World War II, the *Radnik* was renamed and refitted for its new mission.[55] Its first complement of passengers was picked up in February, 1947, along the coast, in San Pedro, Seattle, and Vancouver. Twenty-eight members of the United Fishermen and Allied Workers Union, led by Marijan Ruljanovic and Anton Milkovic, boarded the *Radnik* accompanied by hundreds of friends and relatives who came to dockside to see them off.[56] Perhaps forewarned by the experience of the Japanese fishermen who had lost their property during the war and were now seeking indemnification,[57] these South Slavs sold their property and transferred their funds directly to Yugoslavia. In addition, they carried with them $500,000 worth of fishing equipment and lumbering machinery purchased by the Canadian Council of South Slavs on their behalf, and for the export of which they had had to secure permission from the Canadian government.[58] Also loaded on board were hundreds of parcels of food, clothing, and comforts for their friends and relatives in the old country. The ship then sailed via the Panama Canal and the Atlantic into the Mediterranean, where it picked up further supplies and passengers in Marseilles and Genoa before debarcation in Split later in March.[59]

The first expedition had scarcely landed when plans were afoot for a second and third. With a steadily increasing subscription fund, which totalled $1.2 million in committed funds by July, 1947, and glowing reports from the returnees in the first wave, the pressures mounted to increase the flow of people and material to Yugoslavia. The next voyage of the *Radnik* was slated for departure from Montreal late in May, and 500 returnees travelled by train from Ontario and the West to make their rendezvous with destiny. Unlike the earlier tentative expedition of a few older returnees from Vancouver, this "first group" was a highly organized pilgrimage and more clearly an ideological and youthful crusade.

An impassioned article by a young fisherman from the Vancouver area explained the motivation of the first-generation Canadians leaving for their parents' homeland both in ideological and personal terms:

> As we listened to the [older] speakers, which followed it did not take us long to realize that their stress on us was no mere coincidence, but truly a reality. We were definitely in the limelight. We realized just how much the older people though[t] of us, what their wishes and hopes really were. In other words, we grasped the responsibility that rests on the shoulders of all youth throughout the

world. . . . Why have we chosen to go to Yugoslavia? What is our motivating force? Are we leaving Canada because we are unhappy here? Are we leaving because we dislike the people of Canada? No. We are leaving because we feel that to sleep in times such as these is not only a crime but it is suicidal. We want to look to a future, a better world. We want to have a world where nations can be proud of their national status and still find time to break the black chain of reaction which has strewn our souls with hate, blood and war. This we feel that we can achieve in the new Yugoslavia. The youth of that country realized what we in Canada have just begun to grasp. They paid the price for freedom and independence, we, in turn have learned from their bitter experience. . . .[60]

This new wave of migrants waved their tearful goodbyes to their friends and relatives at railway stations across Canada, who urged them to write as soon as they arrived in their home villages and to give their best regards to long unseen relatives there. Once in Montreal and aboard the *Radnik*, the returnees felt an overpowering sense of community, and they literally sang, danced, and feasted on their voyage home full of belief in the future of their promised land. They arrived finally in Rijeka to a heroes' welcome with 30,000 lustily cheering them and Tito in unison.[61] Almost immediately the younger members, about forty in number, were pressed into service as a volunteer work brigade and went to work on the Šamac-Sarajevo railroad line.[62]

A slightly disquieting note in the euphoria that swept through the left-wing Croatian communities at this time was the position of the Canadian government. While it took a consciously liberal position of admitting any but "war criminals and traitors, and assisting those who want to return to the country," it had to take care to monitor possible abuses of immigration laws.[63] Subsequently, the Minister for External Affairs, Louis St. Laurent, formally announced in Parliament that naturalized citizens would have to return within six years or forfeit their Canadian status. Landed immigrants and aliens would automatically lose any chance of return to Canada as soon as they left Canada.[64] Meanwhile, the Canadian immigration department kept a watchful eye on those emigrating, obtaining where possible ship manifests of the *Radnik* and files on those who left.[65]

In the meantime, plans were laid for yet another wave of *povratnici* in the midsummer of 1947; despite estimates of thousands waiting to return on the next voyage of the *Radnik*, less than a full complement was subscribed for the third sailing.[66] The third group of less than 400 Canadian returnees sailed from Montreal in late October, 1947, and after picking up another seventy passengers in New York it arrived in Split, Dalmatia, in mid-November.[67] It was also apparent that the Yugoslav Reconstruction Fund had begun to falter somewhat late in 1947, for the organizers of the Canadian Council of South Slavs announced that although $1.8 million had been subscribed, six months would be allowed for the collection of the remaining $200,000.[68] Further optimistic estimates were made for another three voyages of *povratnici* in 1948, the first to sail in May. But a sober rejoinder was made to those "who are not willing to make sacrifices for New Yugoslavia, it is better not to go there. It is better for speculators and adventurers to wait here until they get into 'breadlines' and 'old folks' homes."[69] Thus, despite accounts of the superiority of the new communist society that appeared regularly in the left-wing press, [70] resistance had begun to set in to the idea of return to the homeland. By April, 1948, only 100 subscribers had indicated their intention to return in the summer and had arranged for their passports and visas home.[71]

It was also manifest by now that the Yugoslav paradise regained had become a paradise lost for several of those who had returned. Late in 1947, the Canadian immigration department in London received its first formal application for return. Like many of the returnees, the applicant was a naturalized Canadian citizen and had worked for several years on the CNR before returning in 1947. Upon arrival he refused to yield his Canadian papers, and, after several weeks' work on the railways in Yugoslavia, he had another disagreement with authorities and peremptorily quit, indicating his desire to return to Canada.[72] Further indications of whole groups wishing to return were received by April, 1948, and by May of that year a Canadian legation was opened in Belgrade to process emigration applications.[73]

Since the ideological advantage had now clearly swung to the right, requests came from the *Croatian Voice* to examine the books the Canadian Council of South Slavs for unaccounted discrepancies of $30,000 in funds collected for the Relief of Yugoslavia fund.[74] Despite the fact that no irregularities were found in the accounts, and appropriate rejoinders were made to John Diefenbaker's accusations in the House of Commons,[75] the seeds of suspicion had been planted. Further warnings were then issued from the Department of External Affairs that any migrants back to Yugoslavia should be warned that they might be deprived of their Canadian citizenship upon arrival there.[76] Finally, the denial of entry to two officials of the now pro-Yugoslav Croatian Fraternal Union of America by Canadian authorities in May, 1948, appeared to mark yet another step in the direction of reaction in the eyes of the left.[77]

The increasingly negative political climate in Canada clouded the departure of the fourth and last expedition of *povratnici,* which left for Yugoslavia in June, 1948. This group experienced a more negative public reaction than the previous ones, ranging from police refusal in Montreal to allow them to sing their Slavic folk songs publicly to denial by emigration authorities of permission to export a Jeep to Yugoslavia.[78] But despite the clamour of the Montreal daily press, the 1948 expedition achieved a full complement of 500 passengers, which included some of the prominent Yugoslav-Canadian newspapermen and ex-Spanish Civil War volunteers such as Edo Yardas and Ivan Linardich.[79]

As the *Radnik* steamed across the Atlantic, the reasons for the departure of these top-ranking Yugoslav Communists in Canada became more apparent. The replacement on June 14 of the three South Slav newspapers – the Croatian *Novosti (News)*, the Serbian *Herald (Srpski Glasnik)*, and the Slovene paper *Unity (Edinost)* – by *Jedinstvo,* a single Yugoslav newspaper, coincided roughly with the public denunciation by Stalin and the Cominform of the Communist Party of Yugoslavia on June 28 in Bucharest.[80] This public announcement merely formalized a struggle that had been escalating in intensity since February between Stalin and Tito, and now culminated in a formal attack upon bourgeois nationalism, Yugoslav style. In the months that followed, it was readily apparent that the Yugoslav-Canadian editorial cadre of *Novosti,* which had left on the fourth expedition from Canada, was strongly pro-Tito and the new editors of *Jedinstvo* were more inclined to Stalin in the growing rift between Belgrade and Moscow.[81]

After several months of uneasy *détente* in which it appeared possible to reconcile Yugoslav national aspirations with Soviet Communism, the break came in early October, 1948, when several members of the Yugoslav legation in Ottawa resigned over Tito's policies in favour of Stalin.[82] Two weeks later a scathing denunciation of Edo Yardas appeared in *Jedinstvo* decrying his new affiliation with Titoist policies as the new Deputy Minister of External Trade and Commerce.[83] Without a medium in Canada to reply to his critics, Yardas defended himself and other returned immigrants in the pro-Yugoslav Croatian Fraternal Union newspaper in the United States, *Zajedničar.*[84] Further open letters to the editors of *Jedinstvo* were sent by Ivan Linardich from Yugoslavia, condemning the pro-Stalinist policies of the Communist Party of Canada and its leader, Tim Buck.[85] Charges and countercharges were levelled: the Stalinists that Tito had jailed many of their persuasion, including a returnee and a former member of the Yugoslav legation in Ottawa, Major Branko Vukelich;[86] the Titoists that the pro-Soviets had effectively killed the Yugoslav Relief Fund and the *povratnici* movement by refusing to send more machinery or capital or to encourage repatriation.[87] In essence both statements had some elements of truth, in particular the latter, for only twenty-two of 200 original applicants travelled with the last group in November, 1948, and the last donation of machinery left the total at less than $840,000 for 1948.[88] With that donation, the Canadian Council of South Slavs effectively wound up its business, having repatriated 1,869 returnees and donated $1.8 million in total.

The story did not end there, however, for dissatisfaction, whether ideological or economic, with Tito's Yugoslavia mounted, and further applications were made to come back to Canada. Several of the 1,100 Canadian citizens who migrated back to Yugoslavia returned within a year. One of them who had lived in Canada for twenty years admitted he had been in error to return to the poverty of his homeland, where he was greeted with the incredulous query, "Why then did you come here where there is not enough food even for us?"[89] In all, some 450 of those South Slavs who held Canadian citizenship returned to Canada over the following decade and a half.[90] The citizenship of several others was revoked by the Canadian Citizenship Registration Branch in 1952, some of them having been citizens for as long as twenty-two years, and the average for more than ten years.[91] Even from among the non-Canadians, some were readmitted to Canada on compassionate grounds, such as one former volunteer to the Canadian army in 1944-45, who was finally allowed to return in 1956.[92] Yet another petition was lodged with immigration authorities by two children of a British Columbia miner whose mother had died in Yugoslavia shortly after the parents' return to their homeland. They pleaded their case eloquently and apparently successfully, on the grounds that they were born in Canada, were Canadian citizens, "attending Canadian schools and brought up in the Canadian spirit," and that their father, despite the fact that he lived for twenty years in Canada without applying for citizenship, had also "got so used to [the] Canadian way of living."[93] But others who had no such emotional or legal claim had irrevocably burned their bridges for a return to Canada. Because of their leftist connection they also had few political or institutional ties to the organizations accepting and processing refugees who were leaving Yugoslavia in increasing numbers after the war.

The refugee problem that resulted in post-war Europe was an entirely new phenomenon, which in the short term created a temporary hiatus in Canadian government policy. Technically, the Canadian government had provided by Order-in-Council on October 26, 1945, for the granting of permanent status to refugees from enemy countries and occupied territories who had entered Canada prior to 1939.[94] But there was no provision for the hundreds of thousands of stateless refugees housed in displaced persons camps throughout Europe, and in particular the 15,000 or so Croats in Germany, Italy, and Austria. It was not until June, 1947, that the Canadian government took independent action, again in Order-in-Council, for the admission of an initial number of 5,000 displaced persons.

In that year there were established five Canadian immigration teams working in Germany and Austria, out of headquarters in Heidelberg.[95] With the intention of expediting refugee resettlement in Canada, the government had already approved emergency measures to bring to Canada persons admissible under existing immigration regulations. Consequently, the first of the refugees from Yugoslavia sailed in April of 1947, and in all 56,000 displaced persons were processed in the next eighteen months by the International Refugee Organization and Canadian immigration officials. A total of 123,500 were processed for transportation to Canada by 1950, and of these 5,123 were from Yugoslavia, although UNESCO estimates later placed the number at 20,000.[96]

More important than the number of refugees from post-war Yugoslavia was their motivation for leaving and the unique nature of their plight as persons without a state. Unquestionably many of the first refugees were the war's losers, military personnel who had served with the *domobran* army and also those who sympathized with the ousted wartime government.[97] With the Communist reprisals that followed against ideological unorthodoxy, many intellectuals, priests, professionals, displaced politicians, and bureaucrats followed.[98] In addition, various ethnic groups were displaced by the war, such as German-speaking Schwabians from Vojvodina displaced from homes they had occupied since the middle of the eighteenth century.[99] While these naturally returned to Germany, it was equally natural for the Italians of Istria to retreat to Italy after the war.[100] To these were added those peasant refugees who refused to comply with the collectivization of agriculture.[101] Thus, a steady stream of political and economic malcontents swelled the camps in the hundreds and thousands as Yugoslavia went from crisis to crisis in the post-war decade.[102]

The drive to admit the refugees from Yugoslavia to Canada was led by the Croatian Peasant Party of Canada. On several occasions during the year, petitions were sent to the Canadian government to allow the Croatian victims of "Nazi and Communist persecutions" to enter Canada.[103] As well, the Peasant Party regularly advised through the *Croatian Voice* the new arrivals from displaced persons camps in Europe of their rights and their obligations to honour the labour contracts they had to enter upon coming to Canada, "otherwise they might harm themselves as well as others who are still waiting in Europe for permission to enter this democratic country."[104] While their ministrations to the refugees were not without political purpose, they also provided practical assistance to the refugees upon their arrival in Canada.[105]

From the standpoint of the Canadian government, the pressure to accept refugees appeared to be based on a mixture of humanitarian, political, and economic motives. The federal government, for example, allowed thirty-five immigrants into Canada in September, 1947, and another forty-four in November largely on compassionate grounds. The five Croats in the first group had been gainfully occupied in Canada for several years after illegal entry, several of them in wartime industries. Of the second variety was a group of ten priests, businessmen, and intellectuals, in short, political refugees with some status, means, or connection. As such, they were considered potentially valuable as Canadian citizens.[106] In the last category were those refugees who came in 1948 as a result of an economic upswing in primary resource commodities, which in turn created a significant demand for unskilled labour in the Ontario pulp and paper industry. The need for woodcutters by the large corporations such as Abitibi in northern Ontario was particularly acute, and as a result there were sixty Yugoslav woodsworkers in the first five shipments of 3,000 refugees that sailed from Bremerhaven, West Germany, by October of 1947.[107] Several citizens of Yugoslav origin, many of them Croatians, also found their way into northern Ontario railway and hydro-electric projects sponsored by the CNR and Ontario Hydro. These frontier labour camps had been largely depleted of Croats and other South Slavs during the war, but a few older immigrants in their forties and fifties remained, and now mingled with the younger displaced persons coming into camp for the first time.

A typical frontier migrant of this type was a political refugee and former Croatian soldier from Zagorje during World War II who fled Communist Yugoslavia in 1946, spent two years in d.p. camps in Austria and Germany, then came to Canada as a bush-worker and navvy in 1948. After drifting across western Canada for several months, he finally reached the Pine Portage Power development at Nipigon, Ontario, where he joined sixty other South Slavs, who counted for 5 per cent of the total labour force.[108] In general, these younger men, who were often educated to a secondary school level, proved eager and capable of learning at the hands of their Frontier College instructors. One former captain in the *domobran* army of Croatia particularly impressed one of his instructors with the much vaunted hospitality of the South Slavs in contrast to "our emotionless Anglo-Saxon society."[109]

Relations between the Croatian refugees and other Yugoslavs were often much less amiable, as inter-group relations became more hostile and divided. The leftists often identified the newcomers as *ustaša* or war criminals in their newspapers and at their public meetings.[110] One member of the Croatian Peasant Party and a newcomer to Canada was so accused in Welland, Ontario, and at a mass meeting the left strongly denounced the Canadian government for allowing such "European reactionaries" into Canada.[111] The accused subsequently took legal action to clear his name in a libel suit against a prominent member of the Canadian Council of South Slavs. The latter official received six months in prison for libel, although the left still claimed an ideological victory after the well-publicized trial.[112]

In the meantime, the migration of the Croatian refugee settlers continued at a slow but steady trickle in the late 1940's and early 1950's.[113] The demand for cheap unskilled labour continued unabated and more Yugoslavs were imported to work under contract to mining, lumber, construction, and railway companies.[114] Although many more in this new wave from Yugoslavia to North America were Serbian than in the pre-war era,[115] there were nevertheless several hundred Croatian miners, bricklayers, and lumberworkers among them.[116] Their numbers remained at a nearly constant 5 per cent of the total work force of railway extra gangs, pulp-cutting crews, and hydro construction gangs in remote frontier locations.[117]

The movement of refugees had become so substantial by the early 1950's that the older Croatian immigrants to Canada were often angered, as were many other Canadians, at having to compete with non-union "d.p." labour. One naturalized Canadian of South Slav background complained bitterly to the Immigration Department in Ottawa that many native Canadians were out of work "all on account of foreigners taking the jobs . . . because a D.P. is there."[118] The gross exploitation of immigrant railway navvies by railway sub-contractors in northern Ontario was also criticized, although fewer Croatians than Italians, Greeks, and Portuguese were subject to the classic abuses of labour indenture.[119] The left-wing Yugoslavs were particularly annoyed at the influx of thousands of refugee "scab labourers" coming to toil in the paradise "of Canadian primary industry."[120] They were consequently most active in supporting the radical unions of the western resource frontier, the International Woodworkers in British Columbia, the United Mineworkers in Alberta, the steelworkers and mine mill unions in northern Ontario and Quebec.[121] Articles in the left-wing press denigrated the d.p.'s ("dipi-jevci") as professional *declassés* ("lawyers, doctors, dentists, bureaucrats and heaven knows what else") who had come down in the world since their halcyon days during the war.[122] Clearly, so these leftists claimed, a residual peasant distrust of the urban middle class, combined with a sense of prior claim upon Canada's riches and potential as their chosen country, had forced them from their native soil. Also, an inverted sense of social superiority gained from the struggle and hardships of the depression was particularly evident in a fictionalized romanticization of the great Canadian industrial worker "Big Jack," which appeared in *Jedinstvo*.[123] This radical Jack was a Croatian idealization of Jack Canuck, a heroic and progressive worker, who was unimpressed by "schoolboys" but was attracted to workingmen of practical skills and experience. Placed beside such superhuman characters, who symbolized the successful economic and social adjustment of the earlier generation, the new refugees were perceived as a vestige of past class oppression, which posed a direct threat to the present and future aspirations of the left.

For their part the refugees from Yugoslavia, who numbered some 10,000 by 1951, reflected the sudden addition of a significant unassimilated element of perhaps 6,000 to 7,000 Croatians by the early fifties. Like many of their contemporaries who went to Australia, New Zealand, or the United States, they were rootless aliens in a country often "hostile to their presence."[124] The attitudes of many of these post-war arrivals were complex and ranged from feelings of intense ethnocentrism and attachment to their Croatian nationality to a sense of rootlessness that acknowledged no allegiances beyond the immediate family. Among the liberal professionals and businessmen who usually fell into the first category, there was often an evident frustration at the menial occupations and lack of status that had to be endured during the first year in Canada.[125] The case of a former Slovenian industrialist might also be taken as characteristic of some dispossessed Croatian businessmen, for like them he, too, endured the physical stress and psychological penance

183

of a year at contract labour in the northern wilderness. But he sought out urban civilization as soon as the opportunity presented itself. "By now I am saved from my one-year long contract. The first thing I did was move to Toronto. The only job I could this far find here is washing dishes, but yesterday I attended for the first time the singing rehearsals of a Slovenian choir and I felt happy for the first time." Thereafter he reconciled his strong sense of ethnicity with his economic and social drives by becoming an ethnic journalist and travel agent, a happy compromise of Old and New World allegiances.[126]

The response of the working-class migrants of the post-war era was equally critical of Canadian society in its own way. While they were less aware of the larger cultural issues that concerned the middle-class intellectuals, they, too, found some fault with their new environment. While they were astounded with the vast wide-open spaces, the great political freedom, and the liberty of expression they found in Canada,[127] they were concerned with such nebulous factors as the "quality of life," which ran across a large range of issues from the craftsmanship in industrial production to the lack of civilized leisure opportunities. A survey of Ottawa post-war immigrants in the late 1940's revealed them to be hurt by anti-d.p. prejudice combined with an initial feeling of exploitation and job frustration in the first years of work in Canada.[128] Women in particular who served as domestic charwomen after the war felt exploited by their labour contracts, having had to endure heavy physical labour and long hours. They also complained of having been insulted and ridiculed, making their menial tasks all the more unpalatable.[129]

Thus, two generations of migrants – the pre-war migrants of the late twenties and those of the post-war decade – had come to a fundamental impasse regarding a wide spectrum of political, social, and economic issues. The pre-war immigrant for the most part was happy to have a steady job in industry after the insecurity of the depression years. He also sensed the prospects of a better world for his children if he worked hard, and his wife was usually happy to tend the children in a newly acquired home and thereby emulate the ideal of Canadian family life in the 1950's.[130] The older migrants often perceived the new arrivals as having it good in terms of paid assistance for their passage and employment and language opportunities unavailable to them in the depression years. Finally, and perhaps unfairly, they considered the new immigrants solely concerned with getting ahead financially as quickly as possible without contributing to community causes or to Canadian society.[131]

The post-war generation, on the other hand, perceived of the world as an unjust one and considered themselves as the dispossessed victims of oppression. To them, the older migrants were naive in their romanticization of the European past and unaware of the brutal realities of the present. They saw the older generation as favoured by fate and envied them their homes, their knowledge of the English language, and their children's ease in Canadian society. If there were two solitudes of misunderstanding between the two majority cultures of French and English, the two which existed between the two generations of Croatians posed an equally unbridgeable gap by the early 1950's. Time alone would dull the harsh perceptions each group held of the other.

In the meantime, the process of assimilation into Canadian society continued on its forward course in the post-war era. At an historic citizenship ceremony held in Ottawa on January 3, 1947, Prime Minister Mackenzie King celebrated another milestone in his life-long dedication to Canadian nationality by honouring the new Canadian Citizenship Act.[132] After many speeches by dignitaries on the subject of Canada's emergence as a tolerant, multicultural country, citizenship certificates were awarded to Canadians from all walks of life. Prime Minister King rose to receive the first certificate from Chief Justice Rinfret of the Supreme Court, and was followed by Giuseppe Agostini, the Italian-born music conductor, Wasyl Elyniak, the first Ukrainian settler in Canada, Yousuf Karsh, the Armenian-born photographer, and several other notable ethnic representatives. Among the eleven residents selected from the Ottawa district to receive Canadian citizenship was a Croatian shoemaker, Anton Justinić, who proudly stepped forward and received certificate number twenty-two. He thereby became the first Croatian to acquire Canadian as opposed to British nationality at this historic moment in Canada's emergence to full national sovereignty.

Canada's Croatians had entered a new era in more than one sense. The end of the forties and the beginning of the fifties marked a period of sharp upswing in their numbers as the immigration from Yugoslavia swelled to over 2,000 annually, reaching a post-war high of 5,000 by 1952. The rate of citizenship acquisition also shot up suddenly, to over 1,600 in 1955, nearly 300 per cent over the previous year. These figures were to have more than legal significance, for they signalled not only a new social reality of ethnic and cultural invigoration, but also one of rapid demographic change, class mobility, and intergenerational tension. If the Croatian community in Canada had just emerged from a decade fraught with international war and political tension in the forties, they were headed for even more turbulent waters of social change and adjustment in the fifties and sixties. For just as those thousands of new immigrants from the Old World had become increasingly mobile, those who had already been in Canada for a generation or two also became people on the move.

NOTES

1. *Zajedničar,* 18 December 1940: "President Butković's Message."
2. *Hrvatski Glas*, 2 September 1941.
3. *Ibid.,* 4 November 1941, reprinted from Timmins *Daily Press;* also *Hrvatski Glas Kalendar* (1943), pp. 43, 47, 57.

4. *Hrvatski Glas,* 30 December 1941, reprinted from the Yugoslav News Bulletin. See also *ibid.,* 4 January 1943.

5. H.C. Darby, R.W. Seton-Watson, Phyllis Auty *et al., A Short History of Yugoslavia* (Cambridge: Cambridge University Press, 1968), p. 222.

6. PAC, RG 24, D.N.D. vol. 2848, "Yugoslav Military Mission," Dr. Ivan Cankar, Yugoslav Minister, to N.A. Robertson, Under Secretary of State, Ottawa, 3 August 1948 (with enclosure, dated January, 1943).

7. *Ibid.,* RG 27 (Labour), vol. 999, "Aliens – Yugoslavian," Col. P. Savitch to Major Leal, D.N.D., Windsor, 14 July 1943.

8. *Hrvatski Glas,* 19 November 1940.

9. *20 Godina: Kratki Pregled . . . ,* p. 47; *The Fisherman,* 13 January 1942. For the position of the Communist Party of Canada during the war, see I. Avakumovic, *The Communist Party in Canada, A History* (Toronto: McClelland and Stewart, 1975), ch. 5.

10. George Prpić, *The Croatian Immigrants in America,* pp. 300-2.

11. V. Holjevac, *Hrvati Izvan Domovine* (Zagreb, 1968), pp. 277-9. Reports on the proceedings were transmitted to the Canadian government via the Office of Strategic Services in Washington. See PAC, RG 26, vol. 8, ff. 35-Y-1, Dewitt C. Poole to Tracy Phillips, Dept. of National War Services, Washington, 23 March 1943.

12. *Hrvatski Glas,* 2 March, 9 February 1943.

13. *20 Godina: Kratki Pregled . . . ,* p. 48. *Hrvatski Glas,* 27 April 1943.

14. *Hrvatski Glas,* 23 February 1943.

15. *Ibid.,* 5 October 1943.

16. PAC, RG 26, vol. 3, ff. 33-G-1, *Glas Kanadskih Srba,* 1942-44; *ibid.* (Citizenship and Immigration), vol. 10, File 50-2-A Part II. List of Foreign Language Newspapers. In 1941 *Novosti* replaced *Slobodna Misao,* which was banned early in 1940 along with other Communist publications opposing the war. See Avakumovic, *Communist Party in Canada,* p. 142. *Ethnic Press Digest,* X, 1 January, A54, p. 5.

17. PAC, RG 44, vol. 47, ff. "Yugoslav Relief," Frank Foulds, Director of Citizenship, to C.A. Payne, Deputy-Minister, Ottawa, 10 March 1945. See also the RCMP report of surveillance of the "racial antagonism existing between the Croats and Serbs," *ibid.,* RG 26, vol. 8, Mary Black to V.J. Kaye, Dept. of National War Services, Toronto, 27 April 1943.

18. *Ibid.,* RG 44 (National War Service), Mrs. K.E. Archer (Secretary, Canadian Friends of Yugoslavia) to Col. P.L. Browne, Director, Voluntary War Relief, DNWS, Ottawa, 24 August 1946.

19. *Ibid.,* vol. 47, T.A. Bradette, Deputy-Speaker, House of Commons, to Hon. H.R. Lafleche, Minister of National War Services, Ottawa, 4 December 1944.

20. *Ibid.,* T.A. Bradette, Deputy-Speaker, House of Commons, to Hon. H.R. Lafleche, Minister of National War Services, Ottawa, 4 December 1944.

21. See *ibid.,* National War Service, file "Yugoslav Relief Fund – Purchasing and Transport"; *ibid.,* vol. 31, "Funds to Aid the Yugoslavian Army For Liberation, 1943-46."

22. *20 Godina, Kratki Pregled* . . . p. 68; *Novosti,* 25 April, 6, 16 May 1944, 9 August 1945.
23. Prpić, *Croatian Immigrants in America,* pp. 298-9.
24. Department of National Defence files do not list ethnicity in their records of military personnel; however, many regimental histories in their honour and nominal rolls do list specific Croatian names of personnel. See, e.g., Major R.B. Mainprize, *Princess Patricia's Canadian Light Infantry,* vol. IV, 1939-45 records, Pte. A. Pavelick killed in action in Italy, 3 February 1945; G.F.J. Mahovolic, struck off service, Italy, 6 December 1943; R.H. Roy, *Ready for the Fray: The History of the Canadian Scottish Regiment, 1920-55* (Vancouver: Evergreen Press, 1958), Pte. Francis Slogar, wounded, 30/3/45; H.M. Jackson, *The Argyll and Sutherland Highlanders of Canada: 1928-53* (Montreal, 1953), Pte. Frank Penich, POW, captured 7 March 1945; nominal roll, Pte. D. Predovitch, Pte. J. Vlahovich.
25. *Novosti,* 3 March 1944. See also *ibid.,* 30 November 1944.
26. *Hrvatski Glas,* 14 December 1945. *Hrvatski Glas Kalendar* (1945), pp. 41, 161.
27. *Ibid.,* 27 February 1945: "Captain Vicevich decorated, Feb. 13, 1945, Umro Ivan Pavelić." *Ibid.,* 10 November 1943. *Novosti,* 1 July, 7 September, 28 November 1944.
28. Two examples of distinguished military service were: Private Laurence Sanko of Sault Ste. Marie, who served with the American Special Services Force in Alaska, Africa, and Italy from 1940-44; Steve Sarich of Penticton, who was awarded five medals for his service to Canada from 1939-45. Mrs. M. Sanko to G. Kokich and author, Sault Ste. Marie, January, 1975; *Jedinstvo,* 5 February 1971.
29. A good general account of the Partisan war in Yugoslavia is contained in Fitzroy Maclean, *Eastern Approaches* (London: Jonathan Cape, 1950), pp. 275-532. For Yugoslav Canadian contributions, see Roy MacLaren, *Canadians Behind Enemy Lines, 1939-45* (Vancouver: UBC Press, 1981).
30. *Jedinstvo,* 27 October 1967: "Tomo Čačić o Sam Sebi"; "Čačicev-Članak," 26 October 1956.
31. *Novosti,* 7 November 1944.
32. *Ibid.,* 10 October, 14 November, 17 May 1945. *20 Godina, Kratki Pregled* . . ., pp. 58-9.
33. See, e.g., *Srpski Glasnik,* 26 January 1946: "Red Cross Blood Donor Honor Roll"; *Hrvatski Glas,* 30 October 1945: "Buy Victory Bonds"; *Zajedničar,* 31 October, 7 November 1945: "Ninth Victory Loan."
34. Dennison Rusinow, *The Yugoslav Experiment: 1948-74* (London: C. Hurst for R.I.I.A., 1977), p. 19; Darby *et al., Short History of Yugoslavia,* pp. 244-6; Robert L. Wolff, *The Balkans in our Times* (Cambridge: Harvard U. Press, 1956), pp. 191-267.
35. See Ilija Jukić, *The Fall of Yugoslavia,* pp. 274-89.
36. Prpić, *Croatian Immigrants in America,* pp. 309-19.
37. For varying discussions of the Bleiburg massacre, see *ibid.,* pp. 318-19,

ff. 38, references to studies by Benković, Hecemović, Prćela, and Guldescu. See also: N. Dinko Šuljak (ed.), *Croatia's Struggle for Independence: A Documentary History* (Arcadia, California: Croatian Information Service, 1977), pp. 195-6; Richard D. Goodman, *Communist Yugoslavia* (Cleveland: Erie University Press, 1953); M. Djilas, *Wartime* (New York: Harcourt Brace Jovanovich, 1977), and review of same in *Zajedničar,* 21 September 1977; Jerome Jareb and Ivo Omrčanin, "The End of the Croatian Army at Bleiburg, Austria, May, 1945 According to English Military Documents," *Journal of Croatian Studies,* XVIII-XIX (1977-78), pp. 115-82.

38. See John D. Butkovic, open letter of the U.S. Croats to Mr. Byrnes, Secretary of State, August, 1946; cited in Šuljak (ed.), *Croatia's Struggle,* p. 249; "Memorandum of the Canadian Croats," open letter from S. Bradica and Ivan Skačan to W.L. Mackenzie King, reprinted in *Hrvatski Glas,* 25 June 1946.

39. PAC, RG 44, vol. 47, ff. "Yugoslavia Relief Fund," S. Miosich, Secretary, Canadian Council of South Slavs, to Col. P.L. Browne, Director, Voluntary War Relief, Toronto, 23 March, 15 July 1946.

40. *Ibid.,* K. Archer to F.W. Routley, National Commissioner, Canadian Red Cross Society, Montreal, 27 May 1946.

41. *Ibid.,* ff. "Yugoslavia Misc." Geo. Sigmund to National War Services, 31 December 1946.

42. *Ibid.,* vol. 36, ff. "Canadian Council of S. Slavs," P.L. Browne to Deputy-Minister, 14 May 1946; *ibid.,* vol. 31, ff. "Funds to Aid Yugoslav Army for Liberation, 1943-46," C. Payne to S. Miosich, and return 11 January 1946; *Novosti,* 10 January, 19 March, 21 December 1946, 10 April 1947.

43. PAC, RG 76, Immigration Branch, vol. 45, ff. 673931, pt. 18.

44. *Ibid.,* James Mackinnon to Vinko Skarac, Ottawa, 3 November 1948.

45. Hans Kohn, *Pan Slavism, Its History and Ideology,* (South Bend: Notre Dame University Press, 1953), pp. 225-50.

46. *Novosti,* 17 September, 5 October, 19 November 1946.

47. *Hrvatski Glas,* 17, 22 September 1946.

48. *Novosti,* 3 October, 18 November 1946, 1 October 1946.

49. *Hrvatski Glas,* 24 September 1946.

50. *Novosti*, 8, 10 November 1946.

51. *Novosti*, 26 October 1946. See also *ibid.,* 22 August 1946.

52. *Novosti*, 11 November 1946.

53. *Ibid.,* 17 December 1946.

54. *Ibid.,* 19 December 1946, 11 January 1947.

55. See *Zavod za Migracije i Narodnosti* (Zagreb), vol. 146, II, 22, 3c, "Brod Radnik."

56. *The Fisherman*, 10 April 1947; *Novosti,* 3 March 1947.

57. K. Adachi, *The Enemy That Never Was: A History of the Japanese Canadians* (Toronto: McClelland and Stewart, 1976), pp. 307-34.

58. *The Fisherman,* 23 May 1947.

59. *Novosti,* 29 March 1947: Zorica memoir.
60. *The Fisherman*, 22 August 1947.
61. *Zavod za Migracije i Narodnosti,* vol. 148, II 23, 3c (b) "Povratnici I Grupe, 1947."
62. *Novosti,* 12 July 1947.
63. See Canada, Dept. of Immigration, ff. 5830-3-645, "Immigration from Yugoslavia," 22 November 1946.
64. Canada, House of Commons, *Debates,* 23 May 1946; *Novosti,* 27 May 1947.
65. Canada, Department of Immigration, ff. 5830-3-645. One of their concerns was that Canadian passports might be passed on to other individuals who would be trained as spies and return to Canada. Later in 1953, it was claimed by the Toronto *Daily Star* that Tito had in fact admitted that 120 passports were passed on to Soviet agencies for use by Communist spies. See Mrkitch, "History of the Croat Immigration to Canada," p. 52; Toronto *Daily Star*, 19 March 1953.
66. *Zavod za Migracije* . . ., 149, 24, II, 3c (c), "Povratnici, 1947, II grupa," *Borba,* 3/a.
67. *Ibid.,* 150, II, 25, 3 (c), "Povratnici 1947, III Grupa."
68. *Novosti*, 13 January 1948.
69. *Ibid.,* 22 January 1948.
70. *Ibid.,* 13, 31 January, 5 February, 18 March, 6 April 1948; *Zavod za Migracije* . . . v. 151, 26, II, 3c. "Povratnici, 1947-51."
71. *Novosti,* 6 April 1948.
72. Canada, Dept. of Immigration, ff. 5830-3-645. Confidential Report, Government Emigration Office, London, 16 December 1947.
73. *Ibid.,* 14 April, 8 May 1948. See also *Hrvatski Glas*, 13 April 1948.
74. *Hrvatski Glas*, 13 April 1948.
75. Canada, House of Commons, *Debates,* 26 April 1948. *Novosti,* 6 May 1948.
76. *Hrvatski Glas,* 11, 18 May 1948.
77. *Novosti,* 5 June 1948.
78. *Ibid.,* 25 June, 2 July 1948.
79. *Ibid.,* 18 June 1948.
80. Vladimir Dedijer, *The Battle Stalin Lost, Memoirs of Yugoslavia* (New York: The Viking Press, 1971), pp. 129-31; Stephen Clissold (ed.), *Yugoslavia and the Soviet Union, 1939-73: A Documentary Survey* (London: Oxford University Press, R.I.I.A., 1975), pp. 170-215.
81. *Jedinstvo*, 2, 9, 24, 27, 30 July, 20, 24 September, 1 October 1948.
82. *Ibid.,* 5 October 1948.
83. *Jedinstvo,* 19 October 1948.
84. *Zajedničar,* 20 October 1948.
85. *Jedinstvo,* 19 November 1948.
86. *Ibid.,* 2 November, 3 December 1948.
87. *Ibid.,* 21 December 1948.
88. *Ibid.,* 26 November 1948.

89. *Hrvatski Glas,* 21 September 1948. See also *Jedinstvo,* 7, 14 October 1949.
90. Canada, Dept. of Immigration, ff. 552-1-645. Secretariat reference statement, 1 January 1961. See also *Jedinstvo*, 24 April 1956, which claimed a much higher return rate to Canada of 90 per cent. Cited in Mrkitch, "History of Croat Immigration to Canada," p. 53.
91. *Ibid.,* and letter dated 7 April 1945, in ff. 5830-3-645.
92. *Ibid.,* file memo dated, 18 May 1956.
93. PAC, RG 74, D. 2, Records of Parliament, Canada, House of Commons, Sessional Records, 1867-1958, vol. 615, file 13b (23 February 1944), Sess. Paper no. 13b. Letter to Director of Immigration, Zagreb, 20 June 1950.
94. Mrkitch, "History of Croat Immigration to Canada," p. 53.
95. Freda Hawkins, *Canada and Immigration: Public Policy and Public Concern* (Montreal: McGill-Queen's, 1972), p. 239.
96. Mrkitch, "History of Croat Immigration to Canada," pp. 45-57.
97. Ilija Jukić, *The Fall of Yugoslavia,* pp. 277-97.
98. Mrkitch, "History of Croat Immigration to Canada," p. 45.
99. See PAC, RG 76, vol. 287, ff. 251554, "Serbs, Croats and Slovenes 1926-47," Geo. Ruttinger to J. Glen, 27 March 1947, Württemberg.
100. See Canada, Dept. of Immigration Records, ff. 555-54-645-1. Yugoslav Refugees in Italy, Austria and Germany, vol. 1, see, e.g., inter-departmental letter, 15 August 1956.
101. Vladimir Dedijer, *The Battle Stalin Lost,* pp. 112, 204-5.
102. Dennison Rusinow, *The Yugoslav Experiment, 1948-74,* pp. 32-107.
103. PAC, RG 76, vol. 445, ff. 673931, pt. 18, "Refugees Immigration to Canada," Vinko Skarac to Louis St. Laurent, 20 October 1948.
104. *Hrvatski Glas,* 28 March, 6 April 1948.
105. *Ibid.,* 27 January, 15 June 1948.
106. See PAC, RG 14, D. 2, vol. 537, file 61. Canada, House of Commons, Sessional Records, Unpublished; Privy Council Minutes, 23 July 1947, 8 January, 23 December 1948.
107. *Ibid.,* RG 76, vol. 651, ff. B29300, III, "Admission of Bulk Labour from Europe"; vol. 230, ff. 127304, "Lumbermen and Bushworkers general file"; and RG 27 (Dept. of Labour), vol. 277, ff. 12621, Lumberworkers.
108. *Ibid.,* MG 28, I, 124, vol. 162, Frontier College, Instructors' Registers, file 1947.
109. See *ibid.,* vol. 137, Frontier College Ann. Report, 1948. Earl Ryerson report, Stewartville, HEPC, 1948.
110. *Novosti,* 27 May 1948: "Drew Should Know Herceg is an Ustasha."
111. Sayles, *Welland Workers Make History,* p. 196.
112. See *Jedinstvo,* 29 October 1948; *Hrvatski Glas,* 2 November 1948.
113. PAC, RG 27, vol. 276, F. 1-26-13, "Selection of DP's, Special Cases, 1948-50."
114. *Ibid.,* Dept. of Labour, vol. 270, ff. 1-26-6 pt. 1, "Immig. of DP's in metal mining."

115. See, e.g., J.C. Brentar, "The Social and Economic Adjustment of the Croatian Displaced Persons in Cleveland Compared with that of Earlier Croatian Migrants," Western Reserve University, 1951 (San Francisco: R. & E. Research Associates, 1971), pp. 30-1; Linda Bennett, *Personal Choice in Ethnic Identity Maintenance: Serbs, Croats and Slovenes in Washington D.C.* (Palo Alto: Ragusan Press, 1978), p. 65.

116. PAC, RG 27, Dept. of Labour, Box 110, ff. 1-10-I-1-6, International Nickel of Canada, 1948-50; vol. 280, ff. 1-26-11, Immigration of DP's in Building Trades.

117. *Ibid.,* MG 28, I, 124, vol. 137, file, 1948-53, Frontier College Instructors' Reports.

118. *Ibid.,* RG 76, vol. 245, ff. 167-72, Pt. 16, S. Nedimovich to Immigration Department, Matsqui, B.C., 11 December 1952.

119. *Jedinstvo,* 4 June 1954.

120. *Ibid.,* 19 December 1949.

121. I. Abella, *Nationalism, Communism and Canadian Labour,* pp. 188-222.

122. *Jedinstvo,* 24 December 1948, 18 January, 4 February 1949.

123. *Ibid.,* 18 March 1949. See also, 11, 15, 22 March 1949, 22, 26, 29 June, 3 July 1951.

124. *Jedinstvo,* 1, 5 October 1954.

125. See, e.g., Brentar, "Social and Economic Adjustment," pp. 116 ff.; Jean Martin, *Refugee Settlers: A Study of D.P.'s in Australia* (Canberra: Australian National University, 1965).

126. Giles Gobetz, "Adjustment and Assimilation of Slovenian Refugees" (Ph.D. thesis, Ohio State University, 1962), p. 131.

127. Gobetz, "Adjustment and Assimilation of Slovenian Refugees," pp. 3-4.

128. Blanche Borkovich, "The Croatians of Ottawa: A Preliminary Study," unpublished essay, Carleton University, 1956-57, pp. 1-2. (Supplied to author by P. Čulumović, Ottawa.)

129. *Ibid.,* p. 5.

130. *Ibid.,* p. 7.

131. *Ibid.,* pp. 15-16.

132. *The Evening Citizen* (Ottawa), 3, 4 January 1947. The author is indebted for this reference to Mr. Peter Čulumović of Ottawa.

EIGHT

Generations Old and New, 1955-79

The past two decades have witnessed a great transformation and fragmentation of the Croatian-Canadian community. Numerically, this period witnessed a population take-off that matched some of the spectacular percentage increases recorded by other Mediterranean nationalities such as the Greeks, Italians, and Portuguese. Just at the point when it appeared that the group would dwindle and die from attrition among the older migrants and assimilation of its younger sons and daughters,[1] the Croatians experienced an infusion of new blood that quadrupled their numbers over 1951 levels. This swelling tide of migration, which formed but a fraction of the larger outward movement of between a half-million and a million Yugoslav workers into Western Europe, sought in increasing measure the economic fruits of a prosperous and buoyant economy. More importantly for Canada, however, they dramatically reversed the nature and direction of acculturation and assimilation in the older generation. By sheer force of numbers, the new urban migrants to cities such as Toronto, Hamilton, Montreal, Vancouver, Winnipeg, Edmonton, and Calgary fundamentally altered the existing character of the Croatian communities located in the mine towns, mill towns, and lumber towns of Canada.

That small but relatively homogeneous working-class community of some 15,000-20,000 Croatians in 1951 was gradually being diffused into the larger English-speaking society of Canada. Their language, their customs, and more importantly, their children were being transformed by an increasingly urban, secular, and mobile society about them. Their social aspirations were generally those of North America in the 1950's – two educated children, a home, a car, and steady employment.[2] That these social goals were possible was materially visible in the larger Canadian society, and this impression was reinforced by letters and visits to their richer American cousins to the south. At the same time the larger monolithic North American popular culture captured the Canadian-born children, as use of the Croatian mother-tongue declined visibly by the mid-fifties. Even among the older generation the effects of assimilation were visible in its declining language skills and use of a pidgin Croatian-English, in anglicization of surnames, and in adoption of English-Canadian given names for their children. Even the traditional voting preferences and politics of the Croatian Canadians appeared to be altering from the firm allegiances to the Liberal middle way and the radical Communist vote to the more traditionally Anglo-Canadian parties, the Conservatives and the CCF-NDP. John Diefenbaker's "unhyphenated Canadianism" and his vision of the North attracted many ethnic votes in 1957 and 1958, and the more muted brand of trade unionism and socialism advanced by the New Democratic Party increasingly won Croatian and Yugoslav votes in the manufacturing and resource towns of Ontario and British Columbia in particular. The fragmentation of former values and traditions was in fact complete, as the old customs and old ways of the pre-war migrants were being challenged, ignored, or discarded.

Upon this scene of a culture in retreat arrived the new immigrants in steadily increasing number. Slowly and almost imperceptibly the numbers of refugees and sponsored immigrants, almost equal in percentage terms, began to increase yearly, suddenly rising to 4,000 and 5,000 in 1957-58 and then falling back gradually in the economic contraction of the late fifties and early sixties. From 1955-60, over 18,000 immigrants of Yugoslav origin entered Canada, another 16,000 from 1960-65, three-quarters of whom were technically classified as refugees and displaced persons. In the five years that followed, the tide of immigration became a flood, with over 30,000 Yugoslavian migrants entering Canada and accounting for a full 30 per cent of the entire historic migration from Yugoslavia to Canada.[3] Direct recruiting by the new Canadian Department of Manpower and Immigration in Yugoslavia, combined with a curtailment of the refugee influx, was at the root of this historic increase. By 1971, Yugoslav-born immigrants for the post-war period totalled 94,000, and by 1975, nearly 108,000. Overall, the population of Yugoslavian origin in Canada stood at 104,000 in 1971. Of these, 23,380 directly declared themselves as Croatians,[4] but of the total Yugoslav population it is likely that Croatians counted for some 65,000 in 1971, since they also counted for the bulk of the 31,000 post-war refugees and over half of the legally documented emigration from Yugoslavia.[5]

The effect of this massive influx of new immigrants was literally to reverse the prior proportions of old to new migrants in the twenty years between 1951 and 1971. The new arrivals vastly outnumbered the older migrants by the mid-sixties and visible tensions resulted as they began to set up an entirely new set of social and political institutions to serve their own particular needs. As urban migrants and by and large more literate and skilled than their pre-war counterparts, they were often frustrated occupationally by under-utilization of their skills and full earning potential in their first years in Canada. Yet their economic frustrations were heightened by a burning drive to succeed and a more intense and vital ethnic community life within Canada's larger cities. Here they could use their native language to a greater extent within the home, the social groups and clubs, the churches, and even special language schools. By sheer force of numbers, they enjoyed wider opportunities than ever before for the preservation of their language, religion, and culture. This new vitality and hope generated the creative tensions which naturally accompany rising economic expectations and social aspirations. Confronted by an older and by now more passive pre-war generation whose children become deracinated, the new immigrants could neither understand nor appreciate the stoicism and acceptance by the pre-war migrants of inevitable assimilation.

The recent history of the Croatians in Canada, then, has been one of social upheaval and change resulting in fragmented, plural communities across Canada. Suddenly transformed like the larger Canadian community about them into one of the most urbanized societies in the world, the Croatians became, like many small-town Canadians thrust into large cities, urban villagers with extended social networks based upon family ties, kinship, and regional affiliations. Ironically, the assimilated sons and daughters of the older generations clustered into Canada's major cities in search of the same economic opportunity that attracted the new immigrants. But neither party could communicate effectively with the other since they no longer spoke the same language or shared the same life experiences and history. A vague sense of ethnic pride might be excited by the achievements of Croatians in sport, the arts, education, and business. Unity among the Croatian Canadians was, however, as scarce a quantity as it had been in the wake of the first large wave of Croatian immigration in the twenties. A new and brighter mosaic of diversity within the larger Canadian ethnic mosaic was in the making in the vibrant decade of the sixties. Perhaps the passage of time would soften the intensity of its many ideological and regional fragments. For the time being, however, it shone bright and discordant, a testimony to the youth and vitality of its many parts.

THE GREAT MIGRATION AND THE NEW IMMIGRANTS (1955-75)

Refugees and Immigrant Settlers

The most recent wave of Croatian immigration to Canada has been characterized by the same problems of social adjustment that have accompanied every large-scale movement of peoples from the earliest Irish famine migration to the modern post-war refugees. Perhaps the great American historian of immigration, Oscar Handlin, has described the reaction of the new immigrant to the "shock of alienation" best in his classic, *The Uprooted:*

Once landed, the newcomer found himself equal in condition to the natives. Within a short period he could be naturalized and acquire all the privileges of a citizen. In some places, indeed, he could vote before the oath in court so transformed his status. In the eyes of society even earlier than in the eyes of the law, he was an American. . . . Significantly, the newcomers were not compelled to conform to existing patterns of action or to accept existing standards. They felt free to criticize many aspects of life they discovered in the New World, the excessive concern with material goods and the inadequate attention to religion, the pushiness and restlessness of the people, the transitory quality of family relationships. The boldness of such judgements testified to the voluntary nature of immigrant adjustment. The strangers did not swallow America in one gulp; through their own associations and their own exertions they discovered how to live in the new place and still be themselves.[6]

The reactions of the new Croatian immigrants and refugees to Canada were also ones of shock, anxiety, fear, and hope. For some, the rootlessness of modern city life was blunted by a whole host of associations, clubs, and cultural societies. Often, the struggle against alienation was joined by this sense of belonging and clinging to their roots, which served as their only sure anchor in their stormy first decade in Canada. For others, like the single male refugees who had to ride out the storm alone, assimilation often came not at all, or worse still too quickly and at an enormous cost to their own identity and sense of self-worth. As had been the case generally in the history of migration, safety had lain in numbers for the immigrant, and only the very strong or the foolhardy ignored that conventional wisdom, at their peril. Assimilation or alienation, ethnocentrism or rootlessness, these were the horns of the immigration dilemma for the Croatian migrant, and to pass through them in safety without being gored was the trick of their first years in Canada.[7]

The refugee problem created difficulties for immigrants and governments alike from the mid-fifties to the mid-sixties. The numbers of refugees and displaced persons of "Yugoslav" ethnic origin entering Canada reached 10,000 for the years 1953-58, and in the next decade that many again entered this country, mainly from refugee camps in Austria and Italy. Thus, fully one-half of the entire emigration from Yugoslavia in the period up to 1966 was of ostensibly illegal or undocumented emigrants.[8] The persistence of this refugee influx at nearly 2,000 per year for the two decades following the war ultimately meant that 31,000 refugees and displaced persons were admitted by 1968. Only with the establishment of a new immigration act and the creation of a regular immigration office in Belgrade for interviewing prospective immigrants from Yugoslavia was this flow of refugees curtailed.

The continuing interest of Canadian industry and government in attracting cheap and relatively unskilled labour during the late fifties accounted for an unabated flow of refugee migrants. The demand by the railways for construction labour and the demand for agricultural labour persisted throughout the late fifties as it had in the post-war decade. Thus, the availability of refugees with Italian citizenship from the Istrian Peninsula in 1956 and the mounting flow of refugees northward from Yugoslavia into Austria attracted the interest of the Canadian railways. Canadian National and Canadian Pacific subsequently brought in as *bona fide* immigrants a total of 1,000 refugees from Yugoslavia from such camps as Udine and Chieti.[9]

In the meantime, the yearly flow of refugees from Yugoslavia into Austria was closely monitored, for their numbers had jumped from 1,500 in 1944 to 5,300 in 1956 and to 10,000 in the first nine months of 1957. There were already 1,300 applications to come to Canada at this last date, and it was clear from the international refugee organizations monitoring the camps that for 60 to 70 per cent Canada was their country of first choice. In fact, in the first six months of 1957, over 1,000 refugees had left the Austrian camps for Canada, and of these it is likely that at least 600-700 were Croatians since they counted for the bulk of the refugees to Austria. In the subsequent year, Canada accepted an unprecedented number of 4,352 refugees, and immigration officials almost recoiled in surprise in the early part of 1959 when an attempt was made to screen out the genuine political refugees and distinguish them from the economic migrants among them. The result was a sharply reduced intake, coinciding with a particularly severe winter recession in the Canadian economy.

By contrast, World Refugee Year in 1959-60 and increasing international pressure for relaxed immigration controls resulted in looser selection criteria for refugees coming into Canada based on occupational and personality type. The attempt to establish some measure of political controls in the selection process broke down, particularly because it was difficult to rationalize the imposition of such a stricture in the face of universal acceptance of other Eastern Bloc refugees. The Yugoslav authorities for their part also seemed to despair of controlling the outward flow of migrants and began to develop strategies for control of outward-bound economic migrants by means of passport and visa regulations.[10]

By now, Canadian immigration officials were facing increased competition from American and Australian authorities, who were facilitating immigration to their countries by relaxed security clearances and elimination of residency requirements. The spectre of competition for the better migrants thus changed the face of immigrant recruitment, and Canadian officials began to recruit actively in the Italian camps in 1960, when 500 family migrants and 200 single males were accepted for immigration to Canada. Increased pressure from the Austrian government, which now threatened to repatriate many of the refugees from Yugoslavia whom they now considered economic rather than political migrants, added further incentive to Canada to expedite its selection process as Australia and the United States had done. In the face of this increased competition, Canada secured for itself a steady complement of 1,000 to 1,500 refugees and displaced persons per year from Yugoslavia from 1960-65.[11]

Once in Canada, the refugee settlers began to create difficulties of the same order as the large influx of the 1920's. Authorities within the immigration department began to complain much as their counterparts in the twenties had, that the immigrants were not disposed to take on employment in rural and isolated locations in the face of the attractions of the city. Similar tensions between officials and immigrants arose over the tendency of the immigrant refugees to use traditional group models of migration and designate a leader to act as their spokesman. Immigration officials clearly preferred to deal with individuals, and therefore cautioned strongly against groups "to eliminate the possibility of a leader becoming established." One incident in particular demonstrated a classic repetition of the persistence of cultural traditions among the male migrants from Croatia. Apparently, a group of ten or eleven Yugoslav refugees were destined for farm work in the Eastern Townships of Quebec in the spring of 1963 and had taken up rooms at a boardinghouse in Montreal. When work was found for them near Granby, the field officer went to the boardinghouse to arrange their transportation and found that they had suddenly vanished into thin air without paying their rent. The immigration officers thus became extremely disenchanted and despaired of dealing with any group of Yugoslav immigrants, or of placing any migrants on farms, since "it is obvious that when a new arrival spends even one night in Montreal, it is usually impossible to redirect him to employment outside the city."[12]

Reports from western Canada were not much better, and a general disillusionment with refugees from Yugoslavia had begun to set in by the mid-sixties. Some of the objections centred on the rootlessness of the bachelor migrants, their high initial dependence upon forms of social assistance and welfare, and their tendency to default on loans by a sudden move to another city. Complaints also began to surface from employers that immigrants from Yugoslavia, unlike other preferred minorities, were less skilled, had poorer trade qualifications, and were extremely particular about the type of work they would accept. As in eastern Canada, language problems, distrust of government authorities, and a predisposition to trust first the advice of their fellow countrymen were regarded as negative social attributes. Other complaints of their behaviour in the West centred on their strong preferences for particular types of food and a tendency to quarrel among themselves, even on the job.

The impressions being created by the recent refugees from Yugoslavia across the country were not generally positive, and it rapidly became apparent that negative ethnic stereotypes were being formed of the refugee from Yugoslavia. He was coming to be seen by immigration officials as "lazy, arrogant, and is always looking for a handout – believing that if he does not work he won't starve as some agency will look after him . . . argumentative and unrealistic with a tendency to abandon a job at the slightest provocation." Motivation for these poor behavioural syndromes was found often in the protracted periods of time spent in the refugee camps and in the lack of immigration aid organizations in Canada. Yet, in the end, an apparently exasperated department in western Canada promised to renew its efforts "to settle a some-what difficult people in the realization that after initial difficulties most of them eventually find their niche in Canadian society."[13]

Patience was counselled by Ottawa in dealing with the frustrations and problems caused by these refugees and displaced persons, bearing in mind that, "On the whole, they have provided Canada with some very good settlers and over the years have accounted for a substantial portion of the total immigration movement to this country." The intake of refugees was reduced by a third from 1965-67 and eliminated almost entirely in 1968.[14] With the establishment of the new Ministry of Manpower and Immigration and the universal applicability of the point system the refugee movement from Europe, with the exception of the Czechoslovak exodus of 1968, dwindled to a trickle. In the case of Yugoslavia, the establishment of a Canadian immigration office in Belgrade virtually sealed the door to Canada via Austria and Italy.[15]

In the meantime, the tide of regular immigrants remained steady at under 1,000 per year, gradually mounting to over 1,000 by the mid-sixties. With the introduction of the new immigration regulations in 1967 the total of immigrants directly from Yugoslavia rose sharply. In 1968, 6,402 persons of Yugoslav citizenship entered Canada, 4,466 of them coming directly from Yugoslavia and the rest largely from West Germany, France, and Austria, where they had been temporary workers.[16] In 1969, the total of Yugoslav citizens by last country of residence was 5,241 versus 4,053 from Yugoslavia; in 1970 the total reached 6,701, with 5,672 coming directly from Yugoslavia. By 1971 the decline of immigrants from Yugoslavia had set in with the respective totals of citizens versus residents standing at 3,440 and 2,997.[17]

The proportion of Croatians in this total from Yugoslavia was probably over one half, for, according to Yugoslav estimates, of the 41,000 workers estimated to be in Canada in 1971, some 20,050 were from Croatia, and another 3,700 from Bosnia and Herzegovina, 42 per cent of whom were Croatians by nationality.[18] Thus, between 1967-73, approximately 15,000 Croatians left Yugoslavia for Canada. According to the emigration records of Yugoslavia, the greatest proportion of these were from the Croatian coastal region, Lika and Gorski Kotar, and the hinterland of Karlovac. Occupationally nearly half had been in primary production – agriculture, fishing, and forestry – before migrating and another third had been in industry, mining, and construction.[19] In 1966, for example, Canadian records of the 4,332 Yugoslav newcomers indicate that there were among them twenty-seven professionals, ten clerks, seven in transport and communications, sixty-two in sales, fifty-three mechanics, 280 labourers, and 1,222 unspecified.[20] The educational and occupational attainments of some migrants were exceptionally high: it is estimated, for example, that approximately 20 per cent of the Croatians abroad from Yugoslavia in 1971 were in the professions, administration, and the arts.[21] For the most part, however, those from the primary sector had little more than an elementary education, although nearly a quarter did possess some vocational, grammar school, or university training. While these attainments may not have been impressive by other western European standards, nevertheless many emigrants from Croatia possessed higher skills and occupational qualifications than the population that remained.

While it is difficult to estimate the destination and location of the new migrants, and more difficult still to surmise the number of returned migrants to Yugoslavia and serial migrants, a number of hypotheses may be derived from immigration, census, and citizenship records. According to immigration statistics some 94,197 immigrants from Yugoslavia entered Canada from 1946-72, and of these over 31,000 may be classified as refugees and displaced persons, leaving a residual documented migration of 62,885 Yugoslav-born immigrants. Thus, at an estimated 55 per cent of the total, there were at least 35,000 to 40,000 Croatians, plus another 18,000 to 20,000 refugees for a total of 53,000 to 60,000 for the same period. At the same time, Canadian census figures show those of Yugoslav ethnic origin to have risen from 21,404 in 1951 to 68,587 in 1961 and 104,950 in 1971.[22] The number of foreign-born persons of Yugoslav origin rose sharply from less than half to 75 per cent in 1961 and 1971. (See Appendix, Table A.)

The Canadian-born of Yugoslav parentage had increased from 18,000 to 27,000 in the 1961-71 period, an increase of 50 per cent. Although further statistics are unavailable by "Croatian" ethnic group since 1941, this increase approximates the average natural increase for post-war ethnic groups. Thus it is likely that the ratio of Canadian-born to Croatian-born in the Croatian population might be conservatively estimated to have been at about 11,000 to 28,000 in 1961, and 29,000 to 42,000 in 1971.[23] The number of Canadian citizens also increased sharply among those of former Yugoslav citizenship: between 1953 and 1972, 44,677 took out citizenship, 27,246 of them between 1961 and 1971.[24] Thus, approximately 15,000 Croatians were naturalized in each intercensal decade, at a rate approaching one-half of the total number of immigrants coming into the country in the post-war period. (See Appendix, Table C.)

The destination and location of the immigrants were persistently the cities in Ontario and the West. Ontario, which had 64 per cent of the Yugoslav-born migrants in 1951, accounted for 66 per cent in 1961 and

71 per cent in 1971. The bulk of the immigrants were crowded into the cities,[25] even more than the Canadian population at large, Canada having become one of the most urbanized countries in the post-war world at 70 per cent urbanized in 1961. The Croatians inevitably landed, given the logistics of transatlantic air flights, at Canada's major eastern metropolises, Toronto and Montreal. By far the largest number went to Toronto, which absorbed thousands upon thousands of the new immigrants. Although no definitive statistics are available, it is estimated that in 1975 at least 20,000 people of Croatian origin lived in or near Toronto; some estimates run as high as 40,000 for the metropolitan area.[26] Montreal absorbed many fewer immigrants, no doubt because of the increased emphasis upon the French language in Quebec.[27] This community grew to perhaps half the size of that in Hamilton (6,000) and roughly to the size of those in Welland, Windsor, and Kitchener, which had between 3,000-4,000 Croatians by 1971, largely by virtue of their established Croatian communities and continued industrial expansion. The western cities, also easily accessible by international air carriers, gained a solid share in the new immigration, as the community in greater Vancouver grew to 5,000-6,000 and those in Calgary, Edmonton, and Winnipeg to about 1,500 each by 1971.[28]

Smaller urban centres failed to attract more than nominal population increases of sponsored family immigrants because of their more limited economic opportunities. Thus, the more familiar pre-war communities in mill towns and mine towns like Timmins, Sudbury, Thunder Bay, Nanaimo, and Port Alberni increased their numbers only fractionally. The smaller resource towns on the frontier, such as Thompson, Manitoba, and Fort Smith, Northwest Territories, still attracted their share of single male migrants, but they remained, as in the past, only stopping places on the way to urban civilization. For the better-educated immigrants, only the larger cities offered the government jobs, university careers, and professional opportunities for which they had been trained.

The occupations taken up by the new arrivals in Canada were the traditional jobs at which the Croatian immigrants had been employed in the past. Almost none went into farming despite the fact that probably half of the incoming migrants were from agricultural regions or agro-towns:[29] approximately 2 per cent were engaged in farming. Beyond that, less than 5 per cent were employed in such primary resource areas as fishing, forestry, logging, and mining. Thus, in sharp contrast to the pre-war generation of migrants, this new generation had little frontier experience except perhaps for a brief sojourn of a month or two in a northern town. By far the greatest number of foreign-born Croatians were employed in secondary manufacturing and construction in the cities. These occupational sectors accounted for close to one-half of the entire work force of foreign-born Croatians in Canada (industrial processing 9 per cent, machining 9.5 per cent, construction 13 per cent, product fabrication 16.9 per cent; see Appendix, Table F.1). With the exception of manufacturing, which included electronic and textile manufacture, women of Croatian origin were employed largely in the service and clerical sector (14 and 6 per cent respectively), which included a whole host of jobs from cleaning, hair-dressing, and food services to secretarial, library, and postal work. Croatian-born women, like women of all minority ethnic groups, were even less likely than their male counterparts to be found in rural or frontier areas: over 80 per cent lived in the cities and less than a quarter of one per cent on the farm.[30]

These occupational profiles, common to all minorities which had emigrated from Yugoslavia in the fifties and sixties, present a distinct contrast to the Canadian-born Croatians. The latter were under-represented in the manufacturing sector, with only 9 per cent in this category, and were concentrated much more heavily in white-collar pursuits and the professions. In 1971, the clerical, sales, and service sectors accounted for a full third of all those born in Canada, and all of these occupations were dominated by women. By the same token, the professions and administrative and managerial positions were more highly represented, at nearly 18 per cent of the total for the Canadian-born versus only 7 per cent for the foreign-born. In addition, the foreign-born were comparatively underrepresented in the white collar jobs – 3 versus 35 per cent. The socio-economic distribution of the new immigrants thus was basis in itself for different social perceptions and tensions between the settled communities of native Croatian Canadians and the new arrivals.[31]

The regional variations on these general occupational averages for Canada are revealing of the general consistency of the patterns throughout Canada. The number of Croatians or Yugoslavs, either native or foreign, employed in Atlantic Canada appears to be so insignificant as to be incapable of analysis, that is, beyond a few Cape Breton miners and a few urbanites in Halifax, the Maritimes continued to be an unpopular choice for these immigrants. In Quebec, the bulk of population was concentrated in the Montreal area, except for small residual pockets of miners and loggers in the Abitibi and Temiscaming districts. Although the number of immigrants in the work force declaring themselves Croatian in Quebec is small, the economic and social opportunities offered by the large metropolitan centre in Montreal resulted in a larger proportion of professionals, managers, teachers, and artists (18 per cent). Relatively fewer (19 per cent) were employed in clerical sales and service industries, although a similar proportion to the rest of Canada (40 per cent) was involved in manufacturing, processing, machining, and construction. Toronto and Hamilton totals for the Croatian-born, which count for the majority of the 45,000 Croatians in Ontario, reveal a much closer congruence to national totals both for the Croatian-born and those undeclared Croatians in the "Yugoslav ethnic" totals. Virtually the same proportions were evident: 6-7 per cent in the professions; 22-23 per cent in clerical, sales, and service sectors; 47-48 per cent in manufacturing, processing, and construction. Once again, the Canadian-born were less prominent in the blue-collar sector (12 per cent) and more visible in white-collar occupations (37 per cent) and other professional areas (18 per cent).[32] (See Appendix, Table F.2.)

Further to the west, some interesting deviations from the national and central Canadian averages occur in the Prairies. As might be expected for the Prairies, which have a smaller sector of the population employed in industry and relatively higher proportions in service and construction industries and agriculture, the proportion of immigrants engaged in agriculture is higher, at 7 per cent for the foreign-born in both the Croatian and Yugoslav ethnic categories versus 2 per cent of these groups in the country as a whole. There are proportionally more Canadian-born Croatians involved in agriculture because of the prior settlements on the Prairies, and they are, despite very small absolute values, 26 per cent of those Croatian Canadians in the prairie work force. Among those employed in the urban sector, more are employed in construction (15-20 per cent) than in other industrial labour, but fewer on average (35.6 per cent) are employed in that sector as a whole compared to Ontario (48 per cent) and Quebec (40 per cent). At the same time, there appears to have been more economic opportunity in the prairie cities, for educated and skilled workers were slightly above 10 per cent for Alberta, 25 per cent in Saskatchewan, and 3 per cent in Manitoba, for an overall average of 12 per cent. The most distinguishing feature perhaps for the foreign-born Croatians in the Prairies was the high average (23 per cent) employed in the service sector (Manitoba, 18.02 per cent), (Saskatchewan, 21 per cent), (Alberta, 31 per cent) – values that consistently exceeded national averages.[33]

In British Columbia, some distinct areas of difference and specialization emerge in the demographic profile of the new immigrants. There, the major concentration of Croatians was in the lower mainland, with Vancouver and the delta accounting for about 65 per cent of a total population of 10,000 or more Croatians in British Columbia. The breakdown of occupations reveals a very close congruence to the Toronto profile: 6-7 per cent in the professions and administration; nearly 25 per cent in the clerical, sales, and service sectors; and over 47 per cent in industrial processing, manufacture, and construction. The only significant deviation in British Columbia from its eastern counterpart in Ontario occurred in the primary resource areas of fishing, logging, farming, and mining, which absorbed double the energies (6 per cent v. 3 per cent) of the Croatian immigrants in the Canadian work force.[34]

The small community of 200 Yugoslavs in Victoria in the late sixties, which has been the focus of a specific urban study by Pitt and Juričić (see Bibliography) has revealed several interesting quantitative and qualitative factors about new immigrants to the Island.[35] As a community of post-1956 vintage, these recent immigrants from Yugoslavia were, in their view, seeking economic opportunity in this expanding centre of government on the southern tip of Vancouver Island. Just under a half of these were from Croatia, somewhat below the urban average of 50 per cent for recent immigration from Yugoslavia, and 70 per cent were of rural origin. In the absence of a significant industrial sector such as existed in Toronto, Hamilton, or even Vancouver, these immigrants entered unskilled labour (27 per cent) and clerical work (18 per cent), with proportionately fewer involved in skilled work (27 per cent) and 6 per cent in the professions. The authors observed that, without the traditional support systems of a large ethnic community with a language base and means of entry into manufacturing and the trades, significant economic and social frustrations existed. The lack of recognition of existing qualifications or rigorous enforcement of trade examination, combined with traditional prejudice and discrimination in favour of native Canadian or northern European groups, was perceived as a major obstacle to economic advancement and to social integration. While in some cases low wages and poor living conditions led some to re-emigrate back to Yugoslavia, the immigrants generally persisted in relative isolation and overcame their poverty during their first years in Canada.

The new wave of migration had created a constellation of communities across Canada, which were qualitatively similar, each conforming to economic and social imperatives imposed by the peculiar region and city to which they came. The immigrants of industrial centres like Toronto, Hamilton, and Sudbury were alike in both the proportions of new migrants and their place in the economic life and social structure of these cities. The Croatian communities in Toronto tended to be highly segregated residentially by income and region of origin in several locations: the Bloor, Bathurst, and Spadina district; the St. Clair and Weston Road-High Park area; and in such suburban communities as Etobicoke, Rexdale, Mississauga, and Oakville.[36] In Hamilton, similar concentrations were evident in the residential districts contiguous to the steel mills and along the brow of Hamilton mountain, with a gradual dispersal of the upwardly mobile into the suburbs toward Dundas, Stoney Creek, and the Mountain.[37] At the same time, in the older industrial cities of Sault Ste. Marie, Thunder Bay, and Sudbury the Croatian immigrants also moved from their inner city locations near mines and pulp mills to the suburbs with upward social mobility and income. Yet in other cases those small diffused settlements that had persisted and survived in such cities as Ottawa, Winnipeg, Calgary, and Edmonton now became even more scattered with the influx of larger numbers into the suburbs. In these cases, ethnic meeting halls, churches, and clubs became necessary substitutes for the comfortable confines of the ethnic working-class neighbourhood, and where they did not flourish, families were driven back upon themselves for fellowship and maintenance of ethnic identity.

Institutions – Church and State

The numbers, variety, and location of the new urban immigrants began to weave a fresh web of social and political institutions. In the same manner as the mass in-migration of the twenties, the post-1955 migration created by its even greater mass a set of counter-ideologies and parallel institutions, in some cases similar to old ones and in others entirely new. A virtual explosion in the construction of churches across Canada in post-war decades resulted from a fortuitous conjuncture of circumstances – the increasing availability of Croatian émigré priests, vastly increased population of Croatians residing in urban areas, and a rapid increase in social capital available for church construction. The first Croatian-Slovenian church, "St. Francis of Assisi," was established in Windsor in 1950 by the Franciscan priest, Rev. Lujo Ivandić.[38] This was followed by the arrival in Toronto of Father Jure Vrdoljak, a former chaplain in an Irish parish in Sudbury, who spearheaded the purchase of an old church in Toronto by the Croatian community in 1958. Another moving force in the establishment of the Toronto parish was Father Dragutin (Charles) Kamber who arrived in 1961 from Detroit, and when the old church was razed by fire in 1962, he organized the community in the construction of an impressive new church, "Our Lady Queen of Croatia," which was completed in 1965. Reverend Kamber's active parish work among the Croatians in Toronto in the sixties resulted in further purchases of land for a park and a parish graveyard and he earned universal praise for his efforts after his death in 1969.[39] Other churches were constructed or purchased from the late fifties to the seventies, in Hamilton (1958), Nanaimo (1960), Sault Ste. Marie (1962), Montreal (1964), Vancouver (1968), Calgary (1970/81), Winnipeg (1974), and Thunder Bay (1977).[40] The Franciscan priests were the most prominent in the establishment of parishes and missions across Canada and by 1978 had established and served some fifteen of the twenty-two parishes in the major Croatian settlements from Montreal to Vancouver Island.[41] There were, in addition, several other secular priests and religious orders, such as the Dominican sisters who operated humanitarian institutions at Sherbrooke in the Eastern Townships.[42]

The maintenance of a uniquely Croatian Catholic culture has not been without the problems that traditionally beset the church in Canada. A recent report has observed that regional differences and sociological divisions within three generations of Croatian immigrants militated against the formation of "a Croatian ethnic Catholic religious community . . . in Canada."[43] One particular problem that prevented this realization was the lack of formal religious education among the post-war generation brought up in a Communist state, which meant only a nominal affiliation with Catholicism. Often, in fact, the view was expressed by some of the recent migrants of a separatist and anti-ultramontane persuasion that a rigorous division between the affairs of church and state must be maintained in the Croatian tradition of a free state and a free church.[44] Other difficulties preventing the consolidation of a Croatian Catholic community were the peculiar weaknesses of the native-born Canadian clergy in serving the needs of immigrants and the limited linguistic abilities in English and French of the new Croatian priests. The geographical distance between the churches and their parishioners and the gradual absorption of the second generation into the regular English-speaking parishes of their immediate neighbourhood were yet other obstacles in the path of religion as a form of cultural retention. In sum, the restraints placed upon the viability of Croatian Catholicism in the sixties and seventies were not much different from those a half-century earlier. Geographic separation, a scattered and overworked clergy, and the lack of a clerical press were combined with the absence of a common sense of mission and survival that has, for example, fuelled French-Canadian Catholicism.

The latter is perhaps an unfair lament particularly in view of the enduring traditions of Catholicism in conquered countries like Poland and Croatia itself over the last millenium.[45] In addition, a notable exception to this purported lack of messianic religious direction has been the great popularity enjoyed by the Catholic prelates under Communist rule in Yugoslavia. Archbishop Stepinac enjoys a heroic reputation among Croatian Catholics of each generation and political persuasion,[46] and wide reading is done about him in the Croatian press generally and in biographies such as M. Raymond's *The Man for This Moment: The Life and Death of Cardinal Aloysius Stepinac.*[47] Also, the popularity of his successors, such as Archbishop Franjo Šeper of Zagreb,[48] and the recent visits by Archbishop Franjo Kuharić of Zagreb to Canada in the late sixties and the early seventies stand as testimony to the piety of the Canadian Croatians and their respect for episcopal authority.[49]

The émigré priests, intelligentsia, and community leaders of the postwar generation also inspired and led the cultural and economic offensive on several other fronts in a manner similar to their Catholic Action experience in their homeland before the war. They helped begin the work of the Croatian Catholic Union of Canada, an American-based mutual insurance organization similar to the older Croatian Fraternal Union. An organization predominantly centred in eastern Canada, it soon grew to 1,500 members by 1970 and published its own newsletter, *Naša Nada (Our Hope).*[50] Another organization begun in the late forties, the Croatian-Canadian Aid Society, revived its charter in 1954 after a split with the more conservative Pavelić elements, which formed their own society in 1950, the United Croats of Canada *(Ujedinjeni Kanadski Hrvati),*[51] and The Croatian Liberation Movement *(Hrvatski Oslobodilački Pokret).* Ostensibly the former's purpose was to aid and abet the establishment of Croatian immigrants in Canada, although it also published a journal supportive of an independent state of Croatia *(Domovina Hrvatska – Croatian Homeland).* The United Croatians and HOP, on the other hand, published their own journal *(Nezavisna Država Hrvatska – The Independent State of Croatia)* from 1960 on and had formed some twenty chapters across Canada by 1965.[52] Their organization and newspaper advertised a number of Croatian self-help organizations on its pages, notably the Croatian Credit Union of Toronto *(Kreditna Zadruga)*, which by the late sixties had total savings of over a quarter-million dollars. Another enterprise more directly linked to UKH-HOP by the mid-sixties was the weekly radio broadcast "The Voice of a Free Croatia" *(Glas Slobodne Hrvatske)*.[53] This radio hour paralleled others developed by Croatians first in Sudbury, then in Montreal and Windsor in response to changes in Canadian broadcasting regulations. Yet other ventures, such as the development of the Croatian Centre and Development Company in Vancouver,[54] and the purchase of lands for purposes of summer picnics and celebrations,[55] were characteristic of a general enthusiasm for community building projects.

The broadening population base in the cities had produced an expanded source for such capital projects as halls, cultural centres, and churches. By the late sixties, some eighteen Croatian halls had been constructed across Canada, and several of these were of post-war construction or reconstruction. A new Croatian National Home was built on Dupont Street in Toronto in 1956 and dedicated by the parish priest, Father Vrdoljak, and the Mayor of Toronto, Nathan Phillips.[56] Others followed in the early sixties, usually sponsored by either the Croatian Peasant Society, the Catholic parish, or some private capital. In 1961, the "Croatian Home Society" of Port Arthur reconstructed the old home originally built in 1935 and updated its facilities for the use of all Croatian organizations in the Thunder Bay district.[57] The Croatian Peasant Society of Vancouver also revived the idea of a Croatian Cultural Hall, which had closed because of deep political divisions in 1946, with the purchase of a small hall in 1962.[58] The mid-sixties then saw the completion of several other homes and the projection of several more, so that by 1970 there were seventeen in all, three each in Toronto and Windsor, two in Welland, and one in each of Vancouver, Montreal, Sydney, Hamilton, and northern Ontario communities such as Sault Ste. Marie, Sudbury, and Schumacher.[59] Others were added in the seventies, such as the Croatian Peasant Hall in east Calgary and the Croatian Islamic Centre on Jane Street in Toronto.[60] The reciprocal help between Croatian Catholics and Croatian Muslims was demonstrated both in the construction of the Toronto centre and in the building of the Roman Catholic Church on East First Avenue in Vancouver in 1968.[61]

Perhaps the most significant area of activity for the new immigrants was politics. The 1960's witnessed the flowering of aspirations for a free and independent Croatia. In part, this revolution of rising expectations was spurred by developments within Yugoslavia itself. After the fall of the Serbian centralist, Alexander Rankovic, from the vice-presidency of Yugoslavia in 1966 there followed a growing climate of decentralization and liberalism.[62] In part it was based on a widespread consciousness in the small but vocal world community of Croatian émigrés, in the United States, South America, and Australia. Books and periodicals and newspapers dedicated to the overthrow of the Yugoslav state and Communist regime became more numerous and accessible to Croatian migrants abroad.

Canada was no exception in this international movement as a number of organizations and publications sprang up in the 1960's dedicated to the same purpose. The Toronto community was the most prolific in the production of new publications,[63] with *Naš Put*, 1962-72 *(Our Way); Hrvatski Put* (1972-   ), which supplanted *Glas Domovine*[64] *(Voice of the Homeland)*, formerly *Domovina Hrvatska (Croatian Homeland); Država Hrvatska*, 1960-74 *(The Independent State of Croatia)*, begun by the United Croatians in 1960; Božidar Vidov's *Domagojevi Strielci (The Duke's Archers)*; and a short-lived bilingual publication, *Istina (The Truth)*, which was published from 1960-62. Beyond these there were others in Montreal: Dr. Stefan Dubičanac's *Jadran (The Adriatic)*, published by the Federation of Croatian Societies (Savez Hrvatskih Društava) and begun in 1966, and another Croatian newspaper entitled *Zvono-La Cloche (The Bell)*.[65] Other smaller newsletters were published across Canada, including the proceedings of Croatian-Canadian clubs of various political persuasions in Sudbury, Ottawa, Calgary, and Vancouver.

The intense political activities of the new Croatian immigrants in the 1960's may be viewed in part as an extension of the same spirit of Croatian independence that manifested itself in pre-war anti-Yugoslav political dissent of the thirties, both pro- and anti-Communist. It may also be seen sociologically as the first and essential step in the process of acculturation and cultural pluralism, and initially at least a total rejection of the assimilative ideal adhered to by the first generation of migrants to Canada and the United States.[66] The position of the post-war émigrés as a better educated class of immigrants was one of dual allegiance to two cultures, languages, and lifestyles – the preservation of the old and cautious adoption of the new.

The first phase in this development, as described by the sociologists Shibutani and Kwan, is that as minority groups find their ethnicity challenged and broken down by the new culture, there occurs "a transitional period during which people are uncertain about the appropriate modes of thought and conduct. The group loses its solidarity, being split into several factions."[67] Usually this period is characterized by social disorganization and bitter internecine rivalry and is followed by a gradual settling out of a new class structure with integrative linkages into the new community. This transitional phase is also characteristic of dual allegiance to two cultures. The educated immigrants have friendly but infrequent contact with dominant groups; they become acculturated through the media and educational institutions but learn relatively slowly the subtleties of the prevalent values within the dominant social group.

The comprehension of competitive political ideologies is in essence the first concern in the citizenship process, that is, beyond pure economic survival during the first few years within the country. Political beliefs are one of the first points of cultural convergence with the dominant society, and socio-cultural understanding of values and attitudes is one of the last stages in the acculturative process. Thus, a European refugee intellectual would understand through reading and the media a great deal more about Canadian history or politics than those born in Canada, but would fail to intuit many of the simpler cultural norms of the country, which his or her children readily grasped in the school or on the streets.[68] The former might construct a facile political equation comparing living standards in the new and old countries of citizenship and extrapolating political values from this in such terms: the North American standard of living is superior to that of the Old World; therefore, North American and Canadian political systems are superior to Old World political systems.

The conviction was articulated by a young Croatian immigrant active in the HOP (Croatian Liberation Movement) organized in Toronto. He was a displaced person who immigrated to Canada in 1951 and worked at various service and supply jobs, becoming a Canadian citizen in 1957.[69] Six years later, he strongly affirmed to a *Toronto Star* reporter his belief in the free enterprise system that gave his family an economic standard of life they could not have enjoyed in the old country, and then went on to describe his political outlook:

> When I tell you that here I am a free man, you do not pay much attention to that. But I came from a country where I could not talk in the open. I could not dance. Now I can dance wherever I like. I go out when I please and where I please. I come home when I like. And I know when I come home that my family will be here and they will be safe. You know I remember the first time I vote, I stop and I say to myself, "By golly; nobody knows how I voted!" . . . I never finish school, you know, and I once said that the first chance I get, I go to school. But now, I do not worry. I guess I have that hope in my kids and when the day comes for them to take over, they will be able to if we have a good job.
>
> We have many things here. But there are many of us in Croatia still. They have hope: But they have nothing else.[70]

The educated class of immigrants could and did express themselves much more eloquently about the central facts of Croatian history and politics, and the necessity for a separate, independent Croatian state. (Nor did it necessarily follow that proponents in Toronto of a separate Croatia would support the proposition of a separate Quebec when that issue arose after November 15, 1976.)[71] The essential fact, however, was that anyone could affirm individual political beliefs in any form in a democratic state, and if he or she could persuade a sufficient number within an organization to accept a particular position, all well and good. If not, there was also every opportunity to secede and form a new organization. The inevitable result was a proliferation of organizations formed in pursuit of the same political ends, but often in vehement disagreement on the means to attain the ends.[72]

Yet another factor often omitted from discussion of political groupings among emigrants is the convivial spirit involved in political socialization. In contrast to the sober puritanical lifestyle Canadians practised in home, school, and workplace, Croatians were used to a more spontaneous lifestyle, with communal celebrations extending beyond the nuclear family. Heated and passionate discussion of issues ranging from sport to society and politics is as natural to the Croatian as to the Mediterranean character. Thus, political meetings or demonstrations by the United Croats celebrating the establishment of the Croatian Republic on April 10, 1941, were deadly serious occasions, but as often as not they were combined with a picnic, banquet, or some entertainment as a social release. Often telegrams were sent to the Prime Minister denouncing the Communist dictatorship in Yugoslavia, or resolutions such as the following were published in English to advertise the Croatian cause.[73]

Resolution

1. We, the United Croats of Canada, who enjoy freedom and democracy in our great new Homeland Canada, most emphatically condemn the Belgrade Communist dictatorship under which our millenary Croatian people undergo their biological extermination [sic].

2. We beg the freedom loving peoples of the world not to accept as truth the slanderous Belgrade propaganda which through numerous Yugloslav diplomatic representations tries to convince the world that the Croatian people are a part of the so-called "Yugoslav People" which does not and will never exist.

3. Yugoslavia is "a little Soviet Russia" and Great Serbia, ruled by a handful of ruthless Communist criminals against the will of the Croatian people, Macedonians, Slovens [sic], Albanians, and Montenegrins. Yugoslavia is the greatest symbol of tyranny and an enormous concentration camp for the Croatian people and all those who love their freedom.

4. The Croatian people together with other oppressed peoples of Yugoslavia will at the first chance destroy this second and last Yugoslavia as they have destroyed the first one. The United Croats of Canada will give their fullest support to their oppressed brethren in Croatia to materialize this aim.

5. The free world should not think for a single moment that Yugoslavia is of any use to the West in its self defense against world Communism because Yugoslavia is a "Trojan Horse" of Moscow through which this wants to conquer the rest of free Europe and the whole of Africa.

6. There cannot be a successful defence against world Com-

munism unless the West recognizes to the Croatian people and to other enslaved peoples of Yugoslavia their right on self-determination. No Yugoslavia, Communist or non-Communist, can be an ally of the Western democracies, because any Yugoslavia represents negation of democracy.

7. The Croatian State right is older than 1300 years, and consequently older than the artificial great-Serbian Yugoslav or Pan-Slav idea and Communism. Therefore, the Croatian people will never recognize any international agreement which against their wills puts them into the great-Serbian slavery or in the Communist, or Pan-Slav sphere. The Croatian people regard themselves an integral part of the civilized and free mankind.

8. The Croatian people are not fighting for the extermination of the Serbian people, who should live in their Serbian State, but for freedom and independence of Croatia.

9. We regard all the oppressed peoples as natural allies of the West, and their ideals of freedom and independence are far more stronger than all the Communist thermo-nuclear weapons, "sputniks" and rocketry.

10. Therefore, we appeal to the great Powers of the West to give the greatest possible moral and material support to the Liberation Movements of the oppressed peoples, among them also to the Croatian Liberation Movement.[74]

By contrast, the formula for social entertainment, which followed such political rhetoric, ran precisely according to that prescribed by other groups in the past: folk dance ensembles, tamburitza and choral music, a speech or two on Croatian culture, combined with ample quantities of food and drink.[75] A few of the patron saints of Croatian political culture or sports heroes were different from those illustrated by other political factions, but the basic process of socialization was essentially the same as it had been a generation earlier. As the medium can often be considered as important as the message, the process of political socialization was likely a means of easing the immigrants' gradual democratic passage into Canadian society. In anthropological terms, such "rites of passage" might be considered a vital and essential transitional rite of initiation into the new society while retaining elements of the old order.[76]

On the more serious side, outbreaks of violence are also characteristic of those transitional states of inter-ethnic tension and conflict.[77] While in the assimilative older group this tension might be manifested in teen-age rebellion and hostility against their older parents during the 1950's, among the new immigrants the group's hostility was directed at the Communist "Yugoslav" faction. Suspicions of arson behind the burning of the Catholic church in Toronto in 1963 produced commentary in the Yugoslav press on the possibilities of "Ustaša" incendiarism. Similar outrage at the later bombing of the Yugoslav consulate in Toronto in

1967 produced counter-charges against the Croatian terrorists.[78] In general, violence was not sanctioned by either side, nor did there occur the kinds of reprisals and counter-reprisals that occurred in West Germany[79] and even Australia, where a Labour government campaigned against "Ustasha assasin squads" and "bands of Croatian Terrorists."[80] Indeed, on that occasion the United Canadian Croatians urged the Australian government of Gough Whitlam to cease harassing Croatian immigrants and exiles to Australia, and to take a more tolerant example from "YOUR COMMONWEALTH LEAGUE COLLEAGUE NATION: CANADA" and her democratic sister nation, the United States.[81] Thus, despite a decade of strongly antagonistic rhetoric during the sixties and early seventies, the intergenerational conflict has not flared into systematically condoned social violence on either side. A territorial social distance has more often been maintained, with some evidence of residential segregation, as in Toronto, although flare-ups do occur at inter-ethnic picnics, weddings, and banquets where ideological lines have been crossed. The seventies and eighties will likely see less of this transitional social tension as the acculturative and assimilative approaches to the dominant Canadian culture blur and perhaps soften these differences.

A more sophisticated perception of the political social problems inherent in the immigration process was also apparent among Croatian intellectuals and community leaders who attempted to dispel negative group stereotypes held by the larger Canadian society. Emotionally laden newspaper images of the past, such as anarchists carrying lighted bombs behind their backs to destroy Winnipeg in the strike of 1919, were not very different from the popularly held stereotypes of the Croatians as terrorists and hijackers in the sixties and seventies. To their credit, Croatian spokesmen in Canada have attempted to enlighten the Canadian and American public wherever possible about the nature of their objectives and their disapproval of political violence in the name of a free Croatia. Recently, M. Giunio-Zorkin of Nanaimo, of the Croatian Peasant Party, put the record straight in the *Croatian Voice* (also noted in the Croatian Fraternal Union newspaper, *Zajedničar*) by underscoring his party's condemnation of terrorism, hijacking, and other illegal acts.[82] Other Croatian newspapers openly condemned the English-language press for its sensationalist reporting of the activities of the Croatian Liberation Army and its "kamikaze" tactics and arms caches in Hamilton.[83] Several homilies were also delivered attacking Allan MacEachen, the Minister for External Affairs, for his speech of September, 1975, promising to control "activities of right-wing groups opposed to the Belgrade government." *Hrvatski Put (The Croatian Way)* vigorously responded in an editorial, entitled "Advocates of Freedom are not Terrorists," that such efforts by the Jews or the Irish to establish a free state were never the object of official "distaste." Further, the article averred that the bombings referred to in Ottawa and Washington in previous newspaper articles "were never proved to be the work of Croatian groups," and that "if

211

Croatians and Canadians of Croatian descent express their solidarity with the people of Croatia who wish to exercise their right to self-determination and secede from Yugoslavia, they do not infringe on any national or international standard of political morality."[84]

The new elite also made considerable efforts to correct misinterpretations of Croatian history, politics, law, and society. Several scholarly works by the émigré Croatian intellectuals in Canada addressed themselves to more or less contentious issues in the history of the near and distant past. Some spoke to the constitutional complexities of law and society in Yugoslavia, and others addressed themselves to language problems in a federal state.[85] Polemical reviews of current works on contemporary Yugoslavia also appeared regularly in the Croatian newspapers, and dealt with such dissenters as Milovan Djilas, Mihailo Mihajlov, and the Marxist journal, *Praxis*.[86] Nearly always, a critical stance was taken toward the Yugoslav Communist interpretation of events, and critical acclaim was reserved for those who were most eloquent or courageous in their opposition to Tito's government.

Culture: Schools, Folklore, Music and the Arts
The new intelligentsia also made some attempt to provide leadership and understanding of the issues involved in assimilation to Canadian society. Several of them with an understanding of the social process of immigration and firsthand experience with its impact warned the community of the perils of too rapid assimilation or, worse still, none at all. The parish priest was often closest witness to the social problems of the immigrant and gave advice and counsel to his parishioners and even those outside of the parish. They pointed out the risks of "Americanization" and "Canadianization," particularly for the young single males who had drifted through displaced persons camps and perhaps several countries before coming to Canada. An overly hasty marriage to a non-Croatian even before the basic elements of Canadian culture and language were mastered was one of the basic errors according to the clergy.[87] Other bachelors drifted into a demoralized existence, which often bordered on criminality and resulted in incarceration or admittance to a mental asylum.[88] Although the rates of criminality were not high – only 150 indictable offences by Yugoslavs as a whole during a peak year of migration in 1966[89] – they were of concern to Croatian community leaders and priests, who felt some responsibility to curb such antisocial behaviour. The problems were not new ones nor were they confined to Croatians, but they evoked a wider concern and understanding than ever before.

The problem of language retention and loss of mother tongue among the young was another group concern among the immigrant intellectuals. From census statistics that measured mother tongue and language spoken at home, it was apparent that the children of the new generation of immigrants almost universally preferred to speak English as the *lingua franca* of North America. Surveys in the Toronto area demonstrated in

1971 that, in the heaviest areas of new Croatian immigrant concentration, Croatian was only used at home by one-half of the immigrants.[90] Language retention rates across Canada in 1971 were not much more promising, demonstrating again that among even those who were strongest in declaring themselves Croatian, less than half spoke Croatian at home as opposed to English and French (51 per cent). Among even the residual "Yugoslav ethnic" category, which would include the other ethnic groups and nationalities in Yugoslavia, the language retention was somewhat higher (58 per cent).[91] To remedy the very pronounced shift toward English, Croatian communities in the fifties and sixties instituted formal language classes in most urban communities. Usually these language schools were run for children of elementary school age on Saturdays or Sundays in Croatian churches, community centres, and halls. Subjects included Croatian history, culture, religion, and music in addition to some elements of Canadian "civics."[92] By the seventies a more formal institutional structure was established with the formation in 1976 of the Croatian Schools of Canada, which was affiliated to the larger organization of Croatian-American and Australian schools. The executive director in Canada, Reverend Berto Dragičević of Sudbury, was a Franciscan priest, as were two of its program directors in Montreal and Vancouver. Schools were active in several Canadian cities – Toronto, Montreal, Windsor, Kitchener, Sudbury, Sault Ste. Marie, Thunder Bay, Calgary, and Vancouver – and a newsletter of their activities was first printed in the fall of 1977.[93]

In addition, students interested in developing their language skills could avail themselves of language courses in Serbo-Croatian at the university level at Toronto, Carleton, British Columbia, and Victoria.[94] Formal courses in Croatian history, society, and politics were not separately taught for the most part in Canadian schools and colleges, except insofar as they were generally subsumed under the rubric of the Balkans and the South Slav region and its nationalities. The state of advanced studies in both the particular Croatian area and the general South Slavic field, however, was poorly developed by comparison to Eastern European area studies such as Russian, Polish, and Ukrainian.

On the broader social and cultural front, the new immigrants were increasingly active in developing cultural outlets, such as folklore celebrations, for maintenance of ethnic traditions. The Croatian Days festivals organized from 1958 onward by the Croatian Peasant Party were traditional summer outlets for outdoor summer pageants and celebrations throughout Canada and continued to serve a Croatian consciousness-raising function during the sixties and seventies.[95] A typical recent celebration held in Vancouver on June 12, 1977, began with mass at the Croatian Catholic Church and proceeded to the new Croatian picnic ground, where celebrants were welcomed by officers of the society, Dr. Mladen Giunio-Zorkin, the national president, and dignitaries such as the Mayor of Vancouver, Jack Volrich, a Canadian of Montenegrin origin. The large crowd of over 2,000 people ate ethnic foods such as barbecued lamb and suckling pig, listened to the Croatian Choir "Matica Hrvatska," and watched the Croatian Kolo Dancers of Calgary perform on stage.[96] Such folklore celebrations as the one organized for the Montreal "Expo" in 1967 were thus in the gestation process throughout the mid-sixties and came to full flower in the seventies in the Dominion Day celebrations held in Ottawa.

With the expansion of federal government initiatives in the area of multiculturalism and the formation of provincial ministries of culture, a general increase in cultural activities was apparent among all ethnic groups, including the Croatians. These groups at first operated informally within such societies as the Croatian-Canadian clubs. The gradual depoliticization of such local clubs may be witnessed in Sudbury, where the local Croatian committee became more concerned with its social and cultural mission than with the divisive complexities of factional politics.[97] As a result of this new direction in the early seventies the local cultural group was strengthened and resulted in the formation of the Sudbury Croatian Kolo and Tamburitzan group. Soon, the Croatian Folklore Federation crystallized under the leadership of Ante Beljo and the first Croatian Folklore Festival was held in May, 1975, under the auspices of the federal department of the Secretary of State and the Carling Community Arts Foundation.[98]

The immense success of this venture and a spontaneous kolo dance through the streets of Sudbury from the Croatian Church and around the Croatian Hall prompted a return engagement to Hamilton a year later. This festival featured the talents of Joseph Lončarich, Stelco employee and a tamburitza maestro at the Croatian National Home from 1959-76.[99] Added support from seven folklore ensembles such as the Zrinski-Frankopan group from Toronto, and others from Sudbury, Sault Ste. Marie, and Hamilton resulted in a colourful two-day festival. A commentary by a senior Croatian-Canadian resident in Hamilton enthused over the folk mass and festival concert, which ran uninterruptedly for four hours:

> It brought to our youth bigger awareness of the true richness and diversity of our national folklore. They can proudly refer to it as the most visible and lively part of the unique Croatian culture in Canada; it can help them to identify themselves more readily to their own ethnic roots. Besides, such happy and cheerful endings are happy news for a change. They do not scandalize but enrich our lives.[100]

Inspired by this triumph, this increasingly popular and professional form of ethnic entertainment moved to Toronto in 1977 and then westward to Edmonton. The new urban communities of the West had also become more active culturally and founded dance and choral groups in Winnipeg, Calgary, Lethbridge, and Edmonton. The Winnipeg community of some 400 families had suddenly become visible in 1975 with the construction of their church on North Main and participation in Folklorama Week during August of that year. Similar developments had occurred in the Edmonton and Calgary communities, both of similar size and quality. In the latter, for example, the local community had funded a mission and then a church by the early seventies,[101] and had gone beyond the traditional political groupings to form the "Matica Hrvatska" (Queen-Bee Croatia), an organization "where activities are centred around the preservation of the Croatian culture and tradition within the Croatian-Canadian framework."[102] Stressing such cultural activities as drama, dance, choral singing, soccer, and chess, this organization attempted to detach itself somewhat from negative political factionalism to achieve its cultural objectives. These objectives appeared to coincide with those of the Edmonton community, which had undergone a similar evolution toward church and folklore groups, the latter of which was founded in 1973. Thus, the 1978 festival of the Croatian Folklore Federation was jointly held in Edmonton and Ottawa, taking advantage of both federal and provincial funding available for national and local celebrations of the Commonwealth Games.[103]

The formation of cultural clubs and organizations in nearly every Croatian-Canadian community of any size reflected the broader cultural concerns of the new immigrants. Croatian-Canadian clubs were formed in those new communities, like the one in Ottawa (1957), that lacked a solid infrastructure of Croatian ethnic organizations.[104] Others were formed in older, more established communities like Sudbury, where the new arrivals had distinct cultural and literary needs beyond those of the earlier generation.[105] The community in Toronto also established in 1969 a Croatian Cultural Society entitled "Hrvatsko Kulturno Prosvjetno Drustvo," which published a newsletter, *Napredak (Progress)*, of its activities.[106] Shortly thereafter, in May, 1972, several Croatian intellectuals in Toronto established the first Canadian chapter of the Croatian Academy of America, an American organization whose broad purpose was to educate the members and to publish generally concerning Croatian literature, culture, and history.[107]

On an individual basis, the most recent wave of post-war migration also resulted in many cultural contributions to Canadian life. Often these were extensions of earlier arts or crafts begun in the old country, but increasingly they were derived from and adapted to their new environment in Canada. As should always be the case with the true artists, for example, the universality of their statements transcends local and national boundaries and reflects on the broader human condition. Significantly, the greatest contributions by Croatian artists and intellectuals occurred in those areas such as the graphic arts and music and poetry where the limitations of language were least restrictive and the universality of aesthetics, harmony, and imagery most liberating. All three were deeply rooted as well in the fertile soil of Croatian culture and spread their branches into other cultures. In sculpture, the artistic brilliance of Ivan Meštrović enlivened North American culture with his powerful sculptures, as did the paintings of Maximilian Vanka and the violin virtuosity of Zlatko Baloković.[108] Equally, Croatian culture itself was informed by American literary spirit, as the poetry of A.G. Matoš drew from Poe and the verse of Tin Ujević drew deeply from the well of Walt Whitman.[109]

Perhaps the first and most renowned of the post-war Croatian artists was the poet Alan (Alain) Horić, who emigrated to Canada in 1951. A Croatian Muslim from Bosnia, Horić served with distinction in the French army in Indochina after the war. He came to Canada where he entered a career in business and at the same time earned a degree in Slavic literatures at the University of Montreal, choosing as his master's thesis the poetry of Tin Ujević, the great Croatian poet. All the while, he began to write creatively, and some of his early poems written in Croatian appeared in *Hrvatska Revija* (Paris) and in *Hrvatski Glas Kalendar (Croatian Voice Calendar)*, which printed three of his poems in 1955.[110] Some of these early poems were acute reflections of his Croatian heritage, as was a collection, *Nemir Duše,* published in 1959. But his main *métier* soon developed in the French language with the publication of two highly successful collections, *L'Aube Assassiné* (1957) and *Blessure au Flanc de Ciel* (1962), both of which secured recognition for him as a rising new poet in French Canada. This distinction, which was rare for poets of immigrant birth writing in their adopted language, was particularly noteworthy to critics in French Canada.[111] Today he enjoys a prominent place in the anthologies of modern Quebec poetry, a testimony to the cosmopolitan and universal nature of Horić's poetry and of the Montreal literary culture which has acclaimed him as its own.

Very few new poets ventured forth as Horić did into one of Canada's official languages. Nada Stipković of Montreal published a collection of French poems, *Lignes*, in 1961, but must be considered a Canadian poet since she was raised and educated in Canada.[112] Certainly praiseworthy for his monumental efforts at writing some 20,000 poems is Jožo Kutleša of Toronto, who first began to write in English in 1963 after nine years in Canada. His *Mosaic of Life*, published in 1970, is a collection of over eighty poems on life, love, and the hope of the New World in the spirit of Walt Whitman and Tin Ujević. The celebration of the virtues and flaws of his adopted land was characteristically expressed in his poems about Toronto, "a universe of contrasts, many paths," in whose "cosmic heart" was "innocence raging against bias, ignorance and arrogance of mobs clashing."[113]

Beyond these efforts in Canada's official languages there was a virtual explosion of poetry in the Croatian language among the new immigrants. In common with their earlier and humbler counterparts in the twenties, the better educated new arrivals also sang the praises of their new land and poignantly recalled the memories of their homeland. One of the older poets, Stjepan Hrastovec, who studied at the University of Zagreb in the interwar period, settled in Windsor after a distinguished poetic career that included anthologies such as *Budna Zemlja (Awakening Land)*.[114] Of the newer generation of immigrants, many younger poets of all ages were publishing their poetry. One of these was Marijan Šola, who published two of his own collections, *Za Dom (For The Homeland)* in 1960 and *Još Hrvatska Nij Propala (Croatia Has Not Yet Perished)* in 1964. Characteristically the latter dwelt upon themes of the new land, the old homeland, family, and work in Canada.

The Croatian-language newspapers also continued to print poems reflecting the feelings of the immigrants for the new land. Regular contributions from the staff and readership of the Yugoslav-Canadian newspaper, *Jedinstvo*, appeared during the sixties, ranging from simple but eloquent salutes to their new country ("Pozdrav Kanadi"), to celebrations of the working-class pioneers who laboured in the factory, on the farm, and in the fisheries.[115] Several poignant poems also dealt from varying perspectives with unpleasant subjects peculiar to the post-war immigrants, such as the horrors of war and life in the displaced persons camps of Austria after the war. Several of the new Yugoslav poets who contributed to *Jedinstvo* and other Yugoslav periodicals in the United States were gathered together into an anthology by Dr. Želimir Juričić, *Zbirka Lirike iz Nove Domovine (Collected Lyrics from the New Homeland)*. Prominent among these were Joseph Gabre, a native of Šibenik and a regular contributor to *Jedinstvo* after coming to Toronto in 1959.[116] Other younger poets were Šime Negro, a Dalmatian who came to Toronto in the mid-sixties, and Ruba Gverino, a native of Istria who settled in Montreal as a teacher after his arrival in 1967. Their incisive quality and their honest insights into Canadian life from the immigrant perspective will, it is hoped, result in their wider availability in translation.

The aesthetic perspective of the immigrant artists and artisans was further manifested in the realm of sculpture. While he never lived in Canada, the spirit of Ivan Meštrović left its mark with the marble relief he created for the Canadian War Memorial in Ottawa, entitled "The Canadian Phalanx," as well as his figure of a Croatian peasant woman in the Ontario Art Gallery at Toronto and a bust of Cardinal Stepinac at the University of Sudbury.[117] The more significant contribution for Canadian culture, however, was made by a young sculptor, Augustin Filipović, who arrived in Toronto in 1959 at age of twenty-nine after classical study in Zagreb and Rome. Having won encouragement from Henry Moore, with whom he studied briefly in England, and in receipt of international awards before he arrived in Toronto, Filipović's work was soon in great demand at Gallery Moos in Toronto's Yorkville. At that time both a sculptor and painter of wide interests and talents, he expressed his desire for coming to Canada because, "It is a young country and interest in modern art here is reaching its peak."[118] He went on in the next year to establish a post-graduate art school at the University of Toronto with the aid of the Canada Council.[119] By the middle-sixties, he had gained a national reputation as a fine graphic artist, for his realistic busts, and for his freer bronze and steel designs and wash drawings.[120] By the early seventies, he had moved away from the rough edges of his earlier work to more refined surfaces, "almost sensuous and suggestive of the physical rhythm of life."[121] Always colourful and controversial, he continued at the same time the fine traditions of Croatian sculpture in Canada, just as his contemporary, Josip Turkalj, did in the United States.

The international spirit Filipović brought to sculpture was brought to other areas of the fine arts by young Croatian artists on the move. Paul Mostovac, a Croatian-born artist, came to Canada from Bruges, Belgium, in 1956, where he had studied for four years. His paintings attracted good critical reviews during the mid-sixties particularly, in Sudbury, Ottawa, and Toronto, where he taught art.[122] Another young artist trained in the Zagreb Academy of Fine Arts was Anton Četin, who came to Canada in his early thirties in 1968 and soon participated in numerous international shows, notably one dedicated to Copernicus in Krakow in 1972. Others to come from the rich artistic culture of Zagreb were Zlatko Arhanić and Vladimir Polgar, an electronics engineer who migrated to Ottawa in 1968 and was soon exhibiting his paintings, mosaics, and sculptures throughout Canada and the United States.[123] In the Far West there were several other artists, such as Seka Owen of Zagreb, who became an art program co-ordinator in Edmonton, and Peter Bulić, a Vancouver sculptor who designed the monument commemorating the Croatian miners who came to Nanaimo at the turn of the century.[124]

One of the most exceptionally gifted artists of the sixties was Joso Špralja, a neo-renaissance man whose many faceted talents included sculpture, graphic photography, and folk music. A native of Zadar, Špralja showed an early interest in the fine arts and travelled to Zagreb where he studied at the Academy under the well-known graphic artist, Jerolim Miše,[125] and later worked at the archeological museum in Zadar. Upon coming to Canada in 1960, he spent his first two years studying art at Central Tech and the Ontario College of Art before launching into an incredibly varied career. His sculptures in wood, terracotta, and ceramics, which were displayed in various Toronto galleries, showed the historical influences of the Byzantine style and of surrealism in the modern genre.[126] His other passion in the visual arts was photography, for which he had already won a gold medal in Belgrade in 1959. His dramatic photographs, particularly those of the sea and the universal human condition, won him further prizes and a considerable international reputation in this field.[127] But his final area of endeavour gained him his greatest popularity in Canada. As a folksinger, he and his partner Malka, an Israeli, appeared widely on Canadian, British, and American television, at Carnegie Hall, and at the centennial celebrations in London in 1967.[128] All in all, Špralja's meteoric career in the sixties was testimony to his ecumenical interests and great enthusiasm for art and life in every form.

In the sphere of music and the performing arts the new immigrants brought classical as well as folk traditions with them from their homeland. Croatian emigrants had contributed to classical music as early as the 1920's, for Dr. Louis von Kunits (Kunić), a Croatian from Austria and a violin teacher, had become conductor of the New Symphony Orchestra in Toronto from 1923 to 1931.[129] Various talented newcomers entered Canada in the fifties, among them Vlado Miloslavić, who became a music instructor in the Canadian navy,[130] and Emilija Zaharia, who became a professor of music at the Royal Conservatory at Toronto in 1960, only seven years after emigrating from her native Dubrovnik.[131] An exceptionally talented young musician was the child prodigy and pianist, Hilda Irek, who came with her parents to Toronto and composed her own works and played the classics by the age of six. Often a featured performer at Croatian gatherings and at more formal recitals in Toronto and New York, she excited the imagination and pride of the Croatian immigrant community of the sixties.[132] Another highly skilled Croatian immigrant to come in the 1950's was Nenad Lhotka, ballet master for the Zagreb opera company. He was invited to come to Canada to assume duties as ballet master for the Royal Winnipeg Ballet and later organized several productions for the Manitoba Theatre Centre and for television and university in Winnipeg. In the sixties he choreographed his father's famous ballet, "The Devil in the Village," and wrote "Slaveni," a new ballet for the Royal Winnipeg, both of which were well-received in their travels across Canada.[133]

Among the unique contributions to recent Canadian culture has been the work of Maja Seka Miletić, an animator with Zagreb Film who followed her brother to Canada in 1957. After working at various menial jobs, then in Toronto's commercial studios until 1968, she went on to Hollywood to further develop her craft. She and her brother in Hamilton formed a company, Croatian Creations, which in 1973 produced an animated short entitled "Why Not?" that placed in the top sixteen in the Academy Awards competition for animated shorts longer than three minutes. Revised in 1975, it won further international awards in Villiers, Switzerland, in 1976 and in the same year was selected to represent Canada at the twenty-second annual film festival in Oberhausen, West Germany.[134] Other film projects were in the works, including a pilot animation, "1001 Arabian Nights," and the possibility of a comic strip about the legendary folk hero of Croatian steelworkers, Joe Magarac.[135]

Work and Leisure

The post-war migration also included for the first time a steady stream of skilled Croatian professionals and educators who contributed to their fields of endeavour. The first wave of intellectuals and professionals who entered before 1960 tended to include a high proportion of émigrés who were priests, nuns, academicians in the humanities and social sciences, lawyers, and physicians.[136] With the onset of economic immigration in the 1960's the emphasis shifted somewhat to the theoretical and applied sciences, ranging across a wide area from chemistry and geology to agronomy and including researchers and practitioners in the medical sciences, dentists, and engineers. The list of their accomplishments in their several spheres of study and professional activity has become too numerous to catalogue. Some of the most recent arrivals in the scientific community have quickly taken their place at a higher level of Canadian society and consequently have tended to play a more prominent role from the beginning in the leadership of the ethnic community. And often, unlike the pre-1950 migrants who had to struggle with the language as a functional problem in their professional discipline, the scientists could advance more quickly in their fields because of their technical expertise in an international scientific language. Increasingly the possibilities for scientific exchanges of technical information and personnel developed between Canada and Yugoslavia, as in the case of the Electrosond Company of Zagreb, which assisted in the Peace River power project in 1965.[137]

One of the most significant sectors of activity among the modern immigrants was in the area of business enterprise, particularly real estate and construction. Almost every Canadian city had a success story of a post-war Croatian migrant entrepreneur who had struggled, triumphed, and prospered. One of the most remarkable of the enterprising Dalmatian breed of businessmen was Mladen-Giunio Zorkin, a native of the Adriatic coastal city of Boka Kotorska who settled in Nanaimo after the war and within two decades was in command of a commercial and industrial brokerage and real estate empire of considerable magnitude. As well as his many business activities he was also an avid exponent of Croatian culture and history and actively promoted charitable and educational ventures of a multicultural variety. In recognition of his many activities as an ethnic leader he was presented a medal by the Queen at ceremonies held during the royal visit in the fall of 1977.[138] There were others from the Dalmatian coast and inland regions as well who prospered in Canada, men such as Ratomir Babić, also from Boka (Risan), who established an electrical construction company in Vancouver, and Dušan Bezić from the island of Šolta, who established a construction and land development company in Toronto. The post-war immigrants thus continued to demonstrate the capacity of the Adriatic coastline and littoral to generate the elusive quality of entrepreneurship.[139]

On a smaller scale, the business acumen of the new immigrants was shown in the small family partnership. These businesses, usually in the construction sub-trades and service industries,[140] were a direct extension of the *zadruga* or communal family and therefore based on family and extended family relationships. Examples of this type of business enterprise are common to other immigrants from such Mediterranean countries as Italy, Greece, and Portugal and may be found particularly in large concentrations of urban immigrants in Montreal, Toronto, and Vancouver. Whether the business was general construction, a sub-trade, a cleaning service, a butcher shop, or a restaurant, the family partnership nicely matched the small scale of business operation.[141] A brother, brother-in-law, or cousin might be incorporated into the construction business, for example, or alternately, an entire family extending to the parents might be involved if the physical demands were in the less strenuous service sector. Whatever the enterprise, the family and clan stretched and adjusted to match the economic demands placed on it, much as it had over the turbulent last century. A successful business would consequently attract more family members from the homeland during the prosperous sixties, and as the Canadian economy began to contract in the seventies there was often a flow of returned migrants back to the homeland.

The immigrants of the sixties also brought with them strong preferences in leisure as well as in work and achievement. To be sure, imported games were more avidly pursued by the male bachelors who had more leisure time than those who had come in completed families or had married and settled while in Canada. The main sporting passion of the newcomers was soccer; for some, chess was a more intellectual second choice. The latter appealed mainly to the better-educated class of immigrant but was nevertheless very popular in some cultural clubs and organizations.[142] The skill of some of the Croatian players who entered provincial and national competitions was evident in the attainments of Zvonko Vranesić, a Canadian champion and member of the national chess team in the early sixties, and of Branimir Brebrich of Calgary and Ante Zaravić of Vancouver, both of whom won their respective provincial championships.[143] More recently, George Kuprejanov of Don Mills, Ontario, has achieved ranking as an international chess-master and has also won the Canadian closed championship in chess.

Soccer, however, provided the focal point for new Croatian Canadians both as participants and as spectators. The local Croatian soccer club, in fact, provided the male immigrants with their primary access to Canadian society outside of their occupation, for it was here that group conflict with other ethnic groups and the larger society could be played out symbolically on the field and at the same time entertain and reinforce group solidarity among the Croatian spectators. The enormous appeal of this formula to the Croatian urban communities across Canada was such that virtually all of them have successfully sponsored a soccer club in the recent past. Indeed, if any single social activity was capable of producing some unity and community pride among the disparate elements in these communities it was a winning or contending soccer club.

Some of the earliest clubs to organize in the 1950's were the Adria Club of Sudbury in 1950, the Croatian National Soccer Club of Toronto in 1956, and the Croatian National Sports Club of Hamilton in 1957.[144] Other clubs were formed in Welland, Sudbury, Port Arthur, Windsor, and Montreal in the late fifties and early sixties and steadily improved their play and their positions in city and provincial standings.[145] The Toronto-Croatia club climbed slowly from city champions in 1959 to champions of the semi-professional National Soccer League of Ontario in 1970-71 and became Canadian national champions from 1971 to 1974.[146] Further to the west, other clubs were organized in Calgary and Vancouver, with the latter winning the Provincial Cup in the Pacific Coast League in 1970 and the former winning the Alberta Major Soccer League Championship by 1975.[147]

The finest hour for Croatian soccer came in winning the North American Soccer League championship over the Minnesota Kicks in the late summer of 1976. Toronto Metros-Croatia, a team half-owned by the former Toronto-Croatia, was an unlikely victor and unpopular with the league executive and Toronto detractors for being "too ethnic." But Metros-Croatia stolidly overcame every obstacle in the playoffs to reach the final, and to everyone's surprise but their own, the team won. Led by their coach, Marijan Bilić, and bolstered by the former Portuguese great, Eusebio, the Croatians received stellar performances from goalie Željko Bilecki and forward Ivan Grnja. As the first Canadian team and the first Croatian club to win this major international championship, the team and its faithful Croatian supporters in Toronto were elated. The only discordant note in the victory was the slim attendance of 6,000 at the gate in Toronto, and, despite persistent attempts to overcome financial losses, it could not ignore the inevitable.[148] After several takeover offers from Carling-O'Keefe and other interests, the shareholders sold a controlling interest to Global Communications of Toronto for $2.6 million early in 1979, and its name soon changed to the Toronto Blizzard.[149]

Overall, the post-war immigrants have made remarkable strides and have contributed greatly to Canadian life. They have taken much from the economic opportunity the country offered but have also given much back in their work, play, and culture. By the mid-seventies two decades had passed for some, for others even less than a decade, but the tenor and quality of life were still very similar for most. Hard work and an aversion to unemployment and the drive for ownership of a mortgage-free home in the suburbs were their central economic goals. Socially their aspirations were those of the previous generations, an education and a better life for their children and care and concern for their parents, who were brought over to Canada if at all possible. For the most part, particularly for the poorer and less well-educated, this classic immigrant formula worked as it had always worked, and perhaps better than ever before because of Canada's unparalleled prosperity in the sixties and seventies.

Disappointments and frustrated aspirations inevitably occurred, however, particularly among the single migrants and better educated.

Some single male immigrants drifted into far more desperate lives than they had left, and some educated or highly skilled immigrants did not find the work for which they were trained. Some who could return to Yugoslavia did so, and often became serial migrants, citizens of neither the Old World nor the New.[150] Finally there were those for whom the Canadian dream became a tragedy from which there was no return.[151]

The problems of adjustment to Canadian life were not fatal for most, but they were real and persistent nonetheless. The difficulties of occupational exclusion and social prejudice had by no means disappeared, and suspicions of foreign qualifications and hostility toward new immigrants had not diminished, although the hostility had become less overtly violent to Slavs in particular. The problems of ethnic intermarriage were a continuing difficulty for some. Although preferences still ran to in-group marriage, the relative scarcity of Croatian women often promoted arranged marriages with girls in the home country or marriages outside the group. In the latter case the predisposition was to marry native-born Canadians rather than other immigrants,[152] although several hundred married German and other Slavic peoples.[153] Problems arising from such exogamous marriages both for young men and women were not necessarily greater than those in the population at large, although there was a tendency for many in the Croatian group to consider such unions a loss to the ethnic group. It is evident, however, that some native Canadians and other ethnic groups also became closely associated with the Croatian language, mores, and Roman Catholic religion through intermarriage.[154]

Other problems of assimilation and acculturation had become more subtle in the generational tension that pulled between parents and children. The strangeness of a new society gradually gave way to a sense of estrangement between generations as a new language and cultural barrier grew between them. This gap was neither certain nor inevitable since many parents and community leaders made allowances for the rebelliousness of youth in North America. An understanding by some of the inevitability of integration also helped bring enlightenment to this social process. An acute analysis of the interrelated problems of assimilation and the tensions between generations was movingly expressed by Mirko Meheš of Laurentian University, himself a first-generation migrant:

> . . . At the same time, for many years all of us were bothered with the problem of dual loyalty which if it is put in the "old" way creates an unsolvable conflict in every honest person. The loyalty to Croatia and loyalty to the new homeland. Who can live for fifteen years in an airless space and be a typical "castle neither in the sky nor on the earth." . . . We cannot prevent the process of integration, nor can we stop it, and it would be foolish even to attempt that. We would only remove a greater number of people from further battle for Croatia.

223

. . . We the first generation of immigrants must be aware of one more fact: we must always remain in the background of the second and third generations. In the spirit of that people's saying – that a man wants to be better than anybody, but not as good as his son. . . .

No matter how young, we are only a generation of fathers, always the first generations, which splits between the two continents, two homelands, two loyalties, two worlds, but that generation of fathers mustn't be in the spirit of Turgenev [*Fathers and Children*]. Didn't our Majer express it more nicely:

When my father and I go into the forest
For a stroll
Everything around us is solemn and quiet
As if, at any moment, the organ will start playing
Hidden somewhere amidst the leaves.
   My father slightly bent, stops on the gravel
   And listens: a bird sings,
   Sings somewhere high above, on the top of a branch
   Amidst great silence
   Where a butterfly flutters up and down
   In the blue sky.
   I am silent, my Father and I, we are one,
   As if invisible pipes
   Pour blood from his body into mine
   As if I hear the gurgle of our blood.
   Amidst the greenery
      And as it is sad for me to know
      That each step of his,
      Brings him closer to darkness
      While each of mine
      Leads me closer to life
As if full of guilt I turn away from him
While we walk through the forest alone
One uphill, the other downhill.[155]

SECOND AND THIRD GENERATIONS ON THE MOVE

While the drama of the new immigration and its agonies of adjustment were being enacted front stage centre, there was an equally powerful but quiet movement of people in the background. By now, three generations of immigrants and their children mingled together, sometimes vigorously clashing but most often moving silently and anonymously to "strut and fret [their] hour on the stage and then [be] heard no more." The moving silent pantomime of those background actors, who quietly and unobtrusively had become Canadians and were either unwilling or unable to articulate their "Croatianness," was pre-empted by the more spectacular drama occurring upstage. The vocal militancy of the new generation of immigrants tended to obscure the social aspirations and achievements of those 30,000 Canadian-born who made up nearly 40 per cent of the total number of Croatians.[156]

The assimilative process had fundamentally altered the Canadian-born, or those who had come as small children to Canada, so that their language, their manners, and their customs were often very different from those of their parents. Most spoke Croatian, if at all, less fluently and less frequently than their parents, and they seldom read Croatian as a literary language, rarely perusing a newspaper, much less a book. They were frequently less pious in their religious observances and less inclined to observe old customs relating to the Christmas and Easter seasons.[157] They were, more likely than not, married to persons of another ethnic background,[158] and shared a common pride in their dual ethnic heritage. The sense of ethnicity they passed to the third generation was usually based upon family history and genealogy, ethnic cooking, and more subtle attitudes and ways of behaviour learned and adapted from the older immigrants. The process of transformation was not in itself unique, for it had already taken place in the United States, but it was different in the particulars, in the degree and rate of change, and in the way it was perceived by the Croatian Canadians.

There were some elements of stability in the social equation, insofar as core communities of Croatians were still located in areas of original settlement. Thus, the mining and forest frontiers of Canada from British Columbia to northern Quebec still contained viable pockets of settlement. Thus, communities still flourished in the sixties and early seventies, despite attrition among the old-timers, in areas such as Prince George, Timmins-Porcupine, and Rouyn-Noranda. Equally, there were still settlements in rural and small town locations such as the lower Fraser delta, the Okanagan Valley, the Peace River district, and the Niagara Peninsula. Also, in the manufacturing cities of Ontario such as Hamilton, Windsor, Welland, Sudbury, Sault Ste. Marie, and Thunder Bay there were strong and viable concentrations of second- and third-generation Canadians buttressed by immigrant newcomers.[159]

Strong forces for instability existed as well, for Canadian society on the whole was a people on the move, from small town to large city, from east to west, from south to north. Combined with this geographical mobility was a vigorous occupational movement, usually upward but sometimes downward as well. The rapid urban expansion of the sixties attracted many off the farm and from the small town to the large city in search of educational and occupational opportunity. Thus the cities of Toronto, Montreal, Winnipeg, Vancouver, Edmonton, Calgary, and Regina received new immigrants in search of higher wages and improved material lifestyles. And even within these cities and other more moderately sized manufacturing centres there was a vigorous movement upward in income and outward in resettlement to the suburbs as a consequent effect of affluence. The social profile of the second and third generations had assumed a shape and proportion similar to that of the large society, with Croatian Canadians represented in nearly every sector and social life in Canada.[160]

A cautionary note should be added, however, to the optimistic assumption that social mobility was generally upward.[161] In Hamilton during the 1970's it has been demonstrated that approximately 80 per cent of the sons remained either stationary or decreased somewhat in social status, and less than a fifth made the dramatic leap from unskilled jobs to highly skilled managerial and professional jobs. Social slippage was thus as common as social advance, particularly on the margin between the semiskilled and unskilled occupations where most immigrants entered the urban labour force.[162] Intra-generational social tension consequently manifested itself between members of the same families and clans who had established themselves in different occupations and classes. Blue-collar workers might have limited social contact with upwardly mobile relatives in the same city.[163] Equally, those with careers on the rise might in a new city sever themselves entirely from their working-class and ethnic past and develop a new set of social ties. Thus the intense intra-family tensions, which were characteristic of rural and small town social relationships in the pre-1960 era, were gradually dissipated in the much cooler social atmosphere of the modern city. With the conveniences of modern health-care systems, placing an aged parent in an old folks' home increased the social distance between relatives of the same clan or family. Hence, whatever then remained of the old communal family traditions was alive mainly among the first-generation immigrants and was a rapidly disappearing social ideal among the fully assimilated Canadians of Croatian origin.

Of the other sources of tension between generations of Canadian-born and foreign-born, language and religion ranked high as potentially sensitive issues. As the younger children were exposed to the school they tended to introduce and even force English into the home by answering their parents' questions in English.[164] While some parents viewed the situation positively as one in which they could learn a new language, others saw English usage in the home as a foreign intrusion into the family structure, and as a loss of culture.[165] While the Croatian-language schools helped diminish language attrition in the sixties and seventies, they had come too late for the Canadian-born in the 1940's and 1950's.

Whether or not Canada will, because of its dualistic political evolution and recent policies favouring bilingualism and multiculturalism, avoid the pitfalls of the American experience is a moot point, likely to be decided by the current generation of immigrants. Certainly, it appears that the second and third generations of Croatian Canadians are following a similar path to their American cousins, only later in time. As a recent observer of the American linguistic experience has written, "The use of sCr. (Serbo-Croatian) has shifted from all domains of life to a very few and socially marginal ones. Since its functional importance is thus reduced and since linguistic assimilation proceeds steadily and at an ever-increasing rate, the struggle for survival of sCr. is bound to fail with the present generation which is forsaking the ancestral language."[166] With the current lack of hard evidence for language retention among Croatians in Canada such an hypothesis must, however, be ventured very tentatively and without the certainty that exists for other ethnic groups. But, parallel evidence from a recent study of ten other ethnic groups in Canada concludes that, despite the perceived desirability for the retention of language and the means to promote it, "*Under current conditions*, language knowledge will not be transmitted from parent to child in a fully fluent permanent form. It will inevitably be lost to almost all in the natural order of generational succession."[167]

The facets of linguistic assimilation were many and caused considerable debate between the articulate forces for bilingualism and the largely inarticulate assimilationists. The classical purists among the new intellectuals decried the decline in language purity and the formation of a bastardized Croatian grown from peasant roots and grafted with the language of the Canadian streets. The current dialogue between proponents and opponents of *joual* as a folk language of the Québécois might be an instructive starting point for a debate on the value of immigrant "Cro-English." One side might argue that this language provided a middle ground for conversation between the young and old and was often the only means whereby old, lesser educated migrants might good naturedly communicate with their peers of other dialects. Indeed, its convivial value as a source of plain fun was recognized by everyone, as indicated by this humorous passage entitled "Vokali mi i Tokali, Ju Beča!" (We Walked and Talked—You Betcha!")

> . . . Drugi dan i vikend, došlo nekoliko familija sa *banč of kids* koji su, za ono par dana stu su tamu *štapali, rezali hell of a racket*. Jedan od onih *dem ful kids*, da nam je ipak nešto *eksajtmenta* kada je sa *bota* pao *u drink* i bio bi sigurno utopio, da nisu bio tamo dva dobra *svimera* pa ga izvukli iz vode, polegli na *send, pumpali* smu *štomak* i davali *artifičju respiraciju. Ju beča.*[168] [Anglicisms italicized]

Many such examples, laden with more or less English and more or less Croatian, could be used to demonstrate the infinitely flexible quality of capacities and understanding and the speaker's vocabulary and inventiveness, much as in improvisational or unstructured poetry or music. That a great many immigrants and their children speak or have spoken some form of this debased language is testimony to its persistence and effectiveness in Canada and in the United States.[169]

In an indirect way, Croatian Canadians have also contributed to the general process of English-language penetration which has occurred in Croatia since the war. Return migration to particular regions of Croatia has contributed to the general process of English loanwords becoming popular in Yugoslavia, through tourism, the media, and literature.[170] Technological terminology, the international parlance of fashion, sports, music, and dining have all had a massive impact on European languages and have resulted in such loanwords, neologisms, and compounds as "biznismen" (businessman), "lift boj" (elevator operator), "derbimeć" (derby match), "send vić torta" (layer cake), "bikini kostim" (bikini swimsuit), "džez kompozicija" (jazz composition), and "rok opera" (rock opera).[171] In a sense, then, the early Croatian immigrants to North America were linguistic pioneers and a genuine social paradigm of this larger process of linguistic assimilation. While the linguistic effects of language transfer to English were much more devastating for a minority culture in North America and have resulted in a steady and seemingly inevitable process of language loss in the second and third generations, they do offer an example and warning of the larger sociolinguistic process at work.

In the likely absence of long-term language survival, maintenance of ethnic identity among second- and third-generation Croatians has tended to devolve upon other means, such as a consciousness of their family history, their customs, manners, and even foods. As Michael Novak, a Slovak American, has expressed in *The Rise of the Unmeltable Ethnics*, an ethnic group is more than the sum of principals and preferences; it is also a complex constellation of emotions:

> What is an ethnic group? It is a group with an historical memory, real or imaginary. One belongs to an ethnic group in part involuntarily, in part by choice. Given a grandparent or two, one chooses to shape one's consciousness by one history rather than another. Ethnic memory is not a set of events remembered, but rather a set of instincts, feelings, intimacies, expectations, patterns of emotion and behaviour; a sense of reality; a set of stories for individuals – and for the people as a whole to live out. . . .
>
> The network people, among whom are the white ethnics, find it hard to think of themselves as atoms, or of their neighbourhoods as mere pieces of geography. Into their definition of themselves enter their family, their in-laws, their relatives, their friends, their streets, their stores, familiar smells and sights and sounds. These things are not as they are for the atomic people, extrinsic. For the network people these things are identity, *life, self.* It is not that the network people are *attached* to such things. They *are* such things. Take away such things and part of them dies. . . .[172]

In essence, these observations apply equally well to Canada, which, despite its more libertarian British political tradition and unique respect for French-Canadian culture, has exacted a similar price from the second and third generations to Anglo-conformity in Canada.[173] The fact is, however, that despite the formal loss of language, culture, and even history, the pre-war immigrants, many of their children, and some of their grandchildren have paid the nominal price of conformity but carry about with them a personal legacy of emotions, feelings, and ways of thinking that are unique to Croatian Canadians. Unfortunately they are not easily recoverable except by the means of a Croatian-Canadian literature, which remains for the most part unpublished. But at least one observer, who has had experience with both Croatian-American communities and their Canadian counterparts, has suggested that, "Individual Croatians [Americans] express their view that the life of Croatians in Canada may not be as luxurious but is a much more happy life than they experience in America. In addition, they further claim that our Croatians in Canada tend to live a life that is close to the customs and surrounding environment they left in their birth place of Croatia."[174]

One avenue open to the second-generation Croatian Canadian was to assimilate, to succeed, and even to super-achieve. This route to a sense of self-worth has been relentlessly pursued in North America in the field of sporting endeavour, and two sterling Canadian examples may be seen in Frank Mahovlich's hockey exploits and George Chuvalo's long reign as Canadian heavyweight boxing champion. Mahovlich, with his marvelous hockey skills and artistry on ice, played for twenty-two years in professional hockey with Toronto, Detroit, Montreal, and Birmingham.[175] His counterpart in boxing, George Chuvalo, was also a cultural comment upon Slavic strength and durability, having survived over twenty-five years in the brutal sport of boxing. Significantly, both men value their historical roots, both having visited their parents' villages in Žumberak and Herzegovina and having retained a good deal of their culture and language. Their appreciation of ethnic cooking and interest in Croatian history, culture, and art were common "ethnic" features of these two sporting celebrities. Chuvalo's reflections on the importance of ethnicity in his own upbringing in Toronto and the importance of Croatian ethnicity to him are revealing of an entire second generation's thoughts on their ethnic heritage:

You know they say, "Croatian – what the hell is that?" . . . not like you were Anglo-Saxon . . . right? So you are aware of your background in history. . . . So far as Croatian goes, when I was a kid it all seemed pretty nebulous, very hazy, my folks were Croatian and I really didn't know very much about the history, except, I knew the language and that, but I wouldn't know where they came from originally, or what happend in that part of the country. But when I went back, I find out a little more about it. My folks there and the church, and a few other things, but I really didn't understand it that well. It was a chance to study it and to find out the richness of the history and the romance to it, then you can get some sense about it and you can feel it. This is what I want to do with my kids. My kids are only half-Croatian, but they still feel Croatian. . . . If they can hear Croatian spoken they can master it a little and they can take pride in being Croatian, and they can feel more Croatian, you have to *feel* more aligned with the nationality that you are.[176]

To "*feel* Croatian" is perhaps an incongruously sentimental admission from Canada's heavyweight boxing champion in the twilight of a distinguished career. Yet it is the sum and substance of the ethnic durability and pride in the second generation, despite considerable odds against its survival.

The popularity of sport as a proving ground for the second-generation ethnic Croatian Canadians may be witnessed in several fields of endeavour. Professional football in Canada, a sport dominated largely by import players, has seen several American imports and Canadians of Croatian background in the sport – Ken Maglicic, formerly of Notre Dame and later of the Winnipeg Blue Bombers, Mike Cacic and John Cvitanovich of Vancouver, who played with the B.C. Lions.[177] In hockey, Bronco Horvath of Port Colborne played with the Boston Bruins for several seasons, Marty Pavelich with the Detroit Red Wings, Steve Brklasich with New York, Matt Ravlich with the Chicago Black Hawks, and Peter Mahovlich with Montreal and other NHL teams. Currently, Matt Pavelich of Sault Ste. Marie is a familiar face as a prominent NHL linesman, particularly in international matches with Czechoslovakian and Russian teams. In figure-skating the brother and sister team of Val and Sandra Bezic from Toronto won the Senior Canadian pairs championship in the early seventies.[178] In track and field, Jack Stulac from Toronto was a proficient Canadian hammer-thrower, and John Pavelich of Vancouver a shot-putter at the British Empire Games in 1954. In Olympic wrestling a young Ontario foursome born in Yugoslavia, Lacković, Rapajić, Kaljanac, and Pavličić, excelled in Greco-Roman wrestling at national and international levels.[179] Thus Croatian and Yugoslav Canadians have entered competitions in many amateur athletics and will soon produce a list as long and impressive as that of Croatian Americans with the increase in government aid to these sports.

The professions and arts are other areas of endeavour that attract achievement from the Canadian-born as well as foreign-born. Several names may be mentioned, although the list is by no means complete nor comprehensive. In the sphere of music, Andrea Kalanj of Vancouver played with the Vancouver Symphony at nine, then studied music in Kiev and Brussels before going on concert piano tour of Europe.[180] Frances Ginzer of Calgary is a vocalist and operatic singer likely destined for an international singing career.[181] In the visual arts several western talents are emerging, among them a rugged fishing guide in Campbell River, B.C., Jack Jackovich.[182] It is in the professions, however, that the bulk of achievement energy is traditionally directed in immigrant groups, and the Croatians are no exception. Such lawyers as Jack Belobrajdich of

Toronto, John Culina of Sault Ste. Marie, John Filipovic of Thunder Bay, and John Boras of Lethbridge are but a few of the more experienced now practising in Canada.[183] Others have entered the health professions, social work, and the teaching profession and each year become doctors, nurses, laboratory technicians, physiotherapists, case workers, and teachers at all levels of education. Engineering and the physical sciences have also proved popular, with numerous examples of successful professionals in mining, mechanical and civil engineering, and related teaching fields. Every year the list of scholarship students entering Canadian universities has had several Croatian Canadians among them, thus demonstrating the traditional drive for achievement among the second generation.[184]

The field of business deserves some mention as well, for it appears that the drive for economic success is not confined to the first-generation immigrants. A very successful architect-engineer, Nicholas Zunic, Jr., of Winnipeg, has been chairman of the Manitoba Chamber of Commerce and has served on the Board of Directors for CMHC. A highly successful building contractor and executive in the Headway Corporation of Thunder Bay is John Kauzlaric, a second-generation Croatian Canadian. Similarly, a family firm of four Croatian contractors in Toronto, the Znidar brothers, built a flourishing construction enterprise from an automotive repair shop in west Toronto begun by an older brother and his wife. Further to the west, there have been several geologists and engineers in the oil and mining industry, currently among them K.N. Beckie, director of explorations research for Hudson's Bay Oil and Gas.[185]

If business enterprise and self-help were strong Croatian traditions sustained in the second generation, so were trade unionism and radicalism among the Canadian-born Yugoslavs of Croatian ethnicity. These working-class traditions were already transmitted to the third generation by those first fishermen who settled in British Columbia at the turn of the century. By the 1950's and 1960's three generations worked together in the purse-seiner boats that fished along the Pacific Coast, and veterans like Mike Vidulich, John Pavich, and Ivan Colak mixed with younger fishermen like Nick Stevens, Mike Canic, and Peter Pavelich.[186] The place of the United Fisherman's and Allied Workers Union had become steadily stronger in the Ladner-Delta region and penetrated deeply into the social life of the community and even provided assistance to younger members for their education. The continuous perils of fishing accidents and a high mortality rate among fishermen of middle age were but a few of the reasons, beyond the economic issue, for persistent militancy in this union.[187] Some, like Homer Stevens of mixed Greek-Indian-Croatian parentage in the third generation, were virtually born into the UFAWU, for which Stevens became a full-time organizer at the age of twenty-three in 1956. He remained on its executive until 1977, at the same time retaining nearly continuous membership in the Communist

Party of Canada. A dedicated trade unionist, he was respected by competitive unions and management alike, which pay him such tributes as, "He's very firm . . . when he gives his word he keeps it. . . . He's a man with few enemies on the West Coast."[188]

In whatever industry the Croatians or Yugoslavs had been employed since the migration of the 1920's, they continued to play a prominent role in the labour movement. Thus, whether it was the forest or mining industry of British Columbia or northern Ontario, the steel and automobile industry of southern Ontario or the pulp and paper industry across Canada, they were active in such unions as the United Mineworkers, Mine, Mill and Smelter Workers, Pulp and Sulphite Workers, Autoworkers, and International Woodworkers. While their ranks were thinning from retirements and deaths in the 1960's,[189] the industrial unionism they helped to form was very much alive in the second and third generations. In some cases, they had been carried to new fronts, such as teachers' federations and professional associations, and in others directly into the political arena in socialist political activism. Andrew Mihalich, for example, carried the banner of the Hamilton New Ethnic Club to the founding convention of the New Democratic Party in 1961.[190] Perhaps the most prominent of socialist Croatian Canadians is David Stupich, a chartered accountant and son of a miner's family on Vancouver Island, who held a seat in Nanaimo for the NDP in the 1960's and rose to the finance portfolio in Premier David Barrett's administration of the early seventies.[191]

Political participation and voting preference among the Croatian and Yugoslav Canadians had, in fact, become fragmented in the sixties and seventies. The Diefenbaker landslide of 1958 found many converts to the Conservative Party, particularly among older voters of the first generation who were attracted by Diefenbaker's emphasis upon pride in ethnic heritage. Thus, in 1962, the Conservative Party attracted Joseph Mavrinac, Jr., of Schumacher, Ontario, to run as a candidate, albeit unsuccessfully. More recently, Ray Prpic also ran for the Conservative Party in the Humboldt provincial constituency in the Saskatchewan election of 1978.[192] Croatian party preferences for candidates still ran strongly to the Liberal Party, which had at least two prominent Croatian Canadians run federally in the late sixties – John Boras of Lethbridge and M.G. Zorkin of Nanaimo.[193] The Liberal Party proved more attractive to Canadian immigrants arriving after 1945,[194] and the Croatians in Canada's largest cities were no exception to this general rule. Significantly, however, the Canadian federal system has not yet produced second-generation politicians like the governors of Alaska and Minnesota, Mike Stepovich and Rudy Perpich.[195] Canadian politics may follow more closely upon American trends at the local level, where Croatian Americans such as Michael Bilandic and Dennis Kucinich have been elected as mayors of Chicago and Cleveland. Currently, Mayor Nicholas

Trbovich of Sault Ste. Marie is in his third term and appears to be firmly ensconced in office.[196]

The Canadians of Croatian background, whether of pure or mixed ancestry, have thus made their mark upon Canadian society. They continue to demonstrate in that regard some of the positive qualities of *rad* (work) and *strpljivost* (patience), which have been historically prized as cultural virtues. While some individual achievements might be valued more highly than others, a general sense of group pride might be felt by parents and children in their recitation. Each generation placed a different emphasis and value upon those achievements, from the very old to the very young. Those who had come as immigrants celebrated their children's achievements as communal ones and took great delight in informing each other of the latest news of any victory, however small. Interpreted by their children often as outright bragging, it was often not that so much as a common celebration of a better life. For the Canadian-born, inculcated in the beliefs of individual success and the puritan drives of Canadian society, aspiration and achievement were for most a less enjoyable life process occurring under the watchful eye of the community. While expectations were great, disappointments were many, for every success story could be counterbalanced by one that caused anxiety, conflict, and grief between the generations of the Old and New Worlds. For example, limited social aspirations of many families for their daughters meant that upward social mobility was often reserved for the male children. Social deviance and delinquency also were prevalent where fathers were absent for long periods as seasonal workers, and even where they were not the social make-up of a multi-ethnic working district often put children beyond the control of their parents.[197] Thus, the climb upward was neither inevitable nor without problems, despite the mythology of success that fuelled the drive for achievement.

Whether the third and fourth generations will continue in these great expectations is impossible to determine. Indeed, it is hazardous even to guess at ethnic achievement in the pure sense, since many second-generation children were the products of Canadian unions between parents of mixed ethnic stock, which constituted 80 per cent of those marriages consummated before 1940. While exogamous marriage declined markedly in the fifties and sixties to nearly one-half, there are many Croatian Canadians whose ethnic origin extends into Anglo-Celtic, French, and other Slavic stock.[198] Indeed, it is likely that some of the intergenerational tension between many of the Canadian-born and the new arrivals lies in the current high value placed on in-group marriage by many recent immigrants,[199] and the inverse proportion of those in the pre-1945 generation who held similar values. Among the latter and their children many adhered and aspired to a widely held Canadian ideal of assimilative intermarriage expressed as early as Ralph Connor's *Foreigner* and prevalent throughout Canadian society in the twentieth century.[200] Thus, the controversy that has divided native peoples of pure and mixed ancestry in Canada to some degree serves to divide generations of Croatians in Canada. Whatever the many subtleties of the question, it is apparent that many Canadians of even partial Croatian ancestry perceive *themselves* and their achievements to belong within this group and identify positively with those of the ethnic group's virtues which reinforce their Canadian values. The source of the rub with the newcomers is that the assimilated Canadians reject what they perceive as immigrant clannishness, group exclusiveness, and separation from the larger society.

Whether the current and future generations will go further and beyond to a sense of ancestral pride and join the newcomers in a genuine cultural revival is difficult to predict. The parallel growth of consciousness among the third-generation Japanese and Ukrainian Canadians may be held up as an example of the successful recovery of ethnic identity. The literary rediscovery of ethnicity is, after all, the written codification of oral culture and folk experience; in the words of one Italian-American historian, it is something "ethnic groups as well as politicians, priests and realtors who deal with them have known all along."[201] Credit must be given first, then, to those grandparents and parents who kept culture and language and identity alive in face of the considerable odds against their survival, and to those newspapermen, lay poets, priests, realtors, tavernkeepers, and orchestra leaders who sustained them in the dark first decades in Canada. It is possible that the current generation can keep these traditions alive in the process of discovering itself and may possibly convince their children that their ethnicity is not a point of shame but of pride, not a sense of exclusiveness, but of strength.

The beginning of such a social levelling process among the generations – the emergence of a common attitude to the homeland and to Canada – is also becoming more evident. Many are those now of both foreign and Canadian birth who have stood where their ancestors tilled the soil and looked into the faces of close relatives who were long forgotten, a dim memory or none at all. These "sentimental journeys" back in time and into another cultural space are a powerful and positive catalyst in affirming identity,[202] for many such visits home are a firm reminder, as they had been earlier to some of the *povratnici*, of Thomas Wolfe's famous dictum, "You Can't Go Home Again." This process of discovering one's Canadianness among many older immigrants has been found upon returning to the soil they had left a quarter or half-century ago. Ultimately, Croatian Canadians will, like the French Canadians, discover that their homeland lies in Canada not Europe, but that the latter forms a vital part of the ancestral past and supplies a true meaning to the phrase, "Je me souviens" or "Ja se sjećam."

Within Canada itself, cultural assimilation has often taken the form of hybrid cross-generational celebrations of ethnicity: the wedding or the family or clan reunion. Croatians continue to have their separate political banquets and picnics and folklore festivals, all of which celebrate different causes and are in themselves the source of great enjoyment. But Croatian centres and halls have been used in the recent past to celebrate marriages between second- and third-generation Canadians of Croatian background, often to those of another nationality. The clan reunion, long popular among other ethnic groups in North America, has also been adapted to suit the Croatian Canadians' circumstances. In essence, the following description of a recent family reunion in Schumacher, Ontario, is typical of another Canadian clan gathering. Entitled "Auld Family Ties are Never Forgotten," it went on to describe a Canadian-American celebration that brought together seventy-five members of four generations, drawn from all walks of life, from industry and services to the professions, law, and education:

> The high point of the reunion weekend was a banquet supper at the Croatian Hall in Schumacher, the "Little Zagreb of the North." Barbecued lamb and many Croatian dishes were served. . . .
> After the banquet, the family enjoyed other festivities including dancing and singing the traditional songs. Relatives who had never seen one another before met and exchanged stories of the family. . . . Old photographs renewed memories of those family members who have since left for the kingdom of Christ.
> . . . Early members of the family emigrated from Croatia (Žumberak region of Croatia) as early as 1925, settling in such Croatian communities as Schumacher. They kept up their Croatian traditions and in doing so, kept the Croatian identity alive here in the new world. They loved the country of their choice, either the U.S. or Canada, because of the freedom and opportunities available, but they have always retained the loyalty of their mother country, Croatia.[203]

Such informal family gatherings are visible reminders of the speed with which customs alter and adapt, and of how new customs come to fit with the old – the communal family traditions of the highland regions of Žumberak transformed into a unique New World celebration. Indeed, the strong democratic traditions celebrated in both highland cultures are suggestive of the historian Braudel's observation that "the hills were the refuge of liberty, democracy, and peasant 'republics'."[204]

Such cross-cultural comparisons in time and the increasing accessibility of all space on the earth make more and more believable the reality of the "global village." Ethnicity can no longer be an exclusive preserve as it once was to the European villagers who left the old rural areas and simply set up an urban version of the same space in the North American city. The distance that once separated the villages of Primorje, Lika, and Herzegovina from the sea in 1900 could be travelled by donkey and wagon in about the same time as it would take today by modern jet from Zagreb to Toronto. Thus it can only be inferred that human institutions and human perceptions and beliefs, rather than physical barriers, more effectively separate human beings of one generation, religion, or nationality from one another in the modern age. It is, then, perhaps instructive to suggest that ethnicity also must be a shared human condition available to all, not an exclusive one. As the great Croatian poet, Tin Ujević, eloquently pleaded for a new humanism in his *Ispit Savjesti (Examination of Conscience)*:

> Let us stand up for the human soul, for the redemption of the whole man, of the integral man (Svečovjeka), moral and economic. . . . Let us destroy the limitations of hatred, and the landmarks of prejudice; let us organize the legions of learning and of spiritual liberation. Let us be for once and long last what we have never been wholly – but let us this time be wholly: let us be human beings![205]

NOTES

1. Canada, *Census*, Bulletin 92-549. Vol. 1, part 2, pp. 63-1. Serbo-Croatian declined as a mother tongue from 14,863 in 1941 to 11,031 in 1951.

2. A.R.M. Lower, *Canadians in the Making: A Social History of Canada* (Toronto: Longmans, 1958), pp. 423-46.

3. For an overall view, see Leszek Kosiński, "Yugoslavia and International Migration," *Canadian Slavonic Papers*, XX, 3 (September, 1978), pp. 314-38. Specific yearly totals are available from Department of Citizenship and Immigration, *Annual Reports*, 1930-65, and thereafter in Department of Manpower and Immigration, *Immigration Statistics*.

4. *Census of Canada*, 1971, Catalogue 920740, vol. 1, pt. 4, pp. 33-1-2; Catalogue 92-723, vol. I, pt. 3, pp. 1-1.

5. Canada, Department of Manpower and Immigration, Table, "Refugees, Displaced Persons and Stateless Persons Admitted to Canada as Immigrants by Ethnic Origin, 1947-67 Inclusive."

6. Oscar Handlin, *The Uprooted: The Epic Story of the Great Migration That Made The American People* (New York: Grosset and Dunlap, 1951), pp. 266-7.

7. See M.L. Kovacs and A.J. Cropley, "Assimilation and Alienation in Ethnic Groups," *Canadian Ethnic Studies*, IV, 1-2 (1972), pp. 13-24.

8. Canada, Department of Manpower and Immigration, ff. 552-1-645, vol. 2 (closed files), table, p. 9, and table cited in ff. 5, above.

9. Canada, Department of Manpower and Immigration, ff. 555-54-645-1 (closed files), Interdepartmental letter, 15 August 1956; PAC, RG 76, Immigration, vol. 408, ff. 594511, pt. 8, CPR and CNR Admission of Track Workers.

10. *Ibid.*, Letter from Cologne to Ottawa, 4 September 1959.

11. *Ibid.*, Letter from Rome to Ottawa, 26 May 1962; table cited above ff. 5.

12. *Ibid.*, Unreferenced memo from Eastern District: enclosed in depart-

mental memo from Ottawa to Rome, Vienna, Cologne, and Athens, 22 May 1963.

13. *Ibid.*, ff. 552-1-645, vol. 2 (closed file), Western District Report, October, 1964, and reply.

14. See *ibid.*, Table, "Refugees, Displaced Persons . . . 1947-67," above ff. 5.

15. Freda Hawkins, *Canada and Immigration: Public Policy and Public Concern* (Montreal: McGill-Queen's, 1972), pp. 374-5, 381.

16. Canada, Department of Manpower and Immigration, *Immigration Statistics, 1967-68.*

17. *Ibid.*, annual reports, 1969-72.

18. Ivo Baučić, *Radnici u Inozemstvu Prema Popisu Stanovništa Jugoslavije, 1971* (Yugoslav Workers Abroad According to the 1971 Yugoslav Census) (Zagreb: Studies of the Institute of Geography, University of Zagreb, vol. 12, book 4, 1973), pp. 38-87.

19. *Ibid.*, map supplement, no. 15.

20. Canadian Citizenship *Statistics*, Catalogue no. 91-205. Cited in Mrkitch, "A History of the Croat Immigration to Canada," p. 48.

21. Ivo Baučić, *Yugoslav Workers Abroad, 1971*, pp. 72, 123.

22. *Census of Canada*, 1951, vol. X, p. 153; 1961, vol. XII, pp. 40-1; 1971, vol. V, pt. 1, p. 129.

23. See Warren Kalbach, *The Demographic Basis of Canadian Society* (Toronto: McGraw Hill, 1971), pp. 65-6.

24. "Persons Granted Citizenship by Country of Former Allegiance and Period of Immigration, 1953-72," statistics supplied to author, 9 December 1974, by Department of Citizenship, Ottawa. The average residency of Yugoslav citizens applying for Canadian citizenship is seven years, and 88 per cent apply within ten years, a very rapid rate of naturalization. *The Canada Year Book, 1975*, also states the aggregate of citizenship transfers for the period 1945-75 is 54,830. See also *Census of Canada*, 1951, vol. X, p. 442; 1961, XII, p. 49-2; 1971, V, pt. 1, 551-11, p. 24.

25. Leroy Stone, *Urban Development in Canada* (Ottawa: Dominion Bureau of Statistics, 1967), p. 17; Jacques Henripin, *Trends and Factors of Fertility in Canada*, (Ottawa: D.B.S., 1972), pp. 149-50.

26. *Census of Canada*, 1971, Cat. 92-821 (Bull. 2.2), Tables 4-17, 5-7; York University Institute for Survey Research, Statistical Package for the Social Sciences, based upon 1971 census Data, package supplied to author, February, 1979, Toronto-Hamilton by Mother Tongue and Language Spoken at Home. See also *Hrvatski Put*, estimate of 40,000 in "Croatian Street, Anytown, Canada," October, 1977, no. 166, p. 8. *Hrvatski Glas*, 30 November 1968, p. 4, estimated 15,000 Croatians in Toronto.

27. Montreal estimates vary: N. Pavesković, "Croatians in Canada," estimates 1,300 in 1970; Mrkitch (1970), p. 29, indicates "a few hundred"; and the 1976 census indicates a total of 3,790 Serbian, Croatians,

and others by mother tongue: *Census of Canada*, 1971, vol. 2, Catalogue 92-821 (Bulletin 2.2), p. 5-3; *Hrvatski Glas*, 16 April 1969, pp. 1-4. A recent pamphlet advertising *The Canadian Croatian Folklore Festival*, Montreal, May 1980, estimates 6,000 Croatians in Montreal.

28. *Census of Canada*, 1971, vol. 2, Cat. 92-821 (Bull. 2-2), "Population: Demographic Characteristics, Mother Tongue," pp. 5-1, 5-7. *Vancouver Croatian Days*, "History of Canadian-Croatian Origin in the Last 100 Years," pamphlet (Vancouver, 1967); *Hrvatski Glas*, 5 February 1966.

29. See Department of Citizenship and Immigration, *Annual Reports* to 1965; Ivo Baučić, *Yugoslav Workers Abroad, 1971*, p. 68, for occupational origins of immigrants.

30. See Leroy Stone, *Urban Development in Canada*, p. 17.

31. Canada, Statistics Canada, Data Dissemination, Census Field, special cross-classification, April, 1975: "Yugoslav Ethnic Group Broken Down by Ethnic Components by Age, by Sex, by Birthplace, by Occupation, by Major Group for the Experienced Labour Force for Canada and the Provinces." 316 pp.

32. *Ibid.*, pp. 128-63.

33. *Ibid.*, pp. 164-260.

34. *Ibid.*, pp. 261-96.

35. D. Pitt and Z. Juričić, "The Social Adjustment of Yugoslavs in Victoria," *Canadian Slavonic Papers*, XI (1969), pp. 212-20.

36. *Hrvatski Put* (Croatian Way), October, 1977, no. 166, p. 8: "Croatian Street, Anytown, Canada" [by M. Meheš]; York Survey Research for Toronto Census Metropolitan Area, 14 pp. See also Anthony H. Richmond, *Ethnic Residential Segregation in Metropolitan Toronto*, Research Report for Institute for Behavioural Research (York University Survey Research Centre, 1972).

37. See David Bloomfield, "Social Participation: A Problem of Ethnic Identity: The Croatian Case in Hamilton, Ontario," unpublished essay, Guelph University, 1974, 20 pp. For an impressionistic account of the Hastings Street community in Vancouver, see S. Visković, "Život Hrvata u Vancouveru," in *Hrvatski Glas*, 28 May 1966.

38. *Nezavisna Država Hrvatska*, July, 1963, no. 7, p. 5; *Hrvatski Glas*, 12 November 1962, 23 October 1965.

39. See *Hrvatski Glas*, 28 January 1963, p. 3; 4 February 1963, p. 4; 23 October 1965, p. 3; 10 July 1965, p. 4; 23 October 1965, pp. 1-3; *Naš Put*, III (July, 1969), p. 1; *Jedinstvo*, 11 July 1969.

40. *Hrvatski Glas*, 23 October 1965, pp. 1-3: "Prva Velika Hrv. Kat. Crkva u Kanadi." *Ibid.*, 2 July 1962, p. 4 (Sault Ste. Marie); 11 June 1966, p. 5; 9 July 1966, p. 5.

41. Author interview with Rev. Ljubomir Krašić, Director of the Croatian Ethnic Institute of Chicago, Calgary, Croatian Catholic Mission, May, 1978.

42. Nedo Pavešković, "Croatians in Canada," in Eterovich and Spalatin (eds.), *Croatia*, vol. II, p. 492.
43. Vladimir Stankovic (ed.), "Croatian Immigration to Canada," *I.C.M.C., Migration News*, no. 5 (1975), pp. 26-9.
44. Eterovich and Spalatin (eds.), *Croatia*, vol. I, pp. 223-4.
45. For the pervasiveness of Catholicism among the Poles in Canada, see H. Radecki and B. Heydenkorn, *A Member of a Distinguished Family: The Polish Group in Canada* (Toronto: McClelland and Stewart, 1976), pp. 141-68.
46. See, for example, on his death: *Hrvatski Glas*, 29 February 1960, p. 4: "Stepinac je Živio i umro kao Hrvat" (Stepinac Lived and Died Like a Croatian), by Alan Horić; *ibid.*, 18 April 1960, "Svetac-Hrvat" (A Croatian Saint), by Rev. C. Kamber; also, later articles on the anniversary of his death, *ibid.*, 27 March 1961, p. 4; 13 February 1965, p. 5.
47. Linda Bennett, *Personal Choice in Ethnic Identity Maintenance: Serbs, Croats, and Slovenes in Washington, D.C.* (Palo Alto, California: R & E Research Associates, 1978), p. 156.
48. *Hrvatski Glas*, 20 February 1965, 27 October 1965, 19 August 1966; *Nezavisna Država Hrvatska*, February, 1965, no. 2 (Šeper), September, 1969, no. 110 (Kuharić).
49. *Hrvatski Glas*, 17 September 1966: "Uz Konvenciju; "45 god. Hrv. Kat. Zajednice," *Nezavisna Država Hrvatska*, July, 1969, no. 108.
50. Nedo Pavešković, "Croatians in Canada," in Eterovich and Spalatin (eds.), *Croatia*, vol. II, p. 493.
51. *Nezavisna Država Hrvatska*, "Ten Years of Struggle," May, 1960, p. 5.
52. *Ibid.*, "Prigodom Petnaest Godina Obstanka Org. U.K.H.," August, 1965, no. 8 (62).
53. *Nezavisna Država Hrvatska*, June, 1966, p. 4; R. Čuješ, "The Involvement of Canadian Slavs in the Co-operative Movement," in vol. III of *Slavs in Canada*, p. 159; Mrkitch, "History of Croat Immigration to Canada," p. 98.
54. *Nezavisna Država Hrvatska*, September, 1966, no. 75; July, 1966, no. 73.
55. *Ibid.*, July, 1967, no. 85, "Croatian Riverside Inn" (Brampton), also August, September, 1967, nos. 86, 87.
56. *Hrvatski Glas Kalendar* (1957), pp. 76-7; *Hrvatski Glas*, 4 April 1960, p. 2; 26 April 1960, 24 April 1965.
57. "History of the Lakehead Croatian Home Society," in *Grand Opening New Croatian Hall*, Port Arthur, September, 1961, p. 11; *Hrvatski Glas*, 9 October 1961, p. 1; 9, 16 October 1965.
58. *Hrvatski Glas*, 28 March 1960, p. 7; 18 April 1960, p. 6; 30 May 1960, p. 21.
59. *Hrvatski Glas*, "Hrvatski Domovi u Kanadi," 6 March 1965, p. 1; *ibid.*, 29 August 1960, p. 1 (Sydney, Nova Scotia); 31 October 1960, p. 2.

60. *Hrvatski Put*, August-September, 1973, "Hrvatski Islamski Centar, Toronto – Kanada."

61. *Hrvatsko Ozborje* (Croatian Horizon), Vancouver, December, 1969-January, 1970.

62. *Croatia Press*, XX, 250 (1966), "The Downfall of Rankovic in American and British Press," [*sic*] pp. 24-30; Gerson S. Sher, *Praxis, Marxist Criticism and Dissent in Yugoslavia* (Bloomington: Indiana University Press, 1975); *Hrvatski Glas*, 26 March, 17 September 1966, 14 January 1967.

63. "National Library Holdings of Newspapers of Canadian Cultural Communities, Original and Microfilm," January, 1975, typescript, 17 pp.; PAC, RG 26, Citizenship and Immigration, vol. 10, ff. 50-2-A, part II, "List of Ethnic Group Publications in Canada," 1957, 1958.

64. Mrkitch, "History of Croat Immigration to Canada," pp. 73, 86.

65. N. Pavesković, "Croatians in Canada," in Eterovich and Spalatin (eds.), *Croatia*, vol. I, p. 493; *Jadran* (published in Montreal, editor, S. Dubičanac, 1955-   ).

66. T. Shibutani and K.M. Kwan, *Ethnic Stratification: A Comparative Approach*, part V, "The Integrative Approach" (New York: Macmillan, 1965), pp. 469-568.

67. *Ibid.*, p. 480.

68. *Ibid.*, pp. 474, 531.

69. *Nezavisna Država Hrvatska*, October, 1964, no. 52, p. 5.

70. *Ibid.*; and *Jedinstvo*, 9 October 1964, for the left-wing rejoinder on Ante Marković as presented by the *Toronto Star* reporter, Rae Corelli, "Ustaške laži na Stranicama Toronto Daily Star."

71. *Hrvatski Put*, November, 1977, p. 7: "Dva Separatizma."

72. On the theme of factionalism, see Mirko Meheš, *Tražim Hrvate, Homo Titoicus* (Toronto, 1973).

73. See, e.g., *Nezavisna Država Hrvatska*, May, 1962, no. 5 (12), p. 4: "Proslava Hrvatske Državnosti; *ibid.*, November, 1961, p. 1; October, 1961, p. 2; August 8, 1962, S. Hefer to John Diefenbaker.

74. *Ibid.*, November, 1961, no. 11 (17), p. 4.

75. *Ibid.*, e.g., June, 1963, p. 4, cols. 1-4.

76. A. van Gennep, *The Rites of Passage* (Chicago: University of Chicago Press, 1966), pp. 2-3.

77. Shibutani and Kwan, *Ethnic Stratification*, pp. 391-401.

78. *Nezavisna Država Hrvatska*, 3 February 1963, no. 32, p. 1; *Jedinstvo*, 8 March 1963, p. 3; 3 Feburary 1967, p. 1.

79. *Nezavisna Država Hrvatska*, July, 1966, p. 4; August, 1969, no. 109, p. 3; *Naš Put*, 1968, no. 78, p. 1; 1973, no. 131, p. 1.

80. See *Hrvatski Put*, June-July, 1973, nos. 132-3, November, 1973, nos. 136-7; discussion of Les Shaw, *Trial by Slander* (Canberra: Harp Books, 1973); *Journal of Croatian Studies*, XIV-XV (1973-74), pp. 178-80: review by Karlo Mirth.

81. *Hrvatski Put*, March, 1973, no. 129, p. 1: Rudi Tomić, open letter to Prime Minister G. Whitlam.
82. *Zajednicar*, 5 April 1978, p. 2.
83. *Hrvatski Put*, April-May, 1975, no. 154, p. 6: "Hrvatska Tvornica Bomba Hamiltonu."
84. *Hrvatski Put*, 1975, no. 160, p. 2, in response to *Toronto Star*, 19 September 1975. See *ibid.*, September, 1972, no. 123, p. 1: "Terrorists or Heroes"; *ibid.*, January, 1973, p. A. George Prpić, "Ireland, Croatia and Bangladesh."
85. See, e.g., M. Mostovac, "Le Droit Face au Bilinguisme en droit Yougoslave," *Proceedings of the Sixth International Symposium on Comparative Law* (Ottawa: Ottawa University Press, 1969), pp. 59-76. See also F.H. Eterovich, *Biographical Directory of Americans and Canadians of Croatian Descent*, IV (Chicago, 1970), entries for Stephen Krešić, University of Ottawa; Vladimir Markotić, University of Calgary; Nedo Pavesković, PAC, Ottawa.
86. *Hrvatski Glas*, 5 June 1965, p. 2 (Mihailov); *Hrvatski Put*, April-May, 1975, p. 1 (Mihailov); *Nezavisna Država Hrvatska*, February, 1969, no. 103, p. 2 (Djilas); *Hrvatski Glas*, 4 June 1966 *(Praxis)*.
87. *Nezavisna Država Hrvatska*, May-June, 1962, nos. 23-4, Fra Lujo Ivandić, "Hrvatske Mlade Generacije."
88. See *Albertan*, 27 April 1977: "Prisoner Commits Suicide"; Calgary *Herald*, 26 January 1975: "Man Remanded for Tests."
89. See Canada, "Statistics of Criminal and Other Offences," 1966, Annual Catalogue no. 85-2001 cited in D. Mrkitch, "History of Croat Immigration to Canada," p. 49. See also Nicholas Mirkowitch, "Yugoslavs and Criminality," *Sociology and Social Research*, XXV (September-October, 1940), pp. 28-34; H. Lorković, "The Dynamic Psychology of Croatian Discord," *Journal of Croatian Studies*, XVIII-XIX (1977-78), pp. 73-85.
90. *York University Institute for Survey Research*, based on 1971 Toronto C.M.A. data, *Census* Tract 245, p. 6. See *infra* ff. 165.
91. *Census of Canada*, 1971, Cat. 92-776, August, 1975, "Statistics on Language Retention and Transfer," pp. 1-1, 1-2. For a general discussion, see S. Leiberson, *Language and Ethnic Relations in Canada* (New York: T. Wiley, 1970); and K.G. O'Bryan, J.G. Reitz, and O.M. Kuplowska, *Non-Official Languages: A Study in Canadian Multiculturalism* (Ottawa, 1976).
92. Mrkitch, "History of Croat Immigration," pp. 112-13; Sharon Vandervolk, interview re: unpublished undergraduate essay, April, 1979, on the Calgary Croatian School; *Hrvatski Glas*, 12 February 1966, p. 4: "Nikolinjska Priredba Hrv. Škole"; *ibid.*, 4 February 1967, p. 4.
93. Interview, Rev. Ljubo Krašić, Calgary, May, 1978; *CSAC* (Croatian Schools of America and Canada) *Newsletter*, Year 1, no. 1, September-October, 1977. The Toronto and Mississauga schools are outside of this

241

federation. Also, Dr. Grubišić of Toronto introduced Croatian as a credit course in the Toronto urban area.

94. University Calendars, 1977-79 (Toronto, Carleton, U.B.C., Victoria).
95. "Croatian Days" pamphlets celebrating the annual June days held since 1957, e.g., *Twentieth Croatian Day Dedicated to Human Rights, June 12, 1977* (n.p., 1977), supplied to author by Dr. M.G. Zorkin.
96. "Croatian Folklore Day, Expo, 1967" (brochure), 12 August 1967.
97. See, e.g., *Veza* (Sudbury), nos. 1-7, 1965.
98. *Hrvatski Put*, September, 1975, p. 8: "M.M."
99. *Canadian Croatian Folklore Festival, Hamilton, May 22-23, 1976* (n.p., 1976); *Zajedničar*, 7 September 1977: "Tamburitsa King to be Honoured."
100. *The New Perspective* (Hamilton), 2, 4 (June, 1976), pp. 1-7: A. Miletić, "Second Canadian-Croatian Folklore Festival." See also *Canadian Croatian Folklore Festival*, Hamilton, May 22-23, 1976, 74 pp.
101. University of Calgary Special Collections, Canadian Ethnic Studies Archives, "Hrvatska Katolička Misija," Calgary, 1969.
102. *Ibid., Hrvatska Sloga*, Godina 1, 1974; "Croatian Society of Friends of Matica Hrvatska," 18 June 1974, John Rumora, President.
103. *The Fourth Canadian Folklore Festival, Edmonton, May 20-21, 1978* (n.p., 1978).
104. *Naša Riječ,* Year 1, no. 4 (December, 1974), Ottawa Croatian-Canadian Club.
105. *Viesti*, Sudbury, 1964, Sudbury Canadian Croatian Club.
106. *Napredak* (Advance), Year 1, no. 4 (December, 1969).
107. *Journal of Croatian Studies*, XIII (1972), p. 136; V. Markotic, *Biographical Directory of Americans and Canadians of Croatian Descent*, IV (Calgary, 1973), Occasional Monograph no. 1, Research Centre for Canadian Ethnic Studies, p. 107.
108. Eterovich and Spalatin (eds.), *Croatia*, vol. I, pp. 226-352.
109. A. Nizeteo, "Whitman in Croatia," *Journal of Croatian Studies*, XI-XII (1970-71), pp. 105-35; *Hrvatski Glas* (Ujević), 5 March, 9 April 1966.
110. A. Horić, *Pod Tudjim Nebom* (Buenos Aires, 1957); *Hrvatski Glas Kalendar*, XXV (1955), pp. 164-8; *Hrvatski Glas*, 11 February 1963; *Nezavisna Država Hrvatska*, July, 1963, p. 5.
111. N. Paveškovič, "Croatians in Canada," in Eterovich and Spalatin (eds.), *Croatia*, vol. II, p. 498; *Croatia Press*, 20 (1966): "Alan Horić"; Pierre de Grandpré, *Hist. de la Litterature Française du Québec* (Montreal: Beauchemin, 1969), pp. 264-5; Cecile Cloutier-Wojiechowska, "Alain Horić, Le Poète Croate du Québec," *Canadian Ethnic Studies*, IV, 1-2 (1972), pp. 25-33.
112. Nada Stipković, *Lignes* (Montreal: Beauchemin, 1961); *Hrvatski Glas*, 6 November 1961, p. 6: "Lignes" by A. Horić.
113. J. Kutleša, *The Mosaic of Life* (Toronto: F. Vedrina, 1970), p. 89. See also his *Sunrise of Joy and Life* (Toronto: Mystic Press, 1973); and a

brief biography, "Banker Turned Poet – Jozo Kutleša Celebrates Life in His Writing," *Canadian Imperial Bank News* (April, 1974), p. 3.

114. *Danica* (Chicago), 24 December 1974.

115. *Jedinstvo*, 12 February, 8 March 1960, 23 August 1963, 28 February 1964, 23 August 1968. *Naš Kalendar* (Toronto, 1966); *Zajedničar* (Toronto, 1966); *Zajedničar*, 19 October 1977.

116. Z.B. Juričić, *Zbirka Lirike iz Nove Domovine* (Toronto: Lira, 1973).

117. P. Stanković, "Croatians," unpublished ms., p. 14; Gabriel Vrsić, "Yugoslav Contributions to North American Civilization" (Ph.D. thesis, University of Montreal, 1958), LXVI. See also *Jedinstvo*, 22 January 1952: reference to Meštrović exhibition in Toronto.

118. *Hrvatski Glas*, 5 June 1961: "Umjetnik A. Filipović" by Nedo Pavešković; Toronto *Globe and Mail*, 26 March 1960.

119. N. Pavešković, "Croatians in Canada," in Eterovich and Spalatin (eds.), *Croatia*, vol. II, p. 497.

120. *Toronto Daily Star*, 27 February 1965.

121. *Ibid.*, 19 April 1973.

122. *Le Droit* (Ottawa), 2 April 1966; Ottawa *Journal*, 14 February 1966.

123. Ottawa *Journal*, 31 August 1974.

124. Information provided to author by M.G. Zorkin, 3 May 1977; V. Markotić to author, March, 1979.

125. Eterovich and Spalatin (eds.), *Croatia*, vol. II, 288-89; *Jedinstvo*, 24 June, 16 August 1968.

126. *Jedinstvo*, 5 April, 16 August 1968.

127. *Ibid.*, 10 June 1966, 10, 17 December 1965.

128. *Ibid.*, 24 March, 1 December 1967; *Toronto Star*, 17 November 1967.

129. Stanković, "Croatians," p. 14.

130. *Ibid.*

131. *Nezavisna Država Hrvatska*, no. 6 (1960), p. 3.

132. *Nezavisna Država Hrvatska*, September, 1964, March, 1965, July, 1968; *Naš Put*, 1966, no. 48-49, p. 2; *Hrvatski Glas*, 9 September 1963, 8 May, 19 June, 7 August 1965. "Hrvatski Folklorni Dan, Expo, 1967" (Montreal, 1967).

133. Stanković, "Croatians," p. 14; *Hrvatski Glas*, 13, 20 March 1965; *Jedinstvo*, 17 February 1967, reprint of article from Toronto *Telegram*. Max Wyman, *The Royal Winnipeg Ballet: The First Forty Years* (Toronto: Doubleday, 1978), pp. 93-7, 102, 126, 159.

134. Hamilton *Spectator*, 20 July 1957.

135. A. Miletić to author, Hamilton, 23 May, 1976, enclosures, *Vus* (Zagreb), 1972. *Slobodna Rijec* (Buenos Aires, 1976); Hamilton *Spectator*, 1 November 1975. Note, their grandfather, Andrija Miletić, ch. 1, ff. 70, ch. 5, ff. 120.

136. See biographical entries in F.H. Eterovich, *Hrvatski Profesori na Američkim i Kanadskim Visokim Školama* (Chicago, 1963); *Biographical Directory of Americans and Canadians of Croatian Descent* (1970, 1973 editions); *Journal of Croatian Studies*, 1969-

137. *Jedinstvo*, 28 August 1964, reprint from Vancouver *Province*.

138. See Nanaimo *Daily Free Press*, 5, 19, 25 February 1976; Nanaimo *Times*, 14, 19, 25 October 1977. Earlier details of M.G. Zorkin's many business activities may be found in *Hrvatski Glas*, 13, 20 March, 9 October 1965, 17 February 1964, 14 October 1963, 15 February 1960, 28 August 1961.

139. See V. Markotic, *Directory* (1973), pp. 1, 5; *Nezavisna Država Hrvatska*, January, 1963, no. 31, p. 4; *Hrvatski Glas*, 19 February 1966.

140. See Vera St. Erlich, *Family in Transition: A Study of 300 Yugoslav Villages* (Princeton: Princeton University Press, 1966), pp. 372-3; B.C. Bennett, *Sutivan: A Dalmatian Village in Social and Economic Transition* (San Francisco: R. and E. Research Assoc., 1975), pp. 81-94.

141. See business advertisements in *Nezavisna Država Hrvatska*, November, 1966, p. 4; September, 1966, p. 4; 1967, no. 87, p. 6; *Naš Put*, 1974, nos. 148-50, p. 16; N.P. Ivkov, *Privredni Adresar Grada, Toronto za 1949 god* (Toronto, 1949).

142. University of Calgary, Special Collections, Canadian Ethnic Studies Archives, *Matica Hrvatska* Minutes, Calgary, 18 June 1974, p. 5.

143. Telephone Interview, Branimir Brebrich, Calgary, March, 1979; Mrkitch, "History of Croat Immigration to Canada," p. 124; Norris, *Strangers Entertained*, p. 177.

144. *New Perspective* (Hamilton), October, 1975.

145. *Nezavisna Država Hrvatska*, December, 1964 (Windsor), February, 1966, no. 110, 1969, p. 3 (Port Arthur); *Hrvatski Glas*, 2 December 1963, p. 4 (Windsor); 19 September 1964 (Montreal); 18 May 1964; 16 April 1966 (Hamilton).

146. "Prospectus Croatian National Soccer Club" (Toronto, 1973); *Hrvatski Put*, February, 1973, February, 1974; *Jedinstvo*, 11 July, 5 September 1969, 21 August 1970, 27 August, 16 July, 24 September 1971; *Hrvatski Glas*, 23 April 1966: "Kako je Postala Croatia."

147. *Hrvatski Glas*, 30 April 1962, 9 July 1966 (Vancouver Croatia); 24 March 1963, p. 4 (Calgary Croatia); Norris, *Strangers Entertained*, p. 177; Calgary *Herald*, 10 May 1976, p. 27.

148. *Sports Illustrated*, 45 (September, 1976), pp. 24-5.

149. *The Albertan* (Calgary), 2 February 1979. More recently, the soccer exploits of Branko Segota, a native of Zadar and Toronto and star of Canada's national team, have caught public attention. *Calgary Herald Magazine*, 16 May 1981.

150. A.W. Rasporich, "The Croatians in Canada," *Matica Iseljenika Kalendar* (Zagreb, 1975), p. 167.

151. *Nezavisna Država Hrvatska*, October, 1963, no. 10 (40) p. 6: "Ivan Marušić."

152. Mrkitch, "History of Croat Immigration to Canada," p. 104. Warren Kalbach, *The Demographic Bases of Canadian Society* (Toronto: McGraw-Hill, 1971), pp. 278-81.

153. *Census of Canada*, 1971, 92-776 (Sp-6). August, 1975, "Statistics on Language Retention and Transfer," pp. 1-1, 1-2.

154. For American comparison, see Linda Bennett, *Personal Choice in Ethnic Identity Maintenance*, pp. 104-8, 180-2.

155. Mirko Mehes, "Za ili Protiv Integracije? Problem Harvatske Bioloske Ekonomije" (For or Against Integration: The Problem of Croatian Biological Economy), unpublished ms. (Sudbury, 1960), pp. 16-18.

156. Statistics Canada, "Yugoslav Ethnic Group Broken Down by Ethnic Group, by Age, by Sex, by Birthplace for Canada and the Provinces," p. 3, shows that of 23,350 "Croatians," 33.45 per cent or 7,820 were born in Canada, and of 81,570 "Other Yugoslavs," 39.41 per cent or 32,140 were Canadian-born, for an average of 38.08 per cent Canadian-born and 61.93 per cent foreign-born.

157. Rev. Vladimir Stanković (ed.), "Croatian Immigration to Canada," *ICMC Migration News*, pp. 26-8.

158. See above, ff. 152.

159. Stanković, "The Croatians," pp. 3-4.

160. Statistics Canada, "Yugoslav Ethnic Group Broken Down by Ethnic Component, by Age, by Sex, by Birthplace by Occupation Major Group for the Experienced Labour Force for Canada and the Provinces," pp. 1-36.

161. For a general discussion of this problem, see S. Thernstrom, *Progress and Poverty: Social Mobility in a Nineteenth-Century City* (Cambridge, Mass., 1964); D. Ward, *Cities and Immigrants* (New York: Oxford University Press, 1971).

162. David Bloomfield, "Social Participation – A Problem of Ethnic Identity, The Croatian Case in Hamilton, Ontario," Table 1.

163. *Ibid.*, p. 15; B. Borkovich "The Croatians of Ottawa," p. 10. See also W.G. Marston, "Social Class Segregation Within Ethnic Groups in Toronto," *Canadian Review of Sociology and Anthropology,* VI (May, 1969), pp. 65-79.

164. Borkovich, "Croatians of Ottawa," p. 17; Mrkitch, "History of Croat Immigration to Canada," pp. 108-9.

165. Variations are considerable across Canada in the area of language retention and usage, and even within areas within the same city such as Toronto. Language retention rates vary dramatically between some suburban locations such as Rexdale (C.T. 245) with 45 per cent for males versus 50 per cent for females; St. Clair-Weston Rd., 42 per cent males versus 52 per cent, and inner-city locations like Bloor-Bathurst 25 per cent versus 24 per cent. York Survey Research, Toronto, CMA, 1979, pp. 2-11. On the other hand, some census tracts (5, 21) on Hamilton report 90 per cent and 100 per cent language retention rates in the mountain area, and 36 per cent versus 65 per cent in the industrial inner-city of Hamilton East (C.T. 55, 56, 57), and yet other locations on the Mountain (C.T. 8, 11) and near Dundas with 0 per cent language retention rates. *Ibid.*, pp. 11-13.

166. Dunja Jutronić, "Serbo-Croatian and American English in Contact: A Sociolinguistic Study of the Serbo-Croatian Community in Steelton, Pennsylvania" (Ph.D. thesis, Pennsylvania State, 1971), p. 186.

167. K.G. O'Bryan, J.G. Reitz, and O.M. Kuplowska, *Non-Official Languages*, p. 165. Italics the author's.
168. *Jedinstvo*, 18 February 1966.
169. Other studies which examine linguistic change from Europe to Canada are: D. Jutronic, "Serbo-Croatian and American English in Contact," pp. 26-236; Z.B. Juričić and J.F. Kess, "Sociolinguistic Dimensions of Respectful Address; A Comparative Study of Native and Immigrant Croatian," in Z. Folejewski (ed.), *Canadian Contributions to the International Congress of Slavists* (Ottawa, 1978), pp. 103-13.
170. M. Surdučki, "Morphological Adaptation of English Loanwords in Serbo-Croatian: An Analysis of English Loanwords in Serbo-Croatian and in the Speech of Serbian and Croatian Immigrants in Canada" (in Serbo-Croatian) (Ph.D. thesis, University of Novi Sad, 1970).
171. M. Surdučki, "Noun Compounding by Juxtaposition in Serbo-Croatian," *Canadian Slavonic Papers*, XX, 3 (September, 1978); see also Morton Benson, "English Loanwords in Serbo-Croatian," *American Speech*, XLI, 3 (October, 1967), pp. 178-89; R. Filipović, *The Phonemic Analysis of English Loan Words in Croatian* (Zagreb: Inst. of Phonetics, 1960).
172. Michael Novak, *The Rise of the Unmeltable Ethnics: Politics and Culture in the Nineteen Seventies* (New York: Macmillan, 1971), pp. 47-8, 69.
173. Howard Palmer, "Mosaic or Melting Pot: Immigration and Ethnicity in Canada and the U.S.," *International Journal*, XXXI, 3 (Summer, 1976), pp. 488-528.
174. M. Štivorić, Croatian Fraternal Union Director of Member Services to author, Pittsburgh, 25 March 1975, p. 1. See also his "Making of Canadians," *Zajedničar*, 21 July 1976, p. 2, reprinted from Hamilton *Spectator*.
175. On Chuvalo, see *Hrvatski Glas*, 6 June 1960, 5 December 1964, 9 April 1966; *Jedinstvo*, 15 March 1968, p. 3; 9 May 1969, pp. 1, 8; 21 May 1971; *Nezavisna Država Hrvatska*, 14 October 1962; Mahovlich's career is followed in *Hrvatski Glas*, 21 August 1961, p. 2; 22 January 1962, p. 4; 21 June 1965; 23 March 1968; *Jedinstvo*, 8 March 1968, p. 8; *Naše Novine*, 3 November 1971, p. 2; The Calgary *Herald*, 29 November 1979, comments on his retirement; author interview with F. Mahovlich, Calgary, 11 February 1975.
176. Author interview with George Chuvalo, Calgary, 4 March 1975.
177. N. Pavešković, "Croatians in Canada," in Eterovich and Spalatin (eds.), *Croatia*, vol. II, p. 499; Stanković, "Croatians," p. 19; *B.C. Fisherman*, 19 July 1955, re. J. Cvitanovich.
178. See *Jedinstvo*, 7 January 1966 (Ravlich); *Naše Novine*, 3 November 1971 (Horvath); *Jedinstvo*, 29 January 1971; V. Markotic, *Directory* (1973), pp. 5-6 (Bezic).
179. *Naš Kalendar* (Toronto, 1958), p. 142 (Stulac); *Jedinstvo*, 25 May 1954

(Pavelich); *Jedinstvo*, 3 July 1970 (wrestling). Others are the cycling brothers Pokupec of Hamilton, *Hrvatski Glas*, 30 July 1962, p. 4; and the Toronto boxer, Ante Biljak, *Nezavisna Država Hrvatska*, April, 1969, p. 4. *Hrvatski Glas*, 9 July 1969.

180. *Jedinstvo*, 23 July 1971; *B.C. Fisherman*, 26 June 1949, 3 May 1963. The Calgary Herald *Magazine*, 21 June 1980, p. 16.

181. Calgary Philharmonic Society, advertising brochure, 1978.

182. H. Purdy, "King of the Tyee and the Salmon Princess," *The Weekend Magazine*, 24, 18 (May 3, 1975), pp. 8-9.

183. *Hrvatski Glas*, 18 January 1969, p. 3 (Belobrajdich); *Zajedničar*, 8 May 1977 (Čulina).

184. See, e.g., *Zajedničar*, 28 July 1976, 12 February 1975; *Jedinstvo*, 23 September 1958, 11 July 1969; *Hrvatski Glas*, 6 April 1965, p. 2; 29 June 1960, p. 4; 27 May 1967, pp. 2, 4.

185. *Hrvatski Glas*, 4 May 1959, 7 November 1960, 24 April 1961 (Zunić); *Zajedničar*, 28 May 1975 (Znidars).

186. *B.C. Fisherman*, 1 May 1959 (Cosulich); 10 May 1955 (Pavelich); 3 May 1963 (Vidulich); 4 September 1964 (N. Stevens); 8 November 1963 (Canić). *Jedinstvo*, 26 September, 3 November 1959.

187. For accounts of fishing tragedies and accidents, see: *B.C. Fisherman*, 22 November 1955, 3, 30 March 1961, 6 March 1964.

188. Silver Donald Cameron, *Seasons in the Rain: An Expatriate's Notes on British Columbia* (Toronto: McClelland and Stewart, 1978), pp. 42-9.

189. See, e.g., *Jedinstvo*, 29 October 1970 (Thompson, Manitoba); 7 November 1969 (Windsor, Ontario); *ibid.*, obituaries for unionists: Jurić, 13 August 1965; Matovinović, 11 November 1966, Kružić, 7 November 1969.

190. N. Pavešković, "Croatians in Canada," in Eterovich and Spalatin (eds.), *Croatia*, vol. II, p. 499. *B.C. Fisherman*, 22 March 1963.

191. *Hrvatski Glas*, 14 September 1964, p. 5. See also Mr. Stupich's co-operation with M.G. Zorkin on the board of the Vancouver Island School Camp for Special Children: *Nan-Wah-Kawi* (Annual Reports, 1967-71). Currently, Mrs. Ann Marković Hemingway of Rycroft in the Peace River district has been president of the New Democratic Party of Alberta since 1977.

192. *Hrvatski Glas*, 25 December 1957, 19 March 1962 (from Kirkland Lake *Daily News)*, 30 April 1962. K. Beckie to author, Calgary, 17 March 1977.

193. *The Canadian Parliamentary Guide, 1972*, p. 452; *Canada's Twenty-Eighth Parliament* (Toronto: Methuen, 1971), p. 55.

194. John Meisel, *Working Papers on Canadian Politics* (Montreal: McGill-Queen's, 1973), pp. 103-5.

195. George Prpić, "Croatian Immigrants in the U.S.A.," in Eterovich and Spalatin (eds.), *Croatia*, vol. II, p. 456; Prpic, *The Croatian Immigrants in America*, p. 369.

196. *Zajedničar*, 18 May 1977, p. 5. See also *Hrvatski Glas*, 21 November 1964, p. 5, for the aldermanic candidacy of Ed Madronich, a Hamilton lawyer.

197. Author interview with George Chuvalo, Calgary, 4 March 1975; Mrkitch, "The Generation Gap," in "A History of Croat Immigration," pp. 106-11.

198. Inter-ethnic weddings reported in *Hrvatski Glas*, 28 January, 26 August 1963, 7 November, 6 January 1964.

199. *Nezavisna Država Hrvatska*, June-July, 1962, pp. 1-3; *Mlade Hrvatske Generacije*.

200. Kalbach, *Demographic Bases of Canadian Society*, p. 279; Canada, Royal Commission on Bilingualism and Biculturalism, *The Cultural Contributions of Other Ethnic Groups*, IV (Ottawa, 1970), pp. 291-7.

201. R. Vecoli, "Born Italian, Color Me Red, White, and Green," in Sallie te Selle, *The Rediscovery of Ethnicity* (New York: Harper and Row, 1973), p. 123.

202. Several such visits are reported in *Zajedničar* and *Jedinstvo*, as well as some returnees and retirements, e.g., *B.C. Fisherman*, 22 April 1960, 16 March 1962; *Jedinstvo*, 19 August 1966, p. 2; 13 August 1965, p. 2.

203. *Zajedničar*, 15 December 1976, p. 2.

204. F. Braudel, *The Mediterranean and the Mediterranean World in the Age of Philip II* (New York: Harper and Row, 1966), p. 40.

205. Cited in A. Nizeteo, "Whitman in Croatia, Tin Ujević and Walt Whitman," *Journal of Croatian Studies*, XI-XII (1970-71), p. 118.

Appendix

249

TABLE A

Persons of "Yugoslav" Origin in Canada

	a	Born in Yugoslavia	Born in Canada	b	Intercensal Immigration from Yugoslavia		
				Total	Return	Net	
1901	[200]						
				12,420			
1911	[3,600]						
				5,629			
1921	3,906	1,946	1,419				
				20,410	[4,774]	15,636	
1931	16,174	17,110	3,236				
				2,657	[4,280]		
1941	21,214	17,416	6,968				
				9,647 (9,307 refugees)			
1951	21,404	20,912	[9,334]				
				27,764 (14,026 refugees)			
1961	68,587	50,826	17,741				
				42,026 (7,946 refugees)			
1971	104,950 (23,380 "Croatians")	78,285	26,667	120,553			

a Statistics from *Census of Canada*, 1901-71.
b Statistics from Department of Citizenship [Manpower] and Immigration.
Figures in square brackets are estimated totals; figures in parentheses are actual subtotals.

TABLE B

Ethnic Origin of Immigrants from Overseas – Yugoslavic					
1896-1901	23	1926	4,182	1951	4,144
1902-03	1,761	1927	3,149	1952	2,176
1903-04	1,588	1928	4,377	1953	1,999
1904-05	1,130	1929	2,038	1954	1,541
1905-06	1,374	1930	1,285	1955	1,375
1906-07	233	1931	212	1956	1,993
1907-08	2,143	1932	171	1957	5,725
1908-09	1,708	1933	192	1958	4,868
1909	860	1934	286	1959	2,304
1910	886	1935	302	1960	3,517
1911	664	1936	377	1961	2,266
1912	1,981	1937	462	1962	1,965
1913	2,747	1938	576	1963	2,383
1914	657	1939	256	1964	3,055
1915	4	1940	35	1965	3,151
1916	5	1941	—	1966	2,897
1917	—	1942	1		
1918	1	1943	1		
1919	11	1944	3		
1920	72	1945	8		
1921	151	1946	26		
1922	137	1947	146		
1923	714	1948	2,845		
1924	2,183	1949	1,460		
1925	2,132	1950	1,013		
Sub-total 1900-1925	23,165	Sub-total 1926-1950	23,403	Sub-total 1951-1966	45,359
				TOTAL 1900-1966	91,927

SOURCE: Canada, Department of Citizenship [Manpower] and Immigration.

TABLE C

Country of Citizenship and Country of Former Residence, 1940-72 – Yugoslavia*

1940	44	1950	1,489	1960	881	1970	5,642
1941	—	1951	4,908	1961	852	1971	2,997
1942	—	1952	1,617	1962	862	1972	2,047
1943	—	1953	472	1963	781	1973	2,873
1944	1	1954	447	1964	1,187		
1945	9	1955	367	1965	1,230		
1946	12	1956	453	1966	1,502		
1947	147	1957	1,048	1967	2,089		
1948	3,149	1958	984	1968	4,660		
1949	2,110	1959	958	1969	4,053		
1940-49	5,472	1950-59	12,743	1960-69	18,097		

* The cumulative totals for this period for Yugoslavia as country of birth of immigrants are: 1945-55: 24,055; 1956-69: 57,032; 1970-72: 13,110; Total 1946-72: 94,197.

SOURCE: Canada, Department of Citizenship [Manpower] and Immigration.

TABLE D

Country of Last Permanent Residence by Ethnic Origin

	Total Yugo-slavian	Yugo-slavia	Austria	Belgium	France	W. Ger-many	Italy	S. Am.	U.K.	U.S.A.	Aus-tralia
Fiscal Year 1951	1,917	1,144	31	6	5	29	30	4	0	5	0
1952	4,895	3,693	191	97	67	195	239	28	116	35	0
1953	1,318	541	272	55	18	114	76	0	83	30	0
1954	2,132	397	1,132	39	50	167	59	30	115	51	6
Cal. Yr. 1954	1,610	410	614	36	68	122	69	32	88	69	6
1955	1,416	337	585	18	33	121	110	53	82	41	11
1956	2,043	395	924	23	42	254	90	55	140	50	6
1957	5,771	990	3,137	27	52	223	890	71	160	0	30
1958	4,930	958	3,351	10	73	186	106	53	72	62	37
1959	2,360	900	534	73	100	277	235	50	39	56	27
1960	3,572	818	834	35	281	290	1,063	41	39	55	38
1961	2,323	814	496	43	141	172	443	33	33	57	24
1962	2,044	788	285	13	82	223	399	41	10	79	43
1963	2,449	718	238	5	165	517	414	35	45	66	38
1964	3,116	1,119	318	5	282	534	509	65	46	61	66
1965	3,220	1,164	471	6	252	560	417	26	47	69	73
TOTALS 1951-65	45,116	[15,186]	13,413		2,196	3,984	5,149	672	1,115	911	405
Annual Avg. 1951-65	2,820	950	839		138	249	322	42	70	57	26

SOURCE: Canada, Department of Immigration, Annual Reports, 1950-65. (Fiscal years to March for 1951-54.)

TABLE E

Naturalization, 1953-72:
Persons from Yugoslavia Granted Canadian Citizenship by Year and Period of Immigration

	Annual Total of Persons from Yugoslavia granted Canadian Citizenship (col. 2)	Largest numerical bloc of annual total (col. 1) by period of immigration ( )		Second largest bloc of annual total (col. 1) by period of immigration ( )	
1953	245	115	(1945-50)		
1954	570	397	(1945-50)		
1955	1,614	1,349	(1945-50)		
1956	1,653	962	(1945-50)	559	(1951-53)
1957	2,961	2,330	(1951-55)		
1958	2,199	1,684	(1951-55)		
1959	1,806	1,452	(1951-55)		
1960	1,705	1,403	(1951-55)		
1961	1,457	783	(1951-55)	550	(1956-61)
1962	2,268	1,677	(1956-61)		
1963	3,785	3,192	(1956-61)		
1964	3,125	3,615	(1956-61)		
1965	3,167	2,598	(1956-61)		
1966	2,884	1,705	(1956-60)	911	(1961-65)
1967	2,253	1,072	(1961-65)		
1968	2,114	1,256	(1961-65)		
1969	2,738	1,982	(1961-65)		
1970	2,291	1,643	(1961-65)		
1971	2,621	1,267	(1961-65)	1,022	(1966-70)
1972	3,221	2,247	(1966-70)		

TOTAL 44,677

SOURCE: Canada, Department of Secretary of State, Canadian Citizenship Registration Branch, 1974.

TABLE F.1

Ethnic and Demographic Cross-Section, Over Age 15 in 1971

Croatians	Male	Female	Total
Born in Canada	960	580	1,540
Foreign-born	6,310	2,915	9,225
Total	7,270	3,495	10,765
"Other Yugoslavs"	Male	Female	Total
Born in Canada	5,040	2,900	7,945
Foreign-born	20,640	9,675	30,310
Total	25,680	12,575	38,255
Yugoslav Ethnic[s]	Male	Female	Total
Born in Canada	26,945	12,585	39,530
Foreign-born	6,000	3,845	39,845
Total	32,945	16,430	49,375

SOURCE: Statistics Canada, unpublished cross-classification, April, 1975: "Yugoslav Ethnic Group Broken Down by Ethnic Components by Age, by Sex, by Birthplace, by Occupation, by Major Group for the Experienced Labour Force for Canada and the Provinces."

TABLE F.2

Occupations in Canada of Croatians over Age 15: 1971
(per cent)*

	Canadian-born	Foreign-born	Total
n.s. (not specified)	19.81	7.40	9.24
11. Mgr. & Admin.	4.55	0.98	1.49
21. Nat. Sc. & Math	3.57	2.77	2.83
23.-25. Soc. Sc. & Relig.	0.32	0.38	0.32
27. Teaching	7.47	0.71	1.67
31. Med. & Health	1.95	2.01	2.00
33. Art & Literary	0.65	0.49	0.56
41. Clerical & Related	19.16	6.18	8.03
51. Sales	7.79	3.09	3.76
61. Services	7.79	14.26	13.42
71. Farming	4.55	2.06	2.40
73. Fish/Fur/Hunt	0.00	0.28	0.28
75. Forestry & Logging	0.32	0.28	0.28
77. Mining/Gas-Oil	0.64	1.36	1.25
81-2. Processing (ind.)	3.90	9.20	8.40
83. Machining	1.25	9.49	8.26
85. Product Fabric.	4.20	16.86	15.04
87. Construction	3.25	13.01	11.61
95. Crafts and Equip. Oper.	1.95	1.30	1.39
99. Occup. N.O.S. (not otherwise stated)	6.17	7.86	7.66
Total numbers	1,540	9,225	10,765

* Percentages in each vertical column are based on 100 per cent of that category.
SOURCE: See Table F.1.

256

TABLE F.3

Occupations in Canada of "Other Yugoslavs" over Age 15: 1971 (per cent)*

	Canadian-born	Foreign-born	Total
n.s. (not specified)	16.62	6.22	8.40
11. Mgr. & Admin.	3.09	1.16	1.57
21. Nat. Sc. & Math	2.40	2.63	2.59
23.-25. Soc. Sc. & Relig.	0.82	0.35	0.46
27. Teaching	5.54	1.16	2.07
31. Med. & Health	2.58	2.36	2.41
33. Art & Literary	0.89	0.68	0.74
41. Clerical & Related	18.38	6.55	9.00
51. Sales	10.39	4.31	5.57
61. Services	9.88	15.36	14.23
71. Farming	4.54	2.28	2.74
73. Fish/Fur/Hunt	0.51	0.20	0.28
75. Forestry & Logging	0.76	0.52	0.57
77. Mining/Gas-Oil	0.76	1.11	1.04
81-2. Processing (ind.)	3.02	8.42	7.29
83. Machining	2.40	9.90	8.34
85. Product Fabric.	5.16	16.42	14.07
87. Construction	3.97	11.02	9.56
95. Crafts and Equip. Oper.	3.09	1.74	2.03
99. Occup. N.O.S. (not otherwise stated)	5.10	7.71	7.17
Total numbers	7,945	30,310	38,255

* Percentages in each vertical column are based on 100 per cent of that category.

SOURCE: See Table F.1.

TABLE F.4

Occupations in Canada of Yugoslav Ethnic[s] over Age 15: 1971 (per cent)*

	Canadian-born	Foreign-born	Total
n.s. (not specified)	17.19	6.52	8.58
11. Mgr. & Admin.	3.33	1.12	1.55
21. Nat. Sc. & Math	2.59	2.66	2.65
23.-25. Soc. Sc. & Relig.	0.74	0.36	0.44
27. Teaching	5.86	1.05	1.99
31. Med. & Health	2.48	2.28	2.32
33. Art & Literary	0.90	0.64	0.69
41. Clerical & Related	18.51	6.47	8.80
51. Sales	9.97	4.03	5.17
61. Services	9.55	15.12	14.03
71. Farming	4.59	2.23	2.69
73. Fish/Fur/Hunt	0.48	0.22	0.26
75. Forestry & Logging	0.69	0.46	0.50
77. Mining/Gas-Oil	0.69	1.15	1.07
81-2. Processing (ind.)	3.17	8.59	7.54
83. Machining	2.22	9.79	8.33
85. Product Fabric.	4.96	16.52	14.29
87. Construction	3.90	11.49	10.01
95. Crafts and Equip. Oper.	2.96	1.64	1.88
99. Occup. N.O.S. (not otherwise stated)	5.33	7.74	7.28
Total numbers	9,845	39,530	49,375

* Percentages in each vertical column are based on 100 per cent of that category.
SOURCE: See Table F.1.

Bibliography

I MAJOR ARCHIVAL COLLECTIONS OF MANUSCRIPTS AND UNPUBLISHED GOVERNMENT DOCUMENTS

Public Archives of Canada, Manuscript Group 28, I, 124: Frontier College Papers, 1921-57.

_____, Record Group 6, Department of Secretary of State, 1915-20. Record Group 6, E, 1, vol. 42, ff. 182, no. 2, no. 3.

_____, Record Group 14 D-2, Records of Parliament, Canada, House of Commons, Sessional Records, 1867-1958.

_____, Record Group 15 B, Department of the Interior, Dominion Lands Colonization, 1884-1927.

_____, Record Group 24, Department of National Defense, 1914-36.

_____, Record Group 24, Department of Secretary of State for External Affairs, 1884-1929.

_____, Record Group 26, Department of Citizenship and Immigration, 1924-61.

_____, Record Group 27, Department of Labour, 1940-50.

_____, Record Group 44, Department of National War Services, 1942-46.

_____, Record Group 76, Immigration Branch, Correspondence, Memos and General Papers, 1892-1957.

Canada, Department of Immigration files, 1957-66. [Previously closed files. Cited by permission of the Department of Manpower and Immigration. Confirmed by Public Archives of Canada, RG 76, where most of these records now reside.]

Vienna, Staats Archiv, Ministerium des Innern, 1904-14. Verwaltungs Archiv Kriegs Ministerium, 1912-14.

Glenbow Archives, CPR Colonization Papers 31886 – 1958; NWMP Register of Travellers on the Yukon River, 1902-03. [microfilm]

British Columbia Archives, B.C. Police Papers: Inspector's Reports, 1904-11; Correspondence and Reports, 1914-17.

B.C. Archives, Mining Records, 1861-1900.

Saskatchewan Archives, Homestead Entries.

Public Archives of Ontario, Communist Party of Canada Papers, 1929-31.

Immigration Archives, University of Minnesota. Hungarian National Archives, 1902-18. [microfilm] Austrian National Archives, 1848-1914. [microfilm]

Zavod za Migracije i Narodnosti, Zagreb. An inventory of this extensive collection covering the period 1923-65 is described by Zlata Godler in "Archival Materials on Croatian Migration," *Polyphony*, 1, 1 (1977), pp. 41-42.

II UNPUBLISHED INTERVIEWS AND MEMOIRS

Some fifty interviews with common questionnaires were conducted personally by G.J.V. Kokich and by mail with various Croatian migrants of all ages and periods of migration, primarily among those immigrants to Ontario and western Canada. Other interviews were personally conducted by the author with several pioneers and community leaders (e.g., Peter Stanković) as well as with prominent sports figures and personalities. Several of the above kindly provided the author with additional manuscript memoirs and family recollections which have been cited in this history, as have R.B. Nizich, K. Beckie, M. Glibota, K. Smiley; others have written useful letters to the author (M. Stivoric, M.G. Zorkin) or provided useful materials on their communities (M. Meheš, P. Čulumović, A. Miletić).

III NEWSPAPERS

1 **National Library Collection, Ottawa, Canada, includes whole or partial collections of:**

Hrvatski Glas [Croatian Voice], Winnipeg, 1929- .

Borba [The Struggle], Toronto, 1930-36.

Glas Kanade [Voice of Canada], 1934-36.

Slobodna Misao [Free Thought], Toronto, 1936-40.

Novosti [News], Toronto, 1940-48.

Jedinstvo [Unity], Toronto, 1948-71.

Naš Novine [Our News], Toronto, 1971- .

Nezavisna Država Hrvatska [Independent State of Croatia], Toonto, 1960-74.

Domovina Hrvatska [Country of Croatia], Toronto, 1955.

Naš Put [Our Way], Toronto, 1963-72.

Hrvatski Put [The Croatian Way], Toronto, 1962-74.

2 **Newspaper clippings files from *Zavod sa Migracije i Narodnosti,* in Zagreb, Yugoslavia.**

3 **Immigration Archives, University of Minnesota, has:**

Zajedničar [Fraternalist], Pittsburgh, 1907-40 [microfilm].

Croatia Press, 1965-70.

4 **Vancouver City Archives has:**

Nezaposleni Radnik [The Unemployed Worker], 1929-31.

5 **Canada, Department of the Secretary of State, has:**

Review of the Foreign Language Press, 1945-48.

[Ethnic] Press Digest, 1953-62.

Ethnic Scene, 1963-66.

[Canadian] *Ethnic Press Review*, 1972-74.

6 Various Canadian newspapers of local relevance such as:

British Colonist [Victoria].

The B.C. Fisherman [Vancouver].

Delta *Optimist* [B.C.].

The Porcupine Advance [Timmins].

The Port Arthur *News Chronicle*.

Toronto *Daily Star*.

Globe and Mail [Toronto].

The New Perspective [Hamilton].

7 Others:

Hrvatski Radnik [The Croatian Worker], Sudbury [n.d.].

Glas Domovine [Voice of Homeland], Toronto [n.d.].

IV CALENDARS, PERIODICALS, AND MIMEOGRAPHED BULLETINS

Hrvatski Radnički Kalendar [Croatian Workers' Calendar], Toronto, 1938.

Hrvatski Narodni Kalendar [Croatian Peoples' Calendar], Toronto, 1947- .

Naš Kalendar [Yugoslav-Canadian Year Book], Toronto, 1956.

Hrvatski Glas Kalendar [Croatian Voice Calendar], Winnipeg, 1942- .

Hrvatski Preporod [The Croatian Renaissance], Vancouver [n.d.].

Hrvatski Godišnjak [Croatian Yearbook], Vancouver, 1968.

Ozborje Pacifica [Pacific Horizon], Vancouver, 1968- .

Hrvatsko Ozborje [Croatian Horizon], Vancouver, 1966.

Vrijeme [Croatian Canadian Magazine], Vancouver, 1967.

Jadran [Adriatic], Montreal, 1966.

Vjesnik Vijeća [Voice of the Council], Windsor, 1970.

Hrvatska Sloga [Croatian Unity], Calgary, 1974.

Napredak [Advance], Toronto, 1969- .

Viesti [News], Kanadsko Hrvatskog Kluba, Sudbury, 1964-65.

Naša Riječ [Our Word], Ottawa, 1973- .

Vjesnik [The Messenger], Toronto Credit Union.

The Bulletin, Toronto, Lady Queen of Croatia Church, 1964- .

Naša Nada Kalendar, Cleveland, 1925-56.

Matica Iseljenika Kalendar, Zagreb, 1955-75.

V CANADIAN GOVERNMENT DOCUMENTS AND PUBLICATIONS

Berry, J.W., R. Kalin, and D.M. Taylor. *Multiculturalism and Ethnic Attitudes in Canada*. Ottawa: Supply and Services, 1977.

Briant, P.C. *Department of Citizenship and Immigration. Ethnic Groups in Canada, A Bibliography of Research, 1959-61*. Ottawa: Queen's Printer, 1962.

Canada, Department of Citizenship and Immigration. *Citizenship, Immigration and Ethnic Groups in Canada: A Bibliography of Research, Published and Unpublished Sources, 1920-58*. Ottawa: 1960.

Canada, Royal Commission on Bilingualism and Biculturalism. Sum-

261

mary of Book IV of the Final Report of the R.C.B.B. *The Cultural Contribution of Other Ethnic Groups*. Ottawa: 1970.

Canada, Canadian Citizenship Branch. *The Canadian Family Tree*. Ottawa: Queen's Printer, 1967. Reprint, Toronto: Corpus, 1979.

Canada, Department of Manpower and Immigration. *Immigration Statistics*.

Canada, Department of Citizenship and Immigration. *Annual Reports, 1930-65*.

Gregorovich, A. *Canadian Ethnic Groups Bibliography*. Toronto: Ontario Department of Provincial Secretary and Citizenship, 1972.

Henripin, Jacques. *Trends and Factors of Fertility in Canada*. Ottawa:

Dominion Bureau of Statistics, 1970.

Hurd, W.B. "Ethnic Origin and Nativity of the Canadian People," in Canada, *Census Monograph*, 1941.

Kalbach, W.E. *The Impact of Immigration on Canada's Population, 1961 Census Monograph*. Ottawa: Dominion Bureau of Statistics, 1970.

O'Bryan, K.G., J.G. Reitz, and O.M. Kuplowska. *Non-Official Languages: A Study in Canadian Multi-culturalism*. Ottawa: Supply and Services, 1976.

Stone, Leroy. *Urban Development in Canada*. Ottawa: Dominion Bureau of Statistics, 1967.

VI UNPUBLISHED WORKS

Babics, Walter V. "Assimilation of Yugoslavs in Franklin County, Ohio." Master's thesis, Ohio State University, 1964.

Bloomfield, D. "Social Participation – A Problem of Ethnic Identity: The Croatian Case in Hamilton, Ontario." Unpublished essay, University of Guelph, 1974, 20 pp.

Borkovich, Blanche. "The Croatians of Ottawa: A Preliminary Study, 1956-57." Unpublished essay, Carleton University, Ottawa, 1956-57, 20 pp. [Supplied to author by P. Čulumović, Ottawa.]

Cizmić, Ivan. "Emigration to the United States and Canada," *Yugoslavian Heritage in the U.S.*, University of Minnesota, 1977. Unpublished paper.

Čolaković, Branko M. "Yugoslav Migrations to America." Ph.D. thesis, University of Minnesota, December, 1970.

Fitzgerald, Denis. "Pioneer Settlement in Northern Saskatchewan." Ph.D. thesis, University of Minnesota, 1966.

Gobetz, Giles F. "Adjustment and Assimilation of Slovenian Refugees." Ohio State University, 1962.

Godler, Zlata, "Croatia to Canada Migration Between The Wars." Ph.D. thesis, University of Toronto (OISE), 1981.

Horvat, Viktor. "The Croatian Village Community in Yugo-Slavia." Ph.D. dissertation, Cornell University, 1929.

Jutronić, Dunja. "Serbo-Croatian and American English in Contact: A Socio-Linguistic Study of the Serbo-Croatian Community in Steelton, Pennsylvania." Ph.D. thesis, Pennsylvania State University, 1971.

Livingston, Robert Gerald. "Stejpan Radic and the Croatian Peasant Party, 1904-1929." Ph.D. dissertation, Harvard University, 1959.

Marinovich, Charles. "The History of Yugoslav Immigration." Master's thesis, University of California, 1957.

Mehes̆, Mirko. "Za ili Protiv Integracije? Problem Hrvatske Bioloske Ekonomije." [For or Against Integration: The Problem of Croatian Biological Economy.] Unpublished ms., 18 pp., Sudbury, 1960.

Mihanovich, C.S. "Americanization of Croats in St. Louis, Missouri." Master's thesis, St. Louis University, 1957.

Mrkitch, Dan. "A History of the Croat Immigration to Canada." Unpublished ms., Ottawa, September-November, 1970. [Secretary of State]

Palmer, H. "Nativism and Ethnic Tolerance in Alberta, 1920-72." Ph.D. thesis, York University, 1973.

Paves̆ković, Nedo. "The Croats in Canada." Master's thesis, University of Montreal, 1961.

Prpić, George. "The Croats in America," Ph.D. dissertation, Georgetown University, 1959.

Stanković, Peter. "[Canadian] Croatians." Unpublished ms., Winnipeg [n.d.].

Surduc̆ki, Milan. "Morphological Adaptation of English Loanwords in Serbo-Croatian: An Analysis of English Loanwords in Serbo-Croatian and in the Speech of Serbian and Croatian Immigrants in Canada." Ph.D. thesis, University of Novi Sad, 1970.

Vrsić, Gabriel. "The Yugoslavian Contribution to North American Civilization." Ph.D. thesis, University of Montreal, 1958.

VII BOOKS AND PAMPHLETS PUBLISHED IN CANADA

Canadian Council of South Slavs. *Help to the Soviet Union from Croatians, Servians, Slovenians of Canada.* Toronto: Canadian Council of South Slavs, 1942.

____. *20 Godina – Kratki Pregled Historije Naprednog Pokreta Jugoslavenskih Iseljenika U Kanadi.* Toronto: Canadian Council of South Slavs, 1950.

Fourth Canadian Folklore Festival. Edmonton: Croatian Folklore Group, Edmonton, and the Croatian Folklore Federation of Canada, 1978.

Gazi, Stjepan, ed. *Spomenica na Dvadeset Godina Hrvatski Seljac̆kih Organizacija u Kanadi.* Winnipeg: [Croatian Peasant Party], 1952.

Juris̆ić, Z. *Zbirka Lirike iz Nove Domovine.* Toronto: Lira, 1973.

Kutles̆a, Jozo. *The Sunrise of Joy and Love.* Toronto: Mystic Press, 1973.

_____. *The Mosaic of Life*. Toronto: 1970.

Meheš, Mirko. *Tražim Hrvata, Homo Titoicus*. Toronto: 1973.

_____. *I stvori Čovjek Boga*. Toronto: 1979.

Prpić, George. *Tragedies and Migrations in Croatian History*. Toronto: Hrvatski Put, 1973.

Šola, Marijan Emil. *Još, Hrvatska Ni Propala*. Toronto: 1964.

_____. *Za Dom*. Toronto: 1960.

Tovilo, Mato. *Križni Put Hrvatske: Za Dom Su Pali*. Toronto: HOP, 1964.

VIII (A) BOOKS ABOUT CROATIA AND CROATIAN IMMIGRANTS

Adamic, Louis. *The Native's Return: An American Immigrant Visits Yugoslavia and Discovers His Old Country*. New York: Harpers, 1934.

Avakumovic, Ivan. *The History of the Communist Party of Yugoslavia*, vol. 1. Aberdeen: Aberdeen University Press, 1967.

Balch, Emily. *Our Slavic Fellow Citizens*. New York: Charities Publications, 1910; reprint, 1969.

Baučić, Ivo. *Radnici u Inozemstvu Prema Popisu Stanovnistva Jugoslavije, 1971*. [Workers Abroad According to the 1971 Yugoslav Census.] Zagreb: Studies of the Institute of Geography, University of Zagreb, vol. 12, no. 4, 1973.

_____. *The Effect of Emigration from Yugoslavia and the Problems of Returning Emigrant Workers*. The Hague: Martinus Nijhoff, 1972.

Bennett, Linda. *Personal Choice in Ethnic Identity Maintenance: Serbs, Croats and Slovenes in Washington, D.C.* Palo Alto, California: R. and E. Research Associates, 1978.

Bičanić, R. *Agrarna Kriza u Hrvatskoj, 1873-95*. [The Agrarian Crisis in Croatia, 1873-1895.] Zagreb: 1937.

Blanc, André. *La Croatie Occidentale, Étude de Géographie Humaine*. Paris: Institute des Études Slavs, 1957.

Braudel, Fernand. *The Mediterranean and the Mediterranean World in the Age of Philip II*, vol. 1. New York: Harper and Row, 1972.

Byrnes, Robert F. *Communal Families in the Balkans: The Zadruga*. South Bend, Indiana: University of Notre Dame Press, 1976.

Čizmić, Ivan. *Jugoslavenski Iseljenički Pokret u SAD i Stvaranje Jugoslavenske Države, 1918*. Zagreb: 1974.

Clissold, Stephen, ed. *Yugoslavia and the Soviet Union, 1939-73: A Documentary Survey*. Oxford: Oxford University Press, R.I.I.A., 1975.

Crnja, Zvane. *Cultural History of Croatia*. Zagreb: Ured za informaci je Izvrsnog Vijeca Sabora NRH, 1962.

Croatian Fraternal Union of America. *75th Anniversary, 1894-1969 of Croatian Fraternal Union of America*. Pittsburgh: 1969.

Darby, H.C., R.W. Seton-Watson, Phyllis Auty *et al. A Short*

History of Yugoslavia. Cambridge: Cambridge University Press, 1968.

Dedijer, Vladimir. *The Battle Stalin Lost, Memoirs of Yugoslavia.* New York: The Viking Press, 1971.

Eterovich, Adam S. *Croatians and Serbians in the West and South, 1800-1900.* San Francisco: R. and E. Research Associates, 1971.

____. *Croatians from Dalmatia and Montenegrin Serbs in the West and South.* San Francisco: R. and E. Research Associates, 1971.

____. *Jugoslav Immigrant Bibliography.* San Francisco: 1965.

____. *Yugoslavs in Nevada, 1859-1900.* San Francisco: R. and E. Research Associates, 1973.

Eterovich, F.H. *Biographical Dictionary of Scholars, Artists and Professionals of Croatian Descent in the U.S. and Canada.* Chicago: 1969.

____. *Hrvatski Profesori via Amerkanickim i Kanadskim Visokim Školama.* Chicago: 1963.

Eterovich, F.H., and C. Spalatin, eds. *Croatia, Land, People and Culture,* 2 vols. Toronto: University of Toronto Press, 1970.

Filipović, R. *The Phonemic Analysis of English Loan Words in Croatian.* Zagreb: Institute of Phonetics, 1960.

Folejewski, Z., ed. *Canadian Contributions to the International Congress of Slavists.* Ottawa: 1978.

Gazi, Stephen. *A History of Croatia.* New York: Philosophical Library, 1973.

Gewehr, Wesley. *The Rise of Nationalism in the Balkans, 1800-1930.* New York: Archon Books (reprint), 1967.

Govorchin, Gerald. *Americans from Yugoslavia.* Gainesville: University of Florida Press, 1961.

Grado, Arthur Benko. *Migracione Enciklopedija, Kanada,* vol. 1. Zagreb: 1930.

Gross, Mirjana. *Povijest Pravaška Ideologije.* Zagreb: University of Zagreb Institute of Croatian History, 1973.

Guldescu, Stanko. *History of Medieval Croatia.* The Hague: Mouton, 1964.

Gusić, Branimir. *Lika u Proslosti i Sadasnjosti.* Karlovac: 1973.

Holjevac, Večeslav. *Hrvati Izvan Domovine.* Zagreb: Matica Hrvatska, 1968.

Jukić, Ilija. *The Fall of Yugoslavia.* New York: Harcourt Brace and Jovanovich, 1974.

Kohn, Hans. *Pan Slavism, Its History and Ideology.* South Bend: University of Notre Dame Press, 1953.

____. *The Idea of Nationalism.* New York: Collier Books, 1944.

Krekić, Barisa. *Dubrovnik in the Fourteenth and Fifteenth Centuries.* Norman: University of Oklahoma Press, 1972.

Lederer, Ivo J. *Yugoslavia at the Paris Peace Conference.* New Haven: Yale University Press, 1963.

Lojen, Stjepan. *Uspomene Jednog Iseljenika.* Zagreb: Znanje, 1963.

Maclean, Fitzroy. *Eastern Approaches.* London: Jonathan Cape, 1950.

Markotic, Vladimir, ed. *Biographical Directory of Americans and*

Canadians of Croatian Descent, 1970, 1973 editions.

Martin, Jean. *Refugee Settlers: A Study of D.P.'s in Australia.* Canberra: Australian National University, 1965.

Meler, Vjekoslav. *The Slavonic Pioneers of California.* San Francisco: 1932; second edition, R. and E. Research Associates, 1972.

Moodie, Arthur Edward, ed. *The North Western Primorje of Jugoslavia.* Nottingham: Geographical Field Group, 1952.

Nations and Nationalities of Yugoslavia. Belgrade: Medjunaroda Politika, 1974.

Novak, Michael. *The Rise of the Unmeltable Ethnics: Politics and Culture in the Nineteen Seventies.* New York: Macmillan, 1971.

Ostrić, Ante. *La Structure et Les Moeurs de la Société Croate.* Geneva: 1950, Thesis, no. 126, Faculté des Sciences Economiques et Sociales, University of Geneva.

Pomorska Encyclopedia. Zagreb: 1957.

Preveden, Francis Ralph. *A History of the Croatian People,* 2 vols. New York: Philosophical Library, 1956.

Prpić George. *The Croatian Immigrants in America.* New York: Philosophical Library, 1971.

St. Erlich, Vera. *The Family in Transition: A Study of 300 Yugoslav Villages.* Princeton, New Jersey: Princeton University Press, 1966.

Sher, Gerson S. *Praxis: Marxist Criticism and Dissent in Socialist Yugoslavia.* Bloomington: Indiana University Press, 1977.

Shibutani, T., and K.M. Kwan. *Ethnic Stratification: A Comparative Approach.* New York: Macmillan, 1965.

Šuljak, Dinko, ed. *Croatia's Struggle for Independence: A Documentary History.* Arcadia, California: Croatian Information Service, 1977.

Tomasevich, J. *Peasants, Politics and Economic Change in Yugoslavia.* Stanford: Stanford University Press, 1955.

Tomasic, Dinko Antun. *Ethnic Components of Croatian Nationhood.* Bloomington: Indiana University Press, 1965.

____. *Personality and Culture in East European Politics.* New York: G.W. Stewart, 1948.

Vujnovich, M.M. *Yugoslavs in Louisiana.* Gretna, La.: Pelican Publishing, 1974.

Warne, J. *The Slav Invasion and the Mine Workers: A Study in Immigration.* London: J.B. Lippincott, 1904.

Wuescht, Johann. *Population Losses in Yugoslavia During World War II, 1941-1945.* New York: Atlantic-Forum, 1963.

Zganec, Vinko, ed. *Croatian Folk Songs and Dances.* Zagreb: Seljačka Sloga, 1951.

VIII (B) ARTICLES ABOUT CROATIA AND CROATIAN IMMIGRANTS

Adi, Robert. "The Ethnic Press," a study prepared for the Royal Commission on Bilingualism and Biculturalism.

Badovinac, Robert J. "Additional Data on Croatians," *Ethnic American News* (September, 1976).

Benson, Morton. "English Loanwords in Serbo-Croatian," *American Speech*, XLI, 3 (October, 1967).

____. "Problems of Serbo-Croatian Lexicography," *Canadian Slavonic Papers*, XX, 3 (September, 1978).

Bičanić, Rudolf. "Yugoslavia: Croatia-Slavonia; Attitudes to the Zadruga," in Doreen Warriner (ed.), *Contrasts in Emerging Societies*, (Bloomington: Indiana University Press, 1965).

Britovsek, Marijan. "The Process of Individualization of Agriculture in Carniola in the Second Half of the Nineteenth Century," *East European Quarterly*, III, 4.

Chmelar, Johann. "The Austrian Emigration, 1900-14," in Donald Fleming and Bernard Bailyn, *Perspectives in American History*, vol. VII, *Dislocation and Emigration, The Social Background of American Emigration* (Cambridge, Mass.: Harvard University Press, 1973).

Cloutier-Wojiechowska, Cecile. "Alain Horić, Le Poete Croate du Québec," *Canadian Ethnic Studies*, IV, 1-2 (1972).

Colossa, Tibor. "The Social Structure of the Peasant Class in Austria-Hungary: Statistical Sources and Methods of Research," *East European Quarterly*, III, 4.

Franges, Ivo. "Yugoslav Literature: A Review for Foreign Slavists," *East European Quarterly*, VI, 2.

Harney, R.F. "The Padrone and the Immigrant," *The Canadian Review of American Studies*, V, 2 (Fall, 1974).

Johnston, W.B. "Changing Peasant Agriculture in Northwestern Hrvatsko Primorje, Yugoslavia," *Geographical Review*, 44 (July, 1954).

____. "Examples of Changing Peasant Agriculture in Croatia, Yugoslavia," *Economic Geography*, 33 (January, 1957).

Kosinski, Leszek. "Yugoslavia and International Migration," *Canadian Slavonic Papers*, XX, 3 (September, 1978).

Lorković, Hrvoje. "The Dynamic Psychology of Croatian Discord," *Journal of Croatian Studies*, XVIII-XIX (1977-78), pp. 73-85.

Marchbin, Andrew A. "The Origin of Migration from South-Eastern Europe to Canada," *Canadian Historical Association Annual Report*, 1934.

Matesic, Ivan. "Veličanstvena Manifestacija Hrvatska u Kanadskom Životu," *Zajedničar,* 15 November 1978.

Matko, Lorraine. "The Americanization of Croatian Folklore," Part II, *Zajedničar,* 29 September 1976.

Mihanovic, Clement S. "Fortune Telling and Superstitions Among the Peasants of the Poljica Region of Dalmatia," *Journal of American Folklore*, 64 (April, 1951), pp. 197-202.

Mirkowitch, J. "Yugoslavs and Criminality," *Sociology and Social Research*, XXV (September-October, 1940), pp. 28-34.

Mirth, Karlo. "U.S. Census of Population: Americans Whose Country of Origin is Yugoslavia," *Croatia Press*, XIX (1965), pp. 2-15.

Mosley, Philip, E. "The Peasant Family, The *Zadruga*, or Communal Joint-Family in the Balkans and Its Recent Evolution," in Caroline Ware (ed.), *The Cultural Approach to History* (New York: Columbia University Press, 1940), pp. 95-108.

Niland, Billyana. "Yugoslavs in San Pedro, California: Economic and Social Factors," *Sociology and Social Research*, XXVI (September-October, 1941), pp. 36-44.

Nuttonson, M.Y. "Agricultural Climatology of Yugoslavia and its Agro-Climatic Analogues in North America," revised from a report prepared by the author for the Agricultural Rehabilitation Division, United Nations Relief and Rehabilitation Administration, Washington, D.C., American Institute of Crop Ecology, 1947.

Pavešković, N. "Croatians in Canada," in *Slavs in Canada, II* (Ottawa: University Press, 1968), pp. 111-16.

Petrovich, M.B. "Yugoslavia: Religion and the Tensions of A Multinational State," *East European Quarterly*, IV, 1.

Pitt, D., and Z. Juričić. "The Social Adjustment of Yugoslavs in Victoria," *Canadian Slavonic Papers*, XI (1969).

Pusic, Eugen. "The Family in the Process of Social Change in Yugoslavia," *Sociological Review*, 5 (December, 1957), pp. 207-224.

Roucek, J.S. "The Yugoslav Immigrants in America," *The American Journal of Sociology*, XL (March, 1945).

Schöpflin, George. "The Ideology of Croatian Nationalism," *Survey: A Journal of East-West Studies*, XIX, 1 (Winter, 1973), pp. 123-46.

Simic, Andrei. "Country and Western Yugoslav Style: Contemporary Folk Music as a Mirror of Social Sentiment," *Journal of Popular Culture*, 10, 1 (Summer, 1976), pp. 156-66.

Spalatin, Christopher. "The Language Situation in Croatia Today," *Journal of Croatian Studies*, XIV-XV (1973-74).

———. "The Rise of the Croatian Standard Language," *Journal of Croatian Studies*, XVI (1975).

Spalatin, M. "Perspectives on the Croatian Concept of Liberty," *Journal of Croatian Studies*, XVII (1976).

Stampar, Andrija. "Croat Peasant Literature," *Slavonic and East European Review*, 19 (1939-1940), pp. 291-9.

Stivoric, Michael. "Croatians and other Ethnic Minorities in Canada Recognized as Integral Part of Canadian Life," *Zajedničar*, 5 February 1975.

Trlin, A. "Yugoslav Settlement in New Zealand 1890-1961," *New Zealand Geographer*, 24, 1 (April, 1968).

Velikonja, Joseph. "Yugoslavia Emigration," in *Emigration*, Goettingen, Germany, 1975.

Viskovic, S. "Život Hrvata u Vancouver," *Hrvatski Glas*, 28 May 1966.

IX BOOKS AND ARTICLES ON CANADA

Abella, Irving. *Nationalism, Communism and Canadian Labour.* Toronto: University of Toronto Press, 1973.

Avakumovic, Ivan. *The Communist Party of Canada.* Toronto: McClelland and Stewart, 1975.

Bradwin, Edmund. *The Bunkhouse Man, A Study of Work and Pay in the Camps of Canada, 1902-14.* Toronto: University of Toronto Press, reprint, 1972.

Breton, Raymond. *Ethnic Communities and the Personal Relations of Immigrants.* Montreal: The Social Research Group, 1961.

Coats, R.H. "The Alien Enemy in Canada: Internment Operations," in *Canada in the Great War,* vol. II (Toronto: United Publishers of Canada, 1919-21).

Cook, Ramsay, and R.C. Brown. *Canada, 1896-1921: A Nation Transformed.* Toronto: McClelland and Stewart, 1974.

Dumas, Evelyn. *The Bitter Thirties in Quebec.* Montreal: Black Rose, 1975.

Elliot, J.L., ed. *Immigrant Groups.* Scarborough: Prentice Hall, 1971.

England, Robert. "The Central European Immigrant in Canada," *Canadian Ethnic Studies,* VIII, 2 (1976).

Gray, James H. *The Roar of the Twenties.* Toronto: Macmillan, 1975.

Hawkins, Freda. *Canada and Immigration: Public Policy and Public Concern.* Montreal: McGill-Queen's, 1972.

Henripin, Jacques. *Trends and Factors of Fertility in Canada.* Ottawa: Dominion Bureau of Statistics, 1972.

Hoar, Victor. *The Mackenzie-Papineau Battalion.* Toronto: Copp Clark, 1969.

"Immigration in Canada," special issue of *International Migration Review,* IV, 10 (Fall, 1969).

Jones, Frank E. "A Sociological Perspective on Immigrant Adjustment," *Social Forces,* XXXV (October, 1956), pp. 39-47.

____. "Some Social Consequences of Immigration for Canada," in *Proceedings of World Population Conference,* vol. IV (New York: United Nations, 1976).

Marlatt, Daphne, and Caroline Itter. "Opening Doors: Vancouver's East End," *Sound Heritage* [B.C. Prov. Archives], VIII, nos. 1 & 2, pp. 67-72.

Palmer, Howard. "Mosaic or Melting Pot: Immigration and Ethnicity in Canada and the U.S.," *International Journal,* XXXI, 3 (Summer, 1976).

Richmond, Anthony. *Ethnic Residential Segregation in Metropolitan Toronto.* Research Report for Institute for Behavioural Research. Toronto: York University, Survey Research Center, 1972.

Richmond, A.H. *Post-War Immigrants in Canada.* Toronto: University of Toronto Press, 1967.

Roseborough, H., and R. Breton. "Perceptions of the Relative Economic and Political Advantages of Ethnic Groups in Canada," in B. Blishen, *Canadian Society: Sociological Perspectives,* third edition (Toronto: Macmillan, 1971).

Sayles, Fern. *Welland Workers Make History*. Welland: 1963.

Trofimenkoff, Susan M. *The Twenties in Western Canada*. Ottawa: National Museum of Man, 1972.

Troper, Harold. *Only Farmers Need Apply: Official Canadian Government Encouragement of Immigration from the United States, 1896-1911*. Toronto: Griffin House, 1972.

Vallee, F.G., M. Schwarz, and F. Darnell. "Ethnic Assimilation and Differentiation in Canada," *Canadian Journal of Economics and Political Science*, XXIII, 4 (November, 1957).

Index